# PRAISE FOR THE AUTOBIOGRAPHY OF EDWARD R. JONES, THE MAN ALSO KNOWN AS . . .

"THE HOUDINI OF JAILBIRDS . . . TELLS HOW AND WHY HE DID IT IN THIS FRISKY AUTOBIOGRAPHY. . . . *HACKSAW* gustily recounts his cross-country exploits. . . . His portraits of fellow cons crackle. . . . AS ESCAPIST FARE, THIS ONE'S A LOCK."

—*Kirkus Reviews*

"INGENIOUS ESCAPES. . . . AN AUTHENTIC COOL HAND LUKE. . . . The description of the escapes, many of which were remarkable, is deadpan precise. . . . Even if your . . . plans don't include some time on a chain gang or in a federal pen, you might want to file away Hacksaw's helpful hints."

—*The Village Voice Literary Supplement*

"HIS ACCOUNTS OF HIS EARLY ESCAPES ARE ALMOST UNBEARABLY SUSPENSEFUL."

—*Publishers Weekly*

"GREAT ESCAPISM."

—*Wichita Times Record-News*

"The reader cannot help identifying with Jones. . . . *HACKSAW* IS ENTERTAINING, FAST-PACED."

—*Library Journal*

# HACKSAW

## EDWARD R. JONES

**POCKET BOOKS**

New York   London   Toronto   Sydney   Tokyo

POCKET BOOKS, a division of Simon and Schuster Inc.
1230 Avenue of the Americas, New York, NY 10020

Published by arrangement with Donald I. Fine, Inc.
Library of Congress Catalog Card Number: 87-46029

ISBN 0-671-67877-9

First Pocket Books printing January 1990

10  9  8  7  6  5  4  3  2  1

*To my mother:*
*Heddie Bosher*
*who deserved so much more*
*I miss you*

# PART ONE

"*The vilest deeds—like poison weeds,*
*bloom well in prison air;*
*It is only what is good in man,*
*that wastes and withers there . . .*"

OSCAR WILDE
*The Ballad of Reading Gaol*

# CHAPTER 1

*Atlanta, Georgia*
*September 17, 1975, 11:35 A.M.*

DELTA FLIGHT 81 FROM TALLAHASSEE TOUCHED DOWN AT Atlanta's Hartsfield Airport right on schedule. I glanced at my watch as the turbines roared, slowing the forward momentum of the giant DC-10. It would be a day that I would remember for the rest of my life, if I was still alive when it ended. And for what I had in mind, the odds certainly weren't favorable.

I shifted nervously in my window seat as the plane turned onto the taxiway and made its way slowly toward the terminal, finally coming to a halt in front of the large, multi-windowed arrivals building. Most of the passengers in the coach section were already on their feet, stretching and collecting personal gear stored in the overhead compartments. I released my seat belt and threw a questioning look at the two men occupying the seats next to me. Getting no response, I turned and glanced at the third man sitting directly behind me.

"Just wait 'til everyone else gets off," he said. I shrugged and faced forward again, trying to relax. I was in no hurry; it would all be over soon enough. One way or another.

The final passenger disappeared into the jetway, and a pretty flight attendant motioned to us from the doorway. The three men rose and motioned me into the deserted aisle.

"Gimme an arm, Jones," George Peters said. I obeyed, and a steel handcuff was clamped firmly around my left wrist. Peters fastened the other end of the cuff around his right wrist—leaving considerably more slack than he had around mine—then nodded to Simms and Belcher. Together we headed for the exit at the front of the plane, Peters taking the lead with me trailing along like a reluctant bride being led to the honeymoon suite. I smiled brightly at the stewardess standing at the door and saw her blush, averting her eyes. I didn't blame her. It was a blushing situation all around.

We moved through the jetway and stepped into the waiting area inside the terminal. Immediately I saw three men detach themselves from a nearby wall and head purposefully in our direction. Even if I hadn't recognized pudgy, cigar-chewing James Hart, I would have had no difficulty identifying them. The neatly cropped hair, conservative business suits and no-nonsense manner were a dead giveaway. They halted in front of us, and Hart produced a small leather folder from his inside coat pocket.

"Jim Hart, FBI," he said. "These are agents Modine and Blackman."

Peters didn't offer to shake hands, partly because of the cuff fixed to his right wrist and partly because the FBI and U.S. Marshal's Service aren't that fond of each other to begin with. Instead, he made his own introductions and waited for Hart to take it from there. It was the FBI's ball game, and we were in their ballpark. But that didn't mean the marshals had to like it; they would much rather have handled the job themselves. So would I. I certainly hadn't counted on having six men along.

Hart folded his arms and grinned at me from around the dead cigar sticking out of his mouth, nodding his balding head up and down. To have said that he didn't much care for me would have been a gross understatement.

"Well, Hacksaw, how you been? Hear you had a little excitement up there in Tallahassee."

"Just went for a jog, is all," I answered.

Peters made a production out of checking his wristwatch.

"Mind if we hurry this along, Mr. Hart? We got a return flight at four-ten this afternoon."

"No problem," Hart said, keeping his eyes fixed on me. "I'll see you're back in plenty of time. First I want to make sure me and Hacksaw here have a good understanding."

He removed the cigar and delicately plucked a loose strand of tobacco from his lower lip. "Let's get something straight right off," he said. "I personally don't believe for one minute that you're going to lead us to any stash of buried jewels. As far as I'm concerned this whole deal is nothing but a smoke-screen scam of yours to see if you can pull off another escape. What I think happened is you found yourself in a great big jackpot you figured you couldn't get out of and decided to try this angle to see what would happen. But I tell you, if you even look like you're ready to make a break, so help me God I'll personally blow your fuckin' head off. Do we understand each other?"

"I don't doubt that for a minute, Hart," I answered. "From the looks of things, I'd say you aren't taking any chances."

"You told that shit right! I know you." He replaced the cigar between his teeth and thrust his jaw at me. "Now, then. It's not too late for you to turn around and get on the next flight back to where you came from. 'Cause if you lead me on some wild goose chase out in the middle of some fuckin' woods, you're going to regret it. In other words, when we get to wherever it is we're goin', there had damn well better be something there. Now what about it?"

Everyone else was staring at me with detached interest, waiting for my answer. If I had any sense at all I would have just written the whole thing off then and there; there was always tomorrow. But things hadn't been going very well lately, and I was reluctant to let any opportunity slip away, regardless of how slim. So I sighed and shook my head in mock exasperation.

"Believe me, Hart—there's something there."

Hart gave me a long searching look, then abruptly turned and gazed about the crowded terminal. "Then let's get this show on the road. The sooner I get shed of you, the better I'll like it."

* * *

We set out from the airport in two cars and headed south on I-85. Hart, Belcher, Peters and I occupied the lead car, followed closely by Modine, Simms and Blackman. The day was hot and overcast, and the air conditioner was working overtime in an effort to reduce the humidity.

Hart was driving, Belcher sitting next to him with one arm thrown over the seat back. I was in the rear seat, still hand-cuffed to Peters, who was gazing out at the passing scenery like a noiseless, patient spider. The guy really looked cool, confident—not worried about me at all. I wondered if he was the hero type.

I reached up with my free hand and loosened my tie, fumbled with the button and opened the collar of my white shirt. Hart caught the action in his rearview mirror and grinned.

Hart said, "Nervous, Hacksaw? Sweating a little bit back there, are you?"

I said, "The government can't afford freon or something? Why don't you roll the window down a little?"

Without looking at me, Peters leaned away and rolled the rear window down a few inches, then went back to the scenery, his elbow propped on the door rest.

Hart glanced at Belcher. "Hacksaw ever tell you guys how we met?" Making conversation.

Belcher gave him a polite look and shook his head, not looking very interested.

Hart said, "Was about three months—no—*two* months ago. Middle of July." He chuckled and turned his head to glance out the side window, ready to get into it.

I said, "You're going to bore everybody to death, you know it?"

Hart ignored me and made himself comfortable behind the wheel. "We got word from the Lauderdale office to check out a guy named Edward Carlton in an apartment over in Sandy Springs. He was a suspect in a jewel heist went down in Lauderdale the day before. So me and Modine run over there and find Jones. We had a computer composite Lauderdale sent us, and right off I can see this don't look nothing like my man here."

Belcher was nodding now, remembering. He said, "Guy made a phone call from some motel room, didn't he? That's how you guys got on to him?"

"Right," Hart said. "So we get out there and find Jones all nice and polite, inviting us in for coffee, drinks—whatever." He flicked a glance at me through the rearview mirror. "Smooth—real smooth."

Belcher said, "Some people can sell igloos in Africa."

"You got it, that's my man," Hart agreed. "When we ask him about the phone call he starts giving us a bunch of shit about some guy calling for his girlfriend, lives a few doors down from Jones. Said he didn't know the guy very well but had been out on a couple dates with him when they was all living in the same building. Even told us what kind of car the guy drove. Had an answer for everything, right down to some phony note his girlfriend wrote making it look like he'd been in town all the time." He paused a moment, stretching it out for the boys.

"After about an hour," he went on, "we give him the benefit. I give him a card, and we leave, but decide to put him under surveillance and call for a tail team. But old Hacksaw wasn't there when they showed up, were you, Hacksaw? In no time at all he was long gone, taking all that hot ice with him. Turned out I was sittin' right on top of the shit the whole time we were talking."

I heard a brief chuckle and turned to see Peters with a pleased expression on his ruddy face. Hart heard it also and scowled around the cigar. "In case you haven't guessed by now," he said dryly, "Hacksaw did the job himself. The witnesses just fucked up on the composite. It was him made the call—to some broad who was stayin' with him. A couple of days later he was picked up by agents from our Shreveport office at his wife's apartment—along with most of the loot. We're goin' after the rest now . . . ain't that right, Hacksaw?"

"That's right, Hart." His gray eyes were shooting darts through the rearview mirror. What he didn't know—and wouldn't have believed—was that there *wasn't* any more jewelry. The FBI had recovered every piece after they had charged into Susie's apartment at five in the morning and found me sleeping like a hibernating bear. But the "victim" had seen an opportunity to collect a little extra from Lloyd's of London and had padded the actual amount taken by nearly half. I had denied ever having any other jewelry but might just as well have saved my breath. And that wasn't all. So far I had said nothing about the fact that the "victim" had been involved in the heist himself. Hart would have laughed right in my face. So I had pretended to weaken after days of intensive interrogation and had agreed to lead them to the missing gems.

But it wasn't jewelry I was leading them to.

Hart eased into the slow lane, took the I-285 perimeter turnoff and brought the big Plymouth back to speed. Ten minutes later he slowed again for the Roswell Road-Sandy Springs exit. Seeing the Howard Johnson Motor Hotel off to the right reminded me that I hadn't slept in two days, which was a definite strike against me. Then Hart made the wide turn onto Roswell Road, and I put all other thoughts aside.

It wouldn't be long now.

Hart glanced at me through the mirror. "How much further?"

"About a mile and a half," I said, "off to the right. You'll see an International House of Pancakes on the left. Soon as you reach it, slow down. The driveway will be about a hundred feet past."

Peters and Belcher perked up at this, craning their necks left and right, noting landmarks and taking in details—unconscious reactions that reflected good training. Always on the alert for the offbeat, the something that didn't fit.

One more strike against me.

Then we were abreast of the IHOP, and Hart was braking the Plymouth, squinting intently at the wall of vegetation and pine trees to the right.

"There it is," Belcher said, pointing to a barely discernible set of tracks nearly hidden by the dense foliage.

"Call that a driveway?" Hart said irritably. He tapped the brake and cautiously turned onto the pitted dirt road. I shot a quick look over my shoulder on the remote chance that somewhere along the line we might have lost the other car. No such luck. Modine and company were right behind, bouncing over potholes like a cork in a rough sea. A low-hanging branch scraped the roof above my head, sounding like fingernails scratching a chalkboard. Hart cursed and swung the wheel, trying to save the paint.

I would have given anything for one glass of water.

It took several minutes to negotiate fifty yards of driveway, but at last we broke into a clearing about sixty feet in diameter. In the middle sat a pitiful looking wood-frame house, ravaged by time and violated by vandals. Not a solid pane of glass remained in the ancient windows, and the front door had been wrenched from its hinges and tossed aside, as if flung there by some playful giant. What had once been a tidy front yard was now a mini-jungle of mixed vegetation and green trash bags, most of them torn open by marauding dogs and forest creatures in search of a meal.

The two cars came to a halt only inches apart, and the seven of us stepped out amid the cluttered rubble. Modine went to the rear of the second car, fumbled around inside the trunk and returned with an Army trench shovel and Polaroid camera. Everyone looked at me expectantly.

"Over there," I said, nodding to a crippled old elm tree about twenty feet away. My mouth felt as if it were lined with sand. But inwardly I was calm; surprisingly so. The absolute calmness that comes after the final doubt has been shunted aside and the irrevocable decision reached.

I moved forward and to my right a few feet, forcing Peters to move with me, and scanned the old tree intently. I turned to Hart. "See that bare spot just to the right of that old tree? About two feet down you'll find an old hiker's backpack. The rest of the stuff's in there."

Hart regarded me thoughtfully for a moment, then motioned to Modine and headed for the tree. Blackman sauntered over as well and stood next to Hart as Modine plunged the shovel into the soft earth. A startled squirrel scampered along a dead branch of the tree, peered curiously at the men below then scurried away to disappear into a small hollow inside the trunk.

If I was going to move it would have to be soon.

I fumbled in my shirt pocket for a cigarette, found one and accepted a light from Peters. Casually I recorded the positions of the other agents around me. Belcher was standing a few feet to the left of Peters and myself; Blackman several feet off to the right. Both were absorbed with the digging and were paying me little attention. After all, what could I do? As for Simmons, he was standing slightly behind Blackman with his back turned, busy taking a leak.

It was now or never.

Modine had almost reached the two-foot level. I took a final puff from my cigarette and nonchalantly bent down and snuffed the butt out in the dirt. In a pile of rubbish near my right foot was a .357 magnum wrapped in an orange oilcloth. I had tossed it there many weeks ago after the Fort Lauderdale heist. There was only one thing wrong, however. This particular weapon wasn't capable of stopping an angry duck, because the chambers were empty, and the firing pin was broken. But I was betting my life that my escorts wouldn't realize that.

I quickly felt beneath the rag, grasped the handle and straightened up. Incredibly, none of the agents had sensed anything wrong.

"Everybody on the ground!" I ordered, sticking the muzzle behind Peters' right ear. "First one to reach for a weapon gets this man killed!"

Everyone froze for a heartbeat, as if posing for a snapshot. Modine and Blackman were staring at me with mouths gaping, Modine's shovel poised in midair; Simms was looking at me bug-eyed over his right shoulder, his urine flow suddenly interrupted; Hart's face registered sheer amazement, and his clamping jaws had bitten the unlit cigar nearly in half. Belcher, whose only outward reaction was a look of total disgust, turned out to be the coolest of all. As for Peters, he was a complete statue.

I nudged Peters with the revolver, causing his head to tilt to the left.

"Don't make me say it again, Hart. Everybody on the ground—now!"

Hart spat out the wounded cigar and sank slowly to the ground. One by one the others followed suit—except for Peters, who was still a block of stone.

"Facedown and arms spread."

They complied. I removed the gun from Peters' head and stepped backward, extending my left arm.

"You got ten seconds to get this cuff off," I told him.

Peters dug into his pocket and located the key while I kept a wary eye on his companions. His hands trembled slightly, but he managed to unlock the steel bracelet and remove it from my wrist. I reached beneath his jacket and lifted his short-barrel .38.

"Now here's what I want you to do, Peters," I said, stepping back out of reach. "You're going to go over there and very carefully take those guns away from your buddies. One at a time, slow and easy, using the fingertips of your left hand. We don't want any accidents at this stage of the game, do we? Just toss them right over here, understand?"

He nodded.

"Then do it. Just remember—slow and easy."

Peters did as instructed, painfully aware that two revolvers were following his every move. When he finished I had everyone form a tight circle, still in their prone positions.

"Now take out your cuffs and lock yourselves together."

Hart gave me a look as he fumbled his cuffs out from beneath his belt. He fastened one end to his wrist and the other to Belcher's. "You goin' to kill us now, Jones?"

"Why would I do that?" I said. "Just because you wouldn't mind—using your words, now—blowing my fucking head off, doesn't mean I want to do you great bodily harm . . . why you want to act like that anyway?" I looked at the other men lying on the ground. "The rest of you guys hurry up and get those cuffs on . . . Hart, put your face back in the ground, you're making me nervous."

Hart put his face back in the ground.

When everybody was linked arm in arm I gave them a thorough search in case anyone was carrying a backup weapon. Satisfied they were clean, I collected the handcuff keys and threw them as far as I could into the brush. I removed the shells from each weapon and sent them in the same direction. Then I plucked Hart's wallet from his hip pocket, took out fifty dollars and tucked the wallet back.

No one said anything as I moved over to the waiting automobiles. I ripped the ignition wires from under the dash of Hart's car and pulled out the two-way radio mike. Modine had left his keys in the trunk lock. I got them, settled into the driver's seat and started the engine. Then I rolled down the window and tossed out the useless .357.

I said, "Hart, you might want to check out that magnum. I think you'll find it interesting."

I waved at him, acting cocky as hell, and backed out of the driveway, praying I wouldn't break an axle. I reached the

**11**

road safely, caught a break in traffic and headed for downtown Atlanta.

My colossal bluff had worked.

By six o'clock that evening I was unwinding in a Holiday Inn motel room just off I-20, eighteen miles west of Atlanta.

It had been a busy five hours. Twenty minutes after driving away in Modine's car, I had abandoned it at the Broadway Shopping Plaza on Piedmont Road. My first concern had been for a change of clothes, and a Zayre's Discount Store had taken care of that. I had swapped my suit for a pair of jeans, pullover shirt and tan windbreaker. A pair of Adidas tennis shoes and a baseball cap with Atlanta Braves written on it rounded out my new wardrobe. I changed in an empty fitting room and left the store feeling a lot better about the situation.

From the shopping plaza I had taken a cab to Emory University Hospital. A short while later I was on a bus bound for Six Flags, a recreation and amusement park outside the city limits. By then the adrenalin level had returned to normal and delayed reaction had set in, and I said to myself, "What the hell did I do? I could have been killed back there." What I needed was a good stiff drink and maybe five hours' sleep.

I took care of the drink problem by buying a pint of Chivas Regal from a liquor store after I got to Six Flags. Then I checked into the Holiday Inn to see what I could do about sleep.

But I was still way too keyed up for sleep right now.

I poured another Scotch and water—making it about half-and-half—and settled on the bed to watch the six o'clock news. Looked like I was the man of the hour. There I was, staring back at myself from the tube. A serious-looking anchorman was busy describing the details:

"It was a rough day in Atlanta for three U.S. deputy marshals and an equal number of FBI agents. A federal prisoner—Edward Richard Jones, nicknamed Hacksaw—produced a gun in a wooded area of North Atlanta, forced the lawmen to handcuff themselves together then fled in an FBI car. Jones, a thirty-four-year-old drifter and accused jewel thief, had been brought to Atlanta from Fort Lauderdale, Florida, this morning after agreeing to lead the agents to a cache of stolen jewels. Jones is said to be an accomplished

12

escape artist with numerous jail and prison escapes to his credit.''

The scene shifted, and the screen showed the familiar image of the abandoned house, looking indignant at being caught in such a disreputable state by the prying camera. The camera panned the area, showing guys in suits and grim expressions milling around. I didn't see anybody I recognized.

The anchorman said, ''The incident took place around one o'clock this afternoon just off Roswell Road. The agents had been directed there by Jones for the purpose of recovering approximately two hundred thousand dollars in gems taken during a daylight robbery in Fort Lauderdale two months ago. Jones scooped a revolver from a pile of trash and ordered the agents to lie on the ground. He then disarmed them, handcuffed the agents together and fled the area in an FBI car. The missing automobile was discovered abandoned an hour later in a shopping center on Piedmont Road. No one was injured in the incident, but officials have refused to identify the agents involved. A nationwide alert has been put out on the fugitive, who is described as a loner, six feet two inches tall, weighing one hundred ninety pounds, with blue eyes and brown hair. He should be considered armed and dangerous. Anyone seeing this man should notify the FBI or local police.''

I got up from the bed and snapped off the set, staring at the pinpoint of light in the middle of the screen until it faded. I poured another drink from the nearly empty bottle on the dresser, dropped in my last three ice cubes and returned to the bed.

Armed and dangerous. First time I had ever been called that. Shit, *they* had the guns, not me. Before I met up with Joe Morgan, I had never even *carried* a gun. Until today. In every other situation I could ever remember being in, it was always me who ran the risk of being injured or killed. A couple times I came pretty close.

As for being an escape risk, I guess I would have to plead guilty as charged. I had been running from one thing to another for as long as I could remember; if I didn't like something, I simply ran away from it and considered the problem solved—or so I thought. The trouble with running is that, like anything repetitive, it becomes habit-forming. Suddenly it's the great cure-all, the not-so-secret formula that magically causes all of life's unpleasantness to disappear. What it really is, however, is a race with no finish line.

I downed the rest of my drink, set the glass on the formica nightstand, buried my head in the fluffy pillow and tried to will myself to sleep. But the past kept flashing through my mind, flitting across the backs of my eyelids as if cast there by a slide projector. I was becoming melancholy and reflective. I always become melancholy and reflective when I drink, questioning the past and doubting the future. How many jails and prisons had I been in? How many had I escaped from?

Maybe I should count them instead of sheep.

# CHAPTER 2

*Falmouth, Virginia*
*Fifteen years earlier*

THE INSISTENT CLANGING OF THE FIRE BELL WAS SOME-
thing I had come to dread. Every day for the last two years,
except for Sundays and holidays, I had been wakened from a
sound sleep by that nerve-wracking clamor. It was enough to
drive anybody up a wall. For thirty seconds the infernal racket
would continue, leaving no doubt that everyone in the
hundred-man dormitory was awake. Even if you were deaf it
wouldn't matter; you could feel the vibration in your bones.
A hell of a way to start a day.

At last everybody was up, standing bleary-eyed at the foot
of our bunks. A straggler or two had to be hurried along by
a well-placed whack from the floorwalker's wooden cane.
Only then did the damnable bell stop ringing.

The floorwalker went to the front of the dormitory and
nodded to the guard standing outside the barred gate, who
unlocked it and let out a bellow.

"Awright, let's git them bunks made! Five minutes!"

We didn't waste any time carrying out the order, complete
with six-inch white collar over the brown Army surplus blanket and hospital tucks at the foot. When we finished we stood
at attention beside our bunks, a shifty-looking bunch in

scraggly underwear. Then the floorwalker stalked through the gate, and we fell behind in single file, marched into the corridor and down a flight of steps into the basement. We had ten minutes to dress in dirty khakis, douse the sleep from our faces and elbow our way for a turn at one of the three urinals nestled against the back wall. Then we took a seat on our individual cube-shaped wooden boxes that lined the basement and waited.

At five-forty-five Captain Eli put in his appearance at the bottom of the steps, which was our cue to come to attention again. After a nod from him we would march single file back up the steps, past the dormitory and into the chow hall.

Breakfast, like every meal, was conducted in strict silence. "You can't talk if you're yakkin' " was one of Eli's favorite expressions. We ate quickly, slurping our grits, gravy and fatback and sopping up the residue with case-hardened cathead biscuits. The only sound was that of a hundred spoons scraping tin plates and the occasional coughs, grunts and open-mouth belches generally associated with such gatherings. Like a bunch of hungry hogs at the slop trough, watched over by two guards who constantly circulated about the room.

Slop time over, it was back to the basement again, where we grabbed coats, gloves and caps from the cloakroom, parked ourselves back on the little wooden boxes and waited for work call—all in complete silence.

At six-fifteen the camp Lieutenant opened the rear door from outside and stepped into the basement, clipboard in hand. One by one he called out the work gangs, each consisting of ten men.

"Armstrong! Wolfie! Shackleford! Stafford!" and so on. As the gangs were called, the men assigned filed past the Lieutenant and lined up double file on the walkway outside, where ten shotgun guards were spread out in a semicircle to make sure nobody went too far.

When we were all in position the Lieutenant came over to Wolfie's gang and pointed to me with the clipboard. "Fall out, Jones, you're seein' the board today."

Sweet music to my ears! I was finally going to meet with the parole board, something I had been looking forward to with growing impatience for the past two weeks, thinking they would never get here. I fell out of line and walked back into the basement, hearing the iron door clang shut behind me.

I stood on one of the boxes and peered through a barred window, watching the gangs standing quietly on the sidewalk. A yellow dump truck with a slatted wooden cage called a rack loaded on the back pulled to a stop at the end of the walkway, and Armstrong's gang piled inside. A shotgun guard climbed over the tailgate, locked the rack with a chain and padlock, then sat down on a little bench next to the tailgate. As the truck pulled away with its human cargo, another took its place, until finally all the gangs had been loaded and were on their way to another day of backbreaking labor. At least I would get a respite from that. But at that moment I was more concerned about the two-man parole team I would be seeing sometime during the day.

Chain Gang Camp 21, located thirty-three miles outside Richmond, Virginia, was one of thirty such camps scattered throughout the state. They had brought me there two years earlier on a gray bus called The Long Chain, packed in with sixty-eight other recently sentenced prisoners who were being distributed among the camps. A few weeks before, I had been convicted in Richmond Superior Court of grand larceny by possession and given ten years' hard labor. I had married my high-school sweetheart the previous month, both of us figuring we were all grown up, and gave her a stolen wedding-ring set I had bought for seventy-five dollars. I had a hunch they might be hot when the black kid in the shiny green shirt and pegged pants showed them to me in the parking lot of John Marshall High School, but I didn't ask. I didn't tell Gloria, either. How was I to know she was going to take the things to a pawn shop on Third Street and have them appraised? And there they were—right on their Hot Sheet.

From my first day at the camp I realized that I was in for a long haul. Captain Eli put me in Wolfie's gang. Wolfie, who was without question the meanest human I had ever seen, loved to call everybody Shorty; it didn't matter if you were seven feet tall. Being only five feet four himself he no doubt had a short-man complex, which tended to sour what otherwise must have been a perfectly loveable disposition. If Wolfie didn't like how you worked, he would turn to his truck driver and say "Dump that load, Dave," and Dave would dump the rack, and the subject of Wolfie's displeasure would be chained behind the cab. He would then be taken back to camp, turned over to the Lieutenant and placed in solitary confinement—better known as the "hole"—where his staple diet would be bread and water. For a minor offense such as poor work, the average stay was a week to ten days—the first time. Let it happen again, and you were good for thirty. Once was usually enough, however, for the hole was just that; a five-by-eight-foot concrete box with absolutely nothing inside except a one-gallon can in which to deposit body waste.

I was young and strong, so I never went to the hole for poor work. But it was a rare day when I didn't return to camp at sundown wanting to do nothing but fall into my bunk. Many times I had been so drained of energy that I even rebelled at climbing the steps to the chow hall; it just didn't seem worth the effort. I would simply fall onto my box, stuporous from fatigue, and sit there until regaining enough strength to pull off my work clothes.

But at last my day had come, the day I had been praying for. Other than a couple of minor incidents, I had maintained a relatively clean record. There was the time I had gotten into a fight with Tugboat Adams, for which we both wound up in the hole for three weeks. But fights were a common occurrence in camp and weren't considered serious, unless a weapon was used. It had been pretty much a one-sided fight— in favor of Tugboat. He had a punch like a mule's kick and was without question the bull of the camp; it wasn't by chance that he had been nicknamed Tugboat.

The only other mark against my record had occurred a few months earlier, when we were cutting right-of-way on Farm Road 619. I had found an unopened can of Schlitz and tried to chug-a-lug it before anyone noticed. But old eagle-eyed Wolfie put a crimp in that, and I ended up spending another two weeks in the hole. But this too was a minor charge and should have no bearing on a parole decision.

Shortly after nine o'clock the Lieutenant escorted me upstairs to the Captain's office, which the parole board members were using as an interview room. I took a seat in the straight-backed chair opposite Eli's beat-up desk and regarded the two men on the other side with what I hoped was a respectful look. They were both deeply engrossed in the contents of a legal-size folder, which I knew contained not only my record since I had been at camp, but practically my entire life's history as well. I wondered how much of it they were going to hold against me.

The older of the two men finally raised his head and acknowledged my presence. "Good morning, Jones. My name is Mr. Blair, and this is Mr. Hinkel."

"Good morning, sir."

Blair removed a pair of oval glasses and cleared his throat. "As you know, Mr. Hinkel and I are here today to conduct your parole hearing." He motioned toward the file his companion was studying. "We've been looking at your record and, quite frankly, have found a few things that disturb us. We wonder if you would care to comment on them?"

"Yes sir," I said. It was obvious that Blair was the spokesman here, so I focused my attention on him.

Blair steepled his fingers under his chin, leaned back in the chair and continued. "I see you were sent to Beaumont when you were . . . what, eight years old? Juvenile delinquency. What was that all about?"

I said, "A couple of older kids had stolen some military rings from an Army/Navy store on Broad Street, in Richmond. They gave them to me to sell for a quarter each, and I got to keep a dime for each one I sold. What they didn't tell me was that I started selling them on the same block the Army/Navy store was on."

"And they sent you to Beaumont for that?"

"Yes sir," I answered. I was twisting about in my chair, nervous as hell. "My mother had to work—her and my father were divorced, so she had to support us. I used to play hooky a lot, I guess, hanging out at Bird Park, and I'd already been in front of a juvenile judge a couple times for that. I guess he got tired of seeing me there, 'cause when the ring incident came up he told my mother I needed strict male supervision. He said Beaumont was the best place for me."

For the first time Hinkel had something to say. "But you stayed there two years . . . and then you were only out about three months before you got sent back for another two years. What happened? Didn't you learn your lesson the first time?"

I looked at Hinkel, feeling my cheeks flush. "When I was at Beaumont the first time, I had to deal with kids twice my age. I didn't know anything about reform-school life. I was the youngest boy there—and plenty scared. But by the time I left I was talking and acting like a real tough guy—too tough for kids my own age but not tough enough for the older ones. Anyway, I learned how to hot-wire a car at Beaumont and decided to show off for some of the bigger kids. So I jumped the wires of a '51 Ford and was going to drive it over to Bill's Bar-B-Q one Friday night. But I didn't know how to drive and ended up sideswiping a pickup truck as I was pulling away from the curb, and the driver held me for the police. Ten days later, back to Beaumont I went.''

"So you were a car thief at ten," Hinkel said in a flat voice. "And it doesn't look as if your second stint at Beaumont did any good either. Didn't you learn anything, boy?''

"Yes sir," I said, feeling the heat rising. "I learned plenty. How to hot-wire a car before I could even drive, how to pop open storm doors and windows with a screwdriver, how to break the tumblers in a knob-lock with a pair of channel-lock pliers. I also learned what it felt like to be 'stomped' by my cottage Father for not calling him 'Sir,' and how bad it hurt to be knocked to the ground with a bloody head after being hit with a grubbing hoe-handle because I couldn't keep up with the other boys out in the fields. And I learned what it felt like to be beaten with a razor strap until my bottom bled for not making my bunk properly. Other than that I guess I didn't really learn much of anything—not even in school, because the cottage Fathers' wives did the teaching, and even then we only went an hour a day. What they were mainly interested in was how much work they could get out of us in the fields, so they could get a healthy profit from their fruits and vegetables. And when you're constantly told that you're no damn good, it doesn't take long before you start believing it—not at that age, anyway.''

I knew I was sounding bitter, but I couldn't hold back the words. Everything I had said was true. And furthermore, *they* knew that it was true. I wasn't the only graduate of Beaumont they had ever dealt with. Nor would I be the last.

"What they teach at Beaumont is *discipline!*" Hinkel barked. "It's pretty obvious to me that you needed some.''

"What they teach at Beaumont is sadism," I said, "not to mention homosexuality.'' I realized that I might be going too

**20**

far, but at the moment I didn't really care. Prudence had been pushed aside by mental images.

"Did any of the supervisors engage in homosexual acts with you?" Blair asked, leaning forward in his chair.

I hesitated a moment, unable to drive away the visions his question had triggered:

*A tiny two-room apartment adjacent to the upstairs dormitory; a rumpled sofa in front of a portable black-and-white TV with a baseball game in progress. A nine-year-old boy staring stiffly at the screen through terrified eyes while the naked cottage Father sat close beside him, pressing him into the arm of the sofa with his damp body while mumbling gentle assurances. The boy's trembling hand being guided to the man's lap, forced to grip the erect penis; the large calloused hand wrapped around his smaller hand, assisting in the jerky up-and-down movements; raspy breath warm against his neck. Then the hand at the back of his neck, squeezing and pulling, forcing his head downward, down toward the turgid thing that protruded obscenely from the hairy lap—until his face was buried against it, feeling it throbbing against his cheek. The man's throaty demand: "Open your mouth!" and he refusing, lips clamped desperately together; the fingers at the back of his neck squeezing tighter still. Then the spurting semen drenching his face and hair, his head being pressed even harder into the man's lap, until he felt as if he would surely suffocate—and half wished that he would. Then had come the beating, and threats of more horrible tortures to follow if he ever mentioned what had happened to the superintendent; the humiliation of the vileness that had been forced on him, and the frustration of a body not yet strong enough to prevent it from happening.*

"I asked you a question," Blair said.

I pulled myself away from the past. "Sorry. No sir, I can't say that ever happened." Which was true; I *couldn't* say it. Not to these two, anyway.

The two men looked at me in silence for a moment, then Blair closed my file and asked me to wait outside while they made their decision. I walked slowly to the door, closed it softly behind me and leaned heavily against the wall. Now came the hard part: the waiting. Inside, two men were deciding my fate. My entire future was in the hands of two strangers who knew absolutely nothing about me except what had been randomly written in my progress reports dating back eleven years; reports written by men whose thoughts, ideas and conceptions were not necessarily the same as mine; men whose positions of authority permitted them the prerogative of exercising and implementing their own small grudges and prejudices. Men like the cottage "Fathers" of Beaumont.

The door opened, and Blair motioned me inside. I took my seat and regarded the two men apprehensively, trying to look beneath the noncommittal expressions. Hinkel was busy writing in my file and didn't even acknowledge my presence. Blair took his seat behind the desk and studied me gravely.

"Jones, we're going to deny parole at this time. Except for a couple of minor incident reports, your progress here has been satisfactory. But you're only eighteen years old and already have spent six years in custody of one form or another. Because of this, we cannot classify you as a first offender eligible for favorable action at your first appearance before this board. Mr. Hinkel and I would like to be sure that you fully appreciate the seriousness of your actions before placing you back in society. You'll be brought before the board again in one year, at which time you'll be given another review. Any questions?"

I sat there feeling numb, staring at my clenched hands. Oh, I had questions all right, but none that it would serve any purpose to ask. I was stuck here for another year—at least. And I had no assurance that anything would be any different then. Their decision had been reached, and nothing I could say was going to change it now.

"No sir, I guess I don't."

"Then that will be all. Just keep your nose clean and maybe things will be more favorable next year."

I rose stiffly and headed for the door. As I did, Hinkel called to me. "Tell the Lieutenant we're ready for an early lunch, will you?"

I stopped with my hand on the doorknob, turned and looked

at him in amazement. Was he trying to be cute, or was he really that desensitized?

"Tell him yourself . . . sir," I said.

I paused just long enough to see his thin face turn beet red, then turned on my heel and stalked angrily through the door, slamming it shut behind me. It was a stupid, childish move, but the small act of defiance nevertheless brought a measure of satisfaction. It also placed me in an irreversible position, which subconsciously may have been just what I wanted. Whatever chance I had of making parole next year was certainly gone now.

I was perched on my box staring at the opposite wall when the gangs filed into the basement a little after six that evening. We had thirty minutes to clean up, and everyone was scurrying about, jockeying for positions around the large circular sink that dominated one corner of the basement. Many of the men stopped to ask how I had made out with the parole board and were genuinely surprised to hear that I had been denied. And no doubt just a little pessimistic about their own chances. After all, I had one of the best records in camp.

After chow we had two hours of free time in the basement for dominoes, letter writing, reading, or just shooting the bull. At nine o'clock all activity ceased, and we were locked into the dormitory for the night, where sleep invariably came quickly.

Tugboat was sitting on his box thumbing through a year-old edition of *Playboy* magazine when I approached him after chow. He had attempted to escape a few months earlier but hadn't been successful. For three days and nights he had fought the bitter cold of the countryside, leading the dogs on a merry chase through heavy woods that covered nearly thirty miles. But in the end the cold and exhaustion had worn him down, and he had been captured in a farmer's barn, hiding in a grain bin. Those dogs hadn't even hesitated when they entered the barn; they ran right up to that grain bin and started baying like lovesick bulls. When Tugboat had been returned to camp—nearly frozen and carrying the marks of a thorough beating—he was thrown into the hole without so much as a cup of coffee, and there he languished for two months. When he had finally been let out, a set of leg chains were riveted to his ankles. He would have to wear them twenty-four hours a day for six months.

Tugboat lowered the magazine as I took a seat on the box next to him and searched for a way to begin the conversation. "I still can't get over how you get in and out of your pants with those chains on," I said lamely. .

"Nothin' to it, once you get the hang of it," he replied, twisting his bull neck in my direction. "Now, what else you got on your mind? You've been cuttin' your eyes at me all night, and I ain't too sure I like it."

I was glad to see he was in a good mood. Tugboat had become a lot friendlier toward me after our lopsided fight; he was possibly feeling a little guilty about boosting his image by pummeling one so young and inexperienced. I glanced quickly about the noisy basement and lowered my voice.

"Well, there is something you might help me with. I've decided to hit the bushes, and I need a little advice."

He looked at me, surprised. "Why the hell you want to do that? I heard the board turned you down today, but you'll make it sure next time—you ain't got that heavy a beef."

"I don't want to wait 'til next year, Tug. Besides, I already blew that. I backtalked Hinkel today; might just as well have told him to get fucked."

"That was dumb." But Tugboat was smiling nevertheless. That was the kind of reaction he could identify with.

"I know, but I was really pissed. All they wanted to talk about was what happened when I was a kid."

"That long ago, huh?" I saw the flash of amusement in Tugboat's eyes and knew what he was thinking; I was still a kid.

"Anyway, my mind's made up. But I need you to tell me how to beat those damn dogs. I'm not very good at this sort of thing."

Tugboat studied me carefully for a moment, gauging my seriousness. Convinced, he scratched absently at one huge, hairy forearm and nodded.

"All right. I got somethin' stashed in the coatroom that'll do the job. In a mustard jar behind the baseboard, just to the left of the door. Been savin' it for when these damn chains come off. Get yourself one of them plastic aspirin bottles and pour some in—just don't take it all."

"What is it?" I asked, trying to mask my excitement.

"Ammonia."

"Ammonia?"

"Nothin' better. It'll fuck up a dog's nose so bad he won't be able to smell cow shit for a week. Take along a handkerchief when you go. When you get about a mile or so, pour that ammonia over it and drop it where it's sure to be seen. The dog boy'll naturally run the dogs to it for a good sniff. When that happens, it's all over. Just wish I'd had some when I went."

I let this sink in, decided it sounded feasible and nodded. "Thanks, Tug, I appreciate that."

"Just be careful. You're in Wolfie's gang, and Harmon's the guard. He's sharp and don't miss much. If you let him get a shot at you, he'll kill you. He's already got two notches on that stock as it is."

That was a fact of which I was well aware. Harmon was the most dangerous guard in camp, and a crack shot. He was also as cold-blooded as they come; Eddie Meade and Thomas Stacy could attest to that—had they still been alive. Both had been brought down by a single load of double-ought buckshot from Harmon's twelve-gauge pump while trying to escape. Eddie Meade had been wearing leg chains when making his bid, and Harmon could simply have let the truck driver run him down, had he wanted. Instead, he had calmly watched as Meade made a shuffling run across the road we had been working on, trying desperately to reach a ditch on the other side. The two-foot chain around his ankles had rendered his strides about as effective as a three-year-old toddler's. I had only been at the camp about two months and couldn't believe it when Harmon nonchalantly raised the shotgun to his shoulder, took deliberate aim and pulled the trigger. The distance had been no more than twenty yards. The blast tore open the back of Meade's neck and knocked him face first into the ditch he had been so desperately attempting to reach. He had lain there, twitching, fingers hooked into trembling talons as they scratched reflexively at the muddy ditch bottom. After what seemed like an eternity, he lay still.

Wolfie and Dave finally went into the ditch and pulled him out, dragging him by his heels. Dave dumped the rack and pulled the truck over to the mangled body. He and Wolfie lifted it by ankles and armpits and tossed it into the back of the truck like a sack of flour.

The entire incident had been sickening to watch, but you could never tell from Harmon's reaction. He had casually bent down, picked up the spent shell and dropped it into his jacket pocket. All shells had to be accounted for with the Lieutenant.

I wasn't there when Stacy got it; that had taken place five or six months before my arrival. But no one else had attempted to hit the bushes since Eddie Meade. Harmon had made believers of us all.

I managed to locate an empty aspirin bottle and found the ammonia where Tugboat said it would be. I poured a generous amount, making certain there was plenty left for Tug, then placed the two bottles in back of the loose baseboard. I had a pretty good idea when I would be using mine.

I spent the next two weeks watching Harmon's every move. Until now I had never paid that much attention, since escape had been the furthest thing from my mind. But all that had changed now, and I had to face the fact that, in order to be successful, I would have to face Harmon's gun. And that scared me more than just a little.

At last we began work on the project I had been waiting for. A new highway department substation was going up in Falmouth County, and Wolfie's gang would be doing the excavation and foundation work. We would be at the site for about three weeks, and I was certain that within that time I would get my chance. So the day after we began, I retrieved my bottle of ammonia and took it with me when we left camp. During lunch, which consisted of two spam-and-cheese sandwiches, I hid the bottle at the base of a large tree stump I was using as a makeshift table.

My opportunity arrived sooner than I expected and was made possible by Harmon himself. Bulldozers had completed the initial excavation work, and several truckloads of fill dirt had been brought in to level the bottom of the large pit, which measured about fifty yards long and twenty yards wide. An air tamper had to be used to pack the dirt firm as it was shoveled into the pit, and Harmon chose me to operate the machine.

For three days I worked the tamper, which operates on the

same principal as a jackhammer, standing at the bottom of the eight-foot-deep crater, packing the dirt firm as the other men shoveled it in from topside. Harmon always sat on an overturned apple crate about twenty feet from the edge, which placed me out of his immediate vision. But whenever I took my hand away from the trigger, causing the machine to stop its noisy thumping, he would rise and walk to the edge of the pit to make sure I was still there.

At lunchtime on day four I removed the ammonia bottle from its hiding place and slipped it into my back pocket. In another pocket was a six-inch length of baling wire.

I was as ready as I would ever be.

Shortly after returning to work, I paused for a moment to wipe the perspiration from my face, using a bright red handkerchief Tugboat had given me. Harmon strolled to the edge of the hole and watched calmly until I had finished. When I tucked the handkerchief away and started the machine again, he walked away.

As soon as he disappeared I removed the wire from my pocket with my left hand and quickly wrapped it around the trigger on the right handle of the tamper. Slowly I eased the pressure from my right hand and, making certain the machine continued to run, lowered it gently to the ground. A few of the men shoveling near the edge saw what was happening, but I knew they wouldn't give me away. If I made it, they would be returned to camp for the rest of the day.

My heart was pounding faster than the unattended air tamper as I made a dash for the far end of the pit. I reached it, made a leap for the edge and missed. I tried again. My fingers clawed frantically at the loose dirt along the top, couldn't find sufficient grip, and once again I slid back into the hole.

It was then that I noticed the tamper had stopped running. Harmon would be heading over for a look.

In desperation I gathered myself for one final all-out leap. I sprang forward with all the strength my legs could muster, propelled by high-octane terror. I caught the rim with hooked fingers, dug them deeply into the crumbling earth and slowly struggled to the top.

There was a thick copse of pines only a few yards away, and I wasted no time reaching it. I zigzagged my way through the saplings like a man possessed, running close to the ground, heading for the deeper woods beyond. A shot rang out, and the air above my head hummed from the few passing pellets that had not been stopped by the trees behind. Another shot, this one not even close. Then I was in the deep woods, feeling the sting of low-hanging branches slapping my face and the sharp thorns of bramble bushes clutching at my legs. Even in my terror I felt exhilarated as I wildly dodged the oncoming trees. I was free! The words were like a song in my mind, and I sang them over and over as I charged the silent forest. Even so, I knew the difficult part still lay ahead; I had to keep from being captured. But somehow I knew I wouldn't be. I could feel it—taste it! It nestled in the hollow of my tongue like a candy kiss.

And it was oh so sweet!

The rest of the afternoon and well into the evening I continued my headlong plunge into the Virginia countryside; sometimes running, sometimes walking, but always moving. My earlier elation had waned, leaving me sobered by the enormity of the situation. Men with guns were somewhere behind me—perhaps even in front of me. And they wouldn't hesitate to use those guns at the slightest opportunity. The coming night held unknown terrors as well, for I was inexperienced in the ways of the deep woods. My mouth was parched to the point where I couldn't even spit, and I craved water the way a blind man craves sight.

I had decided to wait until I heard the baying of the dogs before using the ammonia. I wanted my scent to be as strong as possible when they came upon it. With a little luck, perhaps they would lose the trail on their own. Then I remembered the book Tugboat had loaned me describing various breeds of dogs and realized that this was only wishful thinking. Unbelievably, the bloodhound's sense of smell was estimated—according to the book—to be six million times that of humans. Six million! They would find my trail all right. And they would keep coming until something interfered with their damnable noses!

At last I took a break and flopped beside a gnarled old pine, breathing deeply of the sweet-scented air. Judging from the shadows, it had to be nearly six o'clock. The gang would be in camp about now. I wondered what Tugboat would say when he heard the news. I certainly knew what Eli would say!

Suddenly, for no explicable reason, I threw back my head and laughed uproariously, the kind that begins in the lower stomach, works its way up through the diaphragm, gathering force as it does, until it explodes in uncontrollable gusts, going on and on until you gasp for air, weak from the effort and with tears drenching your cheeks. But it drains the emotions; love, hate, fear, tension—everything. The steam escapes from the pressure cooker and somehow leaves you feeling better for the experience.

I was still resting some ten minutes later when I heard them. At first I wasn't certain, and I strained my ears for the familiar deep-throated baying until I heard it again. There was no mistake.

The hounds were on the trail.

I jumped to my feet and quickly pulled out handkerchief and ammonia. I doused the cloth, making certain it was thoroughly soaked, and let it fall to the ground next to the pine tree. Then I set out at a fast trot in a direction other than I had previously been heading. I had no idea where I was going. But neither would anyone else.

It was nearly dark when I came upon the stream. And a beautiful sight it was. Wending through a tiny niche in the forest floor some six feet wide and four to six inches deep. I sprawled facedown in its coolness and felt the heat start to fade from my body, drinking deeply, greedily. I could remember nothing ever tasting so wonderful.

Having drunk my fill, I stood and listened to the gathering night sounds that surrounded me. No longer could I hear the dogs. But neither could I take for granted that the ammonia-soaked handkerchief had indeed done its job. So I set out again at a decent pace, keeping to the middle of the small stream, pausing every now and again to scoop a handful of the precious liquid into my mouth.

A few miles further, the stream began to deepen. I took one last drink and returned to the deeper woods, picking my way cautiously through the pitch blackness. Sometime later I came upon an open area surrounded by isolated stands of tall pines. I raked some of the sweet-scented needles into a makeshift mattress and settled down for the night. Within minutes I had fallen into an exhausted sleep.

I was awakened shortly after daybreak by a sharp clash of thunder. Heavy drops of cold rain filtered down through the sheltering pines and jagged streaks of lightning illuminated the ash-colored sky like gigantic flashbulbs. Within minutes I was in the midst of a torrential downpour. But it was a most welcome discomfort, for no one was going to be tracking me in this weather. I got to my feet, brushed at the clinging pine needles and started walking.

By midmorning the rain had stopped, and the sun was starting to break through the parting clouds. I came upon a power line and followed it until I spotted a highway in the distance. Then I abandoned the trail and worked my way closer through the covering forest.

I was within fifty yards of the highway when I noticed a small wood-frame house off to my left. As I watched, a middle-aged woman stepped out on the porch, locked the door behind her and drove off in an old Ford pickup truck. She bounced along the old rutted driveway and carefully joined the rushing traffic on the highway. After she had disappeared into the distance, I hunkered down in a clump of bushes to watch for other signs of life in the house, conscious of my growing hunger.

Fifteen minutes later I was standing beneath the kitchen window. It was down but not locked, and I had no difficulty making an entrance.

It was a small house; a bedroom, living room, kitchen and bath. I checked them one by one and confirmed my earlier opinion that no one else was about. Then I returned to the kitchen and set about raiding the ancient refrigerator. Ham, cheese, leftover navy beans and a quart of milk later, I felt more like my old self. Then I went searching for clothing to replace my prison issue.

In the bedroom I found a pair of patched but clean blue jeans, a plaid work shirt and a hunting cap with earflaps. I changed into the new garb, bundled up my prison khakis and returned to the kitchen. The borrowed clothes were a little large, but much preferable to what I had been wearing.

I made a final ham-and-cheese sandwich, stuck an unopened bottle of Coke in my back pocket, tucked my bundle under my arm and took my leave through the rear door.

Back in the woods I dug a hole in the loose soil and buried my prison clothes. Then I moved as close to the highway as I could without being seen by passing motorists and sat down beside a patch of dogwood trees. I reached for my Coke, popped the cap with the church key I carried on my key ring and thought about what I should do now.

I didn't have long to ponder. I was just finishing the Coke when a tractor-trailer rig loaded with new cars eased off the highway and came to a stop on the graveled shoulder not more than a hundred feet from where I sat. The driver stepped down from the cab with what appeared to be a wrench in his hand. He went to the front of the rig, raised the hood and started tinkering underneath.

I was on my feet in a flash, discarding the empty bottle and fighting my way through the clinging brush to the highway. The rig was only forty or fifty feet away now, and I covered the distance quickly, praying the driver would stay beneath the hood just a few minutes more.

I reached the rear of the trailer and swung up behind the end car. I opened the door and slid into the passenger seat, breathing the clean smell of new leather upholstery. Quietly, I pulled the door shut behind me. I scrunched down in the seat, head against the armrest, and made myself comfortable. A few minutes later I heard the cab door slam. The big rig came to life, and soon I was on my way, knowing not where and caring less. All that mattered was that I had made it.

I was free.

# CHAPTER 3

My DESTINATION TURNED OUT TO BE A NEW-CAR DEALER-
ship in the West End district of Richmond, less than an hour
away. I slipped out of the new Chevrolet while the driver was
inside the office, jumped to the ground and walked off the
lot. I joined the flow of pedestrians on Sheppard Street, feeling conspicuous and out of place. Prison has a way of doing
that to you. When you suddenly find yourself back in the Free
World after years of being locked away, you feel alienated
and confused—out of the comfort zone you've grown used to.
You look upon ordinary things taken for granted by those
outside with a sense of awe. Inconsequential things such as
eating with knife and fork, the simple act of walking through
a department store, the smell of perfume, the sound of kids
laughing, trying to carry on a conversation with a pretty girl
without dribbling all over yourself. You have to develop a
whole new behavior pattern in order to cope with this strange
environment so vaguely remembered. A lot of guys find the
transition difficult to handle . . . others find it impossible,
inevitably leading back to prison. Life in the Free World is
just too complicated, and the feeling of not fitting in, of not
belonging, results in frustration and anger. When you're used
to fatback and beans, it's hard to eat steak and eggs without
gulping and getting a stomachache.

After a few blocks I found myself standing in front of the
State Theater, where I used to watch Saturday matinees as a

kid. It was deserted now, the glass doors and ticket booth painted black. I stared at the empty marquee, remembering temporary heroes in Stetson hats, shiny boots and tied-down forty-fours charging across the screen on speedy mounts to rescue damsels in distress. Not so many years ago, either. And yet I felt ancient as I stood there and for a few moments turned back the clock. Ancient and out-of-date.

I decided that I wanted to see Mom—at least once before leaving Richmond, which would have to be soon. When they finally decided I was no longer in the woods of Falmouth County, the search would shift to my hometown. I wanted to be long gone by then.

I flagged a passing taxi and told the driver to take me to A.H. Robbins Pharmaceutical Company. He gave me a dubious look, then shrugged and started the meter. I knew my ill-fitting clothes didn't exactly inspire confidence.

The meter read nearly four dollars when we pulled up in front of the lobby doors leading inside the long, one-story building. I stepped from the cab and asked the drive to wait.

"I'll do better than that," he said, falling in beside me. "I'll just tag along with you. Wouldn't want you to get lost."

We walked into the lobby; and the cabbie waited by the glass doors as I walked to the reception desk. I asked the lady there for Mrs. Heddie Bosher and waited while she consulted a directory from inside her desk. Then she picked up her phone, spoke to the appropriate department head, replaced the receiver and flashed me a smile.

"Mrs. Bosher works in Packaging. She'll be right out. Take a seat if you like."

I thanked her and took a seat, twirling my stolen cap and watching the cab driver skeptically watching me.

A few minutes later a side door opened, and an attractive lady in a white smock entered the lobby. She noticed me as I stood, her face registering first shock, then joy. She hurried to me and threw her arms around my neck.

"Edward! What in the world are you doing here? Did you make parole?" She quickly lowered her voice and glanced at the receptionist to see if she had heard. "And where did you get those clothes?"

"I'll explain everything in a minute, Mom. But first I need four dollars to pay that cab driver."

She reached into a pocket of her smock and came out with a small coin purse, removed four singles and handed them to me. I walked to where the cabby was waiting impatiently.

"How much?" I asked.

"Three-eighty," he said.

I handed him the bills and turned away. "Keep the change."

"Thanks a bunch, big time." He jammed the bills into his pocket and stalked through the lobby doors.

I steered Mom to a nearby sofa and sat down beside her. I took her hand and carefully explained everything that had happened since my meeting with the parole members three weeks earlier. She listened with a bewildered expression on her face until I finished, then slowly shook her head in disbelief.

"God, Edward," she said. "Why in the world did you have to go and do that? You can't come home now. What about Gloria and Dee Dee?"

Gloria was the high-school sweetheart I had run off to Dillon, South Carolina, with and married. Dee Dee, our daughter, had been born three months after I had been sentenced to prison. But even before then we had been having our problems, arguing and fighting almost constantly. Neither of us had been mature enough to face the responsibilities of marriage.

"That was over before it even began, Mom—you know that. She's back with her parents anyway, where she should be, and there's no point in either of us whipping a dead horse. And I can't go back to that camp now, either. What's done is done, and I'll have to make the best of it . . . By the way, can I get a little money from you? Twenty will do, if you have it."

"What are you going to do when that's gone?" she said. "Steal?"

"I'll think of something. Don't worry."

She was silent for a moment, staring out through the lobby window, deep in private thoughts. She turned back to me, brushed a hand lightly across my forehead. "My car's in the lot just outside. Go wait for me. I'll be along shortly. I'll take you over to Elmo's apartment and try to get you squared away somehow."

"That might not be such a good idea," I said. "The cops probably know all about him, and if they're looking for me in Richmond they just might stop by."

Mom had been unofficially engaged to Elmo Thomas three years earlier, and I was positive their relationship hadn't gone unnoticed by the Richmond police—especially since Elmo was a regular hunting companion of at least one member of the department.

Mom said, "I'm sure you'll be just fine there for a couple of hours—at least until I can go by the house and get you some decent clothes. Now run along, I'll be there in a few minutes."

She patted me on the cheek, then stood and hurried away, disappearing into the side door leading into the factory. The receptionist looked after her, curious, then glanced at me. I gave her a bright smile and left, hoping she hadn't overheard.

I was sitting on Elmo's couch reading his morning paper when Mom came back a little after three in the afternoon, struggling with a huge suitcase. I jumped up and took it from her, amazed at how heavy the thing was.

"What did you put in here?" I asked. "Rocks? This thing must weight fifty pounds."

"You're going to need clothes, son," she panted. "Now for goodness sakes take those things off so I can throw them away! Did you eat anything yet! I'll fix something while you change."

While she fussed about in the kitchen I removed my borrowed clothes and put on some of my own. I had already showered and repaired the worst of the cuts and scratches I had suffered on my flight through the countryside. Then I joined Mom in the kitchen where she had milk, sandwiches and potato chips waiting.

She sat across the table and watched closely as I ate, her face lined with worry. When she spoke, it was with the voice of one resigned to an unpleasant though unavoidable situation.

"Edward, what are you going to do? Where are you going to go?"

"I'll be all right, Mom. I saw in the paper the circus is in town set up over at the Fairgrounds. This is their last day, and I figure I might have a pretty good chance of getting a job. They're always looking for people who can travel.''

"The circus? Your uncle Charlie used to work for a circus when he came home from the service—said it was awful. And speaking of that, why couldn't you join the Army or something? At least you would have a decent place to sleep and three meals a day.''

"Mom, I can't join the Army," I explained patiently. "They take your fingerprints in the Army, and they check them. They'd know who I was the next day. And the circus isn't that bad. At least it's a job, and free transportation around the country. After a while I'll call and let you know where I am." I smiled and reached across the table to pat her hand. "Don't worry—I'll be just fine. I keep telling you.''

She sighed and looked away. "All right. When do you want to go?''

"As soon as I finish eating. I sure don't want to be here when Elmo gets home. We never did hit it off too good.''

"Don't be too hard on him, son. He had his good points. Course he has his bad ones too.''

"I just wish things could have worked out with you and Dick," I said. "I know damn well you two still care for each other. So what's the problem?''

Dick Bosher had married Mom when I was six years old and had been the closest to a father I had ever known. My real father had walked out on us shortly after I was born, and Mom had a rough time making ends meet for a while. Then she met Dick, who was just starting his hauling and trucking business. He also did a little bootlegging on the side, but no one ever held that against him. More than one needy family in Henrico County owed him a debt of gratitude. And when he gave, it was quietly and without fanfare—and most times anonymously. But things had soured between him and Mom after a few years, and right after my eighth birthday, Dick moved out. Divorce soon followed. Neither had ever told me what had happened, and I never asked. I figured it was their business, and if they wanted me to know, they would tell me. But at no time did either start throwing blame at the other, and I respected them both for that.

Mom got up and started clearing the table, falling silent the way she always did whenever I mentioned Dick's name.

So I dropped the subject and pitched in to give her a hand with the dishes. Then I gathered up my old clothes and carried them to the dumpster in back of the building. It was time to leave.

We arrived at the Fairgrounds shortly after five o'clock. Mom found an empty slot in the jammed parking lot and shut off the motor. For a couple of minutes we sat in awkward silence, Mom staring straight ahead, hands gripping the wheel, while I gazed out at the rows of cars reflecting dull sunlight. Finally she reached over and placed a hand on my knee. I looked at her, trying to ignore the wetness in her eyes. I had no idea when I would see her again, and I knew she was thinking the same.

She said, "Edward, are you sure this is what you want? What if they can't use you—what will you do then?"

"They always need people, Mom," I said. "And even if they don't I can always get a couple of meals and a ride to the next town just by helping them tear down. You gotta believe me, Mom—I'll be fine. I don't want you worrying yourself to death."

She nodded and reached into her purse, took out an envelope and handed it to me. She said, "Here's fifty dollars. I'd give you more but I just don't have it."

I took the envelope and stuck it in my pocket, not knowing what to say.

Mom said, "But I want you to promise you'll call if you need more—you hear me? I don't want you ending up sleeping in . . . in alleys, or having to steal to eat. I want you to promise me that, Edward."

I looked at her and said, "I promise, Mom. And thanks, I know you really can't afford this." I put my arms around her and held her, felt her sag against me. "I'll let you know where I am in a few days, okay?"

We untangled ourselves and sat back, looking at each other, both knowing the time for leaving was now. Then I got out and removed the heavy suitcase from the back seat.

"At least I won't need any clothes for about five years," I said lightly. She forced a smile as I walked around to her side and leaned in through the open window. "Do I get a good-by kiss, or what?"

She turned her face up and gave me a kiss on the cheek,

then leaned back and sighed. "You'll call me if you can't take care of things here?"

"Scout's honor," I said, and held up my hand in a mock salute. "If you don't hear from me tonight you'll know everything's fine. And I promise I'll be in touch in a few days."

"Make sure you do."

I gazed down at her for a moment, then leaned in and gave her a quick peck on the forehead. "Good-by, mom. I love you. And don't worry, okay?"

I turned and walked away, heading for the main gate. When I reached it I stopped and looked back. She was still there, a small figure in a white uniform. A mother wondering if she was ever going to see her son again. I gave a final wave and smiled and saw her blow me a kiss. Then I walked through the gate and made my way through the merry circus goers toward the huge Big Top in the background. Maybe, I thought, I'd make a good clown.

# CHAPTER 4

THE CLYDE BEATTY-COLE BROTHERS CIRCUS WAS BILLED as the largest under tent, and I believed it. They had enough canvas to keep Adidas going a year without reordering—at least it seemed that way to me. I was hired to help run one of the concession stands, selling hotdogs, Cokes and candied apples during the shows. I also had to pitch in with the clean-up details after each performance, which usually meant shoveling elephant shit—and believe me there's no shit like elephant shit, especially when one has the runs.

The one job everybody had to help with was tearing down and setting up the Big Top. It was damn hard work, but it beat the chain gang. It was the only part of my new life that I found boring, and only because we had to do it so often. Most of our stops were for one or two days only, and time was of the essence. Often we would pull into a town in the dead of night, weary from travel and lack of sleep, and immediately set to work unloading the caravan of trucks. We had to secure and feed the animals, raise the giant tent of the Big Top, set up the bleachers, erect the concession stands and game tents and a hundred other odds and ends, all ready for show time by ten o'clock the following morning. And when the last performance had ended, and the crowds had all gone home, the reverse procedure went into effect, and the entire show was packed, loaded and on the road, heading for yet another town. It was a hard life, with little of the glamor normally associated with circus life.

Occasionally we would hit a major city for a scheduled week or ten-day stint. These were welcome times, for everyone would have a little extra time to catch up on the more menial tasks that had so long been neglected—such as taking a bath, if you could afford a motel room. Our only other choice was to find an accommodating service station willing to share its bathroom facilities, something most were reluctant to do. For these we had our own way of getting even.

Nearly all of the highest paid performers traveled in their own cars, campers or motor homes. At any given time the Clyde Beatty-Cole Brothers Circus included anywhere between fifty and seventy-five such vehicles—not to mention the twenty-seven giant transport trucks that hauled the animals and equipment. Naturally this huge convoy required a great deal of fuel, and any station that barred its restrooms to circus personnel was guaranteed to watch its competitor break all existing sales records when the show was ready to leave town, regardless of the difference in price. Not one drop of the offending station's fuel would go into any circus vehicle. This was a matter of necessity as well as principle, because most circus workers were dependent on these stations for basic hygienic needs. Most station owners got the message after the first boycott and made their facilities available the following year.

It was late July when we caravanned into the City of Brotherly Love: Philadelphia, Pennsylvania. I had been with the circus a little more than two months and thoroughly enjoyed the hustle and bustle of life with the traveling Big Top. Philly was a ten-day stop, and I was looking forward to seeing the city. I was also savoring the idea of renting a motel room, where I planned to spend a couple of days soaking in a hot tub and sleeping on a real mattress. I was getting a little tired of the stiff Army cot inside the supply tent. I had three weeks' pay in my pocket and was feeling on top of the world, and even the horror of setting up tent city in a torrential downpour failed to dampen my mood.

Another cause for my high spirits came in the form of a seventeen-year-old trapeze artist named Tanya, who had joined the circus at the beginning of the season, along with her mother, father and two grim-faced brothers. They were from Czechoslovakia, and Tanya was the only one who could speak English; well enough to understand that I had slightly less than honorable intentions toward her. Her two brothers understood the same thing, and they couldn't speak a lick of English. You might say it was lust at first sight on my part, aided by the fact that, except for my mother, it had been more than two years since I had even spoken to a member of the opposite sex.

Tanya was a doll, no two ways about it: liquid blue eyes, fluffy blond hair that fell like cotton around her slender shoulders and a fully developed figure. Ever since leaving Wilmington, Delaware, I had been trying to get next to her, with only mild success. I was certain that things would have progressed more rapidly had it not been for the extreme coat of protectiveness her brothers kept around her, and those two boys looked as if they could have easily handled Tugboat. The only time we could scrounge a few moments alone together was in the mess tent, and only then because the other members of her family refused to eat anything prepared by the circus cooks.

Smart people.

Occasionally Tanya and I would sneak out behind the Big Top for a little lightweight petting, but she never permitted things to go any further. She had explained in her halting English that her brothers would "sken us while we live" if they even so much as caught us kissing. This wasn't entirely true, however; they would only "sken" me.

Finally she had given in and agreed to sneak off to a movie with me once we reached Philadelphia. This in itself I considered a major victory, for, hopefully, a movie would only be the beginning of what could prove to be a very interesting evening.

I had already made arrangements with my boss, Sammy Clemons, to borrow his car for the night, and Tanya had agreed to meet me in back of the mess tent after the last performance.

The final show ended at ten o'clock, and the crowd spilled from the Big Top, jamming the midway, flocking to the gaming tents. I was pacing nervously behind the mess tent,

**41**

squeaky-clean in my best sport shirt and slacks, jingling the keys to Sammy Clemons' beat-up station wagon.

At ten-fifteen I saw her appear at the far side of the tent, walking quickly, darting little apprehensive glances over her shoulder. She was wearing a short pale green dress and white highheeled pumps and clutching a green-and-white purse. Her blond hair stirred lightly in the faint summer breeze, giving her an appealing look of sexiness that was totally uncontrived.

She reached me, and I took her elbow, steering her in the direction of the parking lot and Sammy's wagon. Soon we were on our way, bouncing over the rough dirt road, heading for the highway beyond.

When we were out of sight of the Big Top, Tanya seemed to relax a bit and moved closer to me. She reached into my shirt pocket for a cigarette, lit it from the dash lighter and blew a cloud of hazy smoke in my direction.

"I tell my father that I shall be gone to visit girlfriend," she said in her accented English. "But I must be back at twelve-thirty, is okay?"

"Hell no, is not okay!" I said, irritated. "We won't even make the show before eleven. How do you expect us to be back by twelve-thirty?"

"Must we go to movie?" she asked innocently. She placed a tentative hand on my knee and flashed a wicked grin. She knew exactly what she was doing and was loving every minute of it.

I cleared my throat. "Well, we could get a room somewhere, I guess—watch a little TV if you want . . . catch up on some of the programs." I watched for her reaction out of the corner of my eye. There was none. "In fact," I pressed, "I could stop somewhere for pizza—get a large one and a six-pack to go. You like pizza?"

"Pizza what?" she asked seriously.

"Never mind, you'll love it—guaranteed."

Tanya shrugged her shoulders and began twisting the radio dial. All she brought in was static, so after a minute or so she gave up. The old car was missing an antenna, so I wasn't really surprised.

Just then I glanced into the rearview mirror and tensed. A

police car, red lights flashing, had pulled in behind me. "Oh, shit," I mumbled, pulling sedately to the curb.

Tanya gave me a puzzled look and followed my gaze. "Did you break law?" she asked, eyes wide.

"Not that I know of."

But I was definitely worried. For one thing, I had no driver's license; I just hadn't taken the time to get one, nor had I much chance. Even worse, I had no form of identification at all. It was conceivable that I could get around not having the license, but no one goes around without any identification whatsoever—unless he wants to hide his identity.

I watched apprehensively as the officer stepped from his squad car and approached me. I flashed what I hoped was a winning smile as he nodded politely.

"Good evening, officer," I said. "I do something wrong?"

"Not really," he answered. He leaned into the window and gave the interior a brief inspection. "You're running Florida plates with an expired sticker. Could I see your driver's license and registration please?"

I reached across Tanya and removed the registration from the glove compartment, handed it to the officer. "That's my boss—Samuel Clemons. But I'm afraid I don't have my license with me. I work for the circus—we both do, actually. We just got in from Wheeling, West Virginia, a few days ago. Anyway, I either lost or somebody stole my wallet—I think it happened at a rest area on the interstate. Now I have to wait 'til I get back home to get a duplicate."

"Where's home?" he asked suspiciously.

"Sarasota, Florida," I answered quickly. Sarasota was the winter home of the circus.

"Name and address, please?"

"Edward Collins, 1607 Elm Street, sir." I darted a quick look at Tanya and saw her giving me the fish eye. Well, time enough to explain to her later. Right now I was more concerned with the information the cop was writing in his little notebook.

"Phone number?" he asked.

"Well, actually I don't have one at this time because . . ."

"What's the prefix for Sarasota?" he asked.

"Prefix? Well, I really don't know . . ."

"You don't know your own prefix?"

"Look, officer," I said lamely, "I'm originally from Miami; I only moved to Sarasota a few months ago. I really don't know the prefix there." And if you're buying this crap, I thought, you'll go for fried ice cream.

The policeman finished scribbling in his notebook and fixed me with a knowing look. "Wait right here," he said, and returned to his squad car. Tanya started to make a comment, but I silenced her with an abrupt motion of my hand, watching the policeman through the rearview mirror. He had his microphone in his hand, and I knew he was calling in the information I had given him.

In less than three minutes he was back, once again leaning in through the open window. This time he spoke to Tanya.

"Do you have any identification, young lady?"

Tanya fumbled with her tiny clutch purse and removed a thin black folder. I could see she was frightened out of her wits. Being from an Eastern-bloc country, I could imagine that any contact with police there meant nothing but bad news.

"I am from Czechoslovakia," she said, "my family and I. We go with the circus—is okay?"

The officer looked her papers over carefully and handed them back, turning his attention to me. "Okay, son, I want you to step out of the car nice and easy."

I did as he ordered. When I was on the pavement he instructed me to turn around and place my hands behind my back.

"What's this all about, officer?" I asked indignantly. I felt the familiar handcuffs clicking around my wrists, felt his expert hands quickly frisking me for weapons.

"You're under arrest, son," he said.

"What the hell for?" I stormed. "And what's with the cuffs? You act like I'm some kind of murderer or something."

"For all I know you just might be," he answered. "But right now I'm settling for operating a vehicle without a license, failure to give a satisfactory account of yourself—and to see why you find it necessary to lie about where you come from."

He turned me around and looked me full in the face, a slight smile on his lips. "There's no such address as 1607 Elm Street," he said. "Not in Sarasota, anyway."

\* \* \*

**44**

When we arrived at the police station I was led into a holding cell while a female officer questioned Tanya in an effort to learn who I really was. A police car was dispatched to the circus grounds to inform Tanya's parents of the situation and to advise Sammy Clemons that his car had been impounded.

Tanya was nearly hysterical, lapsing every now and again into her native tongue, pleading to be allowed to leave. Patiently the female officer explained that she could go as soon as her parents arrived, but in the meantime would she mind terribly just answering a few questions about her companion. Still sobbing, she was led off to the interview room, the lady cop's arm draped comfortingly around her shoulders.

I spent the next few hours nervously pacing my cramped cell. My last cigarette had long since disappeared, and I wished desperately for a soothing Marlboro. I continued pacing, trying to put cigarettes and the sound of drunken snoring coming from the next cell out of my mind.

Then the outer door leading to the booking area opened, and a uniformed officer carrying a large ring of keys entered. "Come on, sport," he said, unlocking my cell door. "Time to take some pictures and get your hands dirty."

I followed him through the booking office and into a side room where a Polaroid camera on a tripod sat facing a white chart dotted with height measurements. He handed me a numbered card with the day's date written on the bottom, told me to hold it beneath my chin and stand against the chart.

Four pictures were taken, two front shots and two profiles. Then he took my fingerprints. After that I was allowed to wash my hands in a nearby sink while he gathered up my mug shots and fingerprint cards. Then he led me back through the booking office to my cell, after first allowing me to stop by a vending machine where I bought two packs of Marlboros.

As he was locking my cell door I asked about Tanya. He told me that her mother and father had arrived a couple of hours earlier and taken her back to the circus grounds. Likewise Sammy Clemons had wasted no time in claiming his car from the police impound area, after first shelling out sixty bucks in fees. He also had a nice little chat with the investigating officer assigned to my case and verified the information Tanya had supplied; namely that I had been hired in Richmond, Virginia. In fact, the jailer told me, my finger-prints and mug shots were en route to Richmond already. Pending notification from the authorities there, I would continue being held in the police lockup. An answer was expected within seventy-two hours.

After the jailer left I resumed my pacing, chain smoking and cursing myself for not having the foresight to come up with some form of identification. Even something with my own name on it would have been better than nothing at all. Now there was nothing to do but pray that some hungover file clerk in Richmond would goof and overlook my records, which was a slim hope at best.

I grew tired of thinking about the whole mess and flopped on the hard bunk, hoping to find some relief in sleep. The drunk next door was still sawing logs, and I debated whether to pound on the steel wall that separated our cells. I had about decided to do just that when I drifted off into a fathomless sleep, my final thought being that when I awakened, this entire incident would prove to be only a bad dream—which was a dream in itself.

Shortly after noon on the third day the outer door clanged open unexpectedly. A young cop in plain clothes entered and stopped in front of my cell. He was holding a yellow teletype and grinning hugely.

"How's it goin', Ed?" he said. "Catchin' up on your sleep, are ya?"

I ignored the question. "When can I get a shower? And how much longer am I going to have to stay here anyway?"

"Oh, I'd say about another forty-eight hours . . . Mr. Jones."

So much for my slim hope. I turned from the bars and took a seat on the bunk. "My name's Collins, not Jones," I said, reaching for a cigarette and lighting it.

"Let's cut the crap, huh Jones?" He unfolded the teletype and began reading: "Edward Richard Jones, DOB 1/21/43. Sentenced to ten years hard labor for possession of stolen goods in Richmond, Virginia, on 3/18/60. Escaped from State

Road Force 21 on 5/12/63. Upon capture notify Director of Corrections, 501 N. Belvidere Street, Richmond, Virginia.''

He lowered the teletype and regarded me with a smug look of satisfaction. "That about cover it, Jones?"

I took a final drag from my Marlboro and nonchalantly flipped it in the direction of the metal toilet. It missed by about two feet. "You left out Junior," I said. "I'm a Junior. You wouldn't want to arrest my father, now, would you?"

"Tough guy, aren't you? Well, I'm glad to see it. From what I hear about those southern chain gangs, you'll get rid of that attitude soon enough. They don't take too kindly to folks runnin' off like that, do they?"

"I wouldn't know." But I did know. And he was exactly right. Once Eli got me back I had three things to look forward to: a thorough beating, sixty days in the hole and a set of leg irons when I came out—not to mention having another year tacked onto my original sentence.

"You said something about another forty-eight hours," I said. "Does that mean you know when I'll be leaving?"

"You bet I do, smart ass. Day after tomorrow—bright and early. Two guys from the prison system. And I'm gonna meet them personally." He consulted the yellow paper again. "You know anybody named Hope and Jenkins?"

"Sounds like a comedy team to me."

He stepped closer to the bars and flashed his patented grin. "Somehow, Mr. Jones, I don't think you'll find them very funny. No sir—I don't think you'll find them very funny at all."

He was right.

# CHAPTER 5

WILBER HOPE AND RALPH JENKINS ARRIVED A LITTLE AF-
ter nine o'clock on a morning dominated by thunderstorms,
which seemed to fit their mood perfectly. And true to his
word, my little grinning detective friend was on hand when
they entered the station, dripping wet from having to park
two blocks away. After showing the obligatory identification
and extradition papers, they were led back to my cell, sullen
and soggy.

Smiley produced the key and opened my cell door. "This,
gentlemen, is Mr. Edward Jones—Junior," he said. The bigger of the two stepped into the cell, set a briefcase on the
bunk and opened it. He withdrew a leather waistbelt with a
steel ring in back, a pair of handcuffs and a set of leg irons.

"Turn around, Jones," he ordered.

I did as instructed, and he proceeded to harness me in
much the same detached fashion as a farmer hitching a mule
to a plow. When he had finished he stepped back and examined his work critically. Then the four of us adjourned to the
booking desk, where my personal property was turned over
and signed for. Then it was outside, where I waited in front
of the station with Jenkins and Smiley while Hope went to
fetch the car. The rain had stopped, and the air had turned
hot and muggy, and by the time Hope drove up I was already
perspiring. I was helped into the back seat, and the door
locked behind me. Jenkins shook hands with Smiley, climbed

behind the wheel besides Hope, and we were on our way. In the two-and-a-half months since my escape, I had covered a grand total of exactly two hundred forty miles.

We pulled into Richmond a little after three that afternoon. Jenkins had driven straight through, except for one brief stop for gas, and I felt stiff and cramped. The handcuffs had worked upwards around the lower part of my forearms and were cutting deeply into the flesh. When mentioning this to my escorts a couple hours earlier, all I received was a grunt from Jenkins and a laugh from Hope—or maybe it was the other way around. Whichever, the handcuffs stayed where they were, and by the time we stopped at the entrance to the Virginia State Prison, my lower arms and hands were completely numb from lack of circulation.

I was half-led, half-carried up the flight of steps, through two barred gates, and finally into the Captain's office. Only then were the restraints removed. Then I was escorted to inmate reception, where I was again fingerprinted and photographed. My street clothes were taken and replaced with a set of prison khakis. I showered, underwent the indignity of being sprayed with an irritating insecticide, then was taken to a single holding cell in B basement.

A guard opened my cell at nine the next morning. He escorted me to the Captain's office, carrying a manila envelope containing my prison record, mug shots and fingerprints.

Captain Goldie was sitting behind his cluttered desk, chair back, feet up, cleaning his stubby fingernails with a letter opener. He was a big man, with a shock of unruly red hair and an angry purplish scar running from his right temple to a point just below the jaw, a memento from a knife-wielding con he was trying to subdue in the prison machine shop a few years earlier. Goldie had never been particularly fond of prisoners to begin with, but after the knifing incident—which had nearly killed him—his hatred had blossomed into near fanaticism. Since then he had become a holy terror, nearly killing two prisoners himself with a steel gas gun he carried and blinding another with a tear-gas shell fired at point-blank range. His reputation was legendary, and his presence alone had been enough to quell more than one explosive situation within the walls.

We stopped in front of his desk, and the guard handed him the manila envelope. Goldie inspected the contents briefly, grunted and tossed them onto a corner of the desk. He leaned back again, laced thick fingers across his ample stomach and regarded me the way a frog does a fly just before the tongue flicks out.

"Well, Jones," he said cheerfully, "looks like you got yourself in a little trouble, boy. Enjoy your vacation?"

"No sir, not really."

"You mean you didn't like Phil'delphia? Cap'n Eli would probably be real tickled to hear that. Them Yankee states just don't hold a candle to our little summer camps, do they?"

He chuckled and glanced across the room to where two guards dressed in chain-gang uniforms lounged against the wall. "And just to show how much we appreciate your attitude, we're gonna let you visit our most popular camp for a spell. Camp 15, up Chatum way. Real purty country up there."

Camp 15 was run by another man who had become somewhat a legend within the Virginia Prison System, a maniac named W.W. Woodson. It was said that any convict who spent as much as one year under his rule never came away the same. The man was a sadist, and only those prisoners on the administration's Hit List were sent there, usually for either of two purposes: to break them or kill them. The Chatum camp had the highest fatality rate of any in the entire state—all victims of attempted escape. No question about it, Camp 15 was definitely hazardous to a prisoner's health.

One of the guards peeled himself away from the wall and approached me with a set of handcuffs. "Stick your hands out," he ordered. He snapped the manacles around my wrists. He grinned, shifted a half-chewed toothpick to the opposite side of his mouth, then turned and collected the manila envelope from Goldie's desk.

"If that's it, Cap'n, we'll be on our way," he said. "Promised Cap'n Woodson we'd pick up some tractor parts this afternoon."

"Yeah, go on," Goldie replied. "Tell Woody I'll be givin' him a holler before long. And tell him to take good care of my boy here."

"Sure will, Cap'n. Yes sir, I surely will."

He steered me towards the door, his buddy close behind. But Goldie had a final word.

He said, "Hey Jones . . . let me tell you somethin.' " I looked back at him, seeing him all reared back in his chair, head tilted to one side. "I don't know if you still got rabbit in you or not," he said. "But don't press your luck. Cap'n Woodson gonna be keepin' an eye on you. But if you do happen to get lucky and hit the bushes without gettin' your ass shot off—you'd best not get caught. 'Cause if you do I'm gonna see to it you spend the rest of your time right here. And if that happens, I can promise you won't like it one little bit. Now that's the best advice you're likely to ever get, son— and it's free. So you better think about it . . . hear?"

"Yes sir, Cap'n," I said.

"Awright, get him outta here."

The two guards picked up their pistols from the control room outside the double gates. We left the prison and squeezed into a gray pickup truck parked at the curb outside the entrance, with me in the middle. I took a last look at the high walls surrounding the prison as we pulled away, hoping I had seen the last of them. I had heard stories about life inside those walls, none of them pleasant. I was eighteen years old—the age of consent in the outside world. But in there it didn't matter if you were consenting or not, according to the stories, because trying to live at that age behind the walls was about as easy as a one-legged chicken trying to live inside a den of starving wolves. I didn't know how accurate the tales were, but I did know I wasn't anxious to find out.

In twenty minutes the city limits were behind us. We headed north on Route 60, into the heart of the Virginia farm belt. Two hundred miles in the distance lay Chatum, a sparsely populated area of rolling hills and sprawling farms. I was vaguely familiar with the area, having passed through with Dick on the way to Covington many years ago. I remember how taken I had been with the beauty of the passing countryside as we drove through multicolored forests during the peak of autumn. But that had been a different time, a time of untroubled boyhood and innocent dreams. A time forever locked in the past.

Sometime around noon I was asked if I needed to take a

leak. Yes, I said, I certainly did. The driver found a convenient side road, turned off, continued on for another mile or so, then pulled into a small clearing at the side of the road. I followed the guard out of the passenger side and waited until he pointed out a likely looking tree.

"Pull it out there," he said.

I had finished my business and was in the process of zipping my pants when a blow to the back of my head sent me crashing to my knees. Lights were still flashing when I felt a rough hand grab the back of my neck and force my head down into the grass where I had just urinated. I gagged and tried to breathe, but only succeeded in getting a nose full of my own urine. I coughed and sputtered and pushed against the ground with my manacled hands, but the hand held firm. I was beginning to feel in serious danger of drowning in my own water.

The hand suddenly loosened its grip, and I was rolled onto my back. I opened my eyes and found myself staring into the barrel of a .38 revolver no more than six inches from my face. Behind the extended arm I could make out the blurred features of my toothpick-chewing guard.

"This is it, boy," he said, eyes wide and maniacal. He thumbed the hammer back and slowly squeezed the trigger.

The sharp click of the hammer as it fell on an empty chamber seemed to reverberate in the stillness of the forest. The entire scene took on the appearance of a stop-action photograph filled with kaleidoscopic colors, freezing a heartbeat in time. It was a feeling I had never before experienced until that moment.

Absolute, total shock.

"Awright, boy," Toothpick said. "You can git up now—you ain't dead yet."

He stepped back, and the gun disappeared. In the background I could see the other guard leaning against the truck, looking very bored. I struggled to my feet, spitting grass and dirt, and wiped my face on the back of my sleeve. Toothpick looked me up and down and grinned in a mad sort of way.

"How 'bout it, boy—got anything loose runnin' down your leg?" He spat the chewed toothpick out and took another from his shirt pocket, sticking it between yellowed teeth. "Now that was just a warnin'. I coulda blowed your fuckin' brains out, and Hap here woulda swore you tried to take my gun. But it ain't gonna be that easy, boy—not that easy at all. You're gonna sweat and bleed and beg and crawl, 'til the day comes when you just say 'fuck it!' Then you're gonna drop your tool, forget all about the leg chains you'll have on and start hoppin' for the bushes.'' He took a step closer and thrust his narrow face close to mine. "But you won't make it, boy. Nobody in chains makes it—and we've had more'n a few try. But you'll try it . . . oh yeah, you'll try. And that's when the real thing'll happen. And you'll never hear the sound of the shot that kills you.''

He grabbed my arm and jerked me forward. "Now git your ass in that truck. And don't let me hear you say boo 'til we git into camp.''

The rest of the trip was uneventful. But the experience had shaken me more than I wanted to admit even to myself. I had just undergone the worst humiliation of my life—and the worst fear. The smell of urine was still strong on my face as I thought about the speech Toothpick had made. Now I knew what was in store for me at Camp 15, and the knowledge made my fear run deeper. But seeping through the terror was another emotion that would eventually dominate even the fear.

Anger.

# CHAPTER 6

CAMP 15 WAS NEARLY IDENTICAL TO CAMP 21. IN FACT, ALL thirty-one of the state camps were constructed from the same blueprints, with only slight modifications to meet the whims of a few favored Captains.

A feeling of déjà vu came over me as I walked into the basement of W. W. Woodson's camp; even the long row of wooden boxes lining one wall were the same. The camp Lieutenant assigned one to me, pointed out which hook in the coatroom was mine, then issued me khaki uniforms, underclothes and a pair of high-top work brogues. Then I was left alone to pace the basement floor and await the return of the work gangs at the end of the day.

Sometime after six I heard the trucks rumble up to the walkway outside. The door at the end of the basement opened, and a line of weary men filed inside. Unlike Camp 21, here everyone wore chains. They jostled their way to the circular sink opposite the showers, dunking heads and upper torsos under the cool spray, splashing, drinking, shoving and being shoved—like pigs in a mud hole. They cast quick glances my way to see if I were familiar. No one said hello.

I felt a blow across my back that nearly sent me tumbling from my box. I leaped to my feet, ready to defend myself, and came face-to-face with a grinning Tugboat Adams. Except for a botched crew cut he looked the same as when I had last seen him at Camp 21. And he was still wearing chains.

"Goddammit, Eddie!" he roared, "when the hell you get busted?"

In light of the day's events, Tugboat was a welcome sight indeed. I grabbed his hand and pumped vigorously, wincing in pain from his viselike grip.

"How's it going, Tug? Man, you're the first friendly face I've seen in nearly a week! What are you doing here?"

"The same thing you are," he answered, "regrettin' it." He released my squashed hand and beamed at me. "Look, I'm gonna finish cleanin' up and then be right back, okay? We got some talkin' to do." He made a playful pass at my chin, then turned and shouldered his way into the coatroom. Several prisoners swung their heads in my direction, their eyes showing acceptance of the new creature among them. Tugboat's greeting was my stamp of approval.

Tugboat returned in less than five minutes, and we moved to a large wooden table in the center of the basement. Apparently it wasn't mandatory to stay seated on our boxes, nor was the no-talking rule in effect. I thought this was a great improvement over the Falmouth camp, and I told Tugboat the same.

"Yeah, well don't let that fool you," he said, lighting a cigarette. "Before the weeks' out I guarantee you're gonna wish you was back with ol' Eli. This fuckin' Woodson's a stone fool. But I'll run all that by you after chow."

"What are you doing here anyway, Tug?" I asked.

He took a long pull from his cigarette and blew a cloud of smoke at the ceiling. "They finally took my damn chains off a few weeks ago. I told you that's all I was waitin' for. Anyway, I made a move four days later—on a Friday it was. Remember Curly Simmons? He was the shotgun guard. Which was a real break for me because he's got to be the laziest sonofabitch in the world. We was sprawlforkin' a ditch line on 607, throwin' mud left and right. Curly had him a five-gallon bucket to sit on and a 'Do Not Disturb' sign written all over him."

He giggled, took another puff and stared reflectively at the floor. "Ol' Curly shoulda knowed better. He let me get nearly twenty yards away from the rest of the gang and just kept sittin' there, dumb as a sled dog. I ended up right next to a clump of bushes not more'n a jump away. So I looks back at Curly, see he's just now startin' to get up, and that's when I jump. He managed to get off two shots but didn't stand a snowball's chance in hell of hittin' me.''

"So you got away," I said. "How did you get caught?"

Tugboat sighed and crushed out his cigarette. "Would you believe by a farmer?"

"A farmer?"

"Yup. He was comin' outta his house just as I was comin' outta his barn ridin' his new Case tractor. He must of heard me crankin' it up, 'cause he had the biggest damn shotgun you ever saw. He saw me sittin' on top of his pride and joy, squalled like a banshee, and cut loose—and blew a hole the size of a basketball right in the radiator of that Case. How the hell he missed me I'll never know. Anyway, he starts squealin' and shakin' and wavin' that cannon around like the fool he is—tellin' me to come down off that tractor or it's bad news. Meanwhile his ol' lady's callin' the sheriff. And to tell the truth, I was damn glad of it." He paused for a moment, looking sad and serious, and continued, "I tell you, Eddie, don't ever get one of them farmers mad at you. They ain't got a lick of sense."

I was struggling to keep a straight face. "So what happened then?"

The sheriff showed up with a couple of deputies, told the ol' bastard he'd be gettin' fifty dollars from the state for capturin' me and bundled me off back to camp. Eli had the shit beat outta me and threw me in the hole. Next thing I know I got my chains back on and end up here." He made a sweeping motion with his head. "In this shittin' place."

The camp Lieutenant appeared then and gave two sharp blasts from a whistle. Everyone formed a single line at the bottom of the steps, me behind Tugboat, and filed up the steps to the chow hall.

Later that evening Tugboat dragged me into a checker game. We talked about the old days of life under Eli, moving the pieces without much thought, Tugboat giving me a rundown on the camp routine.

Suddenly I heard a strange wailing sound coming from

beyond the barred windows at my back. It started on a low note, then built in pitch until it resembled something out of a horror movie. It took me a few seconds to figure out it was coming from a human being, yet it was like no human sound I had ever heard before. The thing sent goose bumps along the back of my neck. I froze in mid-move and looked around, noticing the basement conversation had waned. Finally the wail faded—like a siren winding down—then stopped.

I rose and walked to a window, stood on tiptoe to look over the sill. There was a funny-looking concrete box out there, about twenty feet away. It looked about seven feet long and two feet high—maybe about two-and-a-half feet across, with a tiny barred window set in a hinged lid made out of heavy wood. There was also a little slot cut in the side, covered by a sliding wooden door.

I stood there gazing out at the strange contraption, trying to figure out what it was, when that spooky wail started again, obviously coming from the box. I watched, amazed, as the wooden lid began bouncing up and down, like somebody in there was trying to get out. This time the screaming was punctuated with words of rage.

"You rotten bastards! . . . oh, *Je*-sus! Fuckin' cocksuck-*errrrs!*"

Then the wail and curses faded again and ended in a spasm of gut-wrenching sobs.

I felt a hand on my elbow and turned to see Tugboat standing behind me. "Come on, Eddie," he said. "Sit down before one of the hacks says somethin'. You ain't supposed to be standin' unless you're goin' one place to another."

I took a final peek before following him back to the table. When we were seated I looked at him and said, "The hell was all that?" He offered me a cigarette, and we both lit up.

"That thing you saw is called The Bunker," he told me. "What they do, you fuck up bad enough, they put you in there buck naked, let you lay a couple days, 'til you have to piss and ain't got no choice but to go all over yourself. Looks like a cement coffin, don't it? Notice that little slot in the side?"

I nodded, fascinated.

"Well, after you piss all over yourself, and the concrete you're layin' on's all good and wet, they open that little slot and throw curin' salt inside . . . got any idea what that does? It makes big red sores pop up all over and burns like you wouldn't believe. Curin' salt and piss—a hell of a combination."

I gave him a long look to see if he was for real. With Tugboat you never knew. "Who's in there now?"

"Guy named Cribbs. He whacked 'ol Shackleford up side the head with a number-five scoop the other day. Damn wonder Lynch didn't blow him away. They'll take him out in a day or two and transfer him to the walls."

I thought about it, then said, "Tug, are you shittin' me?"

Tugboat sighed and turned back to the checkerboard. "I ain't got enough imagination to make up somethin' like that, Eddie." He frowned and concentrated on the board. "Now come on, it's your move. Meanwhile you can tell me your sad story."

So I told him my sad story, trying to shove aside the mental image of the man in The Bunker. I told him everything: about Mom, the circus, Tanya the beautiful, my arrest, the Philadelphia jail, my return to Richmond, and, finally, the event that had taken place earlier that day. I faltered a little there, stammering a little, searching for the proper words to describe the horror and humiliation I had felt. As I relived the experience, still so vivid in my mind, I felt my hands clench into white-knuckled fists, forearms knotting from the effort. When Tugboat saw how the telling was affecting me, he gave me a friendly slap across the wrist.

"Hey, don't let it bother you. You ain't the first to have a run-in with Hap and Willis, and you won't be the last. So forget it."

"I can't, Tug," I told him. "That man rubbed my nose right in my own piss—the way you would a puppy that hadn't been housebroken. Then I just froze. He rolled me over and stuck the barrel of that .38 right between my eyes and pulled the trigger, and I just froze—so scared I couldn't even move. Had it been for real, I would have been dead without a fight."

Tugboat lit a cigarette and passed it to me. "Look, Eddie. There's times when a man's fear gets the best of him, know what I mean? I've seen the time I was so fuckin' scared I nearly shit my fuckin' pants. But I know for a fact I got as much moxie as the next guy. But remember one thing. The braver the mouse, the fatter the cat—and there's times in all our lives when we have to be mice. So forget that shit and chalk it up to experience, and tell yourself it won't happen again. Keep your eyes and ears open, your mouth shut, and train yourself to expect the unexpected. You do that, and I guarantee you'll move when the time comes agin.''

For the first time since I had known him I looked at Tugboat in a different light. There was a great deal of common sense and insight beneath that tough exterior, as well as sensitivity. He could see that I was suffering from a bad case of diminished manhood, which is exactly what Hap and Willis had wanted.

I looked at my improbable friend and smiled. ''Thanks, Tug. I appreciate y—''

''Will you just shut up and move? I got better things to do than just sit and stare at a checkerboard!''

The next morning after chow I was called to the Captain's office, accompanied by the Lieutenant. Woodson was a small man, no more than five-foot-five, and sitting behind his huge mahogany desk made him appear even smaller. He was dressed in an immaculate blue-and-gray uniform, with polished Captain's bars gleaming from the collar of his starched shirt. His hair was pale blond, clipped short to a pink skull that fairly glowed from scrubbing. He had the most penetrating blue eyes I had ever seen, and I had the distinct impression that he would feel right at home commanding a German concentration camp.

I stopped a few feet in front of the desk and waited in respectful silence while the Lieutenant took a position near the door. Woodson gazed at me for several moments, and when he finally spoke it was with the high-pitched voice of a young boy, incongruous coming from a man so widely feared.

''Well, Jones, I hear you got a little rabbit blood in you, that right?''

I didn't know what to say, so I said nothing.

"You'd best learn to answer me when I ask you a question, boy. Now what about it, you got rabbit blood, or what?"

"Yes sir, I have—I mean, I did have . . ."

"You mean you don't have it anymore, that right?"

"Yes sir."

Woodson leaned back and placed one spotless, looking-glass boot on the corner of the desk. "Well, I don't rightly know if I should believe you or not, boy, so I'm gonna give you a nice set of step-chains to kinna slow you down a little. And if I find out you been messin' with 'em, you and me are gonna have a meetin' of the minds—that right?"

"Yes sir, that's right."

Woodson's head snapped back like he had been slapped and his voice dropped an octave. "You wouldn't be mockin' me, now would you boy?"

"No sir," I said. "I wouldn't be fool enough to do that, sir."

"I hope not, boy. I surely hope not."

Woodson reached into a bottom drawer of his desk and came out with a two-foot length of thick chain with two pad-locks connected to the ends. He tossed the works to the Lieutenant, who caught them deftly. The Lieutenant came up behind me, bent down and expertly fastened the chains to my ankles. He snapped the padlocks closed and stood, surveying his work. He nodded, satisfied, and addressed Woodson. "He's got about an inch of play both ways. Plenty room to get his pants on and off."

"Good enough," Woodson said. He turned his attention back to me. "I hear you done buddied up with Tugboat Adams. Used to be wit him at 21, that right?"

"Yes sir, I've known him a couple of years."

"Well, you take my advice and steer shy of him. That 'ol thing's gonna come to no good. He's got rabbit same as you. Sooner or later he's gonna head for the briar patch, and when he does, he's gonna get his ass wiped. And you tell him I said so."

"Yes sir, I'll tell him."

"And one more thing. By rights you got about sixty days hole time comin'. But I'd rather have you workin' on the road earnin' your keep than layin' around restin'. And when I say work, I mean just that. I give you a full bowl, I want a steady roll—that right?''

"Yes sir, Captain.''

Woodson nodded to the Lieutenant, and I was led from the office and back downstairs, walking awkwardly because of the unfamiliar chains.

Tugboat had a foot propped up on his box tying a shoelace when I stopped beside him. "Guess you're going to finally have to show me how to get out of my pants with chains on," I told him.

He looked at me and grinned. "They ain't so bad when you get used to 'em. By the way, I put you some smokes and toothpaste and soap in your box. I had an extra lock so I put that on, too. Here's the key. Keep it locked all the time or some asshole's liable to rip you off. Some of these bastards are so slick they could follow you through a revolving door and come out ahead of you.''

"Thanks, Tug. I'll pay you back when I can.''

"Don't worry 'bout it, I got plenty. Half of these jokers think they're cardsharks, but they can't play mumble-pegs. So you had a talk with ol' Woodson, huh?''

"That right!'' I said, giving a decent imitation.

We moved to a table to wait for the trucks, and I told Tugboat what Woodson said about him. He listened with wry amusement.

"Well, he's right about that,'' he said. "Hell, everybody knows I'm gonna try it sooner or later. My luck can't stay bad forever.''

"It sounds like they want to kill you, Tug,'' I said seriously.

"Of course they want to kill me. The same's they want to kill you or any other motherfucker here. Look around you, Eddie. What do you see? Losers! Nothing but losers, every last man. All of us fuck-ups in one way or another, sent here from every camp in the state. And it's open season all year 'round—no bag limit, no quota. And you'd best remember that when you get ready to make your move.''

"How do you know I'm going to make a move?''

He stuck a cigarette in the corner of his mouth and lit it. "I just know,'' he said. "And so do they.''

* * *

I was placed in Staples' gang. He was a tall rawboned man in his early fifties who was fond of carrying a pick handle. He also took great delight in using it whenever he felt the occasion warranted. Twice during my first three months at the camp I had been whacked across the shoulders with that handle, and each time the pain had lasted for hours. Staples didn't need much excuse; failure to move quick enough with bush-axe or sprawl-fork was usually all it took.

I had hoped to be placed in Tugboat's gang, but Woodson wasn't having any of that. He wasn't about to put two close friends—both recent escapees—in the same gang; too much chance they could team up and distract the shotgun guard. But I ignored his warning to stay away from Tugboat in camp. We ate together, talked together and played poker together, a comradeship born and nurtured by mutual adversity. Woodson extracted his measure of revenge by ensuring that both Tugboat and I worked nearly twice as hard as anyone else in our respective gangs. But this only served to increase our resolve, resulting in a bond of friendship that no amount of pressure could break.

By mutual consent, both Tugboat and I had agreed not to discuss the subject of escape, since this would necessitate the need for whispered conversations—which would be looked upon with great suspicion by the basement guards. We each know what the other would do if the opportunity arose, and since neither of us was in a position to help the other, there wasn't much point in talking about it.

The second Sunday after my arrival, Mom came to visit. It was the first time we had seen each other since our parting at the Fairgrounds. We sat at a small table in an upstairs room adjacent to Woodson's office, constantly watched by a guard with a pistol who sat off in one corner. Serious conversation was out of the question, since every word could be plainly heard by the stoic-looking guard. So we mostly held hands across the table and confined our words to the mundane things that mother and son normally say to each other, trying to keep it light. But it wasn't where our hearts were, and we both knew it. We couldn't say what we really felt, but the message came through loud and clear through intuitive eye contact: we hurt.

The one piece of good news was that she and Dick were

seeing each other on a regular basis, rediscovering each other now that Elmo Thomas was history. It appeared that whatever differences had originally separated them were now being resolved, and I couldn't have been more pleased. She deserved her measure of happiness, and other than my eventual release from prison, I knew that she would only be able to find that with Dick Bosher.

At the end of an hour the guard terminated our visit. We stood and shared a lengthy embrace, neither wanting to break off the contact. She felt small and vulnerable against my six-foot-two-inch frame, frustrated by the forced separation and the holding back of unspoken words. So I kissed the top of her head and told her not to worry and watched wordlessly as the guard ushered her through the door, thinking that whoever said parting is such sweet sorrow was an ass.

There wasn't a damn thing sweet about it.

October was drawing to a close, and with it came the cool evening air that signaled autumn. Leaves were turning a rust-colored gold, and squirrels scurried to and fro, collecting nuts for the coming winter. It was a time of welcome change for the men of Camp 15, a sort of state of limbo between the sweltering heat of summer and the bone-chilling cold of winter.

It was Thursday evening, and our gang was late getting back to camp. A flat tire had put us nearly half an hour behind the other gangs, who had to wait for us before going to chow.

As soon as we entered the basement and headed for the sink, I could tell something was wrong. It was too quiet; guys were sitting on their boxes with sober looks. And nobody seemed to want to look at me. I shrugged it off, finished washing and went into the coatroom for my towel.

I was drying off when Andy Scifo, who worked with Tugboat in Morris' gang, came in behind me. He stood gazing around the small room lined with coats and towels hanging from ten-penny nails, scratching his arm. I looked at him, suspicious.

"Something on your mind?" I said.

Still gazing around he said, "Yeah . . . guess so."

"Well, what the hell is it?" I asked, impatient.

Scifo fixed his eyes somewhere beyond me and said, "Tug tried to hit the bushes today, Eddie."

I stared at him, starting to get a strange feeling that made my scalp tingle. I said, "What happened?"

Scifo, pawing at the concrete floor with a scuffed work-shoe, said, "Puckett killed him, Eddie."

# CHAPTER 7

I DON'T REMEMBER HOW LONG I STOOD THERE, TOWEL poised in midair. I do recall Scifo mumbling something inaudible as he slipped away, the shrill blast of the chow whistle, the shuffle of workboots and clanking of chains as the men fell in line. Little else. Sometime afterward I left the coatroom and walked zombielike back to my box, sat down and tried to work the novocaine from my brain. Tugboat dead? Couldn't be! Just that morning we were sitting at the game table, Tugboat moaning about the full house he had lost with the night before. The biggest pot of the night and Bobby Sifford had won it with four nines; Tug like to have busted a gut over that one. And this evening he ends up dead? Scifo had to be playing games; probably would come back from chow with a wide grin, slap me on the back and tell me Tug was really in the hole: "Gotcha! didn't I, Eddie? Really had you goin there!"

I kept my eyes peeled for Scifo as the men came back from chow, saw him head for his box, cutting his eyes in my direction. It was his look, the ashen pallor of his face, that brought the numbness back. I looked about the basement and saw the grim expressions of the other men, the unnatural quiet, the quick averting of the eyes. And that's when it really hit me. Tugboat was indeed dead.

Scifo saw me coming and made room for me beside him.

"I'm sorry, Eddie." he said. "I know you and Tug was tight. He was good people and didn't deserve to go that way."

"How did he go, Andy?" I asked softly. "Tell me exactly what happened."

Scifo fidgeted about, picking nervously at a book of matches. "Aw, come on, Eddie. You don't need to hear it. Can't no good come of it nohow."

"I want to know, Andy," I insisted. "All of it."

Scifo sighed and leaned forward, elbows on knees. "Well, we was cuttin' right o' way out twenty-seven, you know? Been there all week. Brush's pretty thick around there, and we was makin' slow time. Puckett, the gun guard, had been ridin' Tug all day, tellin' him he was draggin', slowin' everybody down—which ain't true, cause Tug could work the ass off any of us. But Pickett was out to get Tug's goat, only Tug was payin' him no mind. Just kept swingin' away with his bush-axe, tryin' to work off his mad.

"When lunch came, Tug sat off about fifteen feet from the rest of us, next to this big clump of bushes, really starin' a hole through Puckett—and Puckett just stared right back. Anyways, lunch is about over when Puckett gets up, turns his back and walks off about ten feet or so, pulls it out and starts takin' a leak.

"Well, that was just too much for Tug, so he jumps up and makes a beeline for them bushes—kinna hoppin', you know?, on account of the chains. The foreman was sittin' in the truck with Kenny, his driver—they was about twenty yards away and had a clear view of the whole thing. Anyway, Kenny hits the horn soon's he sees Tug make the first jump. Puckett spun around, pecker still hangin' out, and cuts loose on Tug. But Tug's chains got caught on a stub, and he fell hard right on his face, so the shot went over his head."

Scifo fell silent here, flicking matches at imaginary targets.

"Go on," I told him, half wishing he wouldn't.

"Well, Tug knew Puckett had him dead to rights, so he just sits up real calm-like and puts his hands in the air. But Puckett only had one thing in mind—you could see it in his eyes." He cut his eyes quickly in my direction before continuing. "You could see it somewheres else, too. Eddie . . . goddammit to hell . . . I swear on my mother the sonofabitch had a hard-on! He actually had a fuckin' hard-on!"

He straightened up and ran one hand across a beard-stubbled face, took a deep breath and continued.

"Anyway, he pumps another shell into the breech, takes dead aim, and blows a hole in Tug's chest big enough to throw a basketball through. It tore him wide open, Eddie. Knocked him head over heels and left him flat on his face. I don't think Tug even felt a thing, it was that quick. He never knew what hit him."

I sat back and lit a cigarette, conscious of my shaking hands. Suddenly I recalled the speech Toothpick—was it Hap or Willis?—had made to me during that memorable ride from Richmond:

*"You're gonna sweat and bleed and beg and crawl, 'til the day comes when you just say 'fuck it!' Then you're gonna drop your tool, forget all about the chains you'll have on and start hoppin' for the bushes . . . and you'll never hear the shot that kills you."*

Nothing short of cold blooded murder.

"It was a setup, wasn't it, Andy?" I asked dumbly. "A setup all the way."

"No question, Eddie. But Tug shoulda knowed better. Guess he was just so mad he didn't think straight. They pulled it off clean as a whistle."

There was a roaring in my ears, and I could feel the blood pounding in my temples. There was no doubt in my mind that had Puckett been in the basement at that moment, I would have attacked him in screaming fury. But shotgun guards were not permitted in the basement. For the first time, I could understand why.

The night was without end, and I functioned like an automaton. I paced the basement floor, chain-smoking, unmindful of my surroundings. And no one told me to sit down. Later, long after the last exhausted man had fallen asleep, I lay staring at a small crack in the ceiling, wishing for a cigarette.

The five-thirty wake-up bell found me still without sleep. I made my bunk and joined the others as they filed into the basement. During breakfast the seat to my left where Tugboat usually sat was noticeably vacant, adding cruel emphasis to my feeling of loss.

After breakfast the Lieutenant entered the basement and singled me out. "Jones, you're layin' in today," he said then promptly left again. I took a seat and lit a Marlboro, not caring about the reason behind the command.

When the gangs were gone, the Lieutenant returned and led me once again to Woodson's office. He was waiting for me, reared back in the familiar pose.

"Guess I don't have to ask if you know about Tugboat, that right?" he said flatly.

"I heard."

"I told you that sooner or later he was goin' to head for the briar patch, that right?"

"You told me," I said tightly.

"Well, you can see what that got him." He leaned forward, folded his hands on the surface of the polished desk. "You got it in your head to try the same thing?"

I couldn't keep the rancor out of my voice as I answered. "I won't deny that I'd go if I had the chance—you wouldn't have these chains on me if you didn't believe that. But I'll never let anyone drive me to it."

"What's that supposed to mean?"

"I was told that Puckett . . ."

"That's *Mr.* Puckett, boy!"

". . . that Mr. Puckett had been riding Tugboat all day. I was also told that Tugboat was sitting on the ground with his hands in the air when Mr. Puckett killed him. I feel sure the true facts haven't been brought to your attention, and I don't believe you condone outright murder." I didn't believe any such thing, but it was worth a try.

Woodson gave me a level look. "And just who gave you these so-called true facts?"

"I'm just repeating what the basement talk is, Captain."

"Well, the basement talk is *wrong!*" he roared, slamming an open palm on the desk. "I got a full report from Mr. Puckett—as well as from Mr. Kenny and Mr. Morris."

"I know, Captain," I persisted. "But did you ask any of the men in the gang? They were witnesses too." I knew I was going too far, but I couldn't help it. I felt Tugboat would have done the same for me—maybe more.

Woodson lunged to his feet, sending the swivel chair crashing into the wall behind him. His face turned a dark pink as he pointed a trembling finger at me.

"Let me tell you something, boy! I run this goddamned camp, and don't you forget it! I don't explain my actions to you or any other fuckin' convict here, you understand?"

He was shaking with rage, and his girlish voice rose to a near scream as he continued. "You bastards are all the same, that right? Tell any goddamned barefaced lie you can if it suits you, that right? Well, by God, you start bad-mouthin' my guards, you're bad-mouthin' me—'cause I picked every last one of 'em! They're proud, God-fearin' Americans who protect decent folk from rotten sonsabitches like you. Now you shut up, you hear me? You *shut the fuck up!*"

He lowered his outstretched arm and looked about the room as if seeing it for the first time. He retrieved his chair and calmly sat down, composing himself. He lit a cigarette, blew a cloud of smoke in my direction and regarded me the way one might regard a new species of insect.

"You're gettin' the day off on account of Tugboat," he said. "Give you a little time to think about it—get your head straight. Right now you ain't got both oars in the water."

So I went back to the basement and thought about it; about how I would escape, and how to do it without ending up like Tugboat. I couldn't let myself be pushed or goaded, but I knew they would try. I had to plan—create an opportunity instead of waiting for one to present itself. Only then would I have a chance to succeed. Fun and games were over, and the blindfold had been removed. Yesterday I was still a naive kid, but today reality had finally caught up, leaving me slightly scarred but, hopefully, much wiser. Scars you can learn to live with, but wisdom you can't live without.

During the next week I worked like a demon, cutting more right-of-way, shoveling more dirt and sprawlforking more mud than any two men together. I pushed myself relentlessly, refusing to acknowledge the signals being sent to my brain from tired muscles and burning lungs. At night I was asleep within five minutes after my head hit the pillow, awakening only when the five-thirty wake-up whistle sounded. But the effort helped deaden the anger I'd been feeling behind Tugboat's deliberate murder, which had been my purpose. It's difficult to feel anything when you're exhausted.

It was a Saturday, and I was writing a letter to Mom, sitting off to myself at the far end of the long game table. I had become quiet and withdrawn, resisting all efforts of friendship. I had decided that never again would I form close ties with another prisoner. It made you too vulnerable. So I kept to myself, preferring to spend my free time writing letters, reading and dreaming of escape.

I had just addressed the envelope when I looked up to see Raymond Wilshire enter the basement. Wilshire was Woodson's houseboy. He was also the dog boy, responsible for handling the bloodhounds when tracking an escapee. Because of this he was the most despised man in camp, able to survive only because he was under the direct protection of Woodson himself. Attacking Wilshire would be tantamount to attacking a guard, and retribution would be swift and sure. Nevertheless, it was unusual to see him in the basement when the gangs weren't on the road. Most of his time was spent in Woodson's house—or brownnosing in the guards' living quarters.

As I watched him cross the floor heading for the coatroom, my eyes were drawn to the new pair of tennis shoes he was wearing. They were white, with red stripes. And they didn't belong to Wilshire. The last time I had seen those shoes, they had been in Tugboat's box. His sister had sent them to him from Greenville, North Carolina, only three weeks before—and he had never put them on.

But Wilshire had.

Suddenly all logic deserted me, and I became possessed by something I had never before known. I was halfway across the floor without being conscious that I had even moved, skipping and clanking, driven by uncontrollable rage. I was six feet away when I lunged, hitting him in the small of his back like a beserk lineman making a goal-line stand. Wilshire grunted and went down in a heap. I rolled to my feet, aware of a screaming sound in the background, not realizing it was coming from me. Wilshire turned onto his back, looking up in horror and surprise—and caught the downward swing of my clenched hands flush across the bridge of his nose. I swung again, this time catching him behind the ear, and followed with a succession of blows too numerous to count, all delivered with every ounce of pent-up strength and emotion

I could muster. Finally I stopped swinging, leaped into the air and came down with both feet aimed directly at his stunned face. My estimate was a little off, though, and my heels ricocheted off his cheekbone, opening a deep gash that immediately welled with blood. He groaned and rolled awkwardly onto his stomach, and I jumped on his back and continued to pummel his head and neck with heavy blows, incoherent, desiring only to maim, cripple—even kill. I felt hands grasping at my arms, but I flung them off violently and continued to pound away at Wilshire, who now wasn't moving at all. Then the lights went out.

I couldn't have been unconscious for more than a few minutes. I was lying facedown on the basement floor, handcuffs securing my hands behind my back. I felt myself being roughly yanked to my feet by the two basement guards, who half-dragged, half-carried me up the steps. We were met by the Lieutenant, who led the way to the hole, situated within a narrow corridor across from the dormitory. He unlocked the barred door and held it open while the two guards busied themselves with stripping me of my clothing. One reached down and grabbed my leg chains, gave a sharp upward yank and sent me crashing to the floor. I fell on my cuffed hands, and excruciating pain jolted my wrist bones like electrical shocks. After they removed my shoes and socks I was hauled to my feet again, pushed through the door—where I promptly fell on my face—and heard it slam shut behind me. Then the outer door clanged shut, and I was alone with my misery.

In less than fifteen minutes they were back, this time with Woodson leading the charge. The Lieutenant opened the door, and the four men entered. I was lying on my side, trying to relieve some of the agony in my wrists. Woodson stepped up and launched a vicious kick that landed flush on the kidney, driving the breath from my lungs. He grabbed a handful of hair and jerked my head back.

"You want to jump on somebody, that right?" He swung a fist that caught me high on the cheekbone. "Tough guy, that right?" Again the fist. My head was reeling, and my vision blurred, and still he struck—again and again.

I must have lost consciousness briefly, because the next thing I remember was Woodson standing over me, panting heavily and holding his right hand. When he spoke his words sounded distant.

"Nobody jumps on my dog boy, you got that? Nobody! You got a lot to learn, boy, and by God I'm just the one to teach you!"

With that he launched the foot again and started a fire in my rib cage. Then he turned on his heel and stalked angrily from the cell, followed closely by his henchmen. The Lieutenant slammed the outer door, and once more I was alone.

The rest of the day I spent in much the same position as Woodson left me, torn with anger and pain. I made no attempt to stand, convinced that the effort would be futile. I felt a warm trickle of blood at the back of my neck, probably caused by the billy clubs wielded by the basement guards. Occasionally I gained temporary respite from the nameless pain by blacking out.

During the early evening the Lieutenant returned, stopping outside my cell. He ordered me to stand and walk to the door, which I accomplished after considerable struggle. He told me to turn around, then reached through the bars and removed the handcuffs. I brought my hands in front of me and gazed at them dubiously. They were swollen and had turned a sickening blue-white. I tried to move my fingers, but they refused to respond.

The Lieutenant leaned against the barred gate. "Consider yourself lucky, Jones. The Captain came damn close to puttin' your ass in The Bunker, only it's occupied right now."

I made no reply, continuing to gaze at my maimed hands, wondering if the lack of circulation had ruined them for good. I heard the Lieutenant leave amid a jingle of keys, heard the outer door slam. I walked slowly to the far corner of the cell and sat down, forearms across my knees. Close by was the gallon can which served as a toilet, smelling of stale urine and excrement from countless collections. I turned my head away from it and stretched out on the concrete on my side. The coolness of the cement felt good against my cheek. I closed my eyes and concentrated on the small comfort, and somehow fell asleep.

I was awakened the next morning by the Lieutenant's arrival. He stuck two pieces of light bread in the space between the bars and said, "Soup's on."

HACKSAW

"Don't I get water, too?" I asked, aware of my strong thirst.

"You'll get water tonight," he answered. "Wouldn't want you to get too full at one time." He glared at me, waiting to see if I was going to backtalk him. He looked disappointed when I didn't and left.

I left the bread where it was and concentrated on my hands. They looked and felt somewhat better than they had the night before, and after some experimenting I found that I could move my fingers. I gingerly explored the back of my head. There was a lump the size of a golf ball and some dried blood, but no permanent damage seemed to have been done. Along with some bruised ribs and a sore kidney, I also had a splitting headache. Other than that I seemed to be all in one piece.

It was later in the day when the idea hit me. I was shuffling back and forth across the floor, daydreaming and listening to the hypnotic sound of my chain dragging the concrete with each step I took. I dropped to a sitting position and drew my knees up, legs slightly apart. Picking up the slack chain, I isolated one of the oblong links and began rubbing the end against the rough concrete. After about ten minutes I examined my progress. There was very little, hardly more than a shiny spot. But I wasn't discouraged. After all, I had a great many days ahead of me and absolutely nothing to do. Time was no object.

Resolutely, I went back to my rubbing.

# CHAPTER 8

ISOLATION. THE HOLE. DAYS OF MONOTONOUS DRUDGERY and nights of fitful insomnia. Five shuffling steps forward, turn, then five shuffling steps back. Repeat until tired. Rub the sore hipbone, bruised by unyielding concrete during rare moments of sleep. Close the eyes and let the mind drift, projecting itself to some faraway place, a place of beauty and grace where nude girls frolic on sandy beaches, and the air is fragrant and fresh. Dinner for two under evening stars, accompanied by lulling sounds of gently breaking waves. Two-inch steaks with imported wine. No, wait! Never tasted wine before—might not like it. Better make that a pitcher of beer, waiter.

The jingling of keys and the rasping sound of the outer door opening yanked me back to reality. The Lieutenant stuck light bread and a styrofoam cup of water between the bars, peeked over at the gallon bucket, estimating when the trustee will have to empty it; then left, clanging the metal door firmly behind him. Silence again, alone with my thoughts. The hole. Tedious boredom!

On my fifth day the Lieutenant brought a tin plate of food, consisting of exactly one tablespoon of everything served at the evening meal. I wolfed it down with sheer delight, savoring every morsel. Four days of bread and water gives one a great appreciation for prison cuisine. I didn't leave a speck on my plate, and when I finished I looked at it with regret,

74

realizing I wouldn't be seeing anything but bread for the next five days.

The Lieutenant came back with a trustee, who took away the plate and emptied the gallon bucket. When I was finally alone I sat down and for the umpteenth time checked the section of chain I had been working on. No doubt about it, I was making progress. I could see a small indentation in the link and I took heart at the sight. I would make it. I had all the time in the world.

I finished on the twenty-third day. The link was now held together by only a paper-thin sliver. I tested it by holding the link between thumbs and forefingers and slowly applying pressure until it bent. The weeks of effort had paid off. With just a little more force the link would break, freeing my legs for the first time in three months. The impulse was strong to do just that, but I resisted the urge. Once it was broken there would be no way for me to hide the gap from even a casual glance. Better I should wait until I was back on the road. Then I would have the element of surprise on my side, and when I headed for the bushes I would be striding—not hopping. The guards had a great deal of confidence in leg chains. Toothpick had said as much himself: *No man in chains ever makes it.* Well, Toothpick, we'll just have to see about that. Because I have a feeling you're going to be wrong, mister.

The lieutenant brought my clothes on the Monday after Thanksgiving. I had spent fifty-seven days in the hole. I dressed hurriedly and returned to the basement, empty now because of the men working on the road. I took a lengthy shower, put on clean underwear and examined myself critically in the mirror above the sink. A near stranger looked back. The light brown growth on my face made me look older than my years, and the narrowed eyes appeared lifeless and devoid of emotion. Chain-gang life has a way of giving the aging process a little nudge.

I shaved the beard, put on the prison clothes, then grabbed a bar of lye soap and headed for the coatroom. I sat down, located the wounded chain link, pinched off a bit of soap and firmly packed the indentation. I smoothed the surface with loose dirt scraped from the floor and carefully covered the evidence. At a distance it would probably go unnoticed. But if anyone became curious enough to take a closer look, it was all over. Then I would surely go to The Bunker. I would just have to make my move as soon as possible.

When the gangs returned to camp that evening, I was given a warm greeting. Woodson's pet had taken a beating, and the men loved it. Guys who had hardly spoken a dozen words to me before were suddenly slapping my back, asking if I needed anything. It was like old-home week.

Scifo spotted me and came beaming in my direction, clapping his hands. "Hey, Eddie!" He gave me a playful tap on the arm and stepped back, frowning. "Goddamn, I can see right now I'm gonna have to fatten you up some, man. You look like you could dodge raindrops. You eat anything yet?"

"Not hungry, Andy," I said. "Smoked so many of these cigarettes I feel like I'm going to throw up."

"Yeah, it gets like that, you know? Stomach's all shrunk up and all." He gave me a wink and lowered his voice. "Wanna know about Wilshire?"

"What about him?"

"You cracked him some good ones. Fourteen stitches in his cheek—two busted ribs."

"Couldn't have happened to a nicer guy," I said. "But I got a feeling I'm really in deep with Woodson right now."

"No question," Scifo agreed. "You'd best watch yourself good."

The next morning after breakfast I discovered how deep I really was in with Woodson. I was having a final cigarette before work call when the Lieutenant entered the basement. He paused at the foot of the steps and bellowed.

"Jones! Front and center!"

I walked to where he was standing, conscious of my severed chain link and expecting the worst. The hum of conversation ceased, and all eyes focused in our direction.

"Yes sir, Lieutenant."

He looked me up and down slowly, taking his time, stretching the moment. "Cap'n says for you to fall out in Morris' gang today." He swung his head around and bellowed again. "Scifo!"

"Sir, Lieutenant?" Scifo's voice rang out.

"You're moving' to Staples' gang." He looked back at me. "Any questions?"

I stood silent, meeting his level gaze. He nodded, let his eyes roam briefly over the assembled men, then turned and retreated back up the stairs.

I walked back to my box, reflecting on this latest development. It didn't take a mental giant to figure it out. Woodson had launched a psychological war of nerves and was covering all the angles. Now I would be working under Puckett's gun, where I would be constantly reminded of Tugboat's fate. Day in and day out I would labor under his stoic watch, never knowing if Puckett was laying a trap to kill me. Eventually the strain might prove too much, in which case Woodson was hoping I would either break and surrender completely, or that I would become so paranoid that I would make a fatal lunge for the bushes. Either way Woodson figured to win. A diabolical move conceived by a diabolical mind. I was beginning to wonder if I might not be out of my league.

Scifo came over and sat next to me, a questioning look on his face. "Eddie?"

"Don't worry, Andy," I said, "I won't go off on the deep with Puckett—though no doubt Woodson would dearly love that. How's Morris to work for?"

"He's all right. Cracks a mean whip sometimes, but don't believe in bringin' a man in for poor work. Besides, Woodson wants to keep you on the road anyway, so just take it easy a few days and get your strength back. And whatever you do, stay in close to the rest of the gang—and I mean close. Don't give Puckett even a little excuse, hear?"

I nodded, realizing that Scifo meant well. But his advice was unnecessary. I also had no intention of becoming overly friendly with him. All I wanted was to go on my own way, alone, without help or hindrance, and do what I felt was best. Right or wrong, the decision would be mine. So I thanked Scifo for the words of wisdom and excused myself, saying that I had to get my gloves from the coatroom. I also wanted to touch up my frayed chain link.

My first few days back on the road were the most demanding I had ever experienced, mentally as well as physically.

We were clearing ditch lines, some more than ten feet deep, and each forkful of slush and mud seemed heavier than the last. At the end of each day I was barely able to climb into the rack for the ride back to camp. I was weaker than I thought, and my arms and legs felt as if they were encased in lead. Even without Puckett's presence, attempting to escape during those first days was out of the question. The dogs would have run me down within five miles.

After a week I was nearly back to my old self. The aching joints and sore muscles gradually disappeared, and I fell into a steady rhythm, pacing myself so as to conserve energy. Morris left me alone for the most part, apparently satisfied with my work. But every once in a while Puckett would point out a spot I had missed: some loose mud overlooked or a ditch bank I hadn't leveled properly. Each time I flashed a quick smile, said "Yes sir!" and took care of the problem. If Puckett had asked me to jump, I would have smiled and asked how high. A dog will roll over on his back to show that he's harmless; a man will smile. It's smarter to trust the dog.

Winter was in the air, and I wanted to make my move before the bitter cold set in. The dead of winter is no time to be stuck in the deep woods, miles from nowhere, with a pack of dogs and angry hunters behind you. And each day increased the chance of someone inspecting my chains. I resolved that within the next week, regardless of risk, I would test myself against Puckett.

Oddly enough, it was Puckett's desire to play cat and mouse that provided the opportunity. Christmas was nine days away, and we were clearing a large stand of trees and underbrush adjacent to the main east-west highway. The temperature was falling, and a gun-metal sky threatened snow. Scifo and a twenty-year man named Joe Pitts were manning chain saws and had felled several giant cottonwoods. They were lying around in disarray like drunken dinosaurs, distorted limbs in some cases rising more than twenty feet into the air. Except for myself, the other members of the gang, armed with bush-hooks and axes, were trimming branches from the huge trunks. It was my job to drag the cut limbs to a point some thirty feet away and stack them neatly into the pile. Puckett had given me this task because he knew full well how difficult it was to maneuver the bulky branches across uneven ground in leg chains. I was convinced there was also another reason for my selection. Some ten yards beyond was another stand of dense trees and foliage, offering ideal concealment if it could be reached. The prospect of making a dash for this haven was tempting, of which Puckett was very much aware. He was also aware of the length of time it would take for one to bunny-hop that distance in leg chains.

It didn't take long for me to get the picture. Each time I made a trip to the growing stack of branches, Puckett made it a point to have his back turned, shotgun across his shoulder, apparently watching the men in the other direction. Kenny, however, was in perfect position to watch my every move. It was a cute little trap, but one I felt could work for me. All I had to do was get that pile of branches high enough.

During the next hour I was moving constantly between the fallen trees and the mound of branches. I was the picture of clumsiness—slipping, stumbling and falling as I wrestled the bulky limbs across uneven ground. I hoped that Kenny and Puckett were buying my performance. Each time I added a branch to the growing pile I would pause, mop my face on the back of my sleeve, then bend over and pick up a few loose twigs that had fallen off. Then I would shuffle off for another load.

My moment came shortly after ten o'clock. The stack was now nearly eight feet high, and I was having a hard time getting some of the larger branches on top. Any time now Puckett or Morris would tell me to start a new pile, and I had no way of knowing where that would be. I decided on one more trip, then go for it.

I selected a medium-size limb one of the men had just whacked from a thick oak and checked the scene from the corner of my eye. Morris was out of the picture, sitting in the truck that was parked nearly fifty feet away at the side of the highway. Kenny was sitting on a felled tree, chomping on a wad of tobacco and looking around. Puckett was doing his usual: standing hipshot in nonchalant arrogance, shotgun dangling from his right hand. If only he didn't look so damned confident!

I took a firm grip on the limb and set out toward the stack

of branches, pulse racing, breath heavy. The adrenaline was beginning to flow, and objects suddenly took on a stark clarity. My palms grew damp, and I could feel the sweat running down my rib cage. And I was afraid. Would I stumble and fall—only to sit up and find myself staring down the barrel of Puckett's shotgun? I didn't want to die. I didn't want to end up like Tugboat.

"Jones!" Puckett snapped.

I came to an abrupt halt and turned to face him, half convinced he was reading my mind. But his position hadn't changed, and only his head was turned in my direction.

"Yes sir?" I croaked. Puckett's eyes mocked me, and I could tell that he was sensing my fear—and enjoying it.

"Get rid of that branch and start another stack over there," he said, motioning to a spot about fifteen feet further from the tree line I needed to reach. Making a break from there would be out of the question.

"Yes sir, Mr. Puckett." He turned away, and I continued on with my burden.

From the moment I heaved the heavy limb onto the stack, things appeared to move in slow motion. All fear vanished, replaced by a calm detachment. I mopped my face, bent down and grasped the frayed chain link in both hands and separated it with one determined twist. Without hesitation I spun, ducked behind the pile of branches and—using its bulk as a shield—sprinted for the nearby tree line.

I covered the distance in something like three seconds, plunging into its comforting shelter like an enraged bull, praying the trailing leg chain wouldn't become entangled in the thick brush. All hell was breaking loose behind me. Kenny was screaming at the top of his lungs, echoed by three rapid gunshots. I could hear the pellets tearing into the foliage behind me, but I was in no real danger of being hit, for by then I was well into the covering blanket of trees. I ran head-on into one, rebounded, ricocheted off another, then continued my mad charge, dazed but unhurt.

I ran blindly, unchecked, twisting and weaving, narrowly avoiding other trees and low-hanging limbs more by instinct than design. The gunshots had reawakened my fear and added wings to my feet. I imagined Puckett crashing through the woods behind me, shotgun extended, waiting for one clear shot. I resisted the urge to look over my shoulder and continued to run.

The swinging leg chain finally snagged and brought me crashing to the ground. I freed the chain, wrapped the longer length around my right ankle and tied it in place with a strip torn from my shirt. I leaned back against the bole of a large tree, massaging my raw ankles beneath the leg chains, gasping for breath.

After a few minutes the burning in my lungs began to ease. I had no idea how far I had run, and I strained my ears for the slightest sound of pursuit. A squirrel scampered up a nearby tree. Off to my left a field mouse darted for cover. High overhead came the distant sound of a plane. Other than that, all was quiet.

I stood and looked around, orienting myself, then took off at a steady trot, heading east. Somewhere ahead was a railroad track, running north and south, and it was this I hoped to find. This time I had nothing to aid me in throwing off the dogs, and I needed to find transportation fast. I had no illusions as to what would happen if Woodson's crew found me. I would never reach camp alive.

It was well into the afternoon before I stopped again. The short piece of chain on my left ankle was hindering me, so I wrapped it in place as well, trying to think. It would take at least forty-five minutes to an hour to get the dogs from camp; add another fifteen minutes to get them squared away on my scent. As close as I could figure, I had at least a six-mile lead. But I knew how easy it would be to lose that lead. The dogs were relentless—as were the men who would be with them. Also, if they figured out where I was likely to be heading, they would send men ahead to cut me off. Then it would all be over but the shooting. With this thought as incentive, I set out again.

The afternoon waned, then turned to dusk, followed shortly by complete darkness. Night comes early in the winter woods, especially when the sky is overcast. It was turning colder, and I desperately wished for a coat. I slowed my pace to a walk, barely able to see two feet ahead. I was exhausted and disoriented, but I couldn't afford to stop. So I forged ahead blindly, stumbling, arms outstretched, praying I wouldn't run into a bear.

All through the night I kept moving, pausing infrequently to rest. Occasionally I would catch myself nodding off, at which time I would leap to my feet and strike out again, beating my arms against the cold. Once I came upon a farmhouse adjacent to a meandering path. It was deserted, but the old pump well in the back yard was usable. I cranked the handle and brought a small stream of icy water to the surface. I drank greedily and moved on.

Dawn broke clear and cold, the threatening cloud cover of the previous day having dispersed during the night. The growing sunlight filtering through the trees was a welcome sight, but there was one thing wrong: it was rising at a forty-five-degree angle to my left. Instead of east, I had been traveling southeast! I quickly altered my direction, wondering how long I had been off course.

Around midmorning, as I paused for a much-needed rest, I heard the far-off whistle of a freight train. I broke into a run, plowing through vines and honeysuckle and dodging protruding limbs. Gone was the exhaustion, vanquished by the lovely sound of that whistle. Daniel delivered from the lion's den!

I found the tracks in less than fifteen minutes. I fell on my back on the bed of gravel near the rails and gasped for breath, arms flung wide. I rested for perhaps five minutes, then headed south along the tracks. From time to time I would flop on my belly, place an ear against one of the steel rails and listen intently for the vibration that would signal an approaching train.

Soon I heard it. I left the tracks and hid in some nearby bushes, praying it wouldn't be moving too fast. A short while later the engine came into view, rounding a curve far off down the tracks. I took a quick inspection of my tied-down leg chains, assumed a crouching position and waited for the right time to move.

The engine chugged past, smokestack billowing. I could see the engineer with his elbow out the window, attention focused on the tracks ahead. When he was about a hundred yards past, I leaped from the brush and ran hard alongside the moving cars. I looked over my shoulder, saw an empty coal car approaching, reached out and grasped the ladder. The train was traveling faster than I thought, and its momentum yanked me from my feet, my arm feeling as if it were being torn from its socket. But I managed to hold on, grabbed another rung with my other hand and swung myself up and over the top. I dropped to the bottom and sprawled full-length on the metal floor, puffing and blowing like the engine ahead of me.

Then it hit me: I was safe!

I stood and faced forward, letting the icy wind numb my face, bringing tears to my eyes. But on my face was a grin wider than a jack-o'lantern's. Ahead lay miles of empty track, leading far away from Woodson, Toothpick, Puckett— everything connected to Camp 15. Suddenly I laughed, then threw my head back and yelled, the sound carried away by the rushing wind. That's for you, Woodson—that right? You fucking maniac! I yelled again. That's for you, Toothpick, you rotten bastard! How does it feel to eat your own words? Another yell for Puckett. What say you now, you murdering sonofabitch?

Still grinning, I sank to the floor, leaning back against the side of the car. Gradually the smile and exuberance faded as another thought struck me. I tilted my head back and gave one long drawn-out howl. The sound seemed to echo around me, bounding off the steel walls of the coal car before being swept away by the wind.

That's for you, Tugboat.

# CHAPTER 9

As FATE WOULD HAVE IT, I WAS ONCE AGAIN HEADING FOR Richmond, arriving at the city limits sometime after four in the afternoon. The long open-air ride had left me chilled to the core, and I breathed a sigh of relief when the train slowed to a crawl just before reaching the James River viaduct. I uncurled myself from the floor of the coal car and dropped stiffly to the ground. I danced around for a minute, stomping the ground and flailing the air in an effort to get the blood running again, then trotted up the grassy incline and stepped over the railing onto Grace Street.

After a couple of blocks I came to a gas station. I entered the office and smiled at the old man sitting behind the register. He eyed me suspiciously until I told him that I had been in an accident and asked if I could use his phone. He pointed to a small desk across the room and watched silently as I picked up the receiver and dialed.

Mom answered on the third ring and nearly dropped the phone when she heard my voice. Briefly I told her where I was, keeping my voice low, and asked if she would mind picking me up. Of course not, she said, but what on earth? I cut her off in mid-sentence, saying I would explain when she got here, then hung up. I thanked the attendant, told him someone was meeting me. Fine, he said, just wait outside. As filthy as I was, I didn't blame him one bit.

She was there inside twenty minutes, a small figure hunkered over the steering wheel, trying to look every which way at once. I stepped out of the shadow of the men's room, where I had been lounging, opened the passenger door and slipped inside. She looked at me with wide eyes.

"Edward . . . what in the world are you doing here? And look at you, you're a mess! Is that coal you have all over you?"

"Yes, and I'll tell you all about it, but first let's get away from here, that old man inside has been giving me a bad case of paranoia."

She shook her head in wonder and pulled into the rush-hour traffic.

Once again I found myself explaining that I had escaped—as if she didn't know. I left out the parts about Tugboat, Toothpick and my days in the hole, because I knew that would do nothing but upset her. She listened without interruption, only an occasional sigh and inhalation of breath—making mother sounds. When I finished, she remained silent for a while, gripping the wheel tightly, sorting through what she had just heard. At last she spoke.

"Son, you just can't keep on doing this. If you keep running, they'll never let you come home."

"They weren't leaning too far in that direction to begin with, Mom. I was looking at another three or four years anyway, and I'm not so sure I could make it that long."

"What do you mean by that?"

"Nothing," I answered. I couldn't tell her the truth, that I might not live that long. "It's just that three or four years is a long time, that's all."

"What are you going to do now?" We were heading east on Broad Street, the sidewalks lined with shops.

"First of all we have to stop at a hardware store and get a hacksaw blade so I can saw these chains off." She looked down at my exposed ankles and frowned, noticing the manacles for the first time. "Then I'd like to find a motel somewhere off the beaten path so I can get a bath and some sleep."

A few blocks further on I saw what I was looking for. Mom found a parking space, admonished me to stay in the car and trotted into the store. I slouched down in the passenger seat to wait, aware of the coal dust I was leaving all over the place. A police car cruised slowly by. The driver glanced idly in my direction, and I held my breath until he had passed. I would not feel easy until I was far away from Richmond.

Mom came out of the hardware store clutching a brown paper sack. She paused a moment, looked up and down the street then walked rapidly to the car, acting like a minister sneaking out of a porno shop. She handed me the sack, started the engine and pulled out into the flow of traffic.

"Are you sure you want to go to a motel?" she asked. "Wouldn't it be all right if you just spent the night at home?"

"You know I can't take a chance like that, Mom—and neither can you, for that matter. Think I want to see you charged with harboring a fugitive? No. Just find some out-of-the-way motel where I won't have to walk through a lobby. You can pick up a few clothes for me . . . maybe take me to the bus station in the morning . . . maybe let me have twenty bucks or so . . ." I gave her a wry smile. ". . . That's all."

"What about food? Aren't you hungry? You couldn't have eaten anything."

"Right now I'm more tired than hungry. I feel like I could sleep for a week."

We settled on a small motel just off Nine Mile Road, leading toward Highland Springs. The units were located behind the office and were all on ground level. Mom pulled up in front and went inside to register while I waited in the car. When she returned she drove around back, parked in front of the next-to-last unit and we went inside.

It was like a thousand other cheap rooms across the country. Sagging double bed, scarred nightstand and chipper dresser, one easy chair gone hard with use. But to me it was like a suite at the Hilton. I made straight for the bathroom and started a hot tub. Then I sat on the bed and went to work on the chains with the hacksaw blade. Mom fussed with the curtains, making sure they were pulled tight, then sat down in the easy chair, watching me.

The blade made short work of the chain links, and soon I had them off. I gratefully massaged my tender ankles, careful not to agitate the raw areas where the skin had rubbed away.

Mom shook her head. "Putting chains on human beings . . . like they were animals or something. I thought I'd die the first time I saw those things on you. I cried all the way back to Richmond. I didn't think I could stand it, seeing you like that. Even at night—when I would dream of you—they would still be there.''

I went to her and put a dirty arm around her shoulders. "Well, they're off now, Mom. And they're going to stay off.'' I leaned down and kissed her forehead. "So don't think about it anymore, okay? Now, I'd better get that bath before I get you as dirty as I am.''

Mom cracked the bathroom door a few minutes later and called to me. "Edward, I'm going to have to leave now. Sure you don't want me to get you something to eat?''

"Positive, Mom,'' I said, scrubbing away at the stubborn coal dust. "Soon as I get out of here I'm hitting the bed.''

"Promise you won't go out?''

"I promise,'' I said, and smiled to myself. "Now go on before Dick calls or something and starts worrying about you. I don't want him thinking you're seeing somebody on the sly.''

"Well, you get some rest then—and I'll see you in the morning, all right?''

I said, "Make it early, will you? I'm going to have to get out of here as soon as possible.''

In a voice I barely heard through the partly open door, she said, "Yes . . . I know.''

The soft tapping sound awakened me instantly. I padded to the window in my underwear and cracked the curtain, seeing it was not yet full daylight. But there was Mom, dressed in her white uniform and looking nervously up and down the walkway. I opened the door, and she hurried inside carrying a small suitcase. She laid it on the bed and sat down beside it, looking tired.

I said, "This is getting to be a habit, you know it?'' I walked over and gave her a kiss on the cheek, gathered up clean underwear and toilet articles and went into the bathroom to shave off the two-day stubble. Mom came over and stood in the doorway, watching me.

"I got a call from a detective last night,'' she said.

I looked at her, alarmed. "You think anyone followed you?''

"I don't think so. I didn't notice anyone watching the apartment, either. He just asked if I had seen you—and of course I said no, and asked why. Then he told me what I already know."

"They probably think I'm still in the woods around Chatum," I said, splashing on some Old Spice. I moved back to the bedroom and finished dressing. Mom reached into her purse and pulled out one of my old billfolds.

"There's two hundred dollars in there," she said, handing it to me.

I was shocked. "Where did you get that? You don't have that kind of money, Mom."

"I called Dick after I got home last night. I told him about you, and he came right over. He was there when the detective called. So he told me to give you that, and said to tell you to get out of Richmond as soon as you can."

"He doesn't have to say that twice," I said. "I don't guess he's too pleased with the situation, is he?"

Mom shrugged. "He said to do what you feel you have to do."

"And what do you say, Mom?" I asked.

"I can't tell you what to do, son," she answered. "I don't like the thought of you being on the run—not able to come home. But I guess I don't like the thought of you being locked up, either. I just wish there was some way to wipe the slate clean."

"Well, it's too late for that," I said. "Unless I just give myself up right now. And I probably would . . . if it wasn't for a few things I'd rather not go into."

"Are there other reasons why you had to run, Edward? Something I don't know about?"

I was tempted to tell her about Tugboat, about Hap and Willis and Woodson, and how life in general would be for me back on the chain gang. I was tempted, but held my peace. It would serve no purpose other than to add to her fears, and she had enough of those already.

"It's no big thing, Mom," I said. "Guess I just don't take confinement very well."

She sighed and looked away, then said, "By the way, Gloria called last night, too. She got a call from the same detective."

"You didn't tell her anything, did you?"

"No. But she said if you wanted to see the baby, it would be all right. She just said to tell you that if I heard from you."

I placed the filthy prison clothes and leg chains in a bundle by the door. Then I gave her a mock bow, ignoring the subject of Gloria. "Ma'am, would you allow this rich boy to buy you some breakfast?"

She remained serious, toying with the top button of her white uniform. "You don't think it would be a good idea, then?"

I walked back to the bed and sat down beside her, sighing. "No, Mom, I really don't. I'd love to see Dee Dee, but it wouldn't be right. It would just make it harder for me to leave. And Dee Dee's old enough now to remember the strange man who would show up calling himself daddy. What's she going to think when daddy leaves and doesn't come back? She wouldn't understand. No, Mom, it's best I don't go poking around trying to play a role I can't fulfill."

She nodded and stood, smoothing out her skirt. "Maybe you're right," she said. "It was just a thought. Now, what about that breakfast? You must be starved."

"How did you guess?"

After a huge breakfast at a nearby Denny's, Mom drove me to the Greyhound Bus Terminal. She parked at the curb opposite the side entrance and cut the engine.

"Time to say good-by again, I guess," she said. "I should be used to it by now." She looked at me and forced a smile. "Sure you want to go all the way to California?"

"I'm sure . . . and don't say it, Mom. Yes, I'll be careful." I grinned at her and pulled the small suitcase from the back seat. "Tell Dick I said thanks for the money, will you?"

She nodded, then said, "Another Christmas with you not home. I can't think of too many when you were." She pulled out a Kleenex and dabbed briefly at her eyes. "Sorry. I told myself I wouldn't do that."

"Nothing to be sorry for, Mom," I said gently. "Like you said—you wouldn't be a mother if you didn't feel the way you did."

I opened the door and set the suitcase outside, leaned over and kissed her. "I'd better go. I'll give you a call as soon as I get to California."

"If I'm at work, call Dick."

"Will do," I said, and got out of the car.

I stood on the sidewalk and waved until she reached the end of the block, then picked up my suitcase and went into the terminal.

The waiting room was crowded with Christmas travelers, mostly servicemen in uniform. I threaded my way through the mass of bodies and fell in line at the ticket window, checking the departure board on the wall behind the ticket agent. There was a bus leaving for Los Angeles at eight-twenty. I glanced at my watch: seven fifty-five. Plenty of time. I felt an excitement at the prospect of seeing California. Like most, I had heard a great deal about Hollywood and Beverly Hills. And the ocean. I love the ocean!

"Stay right where you are, son, and don't move a muscle."

Powerful hands grabbed me from behind, twisting my arms behind my back. I heard the unmistakable click of handcuffs opening, felt cold steel as the manacles secured my wrists. Then the hands spun me roughly around, and I was looking into the face of two detectives. One flashed a badge and returned it to his inside jacket pocket.

"Planning on taking a trip, were you?"

California would have to wait.

# CHAPTER 10

"WELL, JONES, I SEE YOU DIDN'T TAKE MY ADVICE, DID you?"

Once again I was facing Captain Goldie across his desk. He was in his favorite position, reared back in his chair, fingers interlaced across his stomach.

"I asked you a question, boy. I don't like repeatin' myself."

"I guess I didn't, Captain," I answered.

"Well, that's a damn shame, son—because it was really good advice. Didn't you think it was good advice?"

"Yes sir."

"Then why didn't you take it? Didn't you think I meant what I said?"

"Yes sir, I think you meant it."

He sat up and folded his hands on the desk, a half smile on his face. "And just what did I say?" He spoke softly, almost politely, a manner that I found more intimidating than any shouted obscenities. I had no doubt that he remembered exactly what he had said.

"You said that if I was lucky enough to hit the bushes without getting shot that I'd best not get caught because I'd spend the rest of my time here." I spoke quickly, rushing the words, wanting desperately to get this meeting over with.

He absently fingered the scar along his cheek. "I said somethin' else too, didn't I?"

I hesitated a moment, not wanting to say it, but having little choice. "You said that you could guarantee I wouldn't like it."

He reared back again, looking pleased. "You got a good memory, boy. Too bad you ain't got good sense. I'm just like Sears & Roebuck—when I guarantee somethin', I stand behind it." He turned to a guard standing quietly off to the side. "All through with him in Admissions, Mr. Talbert?"

"Yes sir, Cap'n. His folder's already been sent to the Record office."

Goldie wrote something on a printed form, tossed it into his Out tray and returned his attention to me. "Jones, I'm givin' you thirty days' hole time—plus you'll be gettin' a slip from Records advisin' that another year's been added to your sentence. I'm obligated to tell you that if you don't agree with this, you can write to Mr. W.K. Cunningham, Director of Prisons, and state your case. But I can tell you right now it won't do you a damn bit of good."

He paused for a moment and looked at me thoughtfully. "I'll tell you somethin' else, too," he continued. "Look at it as one more piece of good advice. You've been damn lucky so far, but don't push it. In case you ain't noticed, we got walls here—and automatic weapons to keep you off 'em. You'd best keep that in mind in case you get homesick again. Any questions?"

"Yes sir," I said, shifting about awkwardly. "Could I write my mother a letter and let her know where I'm at?"

"She read the paper?"

"Yes sir."

"Then she'll know where you're at. Anything else?"

"Well . . . can I send my clothes home and get a receipt for my money?"

Goldie looked at Talbert. "He get a receipt for any money?"

"He didn't have any, Cap'n," Talbert answered, lying through his teeth. "Just a suitcase full of clothes."

"I had a wallet with two hundred dollars in it," I said hotly. "This man took it when I went through Admissions."

"Is that a fact?" Goldie said. "And just where'd you get two hundred dollars—and that suitcase?"

I couldn't answer that, and Goldie knew it. To do so would

be admitting that Mom had helped me, leaving her open for a possible charge of aiding a fugitive. And while there was no doubt in Goldie's mind that she had done just that, there was still no proof. So I stood in silence and glared at Talbert, who folded his arms and glared back. Goldie smiled.

"Cat got your tongue? Or maybe you just made a mistake about the money?"

"I guess I did, Captain," I said, and shrugged.

"Well, that little mistake's gonna cost you ten more days' hole time. I don't like people lyin' on my men. We understand each other?"

"Yes sir."

"Get him outta here, Mr. Talbert."

The isolation cells were located in a separate building called "C" Section: fifteen basement cells on either side of a narrow corridor, each cell measuring six by nine feet. There were no windows, and a solid steel door separated each cell from the corridor. The top two floors were reserved for protective-custody prisoners and those considered too dangerous to be housed in general population.

Talbert handed me over to the isolation officer, told him how much hole time I had, then left. I was ordered to strip, given a roll of toilet paper, then escorted to a cell midway down the corridor. The guard warned me that no talking between prisoners was permitted—which I thought unnecessary because how can one talk through twelve inches of concrete? He motioned me inside the cell and closed the door.

The only fixture was a metal toilet attached to the rear wall—which was some improvement over the camps, anyway. I threw the roll of toilet paper violently against the wall and began pacing the floor furiously. I cursed myself for being an idiot. Of all the stupid things to do. Walking into a public transportation lobby like I owned the place! Any moron would have known those would be covered. And what if those detectives had seen me getting out of Mom's car? I cringed at the thought and made a silent vow. Never again would I involve her in one of my harebrained schemes. What I brought on myself was one thing. Having her suffer for my mistakes as well was quite another.

I threw myself onto the floor, cradled my head in my arms.

Hindsight is such a wonderful thing; all mistakes become painfully obvious after the deed has been done. I curled myself into a ball and bit back tears of rage and frustration. Just like a bear in the woods, I thought. Making a lot of tracks but going no place at all.

No place at all.

Time passed with excruciating slowness. Days blended into nights, nights into days, until it became impossible to distinguish one from the other. To further confuse the issue, guards would stagger the twice-a-day bread-and-water schedule until I wasn't certain if it was A.M. or P.M. Eventually the mind becomes bewildered and disoriented, sealed in a vacuum of timelessness where the only reality is the hundred-fifty-watt light bulb imbedded behind wire mesh screening in the ceiling. Soon the light becomes a focal point. You lie on your back and find your eyes drawn hypnotically to its incandescence. Often a near state of astral projection is induced and a feeling of weightlessness invades the body. You lie in a cloud of peaceful oblivion, unencumbered by conscious thought, until the sound of heavy footsteps and jingling keys from the corridor beyond filters through the senses, breaking the spell. Then time catches up, the mood is gone, and once again you're back in the hole.

Some feel the rain, others just get wet.

The days continued to drag. I kept count by keeping up with the meal days. As a result I was waiting eagerly when the guard showed up sometime during the fifth day with a regular tray. Unlike the fifth-day meals on the camps, this tray had a full issue. I dug in greedily, eyes closed, savoring every bite. After I ate my fill, I discovered that there was still enough leftover to make a sandwich, and I did so. I wrapped it in toilet paper and stashed it in the corner where I slept. It was only a small hunk of cheese slapped between two pieces of bread, but in a couple of days it would taste like steak.

Sometime later I awakened from a fitful sleep to find that I had a visitor. A huge black cockroach was nosing around my snack, trying to find a way in through the layers of toilet paper. I watched for a while, then picked up the sandwich and began unwrapping it. The roach scampered away and ducked out of sight somewhere behind the toilet. I pinched off a few crumbs of bread and scattered them in a small circle.

In a few minutes he reappeared, creeping from behind the toilet, testing the air with his long antennae. Hunger overcame caution, and he inched his way toward the goodies, pausing now and again to check for signs of danger. Eventually he reached the pile, latched on to a crumb and dragged it back to his hiding place. Soon he returned for another, and still another. Though he sensed my presence, his confidence grew with every trip, until finally he ignored me all together. It dawned on me what a ridiculous sight I must have made, lying nude on the concrete floor, breaking bread with a cockroach. But it broke the drudgery, and any relief is welcome in solitary confinement.

As time passed, my little friend—who I named Jasper—began trusting me more and more, possibly realizing that I was the source of his new-found bonanza. Eventually he ceased lugging the crumbs back to his hideout and took to eating his fill on the spot. After several days he even allowed me to pick him up. Within a week I had him literally eating out of my hand. Occasionally I would deliberately leave his feeding area empty. When this happened he would stalk about angrily, flailing the air with his antennae, indignant as hell, until I finally sprinkled a few crumbs around him. Never in my wildest dreams did I ever think I would make a pet out of a cockroach. But a pet is what Jasper became, and he helped fill a lot of empty hours. Me and Jasper. Both doing hole time on bread and water.

Then came my fourth meal day. I was sitting with my back to the wall, daydreaming as usual, when the clanking of keys brought me back to the present. The door opened, and I jumped to my feet as the guard entered and handed me my tray. As he turned to leave he paused and looked down. I followed his gaze and was surprised to see Jasper prancing about in the middle of the floor, swinging his antennae, obviously puzzled by the strange presence in the room. Normally he would have been behind the toilet about now, but he had grown comfortable with me as a permanent part of his surroundings, finding no need to hide. I watched in horror as the guard raised one big boot and brought it sharply down on the unsuspecting insect. There was a small popping sound as Jasper exploded. The guard checked the bottom of his sole, scraped it across the concrete, then left without a backward glance.

For several moments I stood there motionless, staring at the flattened object. Slowly I set the tray down, unrolled a small piece of toilet paper, and carefully wiped up the remains of Jasper. It's difficult to explain the sadness I felt over the death of this cockroach. But I was, saddened and angry. To me Jasper had become much more than an annoying insect. He had become my companion. An animate creature on which to focus attention and—to some extent—affection, a vital element in the human makeup. His absence would be sorely felt.

It didn't seem right that I should just flush him down the toilet. So I wrapped him tightly in the toilet paper, got down on my hands and knees and felt around behind the toilet. I found the small hole that had been Jasper's home and stuffed the wadded paper inside, pushing it as far back as it would go. Only then did I turn my attention to the metal tray, only to discover that I wasn't as hungry as I thought.

Three weeks later the guard came in carrying a plastic bag which contained my clothes. "Get dressed," he said. "You're goin' back to the land of the livin'."

Afterward, I followed him along the corridor and up the short flight of steps to ground level. Another guard was waiting for me, and together we walked outside into an overcast winter morning. The shock of a chilling wind made me catch my breath, but I welcomed it with pleasure. I opened my mouth and tasted the air—literally *tasted* it! It was like stepping into another world.

We went straight to Admissions, where I was allowed to shower and shave for the first time in forty days. The property clerk issued me additional clothes, underwear, towels and bedding and a thin Army jacket. Then I was escorted to a section in "A" Cellblock called "Deadhead." Here I would stay until given a permanent job assignment and would only be let out for meals. The guard told me the Classification Committee would probably see me the next day. Then he locked me in my new home to await the noon meal.

Later that afternoon the sounds of boisterous shouting and laughter brought me to the bars of my cell. Hundreds of prisoners were filing into the cellblock, which was five stories high and longer than a football field. The workday had ended, and the men were returning to their cells for the afternoon count, after which everyone would be let out for the evening meal. At four o'clock we would be locked in our cells again, where we would remain until six-thirty the following morning.

The count finally cleared, and I had just stepped from my cell when three hard-looking men in their late thirties and early forties approached me.

"You Dick Bosher's boy?" The speaker was a tall, raw-boned man with prematurely gray hair and a portion of his left earlobe missing.

"His stepboy," I said. "Why?"

"You don't remember us, do you?" He motioned to his two companions. One was of medium build, slightly balding, a look of permanent brooding etched into his homely features. The other was a little taller and sported a crew cut. He also had the deadliest pale green eyes I had ever seen. I thought for a moment, puzzled by the question, then shook my head.

"No reason why you should, I guess," the speaker said. "Last time we saw you, you was no bigger than a wagon wheel. We used to drive for Dick. He'd bring you in sometimes on payday and you use to get a kick outta seein' everybody all hunkered down by the back wall, shootin' craps. You even tossed the bones a couple times yourself, as I recall." He stuck out a bony hand. "I'm Joe Wheelhouse. This here's Norman Whitlock and Henry Miller."

I shook hands all around, vaguely remembering the incidents just described, though not the participants, since I was only about six at the time. Joe Wheelhouse gave me a nudge and said, "Come on, let's get some chow."

We sat four abreast in the chow hall, which was dominated by rows of long metal tables bolted to the floor. Joe and Henry Miller did most of the talking, filling me in on the routines of the prison. Norman Whitlock spoke hardly a word, giving only an occasional grunt in response to some comment made, chewing slowly while his eyes constantly explored the assembled men. I had the impression that very little escaped his sweeping gaze. I finally voiced the question that had been puzzling me since our meeting.

"How did you guys know who I was?"

Joe Wheelhouse answered. "Henry here got a letter from Dick a couple weeks ago. Said you was here and asked if we'd kinna look after you."

I bristled at this. "Look after me? Doesn't he think I can look after myself? I've spent two-and-a-half years on chain gangs without any help in that department. Why should he feel I need looking after now?"

"Whoa, Eddie—don't get all puffed up," Joe said, laughing. "Nobody's doubtin' your manhood. But things are a little different in here than on the road."

"Such as?"

"Well . . . ." he hesitated, toying awkwardly with his food. "Such as the kind of people you got in here . . . I mean . . . let's face it, you're what now—eighteen? nineteen? And you're a pretty good lookin' kid, too. Most guy's here're doin' forty, fifty years, some ain't gonna ever get out. On the road, nobody's doin' more'n a twenty spot—and they usually make parole inside of five years."

I had a hunch what was coming next, but asked anyway. "So what are you trying to tell me?"

"What he's tryin' to tell you is that some dudes in here are gonna try to fuck you," Norman Whitlock said evenly. Evidently he didn't believe in mincing words.

Joe cleared his throat and quickly took command of the conversation again. "It's a different world in here, Eddie. A city within a city, with its own rules and values. The strong take from the weak, and the only way to survive is by bein' just a little bit tougher than the motherfucker next to you. You're gonna see things you've never seen before, and sooner or later some asshole's gonna pressure you for sex. When that happens, we'll help you handle it—and believe me, you'll probably need help . . . at least for a while. That don't make you no less a man."

I pushed my tray away, experiencing a sudden loss of appetite. For years I had heard stories about Five Hundred Spring Street, the beatings, stabbings, younger guys being threatened and raped. Apparently they were true. *"I can guarantee you won't like it.''* That's how Goldie had put it. I had learned to cope with life on the road, adapting quickly. I wondered if I could do the same inside the walls.

That night I lay awake well into the early morning hours, staring at the chipped ceiling, listening to snores and muffled curses as they echoed through the rows of silent tiers. My mind was filled with jumbled thoughts, bouncing around haphazardly inside my head. I didn't want to think about tomorrow, because tomorrow looked too much like yesterday—and the yesterdays hadn't been so hot. Memories are funny things. Private things. We discard as extraneous those things which aren't important to us. I thought about the traumatic incidents of my life that were significantly important now. I counted perhaps three. So much for past events. I had the feeling that the ones that really counted would take place in the not-too-distant future.

Because I certainly didn't plan on staying in this madhouse.

# CHAPTER 11

THE NEXT MORNING I WAS BROUGHT BEFORE THE CLASSI-fication Committee, which was made up of two men in their early fifties who appeared to have been cast from the same mold. They assigned me to "A" Cellblock, and because I had no record of narcotics abuse, they decided that I should work in the prison hospital as an orderly.

I was given a pass to the laundry, where I picked up three sets of whites, the standard dress for hospital workers, then reported to the "A" Cellblock officer. He placed me in a two-man cell on the third tier. The top bunk was open, so I made it up, placed my meager belongings at the foot then reported to the hospital.

Doctor Vanetter was a tall, fragile-looking man with a full head of silver-white hair. He walked with a habitual stoop, as if he were carrying the burdens of the world. He was the chief physician for the prison and well liked by both inmates and staff. Many prisoners owed their lives to this soft-spoken, kindly old man—those who had been carted in nearly hacked to pieces by an assailant's homemade "shank." For those who weren't so lucky, their remains were hauled away by an ancient hearse under contract to the prison. Many a prisoner had taken his final ride in that vehicle, which was nothing but an old Ford station wagon with the rear seats removed. I would see that wagon often.

Doctor Vanetter sat behind his cluttered desk, stuffing a

long-stemmed pipe from a brown tobacco pouch. I sat across from him in a straight-back chair that had seen better times, feeling uncomfortable in the small office. He fired the pipe, released a cloud of sweet-smelling smoke into the air and cast thoughtful eyes on me.

"How old are you, son?" he asked.

"Nineteen, sir."

"Nineteen," he mused, shaking his head. "And unacceptable for the Road because of a couple of escapes, right?"

"I guess that's the reason, yes sir."

He gnawed on the pipe in silence for a moment, then sighed and said, "Kids—they're sending me kids now. You ever work with hospital patients before?"

"No."

"Good," he said. "Then you don't have any bad habits I'll have to break. A prison hospital runs quite differently from one outside—at least mine does. Primarily because security ties my hands. Established procedures—most of them, anyway—have to be dumped by the wayside, and I've had to come up with a few methods of my own."

He opened a side drawer of his desk and removed a folder containing several typewritten pages. He selected one and handed it to me. It was a listing of procedures to follow when dealing with inmates under the influence of various drugs.

"The biggest problem we have here—other than stabbings . . . by the way, how do you handle the sight of blood? Make you sick? You don't faint or anything, do you?"

"I've seen blood, Doctor Vanetter," I answered somewhat testily. "It's a red liquid, right? Like sweat is a clear liquid."

"Good enough. Like I was saying, our biggest problem other than stabbings is with drugs. You name it, and it's here. The most popular is a nose inhaler named Whymine."

"Why is that so popular?"

"Amphetamine, son. Speed. The damn things are loaded with it. They break open the tube, remove the cotton, draw out the liquid with a syringe and inject it into the vein. The effect is more powerful than taking a dozen Bennies—and a hundred times more dangerous. It plays havoc with the nervous system and literally burns away brain cells. Prolonged usage causes extreme paranoia and, in some cases, toxic psychosis. This usually comes in the form of hallucinations, tremendous panic and acute depression. When a man reaches that point, it's important that he receive medical attention fast, as there's no telling what he may do. Obviously he isn't going to come to the hospital voluntarily. So I've detailed some effective measures that my orderlies can take to counteract overdoses and possibly save the man's life, without forcing him to come in to the hospital. It's all spelled out in there. Study it and memorize it, because I'll test you in three days.''

I skimmed over the paper in amazement and said, ''You mean that ordinary meat tenderizer actually works on some of these drugs?''

''That's right. And I'll see that you're supplied with some to keep in your cell; nothing about that violates security. If you know of a man who has overdosed on stimulants, five to seven tablespoons will relax the muscles and stop hallucinations within forty-five minutes. You'll also be given a two-gram vial of alcohol in case you run into an inmate who has lost consciousness from sniffing glue—which is also quite popular. You place the vial directly under the man's nose. The fumes will break down the glue vapor and restore consciousness in minutes.''

An item near the bottom of the page caught my eye. ''What's this about never giving coffee to somebody suffering from an overdose of Darvon? You've got the word 'never' underlined.''

He tapped out the now-spent pipe and dropped it into a jacket pocket. ''Because it can kill him, that's why. You induce vomiting and attempt to keep the victim awake . . . but never by pouring coffee down him. Caffeine will cause convulsions in Darvon overdoses.''

I shook my head again, handed the paper back. ''You must care an awful lot about cons, Doc.''

''Wrong. I care an awful lot about people. Cons just happen to fall into that category. Now, go find Mr. Portus—he's floating about someplace. He'll get you squared away with a memo for the cellblock officer.''

As I stood, he reached a gnarled hand across the desk. I took it without hesitation. I had the thought that he was wasting his time inside these walls, that he should be practicing someplace where his obvious concern would be more appreciated. It was only after I stepped out of his office and closed the door behind me that I thought of something else. Doctor Vanetter was the first prison official I had ever shaken hands with . . . or wanted to.

The next week went by quickly. I was kept busy learning my hospital duties: how to take blood pressure, pulse and temperature; how to draw blood samples; how to give injections—dozens of other incidentals. True to his word, Doctor Vanetter tested me on his emergency drug-overdose procedures, which I passed with no trouble. I found that I rather enjoyed the work and went about my chores eagerly, an avid pupil. After the slavelike routine I had grown accustomed to during my chain-gang experiences, this new vocation was a welcome change.

Joe Wheelhouse, Norman Whitlock and Henry Miller were also assigned to "A" Cellblock, and I spent most of my nonworking hours visiting with them. My cell mate was a small, potbellied man of about fifty who was medically excused from work because of severe asthma. He spent most of the time asleep on the bottom bunk, so I hung around the cell as little as possible. Then, in my ninth day behind the Walls, I saw my first murder.

It was during lunchtime. Joe, Norman, Henry and I had just walked through the chow-hall door when we nearly ran over a thin black guy pulling a twelve-inch shank out from under his shirt. Holding it close to his body, he quietly eased up behind another black guy about fifty pounds heavier standing in line. We watched as the guy with the knife planted his feet for balance and lowered his shoulder . . . me not believing what I was seeing, opening my mouth, saying "Hey . . ." just as Henry dug a sharp elbow in my side. With one quick movement the guy buried the blade almost to the hilt in the bigger man's rib cage.

The big guy spun around, looking angry, not even realizing he had just been stabbed . . . until he saw the bloody knife the smaller man was holding, the guy drawing back for another plunge. Then his eyes bulged in horror, and he held out both arms in reflex, shock taking over, but was too late because now the blade was coming at him again, plowing between the outstretched arms and sinking into the right side of his neck—going all the way through and coming out the back. Blood spurted like red oil from the severed carotid artery and drenched several other cons trying to scramble out of the way. The thin guy was having trouble holding the knife now, the handle red and slippery with blood, so he let go and stepped back a few paces, watching like a matador as the bull sank to the floor and sat there, a vacant stare on his face, arms limp and blood still spurting—though not as far now. Then the bull suddenly slumped forward, still in a sitting position with legs spread, forehead touching the floor, four inches of red steel sticking from the back of his neck.

He didn't move anymore.

Guards were coming from everywhere now, charging through the crowd of watching cons. A couple of tear-gas shells exploded at the feet of the thin black guy who was still staring down at his victim, and everybody scattered. Norman, Joe, Henry and I were ducking out the door back into the open yard, coughing and sputtering, eyes watering. More guards wearing gas masks and carrying three-foot billy clubs rushed past us into the chow hall.

Without speaking, we went back to the cellblock and gathered in Henry's cell. No sooner were we inside than Norman turned to me with an icy stare.

"Don't ever do anything like that again," he said.

"Do what?" I asked.

"Open your mouth about somethin' that don't concern you. You was fixin' to let out a yell back there 'till Henry stopped you."

"Damn right I was!" I retorted. "If some goddamned lunatic ever tips on me like that, I hope the hell one of you guys will yell at me . . . Jesus!" I was still shaken by what I had witnessed.

"That's different, Eddie," Henry said. "Us four, we're kinna like a family. In here there's lots of families—some big, some small. What happens to them ain't no nevermind to us. You see somebody gettin' ready to off another guy—unless it's one of us—you step back and let nature take its course. You see nothin', hear nothin' and say nothin', 'cause if you do, you just might find yourself gettin' some of the same."

Joe was busy examining himself in the mirror and said, "What pisses me off is missin' lunch. Only day in the week we get ham hocks and beans, and we got to miss it. Shit! Cornbread, too.''

I looked at him in amazement. ''You can't be serious. You're thinking about food after seeing *that*? That poor bastard nearly got decapitated!''

''What am I supposed to do, forget my stomach's shakin' hands with my backbone just 'cause some clown gets . . . what was that word?''

''Decapitated.''

''Whatever. Anyway, hell yes I can think about food. Besides, there's an unwritten rule you don't stick somebody in the chow hall—we're gonna be smellin' gas a fuckin' week.''

From outside came a blast of the powerhouse whistle, telling us it was time to go back to work. Joe turned from the mirror, disgusted, and headed out the cell, saying, ''Next time somebody sticks a dude in the chow hall, *I'm* stickin' *him.*''

I believed him.

The next Sunday I got a visit from Mom. I went down the short flight of steps to the visiting room beneath ''B'' Block, handed the guard my slip and went to a small cubicle facing a wall-to-wall section of thick glass. Mom was sitting on the other side, looking small and out of place. I sat down on the metal bench and picked up the phone, motioning for her to do the same.

When she had the receiver to her ear, I said, ''Hi, Mom— not the same as the road, is it?''

She tried to smile but didn't quite make it. She said, ''I guess it does leave a little to be desired . . . how you doing, son?''

''I'm fine—not working myself like a mule, anyway. How about you? You look tired.''

She said, ''Just worried. I'm used to being tired.''

She didn't have to tell me that; it was obvious by the frown lines in her forehead that hadn't been there before, the slight puffiness beneath her eyes. I wanted to say something that would comfort her, so I started telling her about my three friends in an effort to ease some of her fear.

''I know,'' she said. ''Dick told me about the letter he wrote. But Edward, I still wish you were back on the road. I know it was hard, but in here . . ." she let her voice trail off and looked away.

"Are you kidding?" I quipped. "I felt like a damn sled dog! Do you realize guys break legs, cut hamstrings, shoot lighter fluid in their knees just to be able to get transferred here? This is paradise compared to 15, and I can get visits from you more often." I gave her a big grin and winked. "They did me a big favor, Mom—believe me. Hey! I thought you loved me . . . don't go wishing a fate like that on me."

She wrinkled her nose playfully and said, "Just for that, you got a spanking coming when you get back home."

"See there? Now you want to beat me."

We continued that way for the better part of an hour, keeping the mood light, exchanging counterfeit humor. She was seeing Dick frequently now, she said, smoothing old wounds. She was cautiously optimistic about the future. But eventually her mood shifted, and her eyes took on the familiar misty look. She dabbed at them with a tissue, and I joked that if she wasn't careful she was going to get me started, and I didn't even have a handkerchief.

"I'm sorry, son," she said. "I just keep thinking if only I hadn't left you at that darn bus station!"

"I asked to be left there, Mom. If you hadn't taken me I would have found another way to get there. It was my fault, not yours. I made a mistake—again."

She honked daintily and put the tissue away. "I guess you're right." She gave a quick smile. "Dick says you'll probably make parole in a couple of years if you stay out of trouble. That isn't too awfully long, is it son?"

"I'm sure I will," I lied. I knew Dick didn't believe it either. He was just trying to help her through a bad time. In six months her feelings of guilt would be gone, and she would be more accepting of the situation. One of the most valuable assets of the human spirit is that, given enough time, it can adjust to anything. Well, practically anything.

Mom finally brought up the subject that had most been on her mind. "Edward . . . I want you to promise me that you won't try to escape again. Will you do that? Dick said they would shoot you quick in here, and I couldn't take that."

Obviously Dick knew nothing about the chain-gang camps. I thought for a moment before answering, choosing my words carefully. I could count on one hand the guys who had beat the Walls in the last forty years, and I didn't know if I could make it or not. But I did know that I was definitely going to try.

"I'll promise you one thing, Mom," I said noncommittally. "I promise I won't do anything to get shot. I couldn't take that either. Fair enough?"

She gave me a level look, started to say something, then decided not to pursue it. But her eyes showed her disappointment. And I was having trouble looking at them.

The guard stood up from his desk and said visiting hours were over. We said our good-by and promised we would write, and Mom said she would come every weekend. She stood and looked at me sitting there for a moment, then blew me a kiss and walked away, another guard escorting her through the door on the other side.

I couldn't remember ever feeling so depressed.

# CHAPTER 12

THE WEEKS PASSED, AND I GRADUALLY FELL INTO A ROU-
tine of mechanical movements. Five days a week I worked
my hospital duties, cleaning the wards, taking vitals, preparing charts—occasionally even helping Doctor Vanetter stitch
up a knife wound. There were a lot of knife wounds.

I had Fridays and Saturdays off, and usually I spent them
in the small music room underneath the library. There was
an old set of mismatched drums sitting in the corner, and I
used to spend hours at a time pounding the shit out of them,
like they were the cause of all my troubles. Before long I
realized I was getting pretty good at it and started practicing
in earnest. I told myself that playing drums and escaping had
a lot in common. They both required good timing.

If the weather was good I would sometimes play a little
softball in the rec yard. If I wasn't doing that or playing
drums, I would just hang around with Joe, Norman and
Henry. Sunday mornings, though, were set aside for my
weekly visits with Mom.

For a while things went pretty well. I would get a few
whistles once in a while walking down the tier with a towel
draped around my waist, heading for the shower—overhear a
smart-ass remark every now and then that would make me
angry. But for the most part I gritted my teeth and ignored
them. I noticed that none of these incidents ever occurred

when I was with my three friends. I was becoming more thankful for them every day.

There was one exception: a short, blocky-looking lifer named Red Miller (no relation to Henry). The guy really made me nervous, always following me around whenever we were in the rec yard together, smiling and winking—acting like he was in love. Before long I realized he was . . . with me. Not wanting the situation to blossom into full-scale warfare, though, I never mentioned anything to Norman, Henry or Joe. I especially didn't want Norman finding out, because I had a pretty good idea what he would do. But Red was dangerous. I had found out from Doctor Vanetter that he'd already killed one man a few years earlier. I just hoped that he would soon get tired of the game and go after a more willing partner.

Talk about being naive.

It was early April, more like summer than spring, and a serious softball game was going on in the rec yard. I was playing third base and during one turn at bat I made a quick trip to the toilet, which was housed in a small wooden building behind the backstop. I had just finished my business at the single urinal and was turning to leave when I came face to face with Red, blocking the doorway with his bulk, lips curled in a mocking grin. I pulled up short and watched apprehensively as Red slowly walked toward me. At the same time his hand disappeared inside his shirt and came out clutching a slim, wicked-looking shank.

Cautiously I moved backward until I felt my back hit against the wooden wall. My eyes were glued to the steel blade as Red continued to shuffle forward, relaxed and casual, running his thumb gently across the cutting edge of the knife.

He stopped three feet in front of me and said, "Don't look so scared, Hollywood . . . you don't mind me callin' you Hollywood, do you?"

I said nothing, still watching the knife, feeling my heart building up speed.

"I just want you and me to be friends," he continued. "And you ain't been actin' very friendly lately, now, have you?"

I finally found my voice. "I don't mind being friends, Red. You don't need a knife for that."

"But I want us to be special friends—you know? I could treat you real nice." The grin left his face. "Or I could be a real motherfucker."

"I've got some special friends, Red—you know that." I alternated my gaze between the knife and his narrowed eyes, trying to keep calm, ready to say anything that would get me out of there alive.

Red turned his head and spat on the concrete floor. "I know all about those special friends of yours. All they doin' is blockin' for you—think I just got here yesterday? Ain't nobody every seen you behind the blanket with any of them. Am I right?"

I nodded quickly. "You're right, Red."

"Then you ain't really hooked up with anybody, right?"

Again I was quick to agree. The grin returned, and he took a step closer, breathing audibly. "Then ain't no reason why we can't hook up, is it? How about it, Hollywood, gonna let ol' Red take care of you?"

There was a maniacal look in his pale gray eyes as they looked unwaveringly into mine. I flicked a glance downward and saw that the knife was now only inches away from my solar plexus. For a moment I thought of trying to knock the blade away, but suddenly remembered something Tugboat had said: *"The braver the mouse, the fatter the cat—and there's times in all our lives when we have to be mice."* This was no time to act like a hero.

I sighed and managed a smile. "Okay, Red. All you had to do was ask. Christ, you didn't have to come in here waving that shank around."

His grin widened, and he let his gaze roam openly up and down my body. But the knife never wavered. "Now that's more like it! You fuck with Whymine? I got a poker game goin' outside, and Colie's holdin' some for me. I'll run out and get it, then we'll fix up and have a little fun."

"Here?" I asked.

"Somethin' wrong with here?" he said, his grin narrowing.

"No . . . here is fine with me."

"Good. Now you wait right here while I go out and see

**110**

Colie. Won't take me more'n a minute." His breathing had quickened during this, and he suddenly leaned forward, snaked a thick arm around my neck and kissed me full on the mouth. I was taken by surprise and stiffened, lips pressed together, fighting the impulse to jerk away.

Red stepped back and cocked his head, his sour breath heavy in my nostrils. "That wasn't very passionate, Hollywood."

I managed another stiff smile and said, "That's hard to do, Red, with a knife pressing against me."

He gave me a long look, said he would be right back and turned to go. Someone poked his head through the door. "Hey, Eddie . . ."

"Get the fuck outta here!" Red said.

The head disappeared. Red gave me a final look, slipped the knife back inside his shirt and left.

I took a deep breath, exhaled and moved quickly to the open door, peeking around the frame. Red was approaching a small group of men about twenty feet away, sitting at the bottom of the bleacher section, deep in a poker game. I wiped a hand across my mouth, feeling both fear and anger at the same time.

Red had reached the circle of poker players now, squatting down next to one of the men, speaking softly in his ear. His wide back was turned to me.

I knew what I had to do.

Moving with purpose, I stepped from the doorway and walked over to the backstop. I bent down and picked up a softball bat, gripped it firmly in both hands and started walking towards Red's back. I moved cautiously with the bat held at port arms, thinking of the knife under Red's shirt. I focused on a point above his collar, which nearly hid his thick neck, blocked everything from my mind as I watched the collar get closer and closer . . . ten feet . . . eight . . . five. I choked up on the handle now slippery with sweat and drew back for a home run.

At the last moment two of the card players looked up, recognized what was about to happen in a flash and started scrambling out of the way. Red spun to his left, throwing up an arm in instinctive reflex . . . God he was quick! But not quick enough.

# Edward Jones

I heard the forearm snap as the bat caught it squarely before ricocheting off and striking him above the left eye. The second blow caught him alongside the neck and sent him staggering. I stepped in closer and really leaned into it, feeling the shock all the way to my elbow as this one landed solidly on his heavy jaw. I drew back again, ready to end it all, then stopped with the bat poised high over my shoulder.

Red was lying in a heap on his side, motionless except for an uncontrollable spasm in his left hand. I slowly lowered the bat and stared down at him, fascinated, vaguely aware of hurried activity taking place around me. But I only had eyes for Red.

A tear-gas shell went off at my feet, and I was surrounded by choking fumes. Full awareness came back then, and I dropped the bat, not wanting to risk being shot by one of the tower guards. I walked away with my eyes closed, fanning my face, until I felt strong hands grab me, twisting my arms behind my back . . . felt the steel cuffs click around my wrists. Then I was led gagging and sputtering from the area.

They locked me in a cell on the second tier of "B" Block. I would have to wait here until Goldie held "court" in the morning, charged with assulting an inmate with intent to do grave bodily harm.

I sprawled out on the bare mattress, laced my hands behind my neck and stared at the bunk above me, wondering how bad Red had been hurt. He wasn't going to let this go unanswered, that was for sure. As soon as I got out of the hole, and he got out of the hospital, I was going to be in for real trouble. And the way I looked at it, I didn't see any way I could win. Regardless of the outcome.

Just before lock time, Norman Whitlock came by. He stopped outside my cell and gave me a long look, hands shoved deep in his pockets.

He said, "What the fuck happened?"

I swung my legs over the side of the bunk, arms on my knees, and looked at him.

I said, "It's a long story."

"I got five minutes," he said, "But I can probably guess."

So I told him, leaving nothing out, going back weeks before when Red had first began his subtle pressuring for sex.

**112**

"Why the hell didn't you say somethin'?" he asked when I had finished. "I've been lookin' for an excuse to stick that fuck anyway."

"That's why I didn't say anything!" I snapped. "Goddammit, Norman, you act like it was my fault. I was hoping it would blow over without anybody getting killed."

"These things don't blow over, Eddie—they blow up. And if you had to go actin' like Babe Ruth, you coulda at least finished the job. You can't play games with a guy like that."

Norman placed two packs of Marlboros in the bars and said, "Anyway, he'll be on ice for awhile. When they carted him off to the hospital they found his shank. That means he's good for a year in "C" Building. When he comes out, though, you let me handle it, understand? And I don't want no shit about it."

It was getting close to count time, and Norman looked up and down the tier. He pulled a Whymine nose inhaler from his pocket and tossed it to me through the bars.

"What's this?" I asked, noticing the tube rattled as I caught it.

"There's eighteen Seconal in there. Help you do your hole time a little better."

I fingered the tube and smiled. "Thanks, Norman. But how am I supposed to get them in? They're going to strip search me, you know."

"Suitcase 'em before you go to court in the mornin'."

"Suitcase them?"

He looked at me, tired, and said, "Eddie—goddammit, don't you know anything? Stick 'em up your ass. You ain't gonna hurt 'em, the tube's airtight."

"Hope it doesn't cause hemorrhoids," I said dryly.

Norman said, "If they do, then everybody's got 'em. Now if you get lonely over there you can talk to Bucky or Freddy Silva on the phone." He saw me look at him, amazed, and added, "You *do* know about the phone, don't you?"

I shook my head, thinking I was learning as much about the Walls during this conversation as I had in my entire three months in population.

Norman moved closer to the bars. "All right, listen up, I gotta go . . . Just sit on the shit jacket with your legs close together and bounce up and down on it. The pressure'll force the water out of the bowl. Then you put your head down in it and talk through the pipes—anybody on that side."

I said, "Stick my *head* inside? You got to be out . . ."

The warning bell sounded from the guard's station below, signaling five minutes until lock-down. Norman made a fist and rapped it lightly on the bars.

"You take it easy now, Eddie," he said. "We'll probably see you in about sixty days. I'll get Joe to write Dick a letter so your Mom'll know what's going on."

"Don't say anything that will worry her, okay?"

"We'll think of somethin' tame, don't worry."

"Thanks, Norman," I said gratefully. "And thanks for the pills, I'm sure they'll come in handy."

I would have never guessed how handy.

I felt like an idiot. Here I was, stark naked, bouncing up and down on the stainless-steel commode like a mad jack-in-the-box: *whoompa, whoompa, whoompa,* stand up and check the water level, then *whoompa, whoompa, whoompa* some more, until at last the bowl was empty. Unravel some toilet paper and swab out the rancid dampness around the inside of the rim, and I'm all set—I think. I tossed the foul-smelling toilet paper in a corner and sat down beside Five Hundred Spring Street's version of Ma Bell, ear cocked to the opening. Nothing so far. Must be waiting 'til after five when the rates go down, I thought, and laughed. The sound echoed within the small enclosure, strange and tinny. Primitive stereo, I thought, and laughed again.

The hole will do that to you.

Norman's prophecy had proved accurate. I was on my third day of a sixty-day sentence gleefully pronounced by Goldie. I had managed to "suitcase" the inhaler tube of Seconals with no trouble, after first preparing the way with a dab of Brylcream. Four of the eighteen red capsules had already been downed, producing a not-unpleasant grogginess that permitted sleep to come at will. During my more aware moments I fooled around with the "phone," like I was doing now. So far I hadn't worked up the nerve to stick my head in the thing, so I just sat down beside it and listened to all the voices coming up through the pipes, smiling at the dirty jokes, war stories and outrageous lies. The miracle of indoor plumbing being used to its fullest potential.

I must have dozed off because the next thing I remember was opening my eyes and finding my cheek resting against the side of the steel commode. Voices were rattling around inside the bowl like a convention of Tidy Bowl men, and I perked up and listened. There was an added excitement to the conversation now, different from the relaxed bullshit that normally went on. I cuddled closer to the toilet and held my ear above the opening.

Within moments I was fully awake. A con named Mickey Pruitt had gone berserk on Whymine, wired a knife to each hand to ensure against losing them and went on a rampage. He had left the metal shop where he was assigned, marched across the inner yard straight into the Back Office and killed the shift Lieutenant and a civilian clerk. From there he had made his way to the hospital, where he was confronted by Doctor Vanetter. Without hesitation Pruitt had proceeded to slash and stab with both knives, literally cutting the doctor to pieces. It had taken more than a dozen guards with billy clubs and tear gas to subdue him, but not before Doctor Vanetter lay dead on the floor. A gentle, caring man, he had ended up a victim of those he had sought to heal.

My finicky attitude vanished, and I thrust my head into the commode opening and joined the conversation. Rumors were flying, varying according to the teller, as I sought to have the story confirmed. Some said that Pruitt's death toll went as high as half a dozen; others swore that Captain Goldie himself had been a victim. But the one thing all were in agreement on was that Doctor Vanetter had been the last to die, and that dead he was. The voices carried no regret, no sorrow—not even disappointment at losing the finest doctor they would ever have. Only ecstatic glee, and wasn't it a shame that old Mickey couldn't have gotten a few more of the fuckin' bastards. A hero had been born, rising up to slay the stooped old man who did nothing but toil to save their miserable lives.

I heard a sound coming from the door behind me and looked around. The five-inch peephole in the steel door was uncovered, and an eye was staring in at me. The eye disappeared and was replaced by the five-inch barrel of a tear-gas gun being shoved through the opening.

The guard pulled the trigger and a shotgun blast of gas pellets exploded high on my left thigh. A cloud of gray fumes immediately filled the cell, and my leg burned like hot coals. I crawled into a corner and rolled onto my side with my eyes squeezed shut, gripping my wounded thigh.

God, it hurt!

The fumes were choking—like inhaling the vapor from a book of matches the moment they all go up in flames.

I finally managed to draw a full breath, held it a moment, then let out a bellow of rage and pain that could have been heard all the way to "B" Block had it not been for the concrete walls. I rolled to my hands and knees and crawled over to the toilet—reached behind the commode and took out the tube of Seconals. I opened the cap with shaky fingers, dumped half a dozen capsules into my mouth and choked them down. I replaced the tube in its hiding place, crawled back to my corner and curled up again. My breath came in short, rasping gasps, and I clenched my teeth, snarling and grunting at the relentless pain until everything came loose, and I dropped down into a black well of nothingness.

# CHAPTER 13

SUMMER WAS IN FULL SWING WHEN I NEXT CAME OUT OF my solitary cell. It had been a difficult two months to say the least, compounded by the fact that I had received no medical attention whatsoever for my injured leg. The wound was now a dull purplish mass of mostly dead flesh that constantly oozed puss, a source of continuous pain. I was seething over the callous way the attack had been carried out but had held my feelings in check; it would have served no purpose to rant and rave and scream in admirable but futile defiance. So I bore the pain in false stoicism and allowed it to fuel my growing determination to escape.

After hacking off the stubborn beard and struggling through a lengthy shower, I reported to the hospital to have Mr. Portus, the medical technician, attend to my leg. I removed my pants, hopped onto the examining table and let him press and swab and probe the sensitive area.

"That's nasty, son," he grunted, pouring hydrogen peroxide over the wound. "How long has it been this way?"

"Two months. It doesn't seem to want to heal."

"And it won't, either . . . not until it's had a thorough cleaning. The problem with these gas wounds is that once the chemical penetrates the flesh, it just keeps churning and eating away like microscopic parasites . . . which in a sense is exactly what they are."

I watched as he expertly went about the business of tending

the wound, wondering if I should mention Doctor Vanetter. As it turned out, I didn't have to.

"Guess you heard about Doc, huh?" he asked.

"I heard."

"A damn shame, that's what it is. Doc treated everyone the same—like people. It didn't matter if you were staff or inmate." He shook his head and put the finishing touches on a bulky dressing. "Okay, you can get dressed now. I want you over here every day for whirlpool treatments and a fresh dressing. We have to keep that thing clean. It hurt much?"

"Nothing I can't live with," I answered, slipping back into my pants. Then I voiced a decision I had made weeks earlier. "Mr. Portus, I'd like for you to recommend that I be transferred out of the hospital, if you don't mind."

He looked at me in surprise. "Why? I thought you liked it here."

"I did. But I just don't think I'm cut out for hospital work."

He nodded, understanding in his eyes. "Sure that's the reason—or is it because of Doc?"

"A little of both, I guess," I answered truthfully.

"Okay, Eddie, I think that can be arranged. Know where you want to work?"

"I thought I'd try the wood shop, see if I'm any good at making things."

He shrugged, removed his heavy frame glasses and polished them with a sterile gauze pad. "If that's what you want, I'll send a memo to the Committee in the morning." He fixed me with a stern look and added, "But I still want you to come in for those baths, understand?"

"I'll come in," I promised.

It was several days later, and I was playing chess with Joe Wheelhouse in his cell. Henry Miller was sitting on Joe's bunk trying to compose a love letter to his girlfriend, which was a struggle since Henry's vocabulary was limited to something like five hundred words. Pencil poised, he looked over at me with a bewildered expression.

"Hey, Eddie, how do you spell 'appreciate'?"

I told him and turned my attention back to the game. But my mind wasn't really on it; I was thinking about a certain guard. I made a so-so move and sat back to study Joe.

"What would you say the odds were of getting out of here?" I asked.

Joe countered my move before answering. "You mean escape?" He thought a moment and said, "I'd say pretty slim. Your best bet's tryin' to get back on the road and make your move from there. But that's pretty slim too, 'cause Goldie ain't about to put you back out after leavin' twice. Even if he did, you'd just end up right back with that crazy Woodson—and he'd love that."

"Hey, Eddie, how do you spell 'passionate'?" Henry asked. I told him.

"What if I told you I thought I could make it out of here," I said to Joe, making another halfhearted move.

"I'd say you better think again. You ain't even been here long enough to know the place good, much less find a way out. You got guys here been schemin' their asses off for years tryin' to find a hole. Know how long it's been since anybody beat this joint?"

"No."

"Eight years, that's how long." He captured one of my knights and leaned back in his chair, looking smug. "John Holloway went over the wall in back of the laundry. Took him two years to pump his nuts up enough to make the move. Then he goes and gets busted three days later at his old lady's house. Nope, I'd say forget it. You ain't got but three—maybe four—years, and they'll parole you. Now, you gonna move, or what?"

I moved, then said, "Let me ask you something, Joe. If a man can beat the four o'clock count, would you say he had a good chance?"

He thought about it. "Maybe. Depends on what he did then. But the only way to do that is use a dummy, and that's been tried before."

"But not with Myers, I'll bet." Myers was the guard who made the four o'clock count on my tier.

"What about Myers?" Joe asked, and knocked off a pawn.

"He's got one bad habit I've noticed." I spoke eagerly, ignoring the chess board. "A couple of times when he was making the count I happened to be sitting on the john. Each time he kept his head turned straight to the front, like he was embarrassed or something."

"So?"

"So what if I made one sitting on the commode? A dummy, I mean—one that would pass at a quick glance?"

Joe gave me his serious look. "Sounds to me like one's already been sittin' on it. You're serious, ain't you?"

"I sure am."

"Hey, Eddie, how do you spell 'thighs'?" This was Henry again.

"For Christ's sake, Henry!" Joe said irritably. "I got a dictionary here, why don't you just look the fuckin' thing up?"

"How the hell can I look it up if I can't spell it?" Henry demanded.

"He's got a point there, Joe," I said, and told Henry how to spell it.

"Hell of a letter," Joe grumbled. "Appreciate. Passionate. Thighs. Shit!"

"How about it, Joe. Think it will work?" I persisted.

He lit a cigarette and pushed the board away. "I don't know—it would have to be a damn good one."

"Has anybody tried that way before? You know, sitting on the john?"

"Not that I know of—ain't nobody been that stupid. You're talkin' about makin' a full-face dummy that's gonna be lookin' the hack dead in the eye, and what about your cell buddy, how you gonna keep him quiet?"

"For one thing, it doesn't really have to be a full-face dummy. And as for my cell buddy, he isn't going to know a thing about it."

I swept the chess pieces into a cigar box Joe kept them in, leaned on the small metal table and looked at him earnestly. "Look . . . if I could get by the count—make something good enough to pass with Myers, I could hide out down in the wood shop until the all-clear whistle sounded. The two gun-tower guards on the back wall leave after that, and the towers are empty until six o'clock the next morning, right?"

"Right," Joe agreed. "Can't nobody get to that area after lockup, so ain't no need for any hacks to be there all night. But goddammit, Eddie, I keep tellin' you this dummy on the shitter ain't gonna work!"

I nodded my head slowly and said, "I think it will, Joe. I really think it will."

Three weeks dragged by and gradually I accumulated the items necessary to pull off my little deception—if indeed I *could* pull it off. It wasn't much: hair swept from the barber shop floor, a pair of surgical gloves, a small stack of out-of-date newspapers, two coat hangers and a bottle of glue. I continued to keep a close eye on Myers as he made his evening count. Human beings are basically creatures of habit; we are all cursed with little quirks and mannerisms that, to anyone who cares to observe, are as predictable as tomorrow's sunrise.

So I went about helping Myers acquire yet another habit: of seeing me every evening at count time sitting on the john—reading a newspaper. Every day, with the exception of Thursdays and Fridays, which were his days off, he became a little more programmed, until eventually he hardly paid me any notice at all. He would look at my cell mate, cut his eyes briefly in my direction, then move on without even breaking stride. Occasionally I would raise the paper high enough so as to practically cover my entire face. The result was the same. After five weeks I was positive I could beat him. The thought sent shivers of anticipation up and down my spine, and I could feel my pulse rate quicken.

I was as ready as I would ever be.

It was late August, and Joe, Norman and Henry were gathered in my cell. The day before, Norman had approached my cell mate and suggested in no uncertain terms that he should check into the hospital for about a week. The man answered that he wasn't ill enough to be confined to the hospital, to which Norman, in his subtle way, replied that he very well might be if he didn't check in posthaste. Realizing that Norman was not one to have angry with him, he saw the wisdom of it all and checked into the hospital. Now we were going over last-minute preparations, though my friends were frankly dubious about the whole thing.

"It'll never work," Joe said, shaking his head emphatically. He and Henry were standing near the back of the cell, looking doubtfully at the contraption I had propped on the toilet. Norman was standing outside watching for any guards that might appear.

"That piece of shit ain't gonna get you nothin' but a year in "C" Building," Henry added. "And ol' Red's gonna love that."

"The problem is that you guys know it's a dummy," I said, making a small adjustment to my creation.

"You ask me, that ain't the only dummy in here," Joe mumbled.

I had carefully filled a pair of pants with toilet paper rolls to fill them out, belted the waist around a stiff piece of cardboard and sat the thing on the commode. Under the pant cuffs was a pair of my shoes, while a smaller piece of cardboard served as the head. On top of this I had glued the hair taken from the barber shop. A newspaper, supported by two wire coat hangers with surgical gloves acting as hands, covered the cardboard body and top two-thirds of the face. From the tier outside my cell, all that could be seen of the figure was the top of the hair-covered head and the lower portion of the legs. All in all, I didn't think it was too bad a job. But stupidity, in its extreme, often rivals brilliance. I looked at Joe and said, "Are you positive you can sit this thing up right, now?"

"I'm sure. But I'm tellin' you it won't fuckin' work. Hey, Norman! You think this piece of shit'll fool Myers?"

Norman pushed away from the railing and came to the cell bars. "Turn the light out," he said. I reached up and pulled the chain dangling from the single hundred-watt bulb hanging from the ceiling. Immediately the cell was thrown into a hazy dimness. "Looks better now," Norman said.

"I know," I said, turning the light back on. "But I've tested Myers with the lights out. He slows down a little. Besides, I'm supposed to be reading a newspaper." Then I thought of something. "Henry, don't you have a sixty-watt bulb in your cell?"

"Okay, I'll swap you," Henry said. "Might make a little difference."

"When you plannin' on tryin' this nonsense, anyway?" Joe asked.

"Tomorrow. I can't see any reason for postponing it."

"Then your ass will probably be in "C" Building tomorrow night," Henry said.

I grinned and said, "Don't be such a pessimist, Henry. You're beginning to sound like Joe."

"I ain't no pessi . . . pissa—whatever. I just don't think it'll work, either."

The following morning dawned overcast and humid. Heat lightning flashed in the distance, and the sky threatened rain. During the day I performed my routine task of running pinewood planks through the huge planing machine. I had a quick lunch with my three companions, receiving last-minute assurances that all would be carried out as planned on their end—which I never for a moment doubted. Afterward, they walked with me to the open gates that separated the main yard from the industrial shops beyond. We stopped just under the gun tower rising thirty feet above the gates, watching the stragglers coming from the chow hall, hurrying to make it through the gates before they were closed electrically by the tower guard. These same gates would be closed again at three-thirty in the afternoon, after the industrial area had been closed for the day.

Norman looked around, then shoved something into my hip pocket. "There's eight bucks," he said. "I hope you'll get to use it. But if you don't hear the all-clear whistle, stick it behind the first commode in the wood shop toilet. I'll get somebody to pick it up in the mornin'."

"Thanks, Norman," I said awkwardly. "I appreciate everything you guys have done for me." They were looking everywhere but at me, uncomfortable with impromptu farewells. The last group of prisoners was just now going through the gates. "Well, guess I'll catch you guys on a later shift, huh? Thanks again."

Joe reached out and slapped me lightly on the shoulder. "Take care, Eddie," he said, and they turned and walked away without looking back. I heard Joe mumbling, "It'll never work," and smiled to myself, knowing I was going to miss these guys. They were hard men who had committed criminal acts but who still walked with their own peculiar set of values that society would have found hard to understand. Out of respect for a man who had once hired them—and who would again, despite their records—they had taken on the responsibility of playing guardians to a kid they hardly knew. Even to the point of killing or being killed.

I wondered how many on the outside would have done the same.

I crouched behind the stack of freshly planed pinewood and looked at my watch: three twenty-five. The hum of the big planes had ceased, and the men were gathering at the end of the wood-shop area. The banks of overhead lights were flickering off now, leaving only the dim night-lights burning at each end of the building.

I heard the foreman opening the sliding door, listened to the sound of fading conversation as the men filed outside. Then the door was pushed closed and locked.

I was alone.

I stood up and peered around the stack of pinewood, making sure. Then I stepped out into the open shop and looked up and down the length of the building, seeing the giant planing machines now sitting quietly like sleeping monsters. I crossed to the opposite side of the building, crouched beneath a side window and peeked over the sill, cautious.

The wall was twenty yards away. I could see the guard perched on his high stool inside the tower, ten feet above the rim. If the count cleared he would be leaving. I slid to a sitting position with my back against the concrete wall, rested my arms on my knees and waited.

I lost count of the times I checked my watch, willing the minute hand to move. Soon it was four-o-five . . . four-ten . . . four-twelve. I was sweating now, the stuff stinging my eyes as I wiped at it with my shirtsleeve. I raised up and peeked over the sill again. The guard was standing now, talking to someone on the tower phone . . . looking this way!

Shit.

I ducked down, gritting my teeth. They knew. They had found the dummy and any minute now a herd of guards led by Goldie would come charging through the door, searching for the other one.

The sharp blast of the powerhouse whistle caught me off guard, and I leaped to my feet, amazed.

It worked. Goddammit Joe, it worked!

I flattened myself against the wall and once again looked up at the tower.

It was empty.

I sat down again and tried to control the adrenaline flow. Easy, Eddie—you're not home free yet. Think. There's a parking lot on the other side of that wall; move too soon and you risk being seen by an off-duty guard getting into his car. Wait too long and you take the chance of the dummy being found by a guard making rounds in the cellblock. I checked my watch and decided I would give it fifteen minutes.

At four twenty-five I gave the tower another long look, then pushed the window out from the bottom and climbed out, flattening myself against the outside wall. Moving quickly, I ran to the end of the building and turned the corner, feeling naked in the glare of lights coming from the top of the wall. A stack of two-by-fours was piled neatly against the side of the building. I knew from having measured them during cutting that they were thirty-two feet long.

I pulled one from the end of the stack and wrestled it over to the wall. I stood it on end, making sure the bottom was firm against the ground, wrapped arms and legs tightly around the beam and started climbing.

At last I reached the top, stretched full-length along the rim and took a careful look at the other side. When I was satisfied no one was around, I pulled the two-by-four up after me, balanced it across the top of the wall then eased it to the ground on the opposite side. I straddled the beam again and slid carefully to the ground.

I reached bottom, kicked out the end of the beam and sent it tumbling to the ground. It landed with a dull thud in the short grass at the base of the wall. Then I sprinted across the paved parking lot partially filled with cars and pickups, ended up in an open field and set my bearings for the freight yards on the east side of the city.

Four hours later I left Richmond the same way I had arrived.

# CHAPTER 14

IN FOUR DAYS I WAS IN MIAMI, FLORIDA. A SOUTHBOUND freight carried me all the way from Richmond to Jacksonville. I left the train when they unhooked the cars, hiked through a seedy section of the city until I reached I-95, then flagged down an ETMF tractor-trailer rig from the on-ramp. From there it was a straight shot on the expressway all the way into Bikini City, as the tall, skinny truck driver called it.

By the time I reached Collins Avenue in Miami Beach, I had two dollars left in my pocket. It didn't matter. As far as I was concerned, I was rich. All I had to do was steal me a bathing suit somewhere, and I'd be in business—and I did, from a small shop opposite LUM'S restaurant across from the Lido Hotel. Just took it off the rack and put it on in the dressing room and walked out. I tossed the well-worn khakis into a dumpster in back of the hotel and went to the beach to get a tan.

In three days I had a job as a cabana boy at the resort Americana Hotel in Bal Harbour. It wasn't bad work for an escapee. All I had to do was clean the big Olympic-sized swimming pool, set up lounge chairs, pass out towels and generally tend to the whims of the rich, well-oiled bodies that lay around soaking up the sun all day—twenty yards away from the ocean. I couldn't understand why anybody would want to come all the way to Miami Beach to lie by a swimming pool. They got swimming pools in Boise, Idaho.

I didn't get a salary, but the fringe benefits made up for it. I had a cabana to sleep in, got three meals a day fixed by a chef who made more money than the mayor, plus twenty or thirty bucks a day in tips when the season started. I was also treated to a constant flow of long-legged beauties who flaunted themselves by the pool every day, a sight that kept my hormones in a high state of agitation.

A few months later I found another part-time job that I liked even better—as a deck hand on one of the big charter boats over at Castaways Marina. A big man with a solid white beard named Jack Rodgers—called "Cap'n Jack" by the locals—owned the boat. I always looked forward to getting a call from Cap'n Jack saying he had a charter. Standing on the bow of his sleek forty-eight foot Hatteras, feeling the salt spray in my face as we bounced over the waves at thirty knots, was the greatest freedom I had ever felt. I should have been a fish, I thought, as much as I love the ocean. Probably would have been a big guppy.

I thought I also probably would have gotten hooked on a hundred-pound-test line.

Within a year, all thoughts of chain gangs and penitentiaries had vanished. The only time they came to mind were during my infrequent phone calls to Mom. I was caught up in a world of bathing suits, deep-sea-fishing craft and endless ocean. My body had grown lean and tan, accentuated by putting to work muscles that even chain-gang labor had failed to exercise. Now, when I looked into a mirror, I didn't see an escaped convict staring back through haunted eyes. What I saw was a full-blown, dyed-in-the-seaweed beach bum with hardly a care in the world.

Labor Day was drawing near, and I was in a quandary as to what to do. There was a temporary lull in activity at the hotel, and Cap'n Jack's next big charter wasn't scheduled until the end of September. I was bored and restless and decided to put in a quick call to Mom to see how things were going with her and Dick. During my last call, three weeks earlier, I learned that their relationship had reached the point where their remarriage appeared imminent, and I couldn't have been more pleased. But when I stepped from the phone booth in the lobby of the Castaways Hotel, I sported a grin a yard wide. Mom and Dick had indeed retied the knot, a week ago yesterday, she'd said. It was the happiest I could remember her sounding in . . . well, I couldn't remember the last time she had sounded so happy. So I decided to take a Labor Day trip and pay a visit to the newlyweds. Mom was hesitant at first, then said fine, as long as I thought it would be all right. No one had been by the house asking for me in months, she said, and anyway they were now living in a house in Mechanicsville, just outside Richmond city limits. So I got directions and told her to expect me in four days.

I was on the road by five A.M. the following Thursday, determined to beat the early-morning traffic. I took the Coast route, following it all the way to Daytona Beach before switching to the freeway. The temperature gradually began to dip after that, and I raised the top of the maroon '57 Chevy I had purchased several months earlier. I spent the night in a cheap motel on the outskirts of Columbia, South Carolina, slept long and deep, and was back on the highway at six-thirty the next morning.

I made good time and hit the city limits of Richmond a little after seven that night. I called Mom from a gas station, got the all-clear from her and by eight was sitting in a comfortable easy chair in her and Dick's living room. Mom, as usual, insisted on fixing me something to eat and was busy in the kitchen. Dick sat opposite me in an old-fashioned recliner, his six-foot-four-inch frame dominating the room. It was the first time I had seen him in nearly five years, but you wouldn't have guessed it from his actions. His was the calm, seemingly emotionless attitude whose philosophy was never to permit the exterior to reflect the feelings of the interior. Except for when he became angry. During those rare occasions, one would almost rather encounter a berserk rhinoceros.

"You didn't park out front, did you?" Dick asked. " 'Cause you're still as hot as the Lindbergh baby in Richmond."

"I pulled around back," I told him, getting that old uncomfortable tingling around my spine again. I was beginning to get the idea that Mom was right, that I should have just left well enough alone and stayed in Florida.

Dick stretched out his long legs, yawned and said, "By the

way, I got a letter from Joe Wheelhouse about a week after you left. He said that dummy you made wasn't found 'til after midnight. Said the midnight man got to wondering how you could read a paper in the dark, or some shit like that. He also said that that Captain—what's his name?''

"Goldie," I said. "A real peach of a guy."

"Right. He said that Goldie had a fit about you getting away. You better hope you never go back there, Edward."

"I wasn't planning on it."

Mom came in with two beers, handed them out, gave me a kiss and a pat on the cheek, then disappeared back into the kitchen. Dick tasted his Pabst Blue Ribbon thoughtfully, eyes watching me above the rim of the can.

"What name are you using?" he asked.

"Edward Griffin."

"How did you get the papers? You know, driver's license, social security card, things like that?"

"It wasn't too hard. I just went to the public library, checked through some old newspaper death notices that were printed close to the year I was born. I found the name of a baby that had died when he was six weeks old, took down his name, date of birth, hospital he was born in, name of his parents. Then I wrote to the Bureau of Vital Statistics, sent them a money order for two dollars and said I wanted a copy of my birth certificate." I shrugged. "And that was all there was to it—the rest was easy."

"Pretty smart."

"I'm learning."

"But are you learning enough?"

I looked at him curiously. "What do you mean?"

Dick drained the beer and placed the empty can on the stand beside him. "I mean how long do you think you can keep running? They'll probably catch you sooner or later, you know. Then you're right back where you started—only with more time."

"I'll just have to worry about that when and if the time comes. I'm not running, anyway. I've been in one spot for more than a year now—living a pretty normal life, too."

Dick belched politely, then said, "There's no such thing as a normal life when you're wanted, boy. Every time somebody knocks on your door, you're going to wonder if it's the law. Each time a police car pulls up beside you at a red light, you'll want to duck your head and look away. And your heart's going to beat a little faster, and your stomach's going to feel like it's in your throat. And don't tell me you're never felt that way, 'cause I know better. And you know something? There's not a damn thing you can do about it. And what if you decide to have another family? You going to tell your wife who you really are? If you don't, you'll be doing her wrong. And if you do, you'll probably lose her. No sir, that don't sound like too normal a life to me.''

I slumped lower in the chair and studied the half-empty beer can. "So what do you suggest I do, give myself up? Just walk into Five Hundred Spring Street and say, 'Here I am, Cap'n, you can take a joke, can't you?' No thanks, Dick. I'll take my chances outside.''

"I'm not suggesting you do anything," he said evenly. "You're old enough to think for yourself. I'm just saying you should look at the long-term results, that's all. Because right now you're living one day at a time. You can't look to the future, 'cause you don't have one. You can't see any further than today.''

Mom came in bearing a loaded tray of food and placed it on the coffee table. I silently applauded her timing because I was fast becoming very uncomfortable with the conversation. But there are times when we all shrink from hearing the truth.

I spent a restless night in a bedroom that had been set aside as mine—had I been free to claim it—surrounded by familiar objects that now seemed out-of-place. It was as if I were an intruder, invading the privacy of a person I had never known. The old sneakers, the beat-up guitar, the catcher's mitt with the torn webbing—a dozen other once-personal effects. They all belonged to a stranger, some unknown individual who lived in a different world and with an entirely different life-style than my own. By the time I drifted into fitful sleep, I had decided that I was now an alien in my own home.

I was ready to leave by six the following morning. I lingered over breakfast and extra coffee with Mom, told her to say good-by to Dick, who had already left for the garage, and was on my way back to Florida by six-thirty.

It was still dark, and a light rain was falling. The rhythmic sound of the windshield wipers had a lulling effect on my senses as I tried to sort through conflicting emotions. I had the distinct impression that I was leaving Richmond for the last time, which meant that I was also leaving behind those who meant the most to me, and I wasn't quite sure if I was ready for that. On the other hand, I was going out on my own into the Big World, seeing places I had never seen, finding adventures I had never known. But I wasn't sure if I was ready for that, either. I couldn't escape the feeling that I was caught between both worlds, suspended in some nether world that didn't fit in with the others. Which posed the sixty-four dollar question: just where *did* I fit in? The answer had to be somewhere. Someday, hopefully, I would find it.

Maybe.

I was so wrapped up in my thoughts that I didn't notice the stop sign until I was halfway through the intersection. Stopping now was out of the question, so I hit the accelerator and shot through quickly, praying another car wasn't in the vicinity. But there was.

And it belonged to the Chesterfield County Sheriff's Department.

He was perhaps a hundred feet from the intersection when I went roaring through, cruising the quiet streets in solitary boredom. He wasted no time in falling in behind me, red lights winking. I remembered all too clearly what had happened the last time a police car had pulled me over, and I wasn't about to let the same thing happen again if I could help it. So I tightened my grip on the wheel, floored the pedal and felt the Chevy leap forward like a startled rabbit. I was familiar with the county and felt I could lose him amid the side streets and back roads that dotted the area.

A short distance ahead was a secondary road leading off the main highway. The turnoff was obscured because of a sharp dip in the highway, and I hoped to put enough distance between myself and the pursuing policeman to turn onto it without him seeing me.

It almost worked.

I came over the dip with all four wheels airborne, hit the brakes sharply and swung the steering wheel hard left. But I had misjudged the distance, and instead of skidding in a controlled turn onto the crossing road, I slammed into a bank of mailboxes on the opposite shoulder, spun around and plunged tail-first into a four-foot ditch. They make it look so easy on TV. By the time I had collected my wits enough to stumble out the door, I found myself staring into the barrel of the biggest revolver I had ever seen.

The Chesterfield County Jail and Sheriff's Department were located in the same building, a one-story barracks-type structure of brick and concrete. The front third of the building housed the Sheriff's Office, Uniform Division and Booking Desk; the back portion, separated by a solid steel door, contained the jail cells.

I was charged with running a stop sign, failure to stop and resisting arrest. I was fingerprinted, photographed and booked under my new name, for which I had plenty of identification. Then I was led to a small interview room off to the side. I took a seat in a folding chair and stared wistfully out the window. A uniformed deputy sat down on the other side of the small table and produced pen and notebook.

"Ok, sport," he said. "Let's do us both a favor and get this over with real quick like. Now, your name's Edward Griffin?"

"Yes."

"Date of birth?"

"It's on my driver's license," I said irritably. "And I've already given that information to the booking officer."

"So now I'm asking you to give it to me," he said. I told him and watched as he scribbled the information in his little book. "Now then," he continued. "What about this permanent address? It's a hotel. How come?"

"Because I live there—and work there. It's part of my job compensation."

He was silent for a moment, tapping the pen thoughtfully against the notebook. He looked at me from behind thin eyebrows and said, "Why did you run, Ed? You got something to hide?"

"Look," I said angrily, "what's with the third degree? I've been booked already, so why don't you just tell me what my bond is and let me make a phone call? I *do* get a phone call, don't I?"

"Oh, you'll get your call," he said. "But you might not get bond just yet. Not until we're really satisfied that you're who you say you are. Every piece of ID you have is less than a year old. Now, ready to answer a few more questions?''

"I've answered all I'm going to answer," I told him.

He sighed, snapped the notebook shut and put it in his shirt pocket. "Suit yourself. We have the right to hold you seventy-two hours without bond—and believe me, we will.'' He stood and motioned me to the door. "Meanwhile, we got a real nice cell for you to relax in. Let's go, smart ass."

So I declined the phone call and went directly to jail without passing go, knowing that within three days my prints would be fed into the NCIC computers in Washington. After that it would be reunion time with one Captain Goldie of Five Hundred Spring Street.

Only two of the twelve cells were occupied, and I was placed in one near the middle of the row, on the left side of the building. The jailer slammed the door behind me, said "Don't go 'way now," and left.

I started my pacing routine. Pacing is a prerequisite for anybody who gets tossed in a six-by-nine cell. To and fro, teeth clenched, cursing or praying—maybe both. Kick the wall a few times, pound your forehead with the heel of your hand. And worry a lot. After a while the legs get tired, and the brain starts looking for something else to do. So you take a closer look at your surroundings, tilting your head as you gaze at the gutter slogans scratched into the wall, trying to decipher them—maybe scratch one or two in yourself.

Some of us look for a way out. And sometimes we get lucky.

I got lucky.

Just to the right of the metal commode on the wall, where the concrete ceiling and wall formed a junction, was a two-foot-long air vent covered by a recessed grille made of steel mesh. I stood on the toilet and gave the area a close inspection. The grille was held in place by four heavy bolts, sunk perhaps two inches into the wall. The bolt heads had been filed so they couldn't be turned, but the concrete itself was flaked and cracked with age. If I could only get my hands on a good stiff piece of metal—maybe a tablespoon—I was positive I could dig around the bolts deep enough to be able to take out the grille. The vent had to lead somewhere. I was betting it ran the entire length of the building, even to the offices beyond the jail area. I decided to wait for lunch and see if I could get away with keeping the spoon. Whatever, I had to do something soon. Before my fingerprints came back from NCIC.

I ended up having to wait until three-thirty for a meal, because the Chesterfield County Jail didn't feed but twice a day. And the spoon I had placed such high hopes on turned out to be plastic. So much for that. I ignored the bowl of strange-looking soup and cornbread, drank the cup of luke-warm amber-colored coffee and started pacing again.

Wait a minute.

I stopped in mid-stride and sat down on the narrow bunk, remembering something. All well-made shoes have a steel arch support between the sole and insole. It's about six inches long and curved slightly to conform with the arch.

Perfect!

I pulled and clawed at the stubborn lining until it finally came loose. Then I pried the shiny length of steel free, re-placed the insole and slipped the loafers back on.

I was ready to go to work.

I stood on the toilet and began chipping away at the crumbling concrete. I worked feverishly, pausing infrequently to give my aching arms a short rest. The concrete was getting harder the deeper I went. I stripped the skimpy mattress from the bunk, doubled it and laid it across the toilet in order to gain more leverage. Even so it was exhausting labor, taking its toll in finger blisters and skinned hands. After nearly two hours, however, I finally managed to free the first bolt. I took a firm grip and shook it back and forth like a dog worrying a bone and nearly fell off the mattress as the heavy bolt suddenly pulled free.

I was elated and decided to take a five-minute cigarette break to celebrate. But freedom is a lot more stimulating than nicotine, and I was back at work in half the time. I tackled the second bolt with renewed confidence, and in little more than an hour this too came loose. Without pause I started on the third.

Around eight o'clock I heard the jingling of keys, signaling the approach of a guard. I jumped to the floor, tossed the mattress back onto the bunk and fell on top of it, feigning sleep. A few seconds later I heard footsteps coming along the corridor, then stopping in front of my cell. He shook the barred door, grunted, then continued on down the line. He reached the end of the corridor, unlocked another door and slammed it loudly behind him. I waited several minutes to be sure he wasn't coming back, then replaced the mattress on the commode and returned to my digging.

Finally I was on the last bolt. All I needed to do was dig out a small indentation around this one, then I used the loosened grille as a lever and pried it the rest of the way out. I lowered the heavy covering to the floor, stood on tiptoes and peered into the dark opening.

There was little to see, and the forced air blowing through the vent made it impossible to keep a match burning. But by the feeling around inside, I determined that the passage was indeed large enough to crawl through. Barely.

After a great deal of twisting and squirming, I succeeded in pulling myself into the opening and stretched out full-length inside the air passage. I rested a moment, waiting for my breathing and heartbeat to return to normal, allowing the rushing air to cool my sweat-drenched body.

For one tense moment I thought I was facing the wrong way; so intent was I on getting into the vent that I had temporarily lost my bearings. Reassured that I was pointed toward the front of the building and not the back, I began inching forward—slowly, painfully, cautiously. A jagged piece of sheet metal caught my left arm, leaving a deep gash. I ignored it and continued crawling, wriggling my body like a snake. A little further on the metal sides bulged inward slightly, as though struck with a sledgehammer. It was touch and go for a while, but I finally slithered through. A claustrophobic's nightmare, I thought, and kept moving.

After about fifteen minutes of squirming forward, I saw a faint light up ahead. I fixed my eyes on the glow, watched it grow stronger as I continued snaking my way toward it.

Soon I was abreast of another air vent. I peeked through the grille and grinned from ear to ear as I looked down into the interview room I'd been in earlier.

This grille was made of aluminum and secured from the inside by four small screws at the corners. In less than five minutes I had it off and was crawling headfirst through the opening. I hand-walked down the wall until I reached the point of no return, then tumbled the rest of the way into the room. The floor was carpeted so I made little noise when I hit.

I jumped up, unlatched the window I had only been able to look out of earlier and threw it open. I climbed through, flattened myself against the building and looked around. Then, keeping low, I dashed across a small parking lot sprinkled with sheriff's cars—out into the black night, heading for the woods beyond.

# CHAPTER 15

Once the catalyst has caused the chain reaction, its function is over. The reaction, once begun, is self-sustaining. The catalyst in my particular circumstance had been the initial escape from Camp 21; the self-sustaining reaction now was to avoid confinement, and if captured, to escape again as soon as possible. Naturally, this form of life-style presents a great many problems. But contrary to popular belief, the greatest of these is not fear of being hunted, of constantly having to look over the shoulder at pursuing ghosts. Unless provided with solid leads, law enforcement agencies do not pursue the average escapee; they lie in wait for him. Old haunts and neighborhoods, known acquaintances and friends, family members—these are kept under systematic surveillance, hoping the fly will enter the mason jar.

The biggest fear of the fugitive is in not *belonging,* for in constant flight there is no stability. He shifts around like a leaf in a maelstrom, searching for friends he cannot keep, loves he can not possess, roots that cannot take hold, for the danger also lies in remaining too long in one place. For the fugitive, familiarity does not breed contempt—it breeds *curiosity,* which is infinitely more perilous. Backgrounds become suspect, hometowns are questioned and the inconsequential lie he told last month may not hold up today. So he drifts, remaining a stranger to all, his worldly possessions enclosed in the trunk of a car or in a set of used luggage. He takes his comfort where he can and prays that today's reality will not become tomorrow's fantasy. For when all is said and done, it is much preferable to awaken in a strange motel than in a familiar cell.

Such were my experiences for the next two years; drifting aimlessly, crisscrossing the country, wondering who I would be tomorrow. I slept with women but never really knew them; I walked with crowds but was always alone. Identities were shed like discarded socks, depending on mood and circumstance: as Edward Griswald, friendly neighborhood bartender in Denver; Ronald Thomas, quiet handyman on a Santa Fe ranch; Ed Wilson, enthusiastic dock hand in Corpus Christi; Robert Jenkins, willing but somewhat inept carpenter in Atlanta; Ed Colson, drummer and vocalist for a Polynesian rock ban in Los Angeles.

Drummer and vocalist?

It was September 1967, and I had finally arrived in the City of Angels. I took the obligatory stroll along Hollywood and Sunset boulevards, marveling at the weirdness of it all, then drove out to Santa Monica for my first look at the Pacific Ocean. Except for the profusion of surfers, I decided it looked much the same as the Atlantic, so being the water buff that I was, I rented a small efficiency apartment three blocks away. It took less than thirty minutes for me to move in; then I set out to explore this strange new land.

During the next week I haunted the Hollywood area, determined to find out the basis for its widespread appeal. Other than the tropical atmosphere and rather strange garb worn by many of its inhabitants, I found it to be much the same as . . . well, Denver. Beverly Hills was certainly all it claimed to be, but the mystique surrounding the fabled intersection at Hollywood and Vine was baffling, since the most remarkable fixture here turned out to be a shoe store. I wandered through anyway on the off chance that I might have missed something. I hadn't. Then I walked into a local night spot called Whisky-A-Go-Go and fell head over heels in love.

Her name was Linda Arciaga, dancer and lead singer for a small Polynesian-flavored rock band called The Modernesians. They were the warm-up group for another more popular band called The Doors, who were riding high in the music world at that time.

As soon as I set eyes on Linda, I was hooked. Wearing a form-fitting sarong, her raven-colored hair swinging below her bare waist, she was a vision straight out of *South Pacific* as she sang and swayed across the stage. For the next six nights I never missed a performance.

The group was headed by a husband-and-wife team named Lou and Cindy Mahana, who were half Polynesian, as was Linda. The other two members included a ukulele-playing Filipino called Little Joe and an American named Bob Dawson on drums. By the fourth night I had seen to it that we were all on a first-name basis.

As fate would have it, two days before the act was to close at Whisky-A-Go-Go, Bob, the drummer, received a telegram saying that his father was dying. He told Lou that he had to return home at once, agreed to leave his drums in care of the band and booked passage on the first convenient flight to Norman, Oklahoma.

And just like that, the group was minus a drummer.

I learned of the situation during intermission break on the night Bob was scheduled to leave. He had agreed to play the last set of the night, which ended at twelve forty-five A.M. and take a two-twenty A.M. Delta flight from L.A. International. Lou said that he would call the musician's local the next day and hire a replacement until Bob returned.

Without hesitation I asked Lou if he would give me a try. He looked at me in surprise and asked if I could really play drums. Why, hell yes! says I, I'm a regular drummer's drummer! Besides which, I told him, there were three other reasons why it would be beneficial to hire me. Number one, I was willing to work for less than union scale. Number two, I had listened to their material so often that I practically knew the numbers by heart. And three, I also had a pretty fair country voice and could help out on harmony.

So Lou agreed to give me an audition that night after the club had closed, and at three o'clock the following morning, after twenty minutes of impromptu rehearsal, I was the new drummer for The Modernesians.

* * *

As I had hoped, Linda and I quickly became an item. The band had a two-week lull after closing at Whisky's with our next engagement at the Elk's Club in Seattle, Washington, the last week of September.

It was a beautiful two weeks. We cruised the night spots, haunted the beach and took long walks through Griffith Park. She introduced me to her parents, who lived in the Silver Lake district of Los Angeles. We laughed at strange zoo creatures, went rowboating at midnight and went riding through tame forests on rented swaybacked mounts.

I was pleasantly surprised to learn that, despite her extraordinary beauty, her wants were earthly and plain, unmoved by extravagance and luxury. There was a vulnerable honesty about her that made me ashamed of the lies I had manufactured about my past. Fresh out of the Army, I told her, after two tours of duty in Vietnam. Hometown—Wheeling, West By-God Virginia. About as ordinary as a young, red-blooded American male could be, I thought. But still a lie. And as the days went by, and I found myself forced to talk about home, family and friends, I began having difficulty keeping track of the lies. I was breaking the Official Rules of Fugitivism. But I was beginning to think that I might be falling in love.

It was the night before we were due to leave for Seattle that I told Linda the true story. It wasn't a conscious decision on my part, it just happened. We were curled on a blanket, listening to the incoming waves on a deserted Santa Monica beach, a nostalgic post-midnight session of surf, moon and too much Chivas Regal. The combination proved to be more effective than sodium pentathol. Or perhaps I had at last succumbed to the adage that held confession to be good for the soul.

So I poured a Dixie cup half full of Chivas, fixed my eyes on the silver path of moonlight leading across the ocean and told her.

I left nothing out, speaking slowly at first, then more quickly as I became caught up in the story. I didn't look at her but focused instead on the shimmering trail leading to the three-quarter moon. But I could feel her stir beside me as the tale unfolded, heard the quick intake of breath when relating certain gory incidents. We were wearing shorts, and I showed her the scar on my left thigh and told her how I got it; really getting into it, spurred on by the Scotch and her silence and that streak of moon-silver.

By the time I had finished, my face was bathed in sweat, and my heart felt as if it were pounding as loud as the incoming surf. But the demon had been released and I fell back on the blanket, drained but somehow at peace. I closed my eyes and thought about a passage I had read in some long-forgotten book:

> *"The rat stops gnawing in the wood, the dungeon walls recede; the weight is lifted, the pulse steadies, and the sun has found your heart."*

Funny, I thought, that I should remember that particular passage while not recalling the context from which it was taken. But perhaps such is the true essence of life—a conglomeration of bits and pieces, all taken out of context.

It was nearly four A.M. when I dropped Linda off at her house. She had spoken hardly a word after hearing my confession, expressing neither anger nor hurt. She had just sat hugging her knees in silence for several minutes, looking at nothing, then stood and announced quietly that it was time to go. On the drive across town she huddled against the passenger door, head turned to the window. She defied all efforts at conversation on my part, until I eventually quit trying. Better she should work it out her own way, I decided.

She let me walk her to the door but would have gone inside still without a word had I not blocked her path.

"Look, Linda," I said. "I know this has been a bombshell, and I really don't know how you're going to take it. But I want to ask one favor, okay?"

"What?" she asked, eyes downcast.

"Don't turn me in. That's all I ask—just don't call the police. I'll get out of your life, leave the band . . . whatever you want, just tell me. But don't send me back to hell. Will you do that much for me?"

"I won't turn you in, Ed," she said. Then she went inside and closed the door quietly behind her.

\* \* \*

We left for Seattle shortly before noon the same day. Lou and Cindy drove their Volkswagen van with the equipment in back, while Linda and I rode in Little Joe's pretentious cherry red 1967 Lincoln Continental. The trip was one of awkward silence between Linda and me but was more than offset by Little Joe's continuous ramblings. I quickly grew tired of it all and stretched out on the spacious back seat, feeling the effects of a sleepless night.

Lou had made reservations for us at the Lake City Sheraton Motel, on the outskirts of Seattle. We arrived late the following afternoon after spending the night somewhere in Portland, Oregon, checked in and went straight to our individual rooms. I unpacked my two suitcases, took a reviving shower, then called the switchboard and asked to be connected to Linda's room. Receiving no answer, I said the hell with it, stripped to my shorts and fell on the bed for a short nap. I was definitely quitting after this gig, I decided. My true confession had undoubtedly turned Linda off for good. Well, perhaps it was for the best. She would get over it, and so would I. So forget it, Ed. At best the relationship had probably been only passing infatuation anyway. Better it end now while the damage was minimal. On that positive note, I drifted off to sleep.

I was awakened by a steady pounding at the door. I glanced at my watch: five-thirty. Probably Lou, wanting to get things set up at the Elk's Club. I rolled out of bed, slipped into a robe and answered the door.

Two men wearing business suits pushed their way inside, forcing me to give ground. I knew immediately who they were.

"Edward Colson?" one asked.

"That's right," I answered. "What's the deal?" As if I had to ask.

He produced a leather wallet and flashed the inevitable badge. "Police officers, Mr. Colson. Like to ask you a few questions downtown if you don't mind."

"And if I do mind?" I asked.

He smiled and replaced the wallet. "Then I'm afraid we'll have to insist."

I nodded wearily, turned and headed for the small closet. The second detective took two giant steps and moved in front of me.

"We'll get your clothes, Mr. Colson. Just stay where you are, please."

"You guys mind telling me what this is all about?" I asked angrily. "You come charging in here, throwing your weight around without saying anything except 'let's go downtown'! Now what's the charge?"

"All right, Mr. Colson," the first cop said. "We have reason to believe that you may be a fugitive from justice. If there's some mistake we'll have it cleared up in an hour; it's just a question of verifying your identity. If you're clean, you shouldn't have any objections. Now, you want to point out what you want to wear?"

The detective was right. It took approximately one hour for them to learn my true identity. I had been ushered into the computer age, and no sooner had they finished taking my fingerprints than they were on their way to NCIC in Washington, D.C., via teletype. Within twenty minutes the results were teletyped back: HOLD FOR VIRGINIA AUTHORITIES— CAUTION: EXTREME ESCAPE RISK!

From now on there would be no more three-day grace periods.

I was allowed one phone call and asked to make it. The booking officer pointed me to a pay phone at the end of the counter and told me I had five minutes. I dialed the Lake City Sheraton, asked the switchboard to ring Linda's room, praying she would be there. She was.

"Hello?"

"Congratulations, sweetheart," I said. "You just won first prize in the Benedict Arnold sweepstakes."

"Ed?"

"Obviously. Know anyone else who would be calling you from jail? You satisfied now?"

"Ed, I'm so sorry," she said. "I really am."

"Then why did you do it, Linda? I told you that I would get out of your life, quit the group . . . whatever the hell you wanted. And you promised you wouldn't turn me in. So much

**143**

for your fucking word . . . I could fertilize a garden with your fucking word!''

"Damn it, Ed . . . it wasn't me!'' she shouted. "I didn't want to see you in jail!''

"Then who, Linda?''

"It was Little Joe!'' she sobbed. "Or maybe Lou, maybe Cindy . . . I don't know!''

"How the hell did they find out?'' I asked angrily.

She sighed and said, "I told them. I know—I shouldn't have, but I've just been so upset ever since you told me those things that I just *had* to talk to somebody.''

"When did you tell them?''

"Shortly after we checked in today,'' she said. "I just couldn't keep it inside any longer. But I didn't think anyone would do . . . *this!*''

"What did you expect them to do—give me a merit badge? Goddammit, Linda! Do you know what you've done? Didn't anything I told you about what might happen if those people get me back sink in?''

"All I can say is that I'm sorry, Ed,'' she said in a small voice.

The booking officer was watching me narrowly from behind the counter. He pointed to his watch and made a chopping motion with his hand. I nodded.

"Look, Linda,'' I said wearily, "let's just forget it, okay? If anybody's to blame, it's me. But I'd like for you to do me a favor.''

"Anything I can, Ed . . . you know that.''

"Sure. Anyway, I'd like for you to call a lawyer . . . any lawyer, and tell him I'd like to talk to him. I have a feeling I'm going to need one.''

"I'll do it as soon as I hang up,'' she said quickly. Then she added hesitantly, "What name do they have you under?''

I gave a short laugh and said, "The same one I've been using. That hasn't changed—yet. Look, I have to go. Just call that lawyer and ask him to get here as soon as possible. I've got a few hundred dollars; that should buy me some conversation at least.''

She paused for a moment, seemingly reluctant to break the connection, then said, "Ed, I really do . . . did love you. At least I think I did. Please don't hold it against me because I needed to talk to someone about . . . us.''

"I won't, Linda," I said, and knew that I was speaking the truth. "At least you didn't call the police, and that's all I really asked you not to do. Take care of yourself now, hear? And for what it's worth—I'm sorry. I've had to say that a lot lately.''

I hung up and stood staring at the phone, feeling the familiar sinking sensation in the pit of my stomach. A minute later I was sandwiched between two burly guards, en route to the all-too-familiar cell.

It wasn't until the following morning that the lawyer showed up. We were closeted in a small interview room on the thirteenth floor of the King County Jail. He was a small, wiry man in his late thirties with lots of hair and teeth, both of which were immaculate.

He introduced himself as Guy Whitsong, and he motioned me to a chair on the opposite side of the square metal table which, except for two metal folding chairs, was the only other piece of furniture in the windowless room.

I shook his hand and sat down. "I don't think I can afford you, Mr. Whitsong," I said, and smiled. "You look pretty prosperous to me."

He flashed a perfect grin and produced a yellow legal pad from his briefcase. "No harm in talking, Mr. Colson. Or should I say Mr. Jones?"

"Whatever," I told him. "Ed will do fine."

"Okay, Ed . . . let's get down to business." He consulted the legal pad. "I've already taken the liberty of getting a lot of particulars in your case." He scanned the paper and raised his eyes at me. "You've been a pretty busy fella, haven't you?"

"All I want to know is can you block my extradition back to Virginia?" I asked.

He was shaking his head before I even finished asking the question. "Not a chance. Their warrant is valid and, excuse the term, you're an escaped con. Besides which, they want you pretty damn bad, Ed." He gave me a level look and said, "In fact, they'll be here in the morning."

I ran a hand across the beard stubble on my face and sighed.

"They didn't waste any time, did they? Suppose I refuse to sign extradition papers."

"Then they'll take you downstairs to the magistrate and he'll sign them," he said. "Either way they'll go back with you."

"Then what's the point of your even coming here?" I asked, exasperated.

The smile again. Broad and beaming. "Because I think I can help you in an even better way, Ed. Now, according to Miss . . ."

"Arciaga."

". . . Arciaga—very attractive young lady, incidentally. According to her, you were tried and sentenced to ten years' imprisonment when you were seventeen years old, correct?"

"Correct."

He nodded and began flipping pages, found the one he wanted. "Okay. Now I called the clerk of Superior Court in Richmond this morning just to be certain I had the facts, and I do." He looked at me and added, "By the way, I'm charging you for the call," then returned to his notes. "According to the record, you never received a juvenile hearing. Didn't your attorney object to that?"

I shrugged. "I don't know."

"Well, did *he* know that you had never been afforded a juvenile hearing?"

"I have no idea, Mr. Whitsong," I said, sighing. "He was appointed by the court two days before I went to trial. The first time I ever saw him was in the holding tank at the courthouse. Why is this so important?"

"Because if you never received a juvenile hearing . . . and the record reflects that you didn't . . . then you were illegally tried and sentenced."

I sat there and stared at him, feeling an odd sensation. "Does that mean," I said slowly, "that I can get the sentence overturned?"

"That's right," he answered. He reached into his briefcase again and pulled out a legal document of half a dozen pages or so. "This," he continued, "is a petition for writ of habeas corpus. I drew it up this morning after my rather lengthy

146

conversation with the court clerk in Richmond. Look it over, see if there's anything amiss. Dates, names, original charge, et cetera. Go ahead, it's brief.''

I looked the document over, head swimming. This was unbelievable! I thumbed hurriedly through the pages, ignoring the Greek legal jargon, concentrating on names, times and places. At last I handed it back and said, "They're correct. And you're right, I never appeared before any other court—only that one. What now?''

I watched him tuck the papers back into his briefcase, feeling a ridiculous moment of near panic as the lifesaving document disappeared from sight. I had a crazy impulse to reach out and snatch it back, to guard it fiercely as one would guard a hoard of treasure. Those few pieces of paper with their magic words had the potential to accomplish what all the escapes in the world would not.

Whitsong displayed his teeth again. "Now I take it back to my office and mail it to Superior Court. Understand now that I am not representing you, I merely prepared the petition. But it's drawn in pro se litigate—which means that you are acting as your own attorney. However, the court will appoint you a regular attorney as a matter of course when they grant the petition—and they will grant it. He can take it from there.''

I looked at him in amazement, stunned. "You did all this just this morning?'' I asked.

"It didn't require much effort,'' he said, shrugging. "The law is very clear in matters such as this.'' He sat back and winked. "Don't worry though, I'm charging you. I checked your account and you have a total of two hundred and twelve dollars and eighty-three cents, so you can turn over a hundred and fifty dollars and we'll call it even. Fair enough?''

He must have seen the sudden cloud of suspicion in my eyes, for he leaned forward and looked directly at me. "If you think I'm conning you, Ed, I'll walk out of here right now and no hard feelings. You don't even have to pay me for the calls—I don't need your business that bad. I just happened to listen to a very emotional little lady who's carrying a great deal of guilt on her back. And then I made a phone call.'' He reached into the briefcase, snatched the document out and tossed it onto the table in front of me. ''In fact, I'll even give the damn thing to you if it will make you feel better—you can mail me the money when you get out. What the fuck, I don't mind trusting *you* for a hundred and fifty bucks!''

I gazed at the document for several seconds, then picked it up. ''Okay,'' I said. ''You got a deal. If this gets me out, I'll send you the hundred and fifty bucks.''

''Fine, you do that,'' he said, shoving the legal pad into his briefcase. He stood and walked to the door, turned and looked back at me. ''Not that I'll hold my breath until you do. Good luck, Ed.''

He raised one hand to knock on the locked door when I stopped him. ''Mr. Whitsong?''

''Yes?'' he said.

I held out the petition to him, smiling faintly. ''I'm convinced. I'll give you the money now. Hell, I'd give you ten times that much if I had it, and I'd still be coming out cheap.''

He took the papers without changing expression. ''It will probably be about sixty days before the court responds, so don't get discouraged.''

''I don't suppose you could get me another phone call, could you?'' I asked. ''I'd like to call Linda.''

''Not a chance. You're under too tight of wraps for that. They don't want to risk you setting up some escape plot. I understand they even have a guard posted outside your cell. That's quite a tribute.''

''What it is is a headache,'' I told him. ''I can't even go to the toilet in peace.''

He turned and gave two sharp raps on the door. I stood, and we shook hands. He had a surprisingly firm grip for such a small man.

''I really appreciate your help, Mr. Whitsong,'' I said. ''And would you tell Linda I said thanks?''

''I'll tell her.''

The door opened, and two guards stepped inside. Whitsong told them that I would be releasing some money to him and to give me the proper form to sign. One jailer stepped back outside to escort the lawyer out of the jail. As he was about to leave, I stopped him again.

"Mr. Whitsong?"

He paused and looked back.

"Tell her I'm the one who feels guilty."

"I'll tell her that, too," he said.

# CHAPTER 16

FIVE HUNDRED SPRING STREET LOOKED THE SAME AS I RE-
membered it as I clanked up the familiar steps between two
stony-faced detectives. It had been a long and tedious flight
from Seattle, and I yearned for nothing more than about ten
hours' uninterrupted sleep. I had so many chains on that I
felt like a boat anchor. Besides the obligatory handcuffs, I
was also equipped with padlocked leg-chains (not one but
*two* sets) and a lead chain wrapped around my waist. I had
been kept this way during the entire flight, feeling much like
a dangerous animal being transported to a zoo. Even the
stewardesses had kept their distance, cutting little sidelong
glances at me as they passed along the aisle. Eventually I
closed my eyes and tried to sleep, but found I couldn't. The
situation was too embarrassing to permit even that.

I was taken straight to Admissions, where I had an unwel-
come surprise waiting for me. Captain Goldie was standing
near the door, talking to the Admissions officer. They looked
up as we entered, and a huge grin crossed Goldie's scarred
face.

"Well, well," he said, "look who's come back to see us!
You miss me, Jones?"

"Can't say I did, Captain," I replied.

"Well, hell, that really hurts. But that's okay, we'll have
plenty of time to get reacquainted. You fellas can take that
hardware off him now, it's a cinch he ain't goin' nowhere."

I watched him as the chains were being removed. I should have known he would make it a point to greet me. It was seven-thirty in the evening and Goldie never stayed later than five—unless there was a reason.

When the chains were off, I was told to take a seat while the necessary paperwork was signed. Finally the detective left, and I was alone with just the Admissions officer and Goldie. The Captain walked to where I was sitting, reached down and grabbed a fistful of my shirt and pulled me slowly to my feet.

"You smart-ass motherfucker!" he hissed in my face. "You think you're so goddamned cute, don't you?" He lashed out with his other fist and caught me a sharp blow in the solar plexus. I gagged, all breath suddenly gone, and would have slumped to the floor had he not been holding me. Then he put his left foot behind my legs, gave a violent shove and sent me sprawling.

"Get up, you sonofabitch!" he croaked. The purple scar alongside his face became even more pronounced in his rage.

"I said get the fuck up!" he screamed, drawing back a large foot. "Get up or so help me I'll kick your fool head off!"

I stood slowly, still gasping for breath. Whatever he wanted to do, I was determined not to strike back. That would be all the excuse Goldie needed.

He finally got a grip on himself and stepped back, leaning against the low counter that ran the length of the room.

"You get them clothes off, boy," he said, calmer now, panting slightly. "And be quick about it. Then get your ass in that shower. I'm takin' you to 'C' Buildin' personally. Got a special cell all ready for you—and believe me you'll be there for a *while!*"

Welcome back, Ed.

My special cell was a six-by-nine-foot cubicle directly across from the guard's station. The door was heavy wood, with a covered slot cut in the middle so that food could be passed through. The inside was pitch dark, and in place of a toilet there was a hole in the corner of the granite floor.

I was stripped nude, and Goldie shoved me inside. He locked the door, then knelt and pressed his face to the open food slot.

"Things've changed since you left us, Jones," he said. "The longest I can keep you here at one stretch is six months now—and I gotta feed you one meal every three days instead of every five. We also gotta make sure your cell's kept nice and clean—for health reasons. So every two or three days Mr. Slater here's gonna hose you down. That way you get a shower at the same time. Now you take care, hear?"

Then he closed the covering on the tray slot and left.

Two days later I found out about the hosing. I was awakened from a light sleep by a stinging stream of icy cold water hitting against my body. I let out a yelp and leaped to my feet, covering my vital parts of my nude body with my hands. The nozzle of a garden hose protruded from the tray slot, and behind it I could see the grinning features of Slater. I tried to dodge the chilling water without success and eventually quit trying. So I crossed my hands over my groin, stood in the middle of the floor and stared in silence as Slater pelted me from head to foot. At last he tired of the game, shut off the water and withdrew the nozzle. He gave me a final look, grunted in satisfaction and slammed the cover over the slot. This process was repeated every two or three days for the rest of my stay.

I learned about the new feeding procedure also. It was now exactly the same as on the camps—one tablespoon of whatever was being served in the chow hall. The result was to leave one hungrier than ever.

On my forty-seventh day of isolation the door opened, and Goldie entered carrying what appeared to be a legal document. I squinted against the unaccustomed light and wondered what was in store now, praying it was what I had been hoping for.

"Got somethin' from the court, Jones," he said, and held out the paper. I stood close to the door and read the contents, feeling my heart leap at the words. It was a Show Cause Order directed to the warden, Mr. C.C. Peyton, stating that I was to be produced before the juvenile court in Richmond on December 2nd for a hearing. It went on to say that the court was appointing a Mr. Richard Repp to represent me. I read it over a second time to make certain I wasn't seeing things, then handed the paper back to Goldie.

"Gonna try to write your way out now, Jones?" he asked

without humor. "I wouldn't be bankin' on it too strong, was I you." Then he turned on his heel, and Slater closed the door, leaving me once again in darkness.

Thank you, Guy Whitsong. You didn't lie to me!


Two weeks later the door opened again, and Slater stood there with two guards behind him. "Got a visitor, Jones," he said.

I stepped into the corridor, shielding my eyes again, and struggled into my clothes, which were lying in a heap outside the door. My hands were cuffed behind my back, and the two guards escorted me outside, across the courtyard and into the visiting room. The handcuffs were removed, and I was pointed to the end cubicle, where a young man not much older than me waited on the other side of the glass. I sat down on the wooden bench, picked up the phone and motioned for him to do the same.

"Mr. Jones?" he said. "My name is Richard Repp, and I've been appointed by the court to represent you in a pro se action you filed some time ago. I'd like to go over your petition, if you don't mind."

"Believe me, Mr. Repp," I answered, "I don't mind at all. Take all the time you want."

"Good," he said, smiling. "But first perhaps I'd better tell you that I haven't been practicing law very long. I still have a lot to learn. But I assure you that I will give you the very best representation I can."

"Fair enough," I told him. "But how about giving me your honest opinion . . . do I really have a chance of getting out?"

"I think you have an excellent chance, Mr. Jones."

"Call me Ed."

"Only if you call me Dick," he said, flashing a boyish grin.

"That's a good name," I said. "I feel better already."

He pulled out the inevitable legal pad and said, "All right, Ed, now let's take it from the beginning."

Our meeting lasted more than an hour, and by the time we were finished I found myself liking him immensely. His enthusiasm outshadowed his inexperience, and honesty and idealism abounded. I had no question but that he would give his all for my cause.

As the interview concluded he asked about my appearance. I told him that I was in the hole. Seeing his puzzled look, I went on to explain about the cell I was being kept in, about the hosings and the food—or rather the lack of it—even how Goldie had tried to provoke me my first day back inside the Walls. As he listened, I saw his face register disbelief, shock, then anger.

"You're being housed in a bare cell with no light, no clothing or covering, no hygienic materials—and you're doused with water every two or three days?"

"That's right," I said. "Not to mention getting only scraps of food once every three days."

He scribbled furiously on his pad for several minutes, lips set in a grim line. He finished, put the legal pad in his brief-case and gave me a firm look. "First thing in the morning I'm going to petition the court for an injunction against the warden."

"What's that mean?" I asked.

"It means that, if granted, you will be taken out of solitary confinement and placed in more suitable quarters—there are many violations here. At the least I'll get those hosings stopped and see that you are provided with proper hygiene materials."

"You think you can?" I asked hopefully.

"Just watch me!"

Dick Repp was as good as his word. Three days after our meeting, I was taken to the hospital, where I was allowed to shower and shave. Then I was issued a clean set of khakis and a pair of cardboard slippers. Then Mr. Portus, the medical technician, gave me a reserved greeting and took me to a single isolation room on the second floor. I couldn't believe it. Here was a real bed, with a thick mattress, yet! There was a sink and a commode; I was given soap, toothpaste, and a toothbrush. And a little later one of the orderlies came by and slid two packs of cigarettes and several magazines under the door.

I was in seventh heaven!

The next day my court-appointed attorney was back. He

smiled as he saw me entering the visiting room all spruced up. We picked up the phones and greeted each other.

"Well, now!" he said. "You look considerably improved since last time we talked."

"I feel better, too," I told him. "Thanks to you."

"Don't thank me, thank Judge Beltrain. He's the one who granted the petition and issued the injunction. And that's not all."

"So tell me," I urged, feeling his excitement.

"Judge Beltrain was so outraged at the allegations that he ordered a blue-ribbon-committee investigation of the isolation section."

This was surprising news. "How come he's so gung ho all of a sudden just because one person started bitching?"

"Very simple," he said. "Judge Beltrain is the same person who ordered certain changes made in the isolation section just eight months ago. Didn't you hear about that?"

I shook my head no.

"Well," he continued, "our petition really lit a fire under him. I have a feeling some heads are going to roll before this is over. But enough about that, I have other news."

"Good, I hope."

"The best," he said, giving me a wink. "I spoke this morning with the state's attorney who's handling your case. They're not going to retry you."

I felt my heart pounding. "Does that mean I'll be getting out?"

"You can count on it, Ed," he said. "Home free."

Home free! I felt a tingling at the back of my neck, and for a moment I didn't trust myself to speak. So I sat there in stunned silence, a collage of visions dancing through my mind. Dick was saying something else, but I hadn't heard him.

"What did you say?" I asked, pulling myself back to the moment.

"I said your mother will be here to see you Sunday. I spoke to her on the phone just before I left my office."

"How is she?" I asked. There was a huskiness in my voice that hadn't been there before.

"She's fine, Ed. Especially since she knows you're coming home." He looked at his watch. "Look, I have to run, okay?

The main reason I stopped by was to see if Judge Beltrain's order had been carried out. I can see that it has. So you just sit tight until next Thursday, and I'll be seeing you at the courthouse.''

"Dick?" I asked tentatively.

"What?"

"Is this all set for sure? I mean, can anything go wrong?''

"Not a thing, Ed," he said. "Not a damned thing.''

Mom showed up a little after ten o'clock Sunday morning. She looked better than I could ever remember, eyes sparkling, cheeks tinted a natural pink. We both carried smiles a yard wide as I sat down and greeted her.

"Hi, sweetheart," I said lightly. "How's married life?"

"Fine, son. How about you, are you all right?''

"I am now," I answered, still beaming. "I'm coming home, Mom . . . I really am! After all these years. Hope you and Dick have room for me.''

"Your room is all ready," she said. "Just like it was when you last saw it. By the way, Dick said to tell you hello.''

"Have you seen Gloria or Dee Dee lately?'' I asked. "I bet Dee Dee's sprouting like a weed, isn't she?''

She hesitated before answering, as if debating how much to tell me. "I haven't seen either of them since Dick and I moved. The last I heard Gloria was planning on getting married again.''

I nodded. "Well, as long as she's happy. I wasn't thinking about us getting back together anyway, but I do want to be able to see Dee Dee.''

"I know, Edward," she said. "And I just thank the Lord that you're going to have the chance.''

"A lot of chances, Mom . . . for a lot of things to catch up on and make up for. Especially to you.''

We discussed my plans for when I came home. Dick wanted me to come in with him in his trucking business, but I didn't know if I was cut out for that. What I really wanted was to finish high school, then maybe take a college course or two. My education had been drastically interrupted due to the prison sentence I'd received more than seven years before. Mom said if that was what I wanted, then it was fine with her.

We talked and laughed and made dozens of plans, and all too quickly the time came to an end. But this time we said our good-bys with a smile and a lightness of heart, knowing that next time we were together I would be free. I was at peace with the world and all that was in it.

That same evening I received another surprise. I was lying in bed in my hospital room, thumbing through a recent edition of Life magazine, when someone tapped on my door. I looked up and peered through the glass viewing window in the middle of the door, trying to make out who was there. When I recognized the face, I grinned, jumped from the bed and went to the door.

"Norman!" I exclaimed. "What the hell are you doing here?"

"I checked in with the flu, that's what I'm doin'," he said, cupping his hands and speaking through the crack in the door. "And keep your voice down, will you? I'm supposed to be back there in the ward."

"Where's Joe and Henry?" I asked, delighted at seeing him.

"Both made parole earlier this year," he said. "I'm the last one left in this dump."

"You'll make it, Norman," I said encouragingly. "I'll be going soon myself. I have a hearing coming up Thursday, and my lawyer says I'll be cut loose."

"Yeah, I heard," Norman said. "And I also heard Goldie's been shittin' all over himself on account of that stink you stirred up about 'C' Building. They got some committee comin' in to check things out. You better be glad you *are* gettin' out. You need anything?"

"Thanks, but I'm okay right now." Then another thought struck me. "By the way, how's Red Miller doing?"

Norman laughed. "He ain't been doin' too good lately. He went stone buggy over in 'C' Building, and they ended up havin' to ship him to Western State Hospital in a straitjacket. He won't be comin' out of there for a while—if ever. Look, I gotta go before the hack makes his rounds. I'll stop by tomorrow. You need anything, you let me know."

I went back to my bed thinking about Red Miller. Norman was right: once they had him in Western State, a hospital for the criminally insane, it was bad news. For those considered dangerously uncontrollable, a rubber room would be their home for many years to come. A screaming demon inside a giant basketball. I pitied him.

I was eating breakfast the next morning when I heard the key in the door. I opened, and I looked up to see Goldie standing in the corridor. He stepped inside, took a quick look around, then rested his attention on me. It was the first time I had seen him since being moved from isolation.

A tiny grin tugged at the corners of his mouth as he handed me an official-looking document. He said, "Got somethin' for you here, Jones."

I took the paper and read it, feeling the blood draining from my face.

Goldie, looking smug, said, "How you like that? In case you don't know, it's a detainer from Chesterfield County. Forgot about that, didn't you? See what it says? Right there." He pointed a finger at the top of the page. "Resistin' arrest and escape—both felonies. What's that make altogether—five, ain't it? Know what that means?"

I knew what it meant all right. The Habitual Criminal Act, which carried life without parole. All you had to do was commit five felonies inside the state and a Superior Court judge would do the rest.

Goldie plucked the paper dainty-like from my limp hand and continued, enjoying himself. "So you ain't goin' nowhere, smart ass—no matter what happens Thursday. Chesterfield County's gonna be waitin' right at the gate and in no time at all you'll be right back here." He took a step closer and stuck out his jaw. "And then, mister, your ass is gonna be all mine."

He turned around and walked out of the room, slamming and locking the door after him. I stood there a moment, then moved slowly back to the bunk and fell facedown across the mattress. I lay unmoving, numb with shock, the reality of the moment sinking in.

I was more frightened than I had ever been in my life.

Because I knew that if I came back, I would probably kill Goldie.

Sometime later I heard a soft knock at the door. I rolled over and saw Norman Whitlock motioning to me through the viewing window. I got up, tired, and walked to the door, slumping against it with my ear pressed to the crack.

Norman said, "What did Goldie want? Saw him leavin' a little while ago lookin' like the cat that just ate the canary."

Without emotion I told him. He looked off, shaking his head, then back at me.

"He's right, Eddie. Only chance you got is to beat those Chesterfield charges."

I said, "Not a chance, Norman. They got me dead to rights on both of them. Only choice I got is to keep doing what I've been lucky enough to do before."

"You goin' to try to escape?"

I said, "I'm not going to try, Norman, I'm going to *do* it. I have to."

Norman said, "Anything I can do for you?"

I thought about it, then said, "I'd sure appreciate it if you could get me a hacksaw blade."

He smiled and said, "You got it, Cuz."

Late the following afternoon a hospital orderly named Fletcher stopped outside the door. He tapped on the window, looked up and down the corridor, then slid a magazine under the door. He caught my eye, nodded, then went on his way.

I took the magazine to my bed and began flipping through the pages. Midway through I found it, a slightly used tungsten carbide hacksaw blade. I carefully snapped the ten-inch blade in half, then picked up my shoes and started prying away at the insoles.

Two hours later I had both halves of the hacksaw tucked away inside my shoes. Only a minute inspection would reveal that the insoles had been tampered with. Hopefully, no one would think to examine them that closely.

My appearance in juvenile court went pretty much as Dick had said it would. There were only seven people present in the small courtroom: the judge, the state's attorney assigned to the case, Dick and I and three guards from the prison who were acting as escorts. Goldie was playing it very safe.

It was all over in ten minutes. The judge asked the state's attorney if he contemplated bringing me to trial again. The state's attorney said no, due to the age of the case and the difficulty in locating witnesses. The judge then formally granted my habeas corpus motion and ordered that I be released forthwith.

My prison escorts stepped forward and clamped on handcuffs and leg-irons, grinning knowingly. Dick asked for a few minutes in private with me, and the guards withdrew a discreet distance, out of earshot, but keeping a wary eye on my every move.

Dick sighed and placed an arm around my shoulders. "Ed, I'm going to speak with the Chesterfield authorities and see what I can do. Maybe they'll consider dismissing the resisting-arrest charge."

"What are the chances of that happening, Dick?" I asked. "I mean really."

"Honest injun?"

"Honest injun?"

He ran his fingers through his short-cropped sandy hair and sighed again. "Not very good, I'm afraid. They have an open-and-shut case on both counts, and I don't have to tell you that there are some external forces at work here."

"I know," I said. "Goldie. But do you actually think they would give me life for that bullshit?"

Dick looked at the floor and said, "I won't lie to you, Ed. I believe they will. It isn't right, but the law says they can."

I nodded and looked over to where my escorts were waiting and watching, feeling an icy anger sweeping through my body. "I'll tell you something, Dick. I'm not too up on this legal stuff. But it doesn't seem fair that a man should have to spend the rest of his life in prison just for running away from jail. Especially if he doesn't hurt anyone. You put a man in a cage, it's only natural that he try to get out—even animals have sense enough to do that. But you don't take away his life because of it. Do they actually think that's justice? There are guys in the Walls that have raped and murdered, but are still eligible for parole. And my crime is worse than theirs? What kind of fucking system is this? That's not justice—that's insanity!"

Dick squeezed my shoulder. "I agree with everything you say, Ed. But unfortunately there isn't a damned thing I can do about it—and believe me, I wish to God I could."

I stared at my manacled hands pulled tightly into my stomach by the chain cinched about my waist. "Well, there's something *I* can do about it." I said. "At least I'll give it a damn good try. But I'm not going back in that prison. I would just as soon die first, and that's a fact."

"Don't do anything foolish, Ed," Dick said. "Please!"

I looked at him and smiled wryly. "It's a little late for that, isn't it?"

As Goldie had promised, two deputy sheriffs from Chesterfield County were waiting for me as I walked up the prison steps. So was Goldie. He stepped forward as I reached the outer gate and said to the deputies, "Here's your boy. Take good care of him now, hear?"

He handed over a manila folder containing my records and turned to me. "I want you to pay close attention to where I'm standin'," he said. " 'Cause this is where I'm gonna be when they bring you back."

I looked at one of the deputies and asked, "Am I in your custody now, or his?"

"You're ours, Mr. Jones," the deputy said.

I looked at Goldie and said without expression, "Fuck you, asshole. How's that sound to you?"

His nostrils flared like an enraged bull, the scar turned purple and a strange guttural sound came from his throat as he tried to get to me, the deputies holding him back. One of them said, "All right, Jones, that's enough outta you." He turned to Goldie with a placating gesture and said, "Appreciate the help, Cap'n . . . don't worry, you'll get your shot at him."

Goldie stood on the bottom step and glared as they tucked me into the back seat of the sheriff's car. When we pulled away I craned my neck around and looked at him through the rear window . . . saw him standing there with his hands on his wide hips, staring a hole through me. He would be waiting for me all right. The way a hungry cat waits in front of the mouse hole.

The Chesterfield County Jail hadn't changed much since I had last seen it more than two years earlier. Apparently they were expecting me; besides the booking sergeant, there were four other deputies waiting in the booking area when we came in. They stayed there while I was put through the routine procedure of being fingerprinted and photographed, lounging against the walls, cutting their eyes at me as I stood nude for the routine strip search.

I had a bad moment when the sergeant picked up my shoes, then breathed a sigh of relief when he did nothing more than slap the soles together and drop them on the floor. Since I had been brought straight from the prison, they hadn't really expected to find contraband anyway.

At last I was permitted to dress, signed my booking form stating that I had no funds, then was escorted into the jail section by two deputies. They placed me in a cell two doors from the one I had escaped from earlier, closed the barred door and locked it.

"There's been some changes made, Jones," one of the deputies said. "Don't expect to get out so easy this time. See that vent?"

I glanced up at the vent and shrugged.

"There's a quarter-inch-steel insert there now, and the grille's welded to it. You can scrape and dig all you want, but you ain't diggin' through that."

He paused to give his words effect, then motioned to his companion and left. I waited until the steel door at the end of the corridor had closed, then stood on the toilet to inspect the air vent.

As the deputy had said, the opening had been reinforced with a steel insert, with the heavy grille welded to the sides. But it was a sloppy job. Whoever did the work had only used two spot welds on each side instead of a solid line. I jumped down from the commode and stretched out on the bunk, hands behind my head. I couldn't believe it.

This was going to be even easier than before.

I waited until the midnight shift came on, and the jailer had made his rounds before going to work on the grille. Then I coated the teeth of the hacksaw blades with soap to help deaden the sound and started sawing away.

In less than twenty minutes, fingers raw with blisters, I broke through the last weld. I pulled the grille off and placed it on the floor, pausing a moment to listen for the sound of jingling keys.

So far so good.

Experience being the best teacher, I pulled the mattress

from the bunk, doubled it, then laid it across the commode to have a better angle when squeezing through the narrow opening, which was even smaller now because of the quarter-inch-steel insert around the inside edge. At first I couldn't quite make it, so I stripped to my shorts, shoved my bundled clothes in ahead of me and tried again.

I left some skin behind, but I managed to slither through. Then I began snaking my way forward, pushing my clothes ahead of me, feeling the forced air warm against my face.

Soon I was above the familiar interview room. I pushed out the aluminum grille, hand-walked down the wall and dropped to the floor. I dressed quickly, opened the window, checked for lurking jailers and crawled outside.

I sprinted through the same parking lot with the same sheriff's cars—even the model was the same—crossed the road on the far side and trotted into the Virginia woods. Not even feeling the cold yet, I felt so good . . . telling myself, Fuck this shit, I'm not ever coming back to Virginia again, if I manage to get out this time.

People here are crazy. Some of them.

# PART TWO

"I know not whether laws be right
  or whether laws be wrong;
All that we know who be in gaol
  is that the wall is strong;
And that each day is like a year,
  a year whose days are long."

OSCAR WILDE
*The Ballad of Reading Gaol*

# CHAPTER 17

*Las Vegas, Nevada*
*June 1971*

THE GAMBLING AND GLITTER CAPITAL OF THE WORLD WAS a spectacular sight indeed as I stood outside the Trailways Bus Terminal clutching my single beat-up suitcase. This was the culmination of nearly two years of drifting, and I savored the moment to its fullest. I was amazed that even at ten o'clock at night, automobiles could cruise the entire downtown area without once turning on their headlights. From as far away as Hoover Dam, which I had crossed during the ride from Phoenix, the brilliant glow was clearly visible, appearing out of the darkness like the mythical pot of gold at the end of the rainbow. And for many, that is exactly what Las Vegas represents. They come from the world over, these eager gamblers, to cast their bread on the waters of chance, always looking for that one roll of the dice, that one turn of the card, that would spell the difference between pauper and prince. Some find it. The vast majority, however, return from where they came with pockets and dreams equally deflated. For Jason, there had been no Golden Fleece; for Cinderella, the slipper didn't fit. To a fortunate few, Las Vegas is a shimmering neon jewel looked upon as their own personal oasis. To the unfortunate many, it is merely seen as it really is: a

watering hole for the damned, stuck in the middle of nowhere.

I walked to a nearby cab and told the driver to take me to
the Strip. As he maneuvered out of the downtown traffic and
onto Las Vegas Boulevard, I thought about the events that
had taken place over the last two years.

Once again I had become a drifter, sifting in and out of
jobs and cities so often that I was having difficulty coping
with it all. My previously moderate drinking habits had intensified, and I was finding myself turning more and more to
the bottle for solace. Dick's words were taking on meaning,
for indeed I was beginning to realize that I *didn't* have a
future; I could see no further than today. Even the nights
offered little peace without increasing amounts of Scotch to
drive away the demons—most of whom looked like Goldie.
It took a full year for me to finally admit the obvious: *I was
terrified of being caught.* Which perhaps was understandable,
since capture and return to Virginia would result in certain
life imprisonment. My decision to come to Las Vegas was
my way of dealing with the seriousness of the situation. I
needed to unwind from the tension and fear that had plagued
me for two years. And I was tired. So very tired. So I decided
that if I couldn't depend on having tomorrow, then I was at
least going to enjoy today . . . for a little while, anyway.

I had the driver drop me at the Tam O'Shanter Motel, a
reasonably inexpensive lodging, but situated within easy
walking distance of the major hotels and casinos. I took a
much-needed shower, slept for two hours, then dressed in my
one good charcoal gray suit that looked expensive but really
wasn't. Then I hit the midnight Strip, looking for the action.

I found it at Caesar's Palace—at the baccarat tables. This
was a game I had heard of but never played. I bought a tall
Scotch at the nearest bar and sauntered over to the roped-off
pit area where the tables were located. I joined the large
gallery of spectators behind the barrier and watched the play,
fascinated by the stacks of hundred-dollar bills being bandied
about the kidney-shaped tables. My eyes were drawn to the
players: elegantly gowned and bejeweled women and expen-
sively dressed men.

I asked a passing cocktail waitress for another Chivas and
thought about it, mentally counting the money tucked in my

worn billfold: four hundred twenty dollars. By the time the waitress returned with my drink, I had decided. Why the hell not? Go for it, Ed! After all, I reasoned, the odds were pretty much fifty-fifty; either the player won or the bank did. So I downed my drink, placed the empty glass on the tray of another passing waitress and strolled into the gaming area, feeling as out-of-place as a turd on a string of pearls.

I took a seat next to a middle-aged lady who was wearing the largest diamond ring I had ever seen. I smiled at her, pulled out my roll of twenties and waited for the shoe to pass. Almost immediately a cocktail waitress appeared and asked if I wanted a drink.

"Chivas on the rocks, please," I said. "Make it a double. And a pack of Marlboros." I smiled at the lady next to me and added, "It's been a long day."

The shoe passed to a fat man wearing a perpetual scowl who was sitting at one end of the table.

"Place your bets, please," said a tuxedoed croupier. All I really knew about the game was that the player with the shoe represented the bank, and that the other players could bet with him or against him. The closest to nine without going over won. I didn't like the fat guy; they were supposed to be jolly, weren't they? So I stuck two twenties on the square marked PLAYERS and waited for the cards to come out.

"No more bets, please," the croupier said, as the man dealt two cards to the players and two cards to himself. The croupier tossed the two cards for the players facedown to an attractive woman in a black sheath dress. She flipped them over gracefully, showing an ace and a seven.

"The players show eight and stand," the croupier said.

The fat man, who had several hundred-dollar bills resting on the BANK square, turned his cards over: a four and a two.

"The bank shows six and draws one card," said the croupier. The man flicked another card from the shoe, turned over a queen and swore softly.

"Pay the players!" sang the croupier. "The players win, eight over six."

Two crisp new twenties were added to the pair I had resting on the PLAYERS square. I pulled them in, glancing woefully at the five one-hundred-dollar bills the croupier counted out for the lady on the left. My double Chivas arrived, and I tipped the girl a dollar. I leaned back, took a thoughtful sip of Scotch and wondered which little square I should bet on next.

For five hours I played without letup, shuffling bills from BANK to PLAYERS at random and knocking back double shots of Chivas at a rate you wouldn't believe. My vision blurred, and I think I giggled a lot, and sometime during that period I switched from twenties and started betting hundreds. And I hadn't the foggiest idea of what I was doing. I vaguely remembered the pit boss asking if I would like to take a rest, perhaps in one of the hotel rooms. I answered something to the effect that only if he agreed to look after my money. Of course, sir—just sign this receipt, please. Shortly afterward I was being escorted by an obliging bellhop through the crowded casino, up in an elevator that moved much too quickly, and into a luxurious room. As I collapsed onto the huge double bed, the last thing I remembered was the bellhop asking politely if he could get me anything.

I awakened the following morning with the granddaddy of all hangovers. My head felt as if someone were running a jackhammer inside, and the roof of my mouth was like rancid sandpaper. I was still fully clothed, lying crosswise on the comfortable bed. I raised my head cautiously and peered through blurry eyes around the sumptuously decorated room, awareness of how it was I came to be there slowing sinking in.

Groaning, I rose and struggled out of my clothes. Just as I finished, my stomach sent a warning signal to my brain. I stumbled across the plush carpet to the bathroom and reached the toilet just in the nick of time. I heaved, gagged and heaved some more, and when it was over I crawled exhausted into the shower. I fumbled with the knobs, turned the cold water on full force and sat down in the stall, face tilted toward the icy spray. When the worst had passed I lathered with the small bar of sweet-smelling soap provided by the hotel, rinsed thoroughly, then wrapped myself in a fluffy bath towel and padded back into the bedroom, deciding that I would live.

After drying, I took inventory of my personal effects. The first thing I pulled from my pants pocket was a rather large roll of bills. I sat on the bed and counted them: eight hundred forty dollars, all in twenties and hundreds. A further search revealed an even greater surprise tucked away in the bill compartment of my wallet. It was a receipt made out to Edward Willis Jones (which I had began using several months before; after all, I thought, how many Ed Joneses can there be in the country?). It was signed by the friendly pit boss of the night before. It was for thirteen thousand two hundred dollars. I let out a great whoop and flopped backward on the bed, all thoughts of hangover gone.

Downstairs I presented the receipt to a severe-looking dark-haired woman behind the casino cashier's window. I signed a counterreceipt, noticing the alert cashier carefully comparing the signatures, then produced my driver's license. Satisfied, she began counting out crisp new hundred-dollar bills, flicking them expertly onto the counter in individual stacks of ten each. As I stuffed the cash into my pockets, she dutifully asked if I would like a security guard to escort me from the hotel. No thanks, I said, I can manage quite nicely on my own.

I stepped outside into the bright light of day, motioned to a waiting cab and told the driver to take me to the Tam O'Shanter Motel. Unlike Jason, I had lucked out and stumbled over my Golden Fleece. Now it was time to get out of Las Vegas before I lost it.

# CHAPTER 18

I STEPPED OFF THE TRAILWAYS BUS IN KINGMAN, ARIZONA, with four thousand dollars in my pocket and another ten thousand tucked away in my suitcase. After a few inquiries, I found myself on the lot of a Chrysler-Plymouth dealership just off the east-west highway, kicking at tires and peering at price stickers.

Within the hour I was the proud owner of a 1970 Dodge T/A that had been used as a demonstrator. It was the only one of its kind on the lot, and I fell in love with it immediately. The body was white with black racing stripes, black vinyl roof and black fiberglass shaker hood. I listened to the saleman's tale of woe, offered him thirty-seven one-hundred-dollar bills and saw them change hands magically, his final protest dying in mid-sentence.

I drove away like a kid with a new toy, speed-shifting and spewing gravel as I fishtailed out of the driveway and into the street. Anyone watching would have gathered from the way I hung my head to one side and gunned the throaty engine that I was about to run over something. Grinning hugely, I switched on the radio and pointed the nose of the machine eastward.

It was early evening, and a dreary low stratus sky was dumping torrents of summer rain, taxing the windshield wipers to their limit. I was on I-20, between Shreveport and

Monroe, Louisiana, still heading east. I had decided to drive
to Houston, partly out of desire to air out my new wheels,
and partly because Houston was one of the few large cities I
had not yet seen. Ed Jones, the perpetual tourist.

On the opposite side of the interstate, partially obscured by
the blanket of rain, I noticed a car pulled onto the shoulder.
Drawing closer I could see that it was a '69 Malibu, its blinker
lights flashing yellow. I slowed as I went past and peered
across the grassy median, trying to make out the two shadowy figures in the front seat. Being in high spirits, I decided
to see if I could help, so I found a drive-through that crossed
the median about half a mile ahead, ignored the posted sign
that read POLICE AND EMERGENCY VEHICLES ONLY and cut
across to the other side.

I eased onto the shoulder behind the stalled Malibu, which
was listing to starboard because of a deflated rear tire. Two
female heads swiveled around to watch through the foggy rear
window as I killed the engine, undoubtedly wondering if I
were friend or foe. I stepped out into the downpour and
jogged to the driver's side, tapped on the glass and grinned
as the driver lowered the window.

The first thing I noticed was that her brown hair was piled
high with rollers—the large ones that resemble miniature
rubber barrels. Even so I could tell that she was quite pretty,
with large brown eyes, a pert nose and small delicate mouth.
She was also very small, no more than five feet, I guessed,
but well proportioned for her size. I judged her to be in her
early twenties. So captured was I by her doll-like presence
that I hardly noticed her friend, who was also in rollers. Only
she wasn't quite getting away with it.

"Need some help?" I asked, hunching my shoulders
against the driving rain.

"Oh, would you?" she pleaded. "I think there's a spare
in the trunk."

"You *think?*" I asked, accepting the keys from her. "Let's
hope your memory's good."

I went to the rear of the car and opened the trunk. She was
half right, anyway. There was a spare, but I had seen more
tread on a life preserver.

In ten minutes I had the tire changed, looking and feeling
as if I had just taken a shower fully clothed. The pretty driver,

whose name was Susan Black, clucked her tongue at my drenched condition and invited me to follow them to a Union 76 truck stop just up ahead where we could have coffee, and I could dry out. I accepted the offer readily.

Instead of drying out, I made a quick change in the men's room. Then I joined the girls at a table in the cafe.

Susan and her friend, whose name was Bobby, lived in Shreveport, and both worked as legal secretaries for a local law firm. Susan did most of the talking while Bobby seemed content enough to merely smile and nod in agreement with everything that was said. Bobby was about the same age as Susan, but a good five inches taller. But it was Susan who had totally captured my attention.

I told them I was a representative for a development firm in Los Angeles, presently checking out the territory for a suitable place to build a textile mill—which I thought was as good a story as any. I compounded the lie by saying that I was staying at the Alamo Motel in Shreveport, a name I had picked up from a billboard while driving through the city. Susan thought that was marvelous and promptly volunteered her phone number, which *I* thought was marvelous. Bobby smiled and bobbed her head, lending silent approval to the budding affair.

We sat talking and drinking coffee until Bobby finally mentioned that the rain had let up. Neither Susan nor I had noticed. The next thing I knew I was following the Malibu back to Shreveport, staying close and keeping a suspicious eye on the newly changed tire.

We reached the city without incident, and Susan pulled to the curb on a lightly traveled street. I pulled in behind and smiled with amusement as she hopped from the car and dashed back through the sprinkling rain holding a folded newspaper above her head. She leaned partially through my open window.

"We turn off here," she said. "Thank you so much for helping with the tire."

"No problem," I said. "Don't forget to replace it as soon as you can—it won't hold up long."

"I will," she promised. Then, as an afterthought, "You can call later tonight, if you want."

"I was planning on it," I said.

She smiled shyly. "Well, thanks again for the help. Sorry you got so wet."

"My pleasure," I said. But she was already trotting back to her car. I watched her pull away and hang a right at the corner. Shaking my head, I put the Dodge in gear and set out to find the Alamo Motel, wondering what it was I found so special about a tiny girl with rollers in her hair.

I awakened the next morning feeling as though every germ in existence had entered my body. My throat was burning, my eyes were swollen and bloodshot and my skin was warm with fever. The symptoms had begun shortly after I'd checked in the day before and had intensified by the time I called Susan later that night. It appeared that my Sir Galahad routine had left my shining armor somewhat tarnished, and I was convinced that along with my lesser ailments I had contracted at least double pneumonia.

Susan had given me the number of the law firm she worked for, and I gave her a call just before noon. She clucked in sympathy at the sound of my gravel voice, insisting that I stay put and rest until she got off work, at which time she promised to look in on me. Even with my sickness I felt a tingle of excitement at the thought of seeing her again.

It was nearly six o'clock when she finally arrived. I opened the door wearing only a bathrobe. She bounced around me, arms laden with parcels, and promptly ordered me back to bed. I obeyed and soon found a thermometer jammed in my mouth. I watched through puffy eyes as she bustled about the small room, setting out cough medicine, nose spray and various other items. She reached into another bag and withdrew a thermos of steamy broth and a container of hot lemon tea and set them on the nightstand beside the bed, all the while maintaining a constant stream of chatter.

She was a continuous mover, rearranging things, hanging up my crumpled pants, even placing a hospital tuck in the bedspread. Just her presence lent a brightness to the otherwise dreary room. She fussed over me like a mother hen, and, ill or not, I enjoyed the attention. There was nothing pretentious about her; she was really concerned. It was an element that had been missing in my life for quite a while.

"Your fever is a hundred and one! she exclaimed, holding

the thermometer to the light. "And it's all my fault. If you hadn't changed that stupid tire in the pouring rain, this wouldn't have happened."

'I'll get over it," I told her doubtfully, stifling a sneeze.

She set about filling me with broth and tea, then stuffed me with medicine. She called maid service, which I had earlier refused, and had fresh linen delivered. Then she ran a hot bath and hustled me into it while she changed the bed.

When I returned from the bathroom, freshly scrubbed, she shooed me right back into bed and—honest to God—tucked me in! Then she curled up in the only easy chair available, wriggled around until she was comfortable and beamed at me.

"Feeling better?" she asked.

"And smelling better, I'm sure," I answered, regarding her openly. Hers was the dusky skin tone of the true Cajun, and her deep brown eyes shown like polished mahogany. The gently cascading hair, now out of rollers, formed a perfect frame for her delicate face, which was accentuated by only a hint of blush and eye shadow.

"You're staring," she said, a pink tint lightening her cheeks.

"Sorry. I was just thinking how beautiful you are . . . and wondering why you aren't out with your boyfriend instead of playing nurse to some guy you don't even know."

"It just so happens that I'm what you might call in between boyfriends right now," she said. Then added quickly, "Not that there were all that many to begin with." She glanced at her watch and frowned. "Anyway, I won't be able to stay much longer. I promised mother I'd be home by seven-thirty."

I smiled. "Does your mother know where you are?"

"Of course," she said. "I'm not *that* dumb. She even knows the room number, so you'd better behave yourself."

There was banter in her voice, but the implication was clear: if you happen to be a weirdo, mister, best find yourself another girl.

I was thinking of a witty response when the phone rang. I lifted the receiver apprehensively, wondering who could be calling. I listened for a moment, frowned, then handed the phone to Susan.

"It's for you," I said. "Sure you're in between boy-friends?"

There was a puzzled expression on her face as she took the receiver from my hand. I watched in silence as she listened to the voice on the other end of the line. Her cheeks grew darker, and her lips tightened, mute testimony to her growing agitation. Then agitation turned to outright anger as she said, "Well, you just tell J.W. to mind his own business, I'm doing quite nicely, thank you!"

She slammed the receiver down with such force that I was convinced the instrument would never work again, then folded her arms beneath her small breasts, inhaling deeply.

"Oooh . . . that makes me so mad!" she said.

"Mind telling me what that was all about?" I asked.

"That," she explained, "was George D'Atoris," as if that solved the mystery.

"And who the hell is George D'Atoris. An old flame?"

"Hardly," she answered, returning to the easy chair. "He's a friend of my stepfather, J.W. I can't believe he had the nerve to ask Mr. D'Atoris to call here and check up on me!"

"Why didn't he just call himself?" I asked.

"Because J.W. felt it would make a better impression if Mr. D'Atoris did it, since he's the chief of police."

I felt my fever going up another degree. "The chief of police?"

"Yes . . . he and J.W. grew up together. I can't *believe* he did that!"

I struggled out of bed and made a beeline for the door. "Well, Susie," I said, "I appreciate the concern, but I think it's best if you run on home now before Mr. D'Atoris decides to sent a SWAT team over here."

She looked puzzled for a moment, glanced at her watch, then collected her purse from the dresser. She paused in front of me as I stood holding the open door. "Promise you'll stay in bed? And take the medicine and drink the rest of the tea and broth, okay?"

I assured her I would.

"And call me in the morning," she added. "About eleven."

"You got it," I said, not meaning a word of it. Here I was in a town less than twenty-four hours and already the chief of police was interested in me. And that was an interest I could do without.

An air of sadness came over me as I watched Susan cross the darkening parking lot, high heels clicking faintly on the blacktop. She slipped into the Malibu, tapped the horn as she backed out and drove away. Absently I took note that she hadn't yet replaced the defective rear tire. No, Susan, I thought, I won't be calling you in the morning—or any other morning. And the sad part is that you'll never know the reason why.

With a regretful sigh I closed the door and plodded back to bed. I shook four aspirin from the bottle on the nightstand, decided it wasn't worth the effort to retrieve the tea sitting on the dresser and swallowed them dry. Then I snuggled beneath the blanket to try to get some sleep.

If only I had world enough and time, I thought. If only I had world enough and time.

It was a little after nine the next morning, and I had just stepped from the shower when a knock sounded at the door. Belting my robe, I went to answer, thinking it was Susan coming back to check on me.

It wasn't.

He was a beefy man, fiftyish, dressed in a loose-fitting tan suit that had seen better days. A tan fedora was perched atop short-cropped hair graying at the temples, and had he been clutching a cigar between his teeth he would have been a dead ringer for Winston Churchill.

"Mr. Jones?" His voice was heavy Southern.

I nodded and cut loose with a giant sneeze. I wasn't overly concerned that anything was wrong; had he been coming to arrest me, he most certainly wouldn't have been alone.

"Bless you," he offered. "Mind if I come in a minute?" He held out a meaty hand. "Name's George D'Atoris."

His grip was firm as I accepted the hand, trying to keep my expression one of neutral curiosity. I stepped aside and allowed him to enter, closing the door behind him. He paused in the middle of the room and casually looked around, paying particular attention to the various medicines scattered about the dresser and nightstand. He removed the fedora, revealing a deeply receding hairline, and turned to me with an apologetic grin.

"Guess you know it was me that called last night, huh?" he asked.

"So I was told," I answered.

He twirled the fedora, the aw-shucks grin creating a web of lines and wrinkles on his blocky features. Like damp leather that had been left in the sun too long, I thought.

"Well," he said, "could be I was a bit out of line there. Ol' J.W., he's stubborn as a mule sometimes. Sorta had me believin' that Susie might have run into some kinna harm. It ain't like her to just go waltzin' in some strange man's motel room, know what I mean?"

I assured him that I knew exactly what he meant.

"Anyways," he went on, "I just want you to forget all about that call. Wasn't my place to do that anyhow. Fair enough?"

"Fair enough," I agreed. "Can't blame a man for being concerned about someone he loves."

"Exactly!" he said, flashing the wrinkled leather grin. He walked over to the window, parted the drapes and peered out at the parking lot.

"Purty fancy wheels you got there, young fella," he observed. "Might as well tell you I took the liberty of runnin' the plates this mornin'. Nothin' personal, mind you. But you'd be surprised how many hard cases come roarin' through here in cars that ain't rightly theirs. Besides, now I've met you, you seem like a right nice enough fella to me."

He released the drapes and turned back to me, dark eyes reflecting an alertness that belied the country bumpkin attitude. "I'm a little puzzled about one thing, though . . . maybe you can help me out. Your car's proper registered in Arizona, but Susie tells it you live and work in L.A. Guess she was just confused, huh?"

He knew perfectly well she hadn't been confused, and it would have been a mistake on my part to have said as much. I had learned that when it becomes necessary to lie, it is preferable to stick as close to the truth as possible.

"She isn't confused at all," I told him. "My home is L.A., but I've been looking for one of those T/A's for quite a while—and Dodge only produced a limited number. I ran across that one at a dealership in Kingman, Arizona, just about a week ago and bought it on the spot. The Arizona registration is only temporary until I get back to California."

He nodded, replacing the fedora on his thinning pate. "Well, now," he said, "that sure makes sense to me. Figured it must be somethin' like that. You gonna be in town long?"

"I might," I answered cautiously. "If I thought I'd be welcome. Right now I'm beginning to wonder if I might need a lawyer." I smiled to take the sting out of my words and got one back from D'Atoris.

"Guess I've been a mite nosy, ain't I?" he said, chuckling. He gave his sagging pants a hitch and walked to the door. "No harm meant, son. You're welcome to stay long's you want." His voice lowered and he gave me a knowing wink as he opened the door. "By the way, our little Susie seems to have taken quite a shine to you. Could be that's another reason you decided to stick around?"

"Could be," I said.

He nodded, his snuff-colored eyes looking at me frankly. For a moment the good ol' boy twinkle had vanished, lending the weathered face an inscrutable look.

"Susie's a good girl, Mr. Jones," he said. "I wouldn't want to see her hurt."

"Neither would I, Mr. D'Atoris," I said truthfully. "Neither would I."

The grin returned and he stuck out the big hand. "Welcome to Shreveport, Mr. Jones. Anything I can do, give me a holler. I'm the easiest man in town to find. And take care of that cold now, y'hear?"

I watched through the parted drapes as he drove away in a dusty three-year-old Chevrolet with oversized spotlights on either side of the windshield. Then I went back to bed, pleased with the way my meeting with Shreveport's chief of police had gone. Maybe I would stick around at that.

I reached for the phone and called Susie.

Three months later, Susan Black and I were married. It was a simple ceremony performed by a local minister in the living room of her parents' home. Her best friend, Bobby, was maid of honor and her three sisters were the bridesmaids.

J.W. had agreed to go through the motions of giving away the bride, a role he fell into with as much drunken dignity as he could muster. There was a mutual dislike between us from the moment we met, and neither of us tried particularly hard to hide the fact. He was loud and overbearing, especially with Susie's mother, Irene. She was a gentle woman in her late forties who was constantly supplying J.W. with snacks and Budweisers while he slumped in front of the ancient TV set, farting and belching seemingly at will. Irene accepted the abuse with a stoic attitude and an occasional look that said, okay, so he's a slob, but he's my slob and I'll stick with him.

Susie had this same quality, which was one reason I fell in love with her. There would be no questioning her loyalty or faithfulness. If anything she was simply *too* good; she didn't smoke, didn't drink, never used a four-letter word stronger than "darn" and didn't eat much. In my opinion, she was a near saint.

I had rented a small one-bedroom apartment near her house, and it was there that we set up housekeeping. Because of my sinking bank account, which I had opened shortly after arriving in Shreveport, we agreed to postpone a honeymoon until better times. I also told her that I had resigned from the development firm I had invented when we first met—burying one lie with another. Susie had no idea how much money I had, nor did she ask. She simply took for granted the fact that I would be able to provide for our needs, never questioning or badgering, never suspecting that I was a total fraud.

But *I* knew. And I was having problems with it.

It wasn't long before I realized something was going to have to be done about our money problems. Our bank balance was below the four-thousand-dollar level. Bills were coming in like crazy, but money wasn't, and I knew that the smallest crisis could easily wipe us out. Even our planned move to Memphis—a decision Susie had accepted even though it meant being uprooted from family and friends—had to be put off for lack of funds. But Susie wasn't aware that this was the cause; she thought I was just waiting for the right time to break the news to her mother. For years I had barely been able to take care of myself. Now I had doubled the responsibility. I needed money, and I needed it fast.

I decided to gamble.

My mind made up, I told Susie that I had to go back to L.A. for a few days to take care of some loose ends I had left behind. A logical enough excuse, I thought, since I hadn't been "home" in nearly five months.

So it was that on a bright Friday morning, armed with a thousand dollars from our vanishing bank account, I kissed Susie goodbye in the airport lobby and boarded a Delta flight for Los Angeles. That afternoon, depressed from having lied to her yet again, I found myself on a connecting Hughes Air West flight, skimming the peaks of the San Bernardino Mountains. A short time later, in the midst of a heat wave that threatened to scorch the air itself, I stepped off the plane at McCaren Field in Las Vegas, Nevada.

# CHAPTER 19

**D**URING THE TAXI RIDE FROM THE AIRPORT, HEADING BACK to the Tam O'Shanter Motel, I tried not to think about how silly I was acting. Who the hell did I think I was anyway, Nick the Greek? Just because I had been lucky once, aided by the fact that I was also drunk and had no idea what I was doing, could I actually expect to be that fortunate again? Las Vegas had sent the most prolific of gamblers limping home with their tails tucked between their legs. What made me think I could succeed where those with a lifetime of experience had failed? Mine was a desperate, immature and highly irresponsible act, one which reflected just how infantile my thinking really was. But worst of all, I thought, staring moodily out the window at the bleak, daytime desert scenery— worst of all, I had lied to Susie. Again. And because of that, it was imperative that Lady Luck favor me one more time. Only then, I felt, could my deceit be justified. At least to myself.

Later that night I set out again for Caesar's Palace, opting to walk instead of taking a cab. A warm breeze was blowing in off the desert, carrying an occasional sting of sand. The Strip, as usual, was aglitter, bathed in the surreal glow of hundreds of thousands of winking neon bulbs: Flamingo, Dunes, Tropicana—all competing for the highest electric bill. I marveled again at the transformation the place had under- gone, from a boiling caldron of drab concrete and steel by day to an elegant necklace of multicolored, dancing lights by night. A lure for the unwary, a beacon for the strays.

Caesar's was crowded. I stood in the lobby and surveyed the casino area, eyes searching. Wall-to-wall humanity dominated the scene; men dressed in thousand-dollar tuxedos rubbed elbows with bejeaned cowboys, while women in flowing evening gowns exchanged intimacies with young girls in sandals and hiphuggers. It was a charged atmosphere that elevated everyone as equals, for when Lady Luck bestows her favors, she pays no attention to how one is dressed.

I weaved and jostled my way through the perfumed, talcumed and perspiring bodies until I reached the baccarat area. As before, it was attracting lots of attention; spectators lined three and four deep around the roped-off enclosure.

The same pit boss was again overseeing the play, perched atop a high, straight-back chair at one end of the pit. He smiled in recognition as I entered the gaming area and took a seat beside an attractive young lady who bore a striking resemblance to Natalie Wood.

I took out my small roll of hundreds, ordered a double Chivas from the hovering cocktail waitress and prepared myself for some serious gambling.

Thirty minutes later I watched gloomily as the croupier whisked away my last hundred-dollar bill. I glanced at my friendly pit boss and give him a hands-up gesture.

"Guess it's not my night," I said flippantly. I stood and strolled nonchalantly toward the exit, feigning indifference at the thousand bucks I had just blown.

"Shall I hold your seat for you, Mr. J.?" The pit boss spoke in the conciliatory tone reserved for losers and funeral parlors.

"Sure—why not?" I answered. "Maybe they'll run a little better after I get some food inside me. Be back in about an hour."

The night air was still warm as I left Caesar's and ambled up the long driveway leading to Las Vegas Boulevard. I paused beside the huge fountain that stood in the median and looked up at the multicolored rainbow of water. What now, General? I asked myself. You've got a grand total of fourteen dollars in your pockets, and less brain cells than that inside your head. Try explaining *this* to Susie! Sighing, I took off my jacket, loosened my tie and collar button and gave a final glance at the castle of broken dreams. Then I flung my jacket over my shoulder and sauntered out onto the Strip.

I ended up nursing my blues over a tall Chivas and water at the New Frontier Hotel, sitting at a small table in a darkened lounge adjacent to the casino area. Two hookers, one white and one black, were talking in low tones at a table nearby. They had been all smiles and open invitation when I first sat down but quickly ignored me when they saw I wasn't buying. As for me, something entirely different had captured my attention.

Two Japanese men with leather money purses slung on their shoulders were making their way to the cashier's window on the far side of the Casino. The reason I had taken such an interest was because these same two men had been creating quite a stir at one of the crap tables, and those purses were loaded with black chips. I was curious to find out just how much those chips added up to in money.

I picked up my drink and sauntered out of the lounge, picking my way slowly through the crowded casino. A row of quarter slot machines were situated near the grilled window where the men were happily unloading their chips. The cashier quickly separated them into stacks of ten each, then reached for a tray of hundred-dollar bills and began counting them out.

I watched the exchange from the corner of my eye as I slowly fed quarters into the machine, mentally conducting my own count. As close as I could determine, there had to be at least fifteen or twenty grand lying on the counter when the counting was over.

I decided to go after it.

The men scooped up the money and stuffed it into the leather purses, speaking excited Japanese to each other. They bowed to the cashier, slung the bags over their shoulders and headed for the bank of elevators on the other side of the lobby.

Casually, I fell in behind.

I paid them little attention as we waited along with several other guests for an elevator. When one arrived we stepped inside, and I watched one of the Orientals push the button for the sixth floor. Smiling politely, I pushed five.

I got off on the fifth floor and turned left. As the elevator doors closed, I darted across the corridor to a door marked STAIRS and bounded up the steps three at a time, coming out just in time to see my targets halfway along the corridor, heading for their room. Watching through the half-open door, I saw them enter a room at the far end of the corridor, pausing long enough to drape a DO NOT DISTURB sign over the outer door-knob.

I pushed through the stairway door and walked along the plush carpeted corridor until I reached their room. I took note of the number and studied the location carefully. Theirs was the third room from the end of the wing, which was all I needed to know. I turned and went back to the elevators, my head buzzing with possibilities.

I returned to the darkened lounge and found my table still vacant. The two hookers were right where I'd left them, only now they had company: two middle-aged executive types out for a little fun and games. I ordered another tall Chivas and water and amused myself by eavesdropping on the sales pitch being offered by the two executives. Their game was weak, but in the end it wouldn't matter. Just as long as they had the going rate.

And so I waited, sipping Scotch and arguing with myself about what I had already made up my mind to do. Any action can be justified if you think about it long enough.

At two-thirty I walked out to the pool area, pulled one of the aluminum lounge chairs to a shadowy spot at the back edge of the apron, stretched out and waited some more. The courtyard was deserted now, lighted only by a few scattered lamps and the underwater lights of the Olympic-sized swimming pool.

The hotel was oval-shaped with the guest-room balconies facing inward, overlooking the pool and grassy courtyard. I lit a cigarette and gazed up at the rows of balconies on the east side . . . there it was, sixth floor, third from the end. The sliding glass door was half-open, a small breeze causing the drawn curtain to billow outward through the opening. There were no lights on. Still, I decided to wait another thirty minutes to be safe. Well, as safe as I had any right to expect.

Three o'clock.

I snubbed out my third cigarette and stood, arching my

back and checking for signs of movement within the courtyard. I was a little concerned because I hadn't seen a security guard anywhere, and I knew they regularly patrolled the area. Then I forgot about it and concentrated on getting the deed over with as soon as possible. ·

I walked across the courtyard and stopped in front of the ground-floor patio, third room from the left, took a last look around, then leaped for the lower railing of the balcony above. I caught it on the second try, pulled myself up and over, then looked down again at the empty courtyard.

Still nothing moving.

Moving cautiously, I worked my way up balcony by balcony, until I finally crawled over the sixth-floor railing and flattened myself against the wall next to the partially open door, arms aching. The front of my suit was covered with patches of chalk-colored dust, and I wished I'd had the foresight to change into something more suitable . . . maybe a black jumpsuit with zippers everywhere, suction cups on the knees, neat little gadgets tucked away here and there. Just like Robert Wagner.

Sure.

After a minute or two I eased the sliding door open wider until I could slip through without snagging anything. I put my ear close to the curtain and listened, hearing the sounds of heavy breathing. I eased the curtain aside and stepped lightly into the room.

I closed my eyes and counted to ten, letting my eyes adjust to the darkness, then looked around. There were two double beds, each containing the outline of a sleeping figure. Across the room, off to the left, was the bathroom, a crack of light spilling from the slightly open door. From the back glow I could see the dresser opposite the beds, not a dozen feet from where I was standing. The leather bags were sitting on top.

I walked on thick carpeting over to the dresser, opened one of the bags and felt inside. The money was still there. I fastened the strap, draped the two bags over my shoulder and headed for the hallway door . . . then stopped. The door was on a direct angle with the bed where the two men were sleeping. If I opened it, the light coming in from the corridor would wash across the bed like the beam from a giant flashlight. I pictured two enraged Orientals leaping from those beds, screaming *Haaaaaa!*, throwing karate chops.

I decided to go out the way I came in.

I moved back to the balcony door and stepped outside, not bothering to close the door behind me. I took a long look at the grounds below, then went over the rail and started working my way back down.

Going down was a lot easier than coming up, even with the two money purses getting in my way. I had a bad moment on the third landing when my foot slipped on the metal railing, but I caught myself by wrapping both arms around the support rail and hanging on for dear life. I finally reached the second landing without further incident, dangled from the ledge, then dropped lightly to the ground.

Then everything went black.

There was an echo chamber where my head used to be. Fragments of conversations faded in and out as if coming from a bottomless well: ". . . clobbered the bastard good, I'm tellin' you! . . . did you see that money? . . . fuckin' thief! . . . swing your end around a little more, Lennie! . . . hell of a gash, ain't it? . . ."

And so it went. Broken sentences and hollow words that made no sense whatsoever. A feeling of motion, then a sudden jolt that sent needles of pain through my skull.

Then darkness again.

I regained consciousness slowly. I struggled from the pit of absolute blackness, waded through a swirling gray fog, and at last emerged into a world of blinding light that seemed to penetrate through my very eyelids. Then came the pain—sharp, stabbing pain—somewhere in back of my skull. And more voices, only this time better understood.

". . . and so he winds up like Sandy Koufax and lowers the boom."

"What did he hit him with?"

"Fuckin' time clock! One of those five-pound jobs on a strap. Wonder it didn't tear his head off."

"It almost did . . . sutures, please."

It didn't take a lot of thought to realize where I was—or what was happening. At least I could still think. I decided not to let anyone know I was conscious just yet. Which wasn't going to be easy, because no one had bothered giving me an anesthetic. I could feel every plunge of the needle, the firm tug as each suture was pulled firm and tightened, the poking and probing of gloved fingers. I told myself it didn't hurt—just before things started swimming, and I passed out again.

The next time I came to I was in the intensive care unit. My head was one gigantic mass of pain, and I could feel the pressure of the bandages wrapped turban-style around my skull. Through slitted eyes I could see nurses and interns dressed in green moving back and forth between the double row of beds, some with drawn curtains. No one seemed to be paying any attention to me, so I took the opportunity to take stock of my situation.

There was an IV tube going into my right arm and another tube in my nostril. I also had a catheter. But my biggest concern was for my legs, which were chained to the bed with two sets of leg irons.

A nurse and an intern were coming my way, so I closed my eyes and played possum again.

While the nurse fiddled with the IV bottle, the intern peeled back my eyelids and directed a small beam of light into the pupils.

"He's dilating," he muttered. "Should be coming around now." His breath smelled of cigarettes and coffee. His observation was my cue to wake up; otherwise he would know for certain that I was faking.

I let out a groan, rolled my head from side to side and let my eyes flutter open. Both were watching me intently with nothing more than professional interest.

"Welcome back," the young intern said. "How do you feel?"

"What are the chains for?" I asked, ignoring the question. "Afraid I'll dash away?"

"Not our doings, I assure you," he replied. "But it appears that you have been a naughty boy, Mr. Jones . . . if that's really your name."

Beautiful, I thought. I didn't even have sense enough not to carry my identification. The only consolation I had was that the police couldn't run a thorough check on me until I was booked. After that, it wouldn't take long for them to realize that I was indeed a Jones. And once they found out that I was a fugitive from Virginia, I was sure they wouldn't object to letting them take custody of me. A picture of Goldie's grinning face came to mind, and I cringed at the thought of getting back in his clutches again.

I was determined that I wouldn't.

Off to my left was a glass-paneled door. I gazed at it thoughtfully, wondering if I were in any condition to make it even that far—assuming that I could first get out of the chains. As I watched, two uniformed figures appeared on the other side of the door. They looked at me through the glass for a moment, whispering to each other, then moved away.

I looked at the intern. "I got an armed guard too?"

He hung the chart on a hook at the foot of the bed, saying, "We don't have a jail ward here, Mr. Jones, so the authorities don't like to take chances. The restraints are just to make sure you stay put. Are you having any pain?"

"Yes."

"I'll tell Doctor Fintch. Meanwhile, Miss Gary here is going to take your vitals and give you a sponge bath, see if we can't get you cleaned up a little. We'll have something for your pain shortly."

The intern moved away leaving Miss Gary checking the tubes running to my body. She was about twenty-five, pretty, with wide-set brown eyes and short cropped sandy hair.

Looking at her I said, "If it's all the same with you, I'd just as soon bathe myself."

She said, smiling, "You shy?"

"We just don't know each other that well," I said.

She took out a green plastic washbasin from the bottom of the metal nightstand. "Suit yourself," she said. "As long as you feel up to it."

She left with the basin and returned a few minutes later with soap, water, washcloth and towel. She placed the basin of water on the nightstand and handed the other items to me.

"Sure you can manage?" she asked.

"I'm sure," I said. "I've been doing this a long time."

"Five minutes then," she said. "And please don't disturb your support systems."

She grasped the curtain hanging from the horseshoe rod above the bed and pulled it around me, hiding me from view.

"Five minutes," she reminded me, and I heard the faint rustle of her starched uniform as she moved away.

I immediately went to work.

The standard restraints used by police departments nationwide are manufactured by Peerless, which advertises its legirons and handcuffs as being "pick proof." Nothing could be farther from the truth. There are three perfectly good ways to open these manacles without a key: with a ballpoint pen filler, with a thin piece of spring steel that can be used to "shim" the tumbler or—with a little practice—with a simple paper clip. I didn't have a paper clip. But I did have something nearly as good.

I removed the IV needle from my arm, wasted a few precious seconds to stop the bleeding, then—using my teeth—I bent the tip backward until it resembled a miniature fish hook. Ignoring the pain in my head, I sat up and reached for the chains that were holding me captive.

It took about two minutes for the first lock to give way, freeing one leg, But the effort had taken its toll, leaving me lightheaded and dizzy, and for a moment I was terrified that I might pass out again. And time was running out.

I decided not to bother with the other lock; someone might come to check on me at any time. So I pulled the length of chain through the foot rail of the bed, coiled it about my ankle and tied the chain in place with a strip of bed sheet. Then I went about the painful business of removing the tube from my nostril and the catheter from my penis.

I eased the curtain back and peeked out at the glass-fronted door leading to the hallway. No one was around, and apparently my nurse was busy tending to more needy patients. I lowered the safety railing, swung my legs cautiously over the side of the bed and stood, fighting back a new wave of dizziness. Taking a deep breath, I headed for the door.

My hospital gown was backless, which was undoubtedly going to raise a few eyebrows, since I had nothing on beneath it. There was a turban around my head, a chain around my ankle, and my ass was shining like a new moon. But there was no time for modesty or hesitation. I reached the door, pushed it open and stepped boldly into the hallway.

The two policemen were flirting with a pretty receptionist down the hall to my right, their backs turned partially in my direction. I turned left and moved at a fast walk toward an exit sign at the other end of the corridor. Several people passed me by, and I could feel their amused stares as they gaped after me. I didn't care. All I wanted was to reach that door with the beautiful red sign above it.

I was a body length away when all hell broke loose behind me. A scream, angry shouts, then the sound of running feet echoing through the corridor. I risked a quick look over my shoulder and saw my nurse standing outside the ICU door, one hand clutched against her breasts and the other pointing an accusing finger in my direction. The two policemen were sprinting past her, shouting as they ran. One collided with a patient in a wheelchair, and they both went sprawling to the floor.

I pushed against the locking bar, shot through the door and found myself in a parking lot. I dashed through a row of parked cars, keeping low in case bullets started flying, until I reached the other side. I scrambled over a low wooden fence into someone's back yard, fell and came up running. I couldn't see my pursuers, but I could hear their feet pounding the asphalt behind me.

I bounded across the lawn, clambered over the far fence into another yard and continued running . . . through two more yards, across a side street, into an alley and over another fence into yet another back yard. I pulled myself to a sitting position and leaned back against the cyclone fence, gasping for air, the world swimming before my eyes.

I could run no farther.

A faint wailing of sirens reached my ears, distant, but drawing nearer by the second. I had to find cover.

Inside the yard was a small wood-and-brick house with a screened-in back porch. I pushed myself erect and lurched drunkenly to the rear steps. The screen door gave a small squeak as I pulled it open and stepped inside, but the sound was masked by a stereo blaring out a rock tune from inside the house. I let the screen door swing shut and looked for a place to hide.

The porch was a cluttered mess: banded stacks of newspapers, a child's red wagon with two wheels missing, a motorcycle engine resting in a puddle of black oil and—against the far wall—a dilapidated couch with springs protruding from the faded upholstery.

The sirens had stopped now, and I knew that the area would soon be swarming with police. The only possibility was the rustic couch, which offered a small space between it and the wall.

It was a tight fit, but by stretching full-length on my side I managed to wriggle my way snakelike into the opening. By now my head was feeling like it was about to explode, and my vision was beginning to blur. I heard voices shouting in the distance, the muted slam of car doors. Then another sound, like a giant bee searching for nectar. It took several moments before I figured out what it was.

A helicopter.

The posse was gathering, and the hunt would soon be in full swing, probably resulting in a house-to-house search of the immediate area. Praying my luck would hold, I rested my throbbing head against the rough wooden floor, and with the foul odor of mildew in my nostrils, I lost consciousness.

During the rest of the day I drifted in and out of awareness, confused and disoriented, mouth like dried concrete. Time was of no consequence, the hours passing like a series of time-elapsed photographs. Reality merged with fantasy until it became difficult to distinguish one from the other.

Reality won out at last and I finally snapped out of my stupor. I gradually became aware of my cramped body, the musty floorboards and the constant ache inside my head. Summoning my strength, I raised my head and peered out.

Night had set in and a small yellow light glowed above the screen door, attracting hoards of inquisitive moths. Nothing moved, and the only distinguishable sounds were those of clinking dishes coming from inside the house.

The search was over.

I rested a couple of minutes more to get my thoughts together, then began the painful task of unpinning myself from behind the smelly couch.

Carefully I wriggled my way backward, at one point catching my hospital gown on one of the jutting springs. While freeing myself I accidentally banged my elbow against the wooden clapboards of the house. I froze for a count of ten, and when all seemed normal I continued working my way backward until I finally slithered into the open. I stood up and breathed deeply of the cool night air, arching my back to relieve the stiffness.

"Right there, man—don't move an inch!"

I jerked my head around and gaped at the figure standing in the kitchen doorway. It was a man, one hand holding the door slightly ajar, the other pointing a .38 revolver at my chest. The gun didn't waver as he called over his shoulder.

"Call the cops, Doris! It's the one they've been after all day!"

Strangely, I felt no fear. Instead there was a smoldering rage that all my efforts should come to an end like this. Tomorrow this man would be looking at his picture on the front page of the newspaper, smiling for the camera while shaking hands with the Commissioner. And I would be on my way back to Goldie.

I decided not to make it that easy for him.

Deliberately I turned my back and moved slowly toward the screen door, careful not to make any threatening gestures.

"I said hold it, man!" There was slight desperation in his voice. This wasn't going right. When you point a gun at someone, they're supposed to do as you say. Now he had to choose; either I walked away peaceably, or he was going to have to shoot me in the back . . . and it takes a special kind of killer to shoot an unarmed man in the back. I was betting my life that he wasn't that special kind of killer.

I reached the screen door, pushed through and stepped out into the night, still moving slowly.

"One more step and you've bought it!" he said. But now I was positive he didn't mean it.

"If you shoot, it's murder, mister," I said evenly, still walking. I was three steps into the yard now, nearly out of the yellow circle of light cast by the night-light above the door.

I heard a sharp banging sound behind me, and I jerked involuntarily, thinking I had drastically misjudged the man. When I finally turned to look back, the man was gone, and the kitchen door was closed.

I wasted no time in scrambling over the back fence into an alley that ran behind the yard. I trotted to the other end, crossed a deserted street and entered another alley. After several blocks I slowed to a fast walk, breathing heavily and with my head feeling as if it were splitting open. But I had to keep moving. The man with the gun would have alerted the police by now, and once again the hunt would be on. I had to get out of the area as quickly as possible.

Side streets, back alley, front lawns and driveways—all came and went as I plodded through the deepening night. An occasional dog would bark menacingly as I approached its territory, then track me with deep-throated growls as I passed out of sight, an automaton without direction.

I almost missed the water faucet. It was sticking out from the side of a brick house, half-hidden by a small bush. I turned it on and knelt under the cool water, letting it run over my entire upper body, turning my face up from time to time, drinking deeply.

When I was finished I shut the water off and dried myself on the hem of my gown, peering into the back yard that was softly lighted by a half-moon. I could see an aluminum clothesline back there, heavy with the day's wash. I moved cautiously through the fence gate, stepped around a wheelbarrow that was in the way and went to examine the clothes. Most of them were men's. I took a pair of work jeans, a plaid shirt and a pair of athletic socks.

I dressed quickly, keeping an eye on the back of the house. The pants and shirt were a little large, but at least the chain coiled around my ankle was hidden. Then I spotted a pair of freshly washed tennis shoes drying on the back steps and went over and got them. These were too large also, but it was better than being barefoot. I buried the gown in a flowerbed next to the porch and set off again into the night.

A fractured dawn was visible in the east when I next stopped to rest. I had skirted the main stream of houses by taking to the desert, making certain I kept the bright glow of Las Vegas Boulevard constantly in sight over my left shoulder. In this fashion I soon put the city of Las Vegas behind me. Ahead stretched nothing but open desert all the way to Stateline, Nevada, some thirty miles distant.

My head had subsided to a tolerable ache as I sat in the pale shadow of a spiny cactus and adjusted my turban. The orange sun was rising quickly now, rapidly dispersing the coolness of the night. When it reached its zenith, the temperature on the desert floor would be well over a hundred ten degrees. In that kind of heat the body loses approximately three pints of fluid per hour. It didn't require a calculator to figure that I had better be out of that inferno before the next nightfall. With this thought as incentive, I struggled to my feet, said good morning to an inquisitive lizard watching me from a nearby rock, and headed for the sun—where I-15 had better be.

It was close to noon when I topped a slight rise in the desert floor and peered through hooded eyes at the ribbon of blacktop ahead of me, stretching into the distance seemingly without end. I was exhausted, dehydrated and nearly at the end of my endurance, but the sight of that lovely interstate was like a shot of adrenaline.

I bounded down the opposite slope, broke into a stumbling run and at last fell gasping onto the graveled shoulder of the highway. My turban had loosened again, and I tore it off and flung it away. It was much too conspicuous anyway. I tenderly fingered the bald spot near the crown of my skull and winced, praying someone would come along soon. Using my shirt as a makeshift hood, I rested my head between my knees and waited.

Sometime later I heard the deep-throated purr of an eighteen-wheeler approaching, coming out of Vegas. A moment later it came into view, a tiny insect lumbering out of the desert, twin stacks belching smoke.

Instead of standing and showing my thumb, I rolled over onto my stomach and rested my head in the crook of my arm. I heard the down-shift of gears as the rig approached, the hiss of air brakes being applied. Then I was bathed in a giant shadow as the eighteen-wheeler halted beside me. I rolled over and blinked owlishly at the skinny young driver looking down at me from the cab.

"You okay, pal?" he asked.

"I've been better," I answered, rising shakily to my feet. "I was hitching to California and guess I must of passed out. Got caught in the middle of a brawl in Vegas the other night and sorta came out on the short end of the stick."

"I'm goin' to Glendale, if that'll help," he offered.

"Glendale's fine," I told him. "Wouldn't happen to have any water with you, would you?"

"Nope," he said, flinging open the passenger door and sliding back behind the wheel. "But I got a quart of vodka under the seat."

"Even better," I said, and crawled into the cab.

# CHAPTER 20

$B$Y THE TIME WE REACHED L.A. I WAS FEELING NO PAIN—literally. My Good Samaritan truck driver, whose name was Bailey, had seen to that, plopping the quart of Smirnoff's on the seat and telling me to help myself—which I did rather frequently. He was also very observant and spotted the chain around my ankle within the first mile. So I told him about my escape from the hospital but stuck to my original story about getting into a brawl in one of the downtown casinos. I don't know if he bought it or not, but he didn't press the issue. He was more interested in how I intended to get the chain off. There was a ballpoint pen attached to a clipboard on the dash. With his permission I removed the metal filler, peeled back a piece from the end with my teeth until it took on the shape of a crude question mark, then inserted it into the keyhole. A single clockwise twist was all it took to pop the cuff open. I tossed the chain out the window, apologized for ruining his pen, took another healthy drink from the bottle and made myself comfortable. Bailey was suitably impressed.

We made a stop in Stateline for fuel, and I took the opportunity to make some quick repairs in the men's room. I kept a close eye on Bailey, making sure he didn't use the phone. He seemed like a regular good ol' boy type, but I still wasn't ready to trust him completely.

Before we left, Bailey bought two cheeseburgers and a six-pack of Miller's, then stood by feeding dimes into a slot machine while I made a collect call to Susie. I caught her at home and, in between huge bites of burger and gulps of beer, asked her to buy a prepaid ticket from Delta Airlines and have it waiting for me at L.A. International. I brushed aside her questions, told her I had to hurry and hung up. Then Bailey and I were on the road again, charging through the California desert in his monstrous rig.

I left Bailey at an off-ramp on the San Diego Freeway in Inglewood just outside L.A. He had two parting gifts for me: a five-dollar bill and an orange baseball cap with CAT written on the front. I raised a hand in farewell as the big rig pulled away and received two sharp blasts from the foghorn in return. I watched until he disappeared into the bumper-to-bumper traffic, then walked slowly along the off-ramp to the street beyond, wondering what I was going to tell Susie.

Two hours later I was on board a Delta 727, climbing through the L.A. smog, heading back to Shreveport.

It was nearly eleven P.M. when we touched down in Shreveport. Susie was waiting for me inside the terminal, looking fresh and appealing in a red halter and white pedal pushers. Her eyes widened as I approached.

"What in the world happened to you?" she asked. "You look awful." She wrinkled her nose. "And you need a bath."

"Yeah," I said. "That's probably what the people on the plane thought. And that's not all I need." I took her arm, and we went out.

I put off her questions until we reached our apartment, saying I would tell her all about it then. When we got there I headed for my bottle of Chivas in the kitchen cabinet while Susie went into the bathroom to run a tub.

I sat surrounded by bubbles, nursing my Scotch, while Susie nursed the gash in my head. The water had been aqua blue when I got in the tub, but now it was a murky brown from all the sand and grime that had come off me.

I had done a lot of thinking on the flight to Shreveport, sitting in a rear window seat staring out at the clouds, ignoring the stares I was getting from the passengers and flight attendants. I decided to tell Susie everything. She had to know—and I owed her that much. I didn't know how she would take it, but at least I knew she wouldn't turn me in.

So I told her, sitting there in the tub of bubbles now gone flat. Stumbling at first, not sure, then picking up speed as I went, wanting to get it out and over with as soon as possible. Halfway through the story she left to get me another drink, and when she came back I noticed without comment that she had a glass of her own. She sat down on the edge of the tub and listened in silence while I continued, her face showing no expression.

After I had finished, she sat there a moment staring into her empty glass, trying to absorb it all. Then she stood and, without a word, walked out.

I raised the plug and sat there listening to the water gurgle down the drain, absently rinsing away the ugly ring my filth had created. I wished I could rinse away as easily the ugliness I felt inside. I dried off, donned the blue silk bathrobe Susie had bought for me shortly after our wedding, then shaved carefully. When I had stalled as long as I could, I picked up my empty glass and went to find Susie.

She was sitting on the couch in the living room, hugging herself and staring at the floor. I walked into the kitchen and made another drink, returned to the living room and sat down in the easy chair across from her. She looked so small and defenseless. I wanted to take her in my arms and hold her, to whisper reassuring words of comfort and stop her world from falling apart. But she would never permit that. All I could do was sit there in silence, gripping my glass of courage and wishing I were someplace else.

Finally she raised her head and looked at me, eyes red and slightly swollen. "Why don't you go to bed?" she said quietly. "You look tired."

I couldn't believe my ears. "Go to bed? Is that all you have to say?"

"No!" she snapped. "It is *not* all I have to say, darn it! But I don't want to talk about it now. I need time to think . . . to come to some kind of grips with this thing. It isn't every day that a woman has the man she just married turn up bloody and beaten—smelling and looking like something that just crawled out of the sewer—and have him tell her the reason he's that way is because he tried to rob somebody . . .

and then find out he's a fugitive on top of it!'' She gave a short laugh and spread her arms. "I mean, what do you expect? Am I supposed to be clever and flippant about the whole thing? . . . say, That's all right, Ed, so I married John Dillinger? Big deal! Is that how you expect me to act?''

She was standing now, hands on her hips, getting it all out.

"Well, it doesn't work that way, Ed. Not with me, anyway. I thought I was marrying Doctor Jekyll, not Mister Hyde. All I wanted was . . . was kids and—PTA meetings. Maybe a little house with a white picket fence. Does that sound corny to you?''

I shook my head no, not saying anything. Letting her go on.

She started pacing in front of me, arms folded. "It wasn't really important if the man I fell in love with had money—or even that he be particularly good looking. What *did* matter is that he be honest and loving. The kind of man my mother never had. I just wanted . . . I just . . . oh, *shit!*''

She turned away and buried her face in her hands. She tried to hold back the sobs but couldn't, and I closed my eyes and squeezed the glass until my knuckles turned white. I wanted to run and hide, and at that moment I would have willingly walked into Goldie's open arms if it would have taken away the torment she was going through.

She pulled herself together with an effort, hunching her thin shoulders and wiping at her cheeks. She sniffed and focused on our wedding picture sitting on the TV.

"I'm basically a pretty simple person, Ed," she said quietly. "It doesn't take a whole lot to make me happy. But this . . . this is something I'm not sure I know how to deal with. I need to be alone—to think. And that's why I want you to go to bed. Don't worry, I won't call the police, or sneak off while you're asleep. I might leave you, but if I do, I'll tell you first. Now will you please go to bed and leave me alone? Before I start throwing things.''

I stood and set my empty glass on the coffee table. It took every bit of willpower I had to keep from going to her, but I fought the urge. She was right; this was something she had to deal with herself, without interference from me. So I slinked across the floor to the bedroom, closed the door softly behind me and went to bed. But it was a long while before I went to sleep.

Quite a long while.

It seemed as though my eyes had barely closed before they flew open again. But the sun shown brightly through the closed curtains, casting a subtle glow about the room. Something had wakened me—a movement, a touch, something. I rolled onto my back and blinked away the sleepiness, sensing another presence on the bed.

Susie was sitting there, looking at me through solemn eyes. Gone were the halter and pedal pushers, replaced by a wispy, pale green nightgown. She was fresh and scrubbed and smelled of lotion, and she held a mug of steaming hot coffee.

"Are you awake?" she asked.

"I'm getting there," I answered. "Is the coffee for me?"

"Yes," she said, handing it to me. "And I've decided what I want to do. So just listen to what I have to say and then tell me if my terms are acceptable."

There was a no-nonsense, matter-of-fact tone in her voice that had never been there before, but her words were promising. I sat up and took a sip from the steaming mug, daring to hope for the first time since stepping off the plane the night before.

"I'm not leaving you, Ed," she began, still favoring me with her direct gaze. "I should—but I'm not. The fact of the matter is that I still love you. You may not be the man I thought you were, but you're still *my* man. And regardless of what you've done, I know there's a lot of good in you. I couldn't be that wrong. So I'm going to stay with you—but only if you make me two promises."

"Name them," I said quickly, returning her look.

She shifted about, making herself comfortable on the edge of the king-size bed. "Number one, I want to leave Shreveport as soon as possible. We can go someplace else—anyplace, I don't care. We can change our names and start a new life. You're good at that sort of thing anyway. You *can* get us a new identity, can't you?"

I nodded. There was a trace of sarcasm in her voice but I let it go.

She nodded back and said, "Good. Now, number two. I

202

want you to promise me here and now that you will never commit another crime as long as we're together. You don't *need* to make a living that way . . . and I won't accept it. I told you last night that it doesn't take much to make me happy, and I meant it. Just love me and never let me regret that I've made this choice. I won't even ask for the little house with the white picket fence. Will you promise me that?''

She tried to remain stern but wasn't quite succeeding, so she folded her hands in her lap and stared at them, gently biting at her lower lip the way she always did when she was nervous. I watched her and realized not for the first time that I loved this little lady very much indeed.

"I promise, Susie," I told her. "And I swear to you, I'll keep it."

She let out a small sigh, took the coffee mug from my hand and set it on the nightstand.

"Then that's it," she stated calmly. "Now will you please hold me before I start blubbering again?"

I pulled her to me and stretched out on the bed beside her, holding her close and buying my head in the soft fragrance of her hair. There was a warm wetness against my shoulder as she hugged me back.

"You better not ever put me through this again, Ed," she whispered fiercely. "Damn it, you had just better *not!*"

I gently rolled her onto her back and kissed her long and deeply. I drew back and made a face, loving her so much I felt I could burst.

"Hey! I thought you didn't swear," I teased.

"I didn't use to drink either," she sniffed. "But you're driving me to it." She raked a gentle finger across my chest and looked thoughtful.

"While we're at it," she said slowly, "there's something else I should probably tell you about."

"What?" I asked, kissing the tip of her nose.

"I'm pregnant."

It took three days for Susie and me to get our things together, close out our bank account and say our good-bys to her friends and family. Our story was that I had landed a good job in Dallas, leasing commercial property for a large real-estate firm. But what we didn't tell them was that Dallas would only be a quick pit stop for the purpose of putting together a new identity. From there we planned on heading for Memphis, Tennessee, a city we had mutually agreed on as being most suited for building our new life.

So it was that on a bright Sunday morning I hitched the small U-Haul trailer to the back of my Dodge and off we went to Dallas, Susie bringing up the rear in her Malibu. For the first time the full impact of my actions was beginning to register. I was assuming responsibilities I had subconsciously avoided all my life. I had little doubt about being able to look after myself, but was I ready to handle the role of husband and provider—and soon, father? With no job, little money and the assumed identity of yet another person long dead? It was a scary feeling. But I had promised Susie a new life, and I was determined to give it my best shot. It was out there— somewhere. All I had to do was find it.

But I knew it wasn't going to be easy.

We checked into the Executive Inn, a small hotel on Mockingbird Lane, where I paid three weeks in advance. Then I set out for the public library to begin the familiar routine of searching old death notices, looking for a likely candidate to resurrect.

Five days later, I made yet another mistake.

I had selected a suitable name from the obituary column of a 1944 edition of the *Dallas News*, purchased a money order for the appropriate amount and sent it off to the Bureau of Vital Statistics. There was nothing left now but to wait for the birth certificate to arrive, after which a driver's license and social security card could easily be obtained. But with the waiting came restiveness, and I responded to the mounting pressure of the situation by hanging out in a local tavern in nearby Irving. Susie was whiling away the idle days by shopping for maternity clothes, and I found it preferable to drink among company than to sit alone in a sterile hotel room. The patrons were friendly, the atmosphere subdued and congenial, and for a few hours I could forget that a world of reality lurked just outside the darkened doorway.

It was late afternoon, and I was returning to our hotel after a particularly lengthy engagement in my favorite bar, weaving in and out of the growing LBJ-Freeway traffic with abandon. Suddenly I caught the familiar red-and-blue flashing lights of a police car through my rearview mirror, closing in fast. I experienced a moment of dread and for an instant thought about making a run for it. But I was sober enough to realize that there was no way I could do much running in that congested traffic. So I eased to the shoulder, cut the engine and waited, trying to appear casual and unconcerned.

The cop was young, probably still a rookie, I thought, as I watched him approach from the driver's side. I rolled down the window and smiled.

"What's the trouble, officer?" I asked, trying hard not to breathe in his direction.

"May I see your driver's license and registration, please?" he asked.

I fumbled the items out and handed them to him, confident in the knowledge that he wouldn't run a check through NCIC on a simple traffic violation.

He examined the documents carefully. "Mr. Jones, do you always drive in such a reckless fashion? You nearly caused an accident at that last on-ramp."

"Sorry, officer," I said. "I guess I was a little careless."

He grunted and walked back to his patrol car to call in a local check on my license. Well, at least I was clean in Texas.

In a few minutes he returned, looked at me thoughtfully for a moment, then leaned over and placed his head inches away from my open window.

"Sir, have you been drinking?" he asked.

"Only a couple," I admitted. "But I assure you I'm completely . . ."

"Would you step out of the car, please?"

"Look, officer, I'm not drunk."

"Just step out of the car, please," he repeated, taking a step backward. I had the distinct impression that he did not want to repeat the order a third time.

I stepped out of the car.

He put me through a series of motor tests: walk to the back of the car, spin around, then walk back; stand straight, eyes closed, and touch the nose with the index finger of each hand. The first time I hit my upper lip. The second time I nearly poked out my left eye. Then he had me stand on one foot and extend my arms straight out. I started waving like a flag in a gentle breeze.

"Mr. Jones," he said finally. "I'm placing you under arrest for suspicion of driving while under the influence. Would you step back to the squad car, please?"

I placed both hands on my hips and glared at him. "I'm not drunk!" I said indignantly. "I've only had two or . . ."

He took another step backward and loosened the strap on his service revolver.

"I asked you to step back to the squad car," he said forcefully. "I won't ask you again."

I stepped back to the squad car. You don't want to get into any hassles with police officers in the State of Texas.

I sat in the rear seat of the Irving police cruiser, hands cuffed in front of me, and listened while the officer called for a tow truck. A wire-mesh screen separated the front and rear seats, and the door and window handles had been removed from the inside rear doors. By now I was sober as a priest, but continued to feign drunkenness. I was beginning to feel a slight panic, for there was no question of what would happen once I was booked. My fingerprints would then be run through the computers at NCIC and it would be all over. Goodbye, Susie. Hello, Goldie.

While the officer stood outside waiting for the tow truck to arrive, I removed the gold Cross pen from my shirt pocket, took out the filler and quickly fashioned a key. In a matter of minutes I had the cuffs open. I refastened them on the first notch so that my hands could slide through easily, put the pen away and waited.

Soon the tow truck arrived, and after supervising the removal of my car, the officer climbed behind the wheel, gave me a quick glance, then set out for the Irving police station.

I rested my head against the rear window and watched the unfolding landscape as we drove, peeking through lowered eyelids. Within a couple of miles we swung onto an off-ramp, turned left onto a side street and were soon passing through a residential neighborhood of green lawns and sparse traffic.

I raised my head, let out a loud groan and doubled over, gagging and retching.

"What's wrong with you?" the policeman asked, risking a quick glance back at me.

I answered by gagging again, a rasping "aaawwwkkk" sound that damn near caused me to upchuck for real.

"Sonofabitch!" he muttered, pulling quickly to the curb. "Don't you go pukin' in my goddamned car!"

He stopped behind a white Wonderbread truck, jumped out and opened the left rear door. An elderly couple sat on plastic lawn chairs directly across from us, gazing curiously in our direction.

I tumbled from the car and landed in a heap on the blacktop, still gagging and retching.

"Dumb shit!" the policeman muttered, then stopped and grabbed me beneath the armpits. As he struggled to lift me I slipped my right hand out of the cuff, turned slightly toward him and grasped the handle of his service revolver. He wasn't such a bright shit himself, since he had neglected to refasten the holster strap.

I jerked the weapon free, spun away and leveled the .38 at the center of his chest, flinging the dangling handcuff from my left wrist into the street. He stood frozen, hands held stiffly in front of him, eyes blank with shock.

"In the car, mister," I said. "Quick!"

He came to life in a hurry and scrambled through the open rear door. I slammed the door shut, tossed the pistol into the front window and trotted away in the opposite direction. I reached the end of the block and turned to look back. The elderly couple were on their feet, shading their eyes as they looked after me in amazement. The irate policeman was pounding furiously on the rear window trying to attract their attention.

I turned the corner and broke into a full run, wanting to get as far away as possible before the troops arrived.

Two taxis and one bus later, I strolled into our room at the Executive Inn. Susie was sitting on the edge of the bed, glued to the swivel TV mounted on the dresser. She looked up as I came in and pointed in amazement at the TV.

"You . . . you were just on the news!" she said incredulously.

I walked to the closet and began peeling off my soiled clothing. "They show a picture?"

"No," she answered, turning back to the set. "Just your name . . . and a picture of your car. God, Ed—I don't *believe* this!"

Seeing that nothing further was forthcoming on the subject, Susie jumped up and snapped the set off. "Why in the world did you have to go and do something like that?" she demanded, focusing her attention on me. "Are you suicidal or something?"

I finished stripping to my shorts and headed for the bathroom. "What was I supposed to do, let that cop take me to jail? They would have known who I was in thirty minutes."

I stepped into the shower and adjusted the water as hot as I could stand it. Susie padded in right behind, continuing the conversation through the shower glass.

"What I would like to know is what you were doing drunk in the middle of the afternoon anyway. What I think is that you're turning into an alcoholic, that's what I think."

I bit my tongue and said nothing. There was no point in getting into a shouting match. Besides, I thought, she might have a point.

"So what do we do now?" she asked sarcastically. "Get out of town by sundown, I suppose?"

Without waiting for an answer, she stormed from the bathroom, slamming the door behind her. I didn't blame her. This was turning out to be a lot more than she had bargained for.

My shower over, I slipped into my robe and went back into the bedroom. Susie was sitting in front of the dresser mirror, brushing her hair with short angry strokes. I perched on the bed behind her, lit a cigarette and spoke to her reflection in the mirror.

"Look, Susie, I'm sorry about what happened, all right? I didn't want it to turn out this way. But maybe you're right about my drinking. It seems like every time I have a few, I do something else to screw the situation up even more. Las Vegas was a classic example of that. It wasn't me who went into that hotel room and stole the money—it was who I had become. I justified the action by listening to a little voice that said, 'Go ahead, you're facing a life sentence anyway, so what the fuck's the difference?' "

I slid back against the headboard and snubbed out my cigarette in the ashtray on the nightstand, searching for words.

"I've pretty well made a mess out of my life, Susie. I was kind of a wild kid, I guess, and I did some stupid things. But I was no different from a lot of other kids—certainly no worse. And yet, somewhere along the line things got out of hand, and the next thing I knew I was doing a ten-year bit on some chain gang. The problem was that I couldn't relate the crime to the punishment. I did wrong, sure, but not ten years worth of wrong. Hell, I'd seen grown men convicted of armed robbery didn't get that much time."

I lit another cigarette and tossed the lighter onto the nightstand, feeling myself getting worked up.

"So I took matters into my own hands and escaped—which is what started this whole stupid mess. Ever since things have been just kind of snowballing, I guess, picking up speed . . . a fucking bottomless mountain. I don't like being where I am, Susie, what I've become. But can you tell me how to get back to the other side? I've made myself an outcast from everyone I've ever loved, and until I met you I wondered if I ever *would* love again. And that's something we all need. Even a fugitive. So where do I go from here, Susie? More important, where do *you* go from here?"

For several moments there was a silence in the room, and I could hear the faint crackle of electricity with each stroke of her hairbrush. Only now they were slow, thoughtful strokes.

She finally placed the brush on the dresser and turned to face me. "I go with you," she said softly. "But you're really going to have to do something about your drinking, Ed."

I nodded and said, "And what if the same thing happens again? Or what if I shake you awake in the middle of the night sometime saying we have to leave again . . . how you going to feel then?"

"I'll worry about that when the time comes," she said. "But right now all I want to do is go somewhere where I can be with you and have my baby in peace."

"Memphis?" I asked.

She shrugged and said, "That's where we were heading,

wasn't it?'' She gazed about the room and sighed. "So, do we leave tonight, or what?''

"I think it would be best. As soon as they put together some composites, every cop in the Dallas area is going to be after me.''

"You've lost your car,'' she said solemnly.

I looked at her fondly and grinned. "I know. But I still have you.''

# CHAPTER 21

*My name is Edward Charles Johnson. I am a thirty-two-year old white male, married, the father of a six-month-old baby boy. Occupation: property manager. Previous experience: two years with Lincoln Realty—Denver, Colorado . . . two-and-a-half years with Center City Development—Santa Fe, New Mexico. Brief description of duties: directly responsible for the orderly running and maintenance of multiple apartment complexes, including—but not limited to—supervising of resident managers, conducting area market surveys, controlling rental schedules and contracting for major renovation work. Military service: two years United States Army, including one tour of duty in Vietnam. Honorably Discharged April 1967. Current occupation: resident manager of sixty-unit apartment complex—Bartlett, Tenn. How long? eleven months. Reason for leaving? No opportunity for advancement.*

THE ABOVE IS A PARTIAL EXCERPT FROM THE RESUMÉ I SUBmitted to Wallace E. Johnson Enterprises of Memphis, Tennessee. Except for current occupation, all the information, including my personal references, was phony as a padded bra. It's amazing what a second-hand typewriter and bogus letterheads with glowing recommendations listed beneath them can accomplish. That, and making a positive impression on the person sitting across the desk from you, who really needs those skills.

And the man sitting across the desk from me definitely needed those skills. I sat in polite silence and gazed appreciatively about the opulent office while he read my creations. The resumé and letters of recommendation were indeed impressive, but I knew that they alone would not guarantee me the job. I had to sell myself as well as my doctored credentials, and thanks to a quick stop at the downtown office of the Better Business Bureau, I was armed with enough information to help do just that. Deep references are seldom checked, especially if they are from out-of-state. But, human nature being what it is, the bottom line dictates that it matters not at all who you are—it is who people *think* you are that really counts.

Jim Bailey grunted and tossed the folder on his desk, favoring me with a wide smile. He was a tall man, only slightly older than myself, with dark hair combed straight back. He had a relaxed, confident attitude and went in for sport jackets and open collars rather than business suits.

"Good stuff there, Ed," he said. "You don't mind me calling you Ed, do you?"

"Not at all, sir," I told him.

"Drop that 'sir' stuff—call me Jim. By the way, you wouldn't happen to be related to Mr. Johnson, would you? You got the name for it."

"I should be so lucky," I said.

He nodded. "A beautiful man, Ed—a *great* man. You'll be meeting him shortly, since he's the one makes the final decision about who we take on. But as I'm Regional Director, he usually accepts my opinion on these matters." He unwrapped a stick of Juicy-Fruit and put it in his mouth. "Tell me, how much do you know about our company?"

I jumped at the opportunity. "Quite a bit," I told him. "Mr. Johnson's about as close to being a legend as you can get in this business—which is why I'm excited about the possibility of coming to work for him. He only hires the best people."

Jim Bailey practically beamed at this.

I said, "If I'm not mistaken, Mr. Johnson . . . along with a gentleman named Kemmons Wilson . . . founded Holiday

Inns—sometime in the mid-fifties, wasn't it? Anyway, he realized there were hardly any places around where a person could find a decent room for the night that could accommodate families—especially children. So he had an idea that eventually grew into the largest motel chain in the country. Mr. Johnson sold his holdings in the chain several years ago, but I believe he's still an active member on the board of directors. Like you said, he's a great man.''

Jim Bailey gave me a look. ''You sure you're not a relative?'' Then he grinned. ''You did your homework, didn't you? I like that—shows initiative. Where'd you get your information?''

''Better Business Bureau,'' I told him, and grinned back. ''I really want this job.''

Susie was in the bedroom putting the finishing touches on Derek's Pamper when I got back to the apartment. He stopped kicking and gave me a toothless smile when I walked in, giving Susie the extra second she needed to press the final tape in place.

''Well, I got the job,'' I said. I sat down on the bed and tickled Derek's pudgy stomach, getting a squeal of laughter as reward.

''Thank God!'' Susie exclaimed. ''I hope it's in a better place. I think there's a Hell's Angels convention in the next building. I've never seen so many motorcycles in all my life . . . Come on, sport. Time for your nap.''

She got Derek squared away in his crib and walked with me into the kitchen. Feeling the urge to celebrate, I fixed a mild Chivas and water and sat down at the table. Susie gave me a disapproving look, got a Coke out of the fridge and joined me.

''So when do you start?'' she asked. ''And how large is the property?''

''They want me in two weeks—and the property's plenty big. Eight hundred and sixty units. It's really a good deal, Susie. Twelve hundred a month—plus a townhouse apartment. And are you ready for this? It even has its own swimming pool . . . our apartment, I mean. The guy who originally built the complex used to live there.''

''Oh, Ed—that's great!'' Susie squealed.

**213**

"There's one catch, though," I added.

"I might have known," she sighed. "What is it?"

"The property is in Houston—or rather, right outside Houston. A place called Spring Branch. And you know what happened the last time we were in Texas."

Susie's face clouded and she was thoughtful for a moment. "But that was in Dallas," she said. "And under another name."

"Oh, I can live with Houston," I said, quickly. "I just want to make sure you can. I don't want you having any fears that some policeman might show up any day."

"I won't," she said. "Lord knows I'm used to it by now. Are you sure it will be all right?"

I shrugged. "As sure as I am about anyplace else."

Susie brightened. "Then I have an idea. Let me take Derek and visit mother. You can pack up our things, have them shipped on ahead, then pick us up on the way to Texas. What do you think?"

I could see no real reason to object. Besides, I could well understand Susie wanting to see her mother—especially now that we had Derek.

"I guess that's all right," I told her. "The company is paying our moving expenses, so I guess we can afford a plane ticket. When do you want to leave?"

"How about tomorrow?" she asked. "I'll check with the airlines right now and call mother tonight."

"All right," I said. "Just don't go getting into any long-winded conversations with J.W., okay? The less he knows about us, the better I'll like it. Meanwhile, I'll give my notice here and let you know when I'm coming."

She wrinkled her nose and smiled. "Gonna miss me?"

"Very much," I said, and I wasn't smiling.


The next morning I took Susie and Derek to the airport and watched with a feeling of apprehension as the 707 roared down the runway and disappeared into an overcast sky. Then I went back to the complex and went through my normal routine. Which wasn't much, really; the property pretty well ran itself. It was made up of sixty one- and two-bedroom apartments contained in two separate buildings that faced each other across a square grass courtyard with a small swimming pool in the middle. It was an easygoing kind of complex, comprised mostly of lower-middle-class blue-collar workers. There were no vacancies, the tenants paid their rent on time, and there were few complaints—a dream combination of any resident manager.

So I went into the little cubbyhole adjacent to our one-bedroom apartment that served as my office, picked a few random envelopes off the floor that had been dropped through the mail slot in the door and sorted out rent checks and maintenance requests. I wrote out receipts for the checks to stick in the appropriate mailboxes later, then filled out work orders for the normal leaky faucets and jammed dishwashers and tucked them into the maintenance man's pigeonhole. Then I went into my apartment and fixed myself a tall Chivas and water.

I still had a few ghosts to chase away.

I moped through the empty rooms with glass in hand, the familiar scent of Susie's perfume and Derek's baby powder heavy in my nostrils. I missed them already; it was the first time Susie and I had been apart since the Las Vegas fiasco fourteen months ago. And you still haven't learned, I thought, staring at the now nearly empty glass. I walked to the small bedroom dresser—part of the mismatched furniture that came with the apartment—and picked up the eight-by-ten color photograph we had posed for shortly after Derek had been born. I had sent Mom a five-by-seven of this same picture to remind her that she was once again a grandmother. And now I couldn't even give her an occasional call; the last time I had tried, six weeks ago, I got one of those impersonal recordings saying that the number had been changed and was unpublished. And Dick had sold his trucking company nearly a year ago, and the new owner had no idea how to get in touch with him. Which meant that I was now effectively cut off from the only roots I had ever known.

I sighed and replaced the picture. I was sure the whole thing had been Dick's idea; his tone of voice during our last phone conversation left little doubt but that he was fed up with the entire situation. And who could blame him? The last thing I wanted to do was interfere with the happiness he and Mom had found with each other, so maybe it was for the best. There was no going back now, and we all knew it.

Edward Jones

Besides, I had my own little family to worry about now. And please, God, I thought, if you're really up there . . . please don't let me lose them, too. Because if I do, I just don't think I'll care anymore.

Feeling more sober than I wanted, I went back into the kitchen and poured myself another stiff Scotch. Then I called the property owner—a popular Memphis disc jockey who had taken an immediate liking to me—and gave my notice.

It turned out that a replacement was found for me in four days, which was somewhat of an ego bruiser. There was certainly no danger of apartment managers becoming an endangered species, I thought, as I went about boxing up our personal effects. Certainly not for small, untroublesome properties such as this. But Jim Bailey had promised a far more difficult challenge in Texas. "A real pisser of a complex, Ed," he had said, "and it's going to take a lot of energy to get it running the way we do business." I felt a real sense of excitement at the prospect, for the truth was I was starting to get bored. Eight hundred sixty units. Now *that* was something I could sink my teeth into!

Which reminded me that I still had not gotten the exact address of the Houston property, so I put through a call to Jim Bailey. He wasn't in, but his secretary was able to give me the information I needed. I told her that I was leaving early, and she gave me the name of the moving company the firm used in such cases. Just have them confirm the billing through her, she said. I thanked her and hung up, then called the moving people. A pleasant female voice told me that they could come out first thing in the morning, but that it would take six days before they could deliver to Houston. Would that be all right? That would be fine, I said, then broke the connection and placed a final call to Susie in Shreveport.

Two mornings later, nursing a mild hangover and a loaded-down Malibu, Memphis became another part of my nomad history. I drove with a fourteen-ounce styrofoam cup filled with vodka and Snappy Tom clutched firmly in my hand. I had also added a dash of practically everything I could find in Susie's spice rack before packing it away in the trunk, alongside the silverware, mismatched dishes, towels and other sundry items we would need until the moving people arrived. The resulting concoction was a fiery, foul monster that tasted something like burnt metal, but I figured it would at least make me forget about the hangover.

By the time I hit Jackson, Mississippi, I felt that I had a good chance of surviving, and when I roared across the Louisiana state line a short while later, I was sure of it. All that remained of my earlier misery was a sour spot at the back of my mouth and a strange grumbling in the pit of my stomach. Naturally I had to do something about that, so I pulled into a small mom-and-pop café outside Monroe for a large Dixie cup of ice. I filled it halfway with Chivas from the bottle I had conveniently placed under the seat and hit the road again. In no time at all the sour spot and grumbling were gone.

My late start from Memphis had put me somewhat behind schedule, and I pushed the little Chevy as hard as I dared, zipping along I-20 at better than eighty miles an hour, wanting to make Shreveport before dark. So it shouldn't have come as any great surprise when I glanced into the rearview mirror and saw the red-and-blue flashing lights of the state trooper car closing in fast.

I swore under my breath, backed off the accelerator and eased to the shoulder of the interstate. I killed the engine and popped a Certs into my mouth, thankful I had gotten rid of the damning Dixie cup several miles back.

I watched through the mirror as the trooper pulled in behind me and stepped out of the white cruiser, a small clipboard in his hand. He paused at the rear of the Malibu and jotted down the license number, then sauntered up to my window and peered inside.

"Registration and driver's license, please," he drawled.

I reached into the glove compartment and took out the brown envelope Susie kept her registration in, opened the flap and shook out the contents . . . and out fluttered the old Edward Willis Jones driver's license I had gotten in Shreveport to replace the California license that had been confiscated in Las Vegas . . . the one I thought I had destroyed after the Irving, Texas, incident. What the hell was it doing in with Susie's registration slip?

But it was too late to think or do anything about it now, because the trooper had spotted it. So I plucked it and the registration from my lap and smiled as I handed them through the window. He attached them to his clipboard, excused himself and went back to his patrol car to run a local check. All I could do was sit there and pray there were no wants or warrants out on me in Louisiana.

In a few minutes he returned, ticket book in hand.

"Clocked you at eighty-four back there, Mr. Jones," he said, scribbling away in his ticket book. "Seein' as how you're from out-of-state, I'm afraid you're gonna have to follow me up the road to Lincoln Parish and post fine money."

I exhaled softly in relief and nodded. I was still clean in Louisiana.

I followed the trooper into a little town called Ruston, a tiny spot in the road that couldn't have boasted a population of more than five thousand. After a series of quick turns, we pulled into a small parking lot behind a one-story building of pockmarked brick. I parked next to a four-year-old Dodge with Ruston Police Department written across the door and joined the trooper at the rear of the building. A sign above the door spelled out RUSTON P LICE DEPARTME T & JAIL in chipped white letters. I hesitated and looked at the policeman suspiciously.

"Courthouse's closed," he explained.

I nodded and went inside. There wasn't much I could do about it anyway.

We were in a dimly lit corridor with closed office doors on either side. Up ahead was a small room separated from the hallway by a barred gate. A large-bellied man in his fifties looked up from an ancient desk, rose laboriously to his feet and unlocked the gate.

"Got a Richard Petty fella for you, Del," the trooper said as we stepped inside. "Fix him up, will you? I gotta piss."

Del grunted and returned to his seat. "Lemme see it," he said wearily.

I dropped the ticket on the desk. He looked at it, made a few scribbles on the graffiti-laden ink blotter in front of him and looked up at me.

"That's gonna cost you about sixty-seven dollars, young fella," he said. "Hope you got that much cash, 'cause we don't take checks."

"I have it," I said, and reached for my wallet. I took out

four twenties and dropped them on the desk. "When do I get this back?"

"Soon's you go before the judge, sonny," he answered. He pulled out a metal box from the bottom drawer of the desk, mumbling that he might not be able to make change.

I felt something stiff poking into my back, as if someone had jabbed a large finger just above my right kidney.

"Lean over, put your hands flat on the desk and spread your legs," the trooper said.

I did as he ordered, feeling the old familiar sense of dread. The man behind the desk was looking at me slack-jawed, the metal box poised in midair. He let it fall to the desk, leaped to his feet and fumbled the strap from the service revolver on his hip.

"Hot damn, Carl!" he shouted. "What we got here?" The revolver came out and centered on my chest.

"Don't rightly know for sure, but it's a hit. He's listed bigger'n hell with NCIC. Now keep that piece on him while I see what he's carryin'."

He gave me a thorough search, then told me to place my hands behind my back. He fastened a set of handcuffs around my wrists, spun me around and pulled a card from his shirt pocket.

"Mr. Jones, you're under arrest. There's a warrant out on you in Irving, Texas, for assaultin' an officer and escape." He looked smugly at Del. "That hook-up Sheriff Houck got last week's done paid off already."

"You ran me through NCIC?" I asked incredulously. I couldn't believe they even had a terminal. Not *here!*

"Sure did, friend," the trooper answered. "Just plum bad timin' on your part. We just got it a week ago and been havin' a few problems with runnin' it right. Guess I picked the right one to practice on. Now keep still for a minute while I read you these rights."

Within thirty minutes I had been booked, fingerprinted and photographed and placed in a small two-man holding cell separated from the booking office by a heavy steel door. I was the only occupant, and immediately I began pacing the floor furiously, chainsmoking and cursing myself for the fool I was. I had finally solved the mystery of how my old driver's license had gotten in the glove compartment. I had given it to Susie just before we left Irving, Texas, and asked her to tuck it away somewhere until we got out of Texas. And since Edward Charles Johnson had been born three days after we arrived in Memphis, I had simply forgotten about it. Great thinking, Ed.

I stopped pacing and pulled out my wallet. I thumbed quickly through my new identification: driver's license, social security card, Texaco credit card, international driver's license purchased from the AAA Auto Club for three dollars—all in the name of Edward Charles Johnson. Thankfully no one had taken them . . . or even bothered to look at them. So far there was nothing to point to Memphis, Wallace E. Johnson or Houston.

I tucked the wallet back in my hip pocket and sat down on the bunk, thinking. All wasn't lost yet. If I could just get out of here. And there *had* to be a way out!

But first I had to call Susie.

I moved to the barred door and began yelling for the jailer. After a few minutes the outer door opened and Del stuck his head in.

"What's your biggest problem?" he asked, obviously irritated.

"I'd like to call my wife and let her know where I'm at," I told him.

"I'll see you get one in a while," he said. "I'm busy right now. And stop all that hollerin'."

I watched as he slammed the heavy door closed again, noticing that it was self-locking. Then I went back to the bunk and stretched out, a vague idea forming in the back of my mind. From somewhere behind my cell I could hear the faint sound of laughter and muted conversation. Probably from the main tank, I thought. Willing myself to be patient, I lit a Marlboro and waited for Del to return.

It was nearly an hour before I heard the keys outside. The outer door opened, and Del came in. He unlocked my cell door and stood aside, his right hand hovering near his loosely holstered revolver.

"Come on out," he said. "You got ten minutes, then back you go—I got things to do."

I walked into the office ahead of him and over to a pay phone attached to the wall across from his desk. Directly under the phone was an old steam radiator, clanking and hissing. A small puddle of water had formed on the bare floor beneath where the pipe disappeared into the wall. Del produced a set of handcuffs, fixed one end to the pipe and locked the other around my left wrist.

In about ten minutes those cuffs are gonna get pretty hot, fella," he said. He grinned, displaying a set of teeth too good to be true. "Helps keep folks from talkin' too long."

"Thanks a lot," I said, fumbling in my pants pocket for a dime. I found one, dialed the operator and had her place a collect call to Susie's mother. Del went back to his desk and flopped down in the swivel chair, watching me with mild interest. He really looked as if he had a lot to do.

It was Susie herself who answered. She accepted the charge and in a cheerful voice asked where I was.

"At the moment I'm standing in the booking office of the Ruston Parish Jail, handcuffed to a radiator," I answered, then briefly gave her the details of what had happened. She listened in stunned silence until I had finished.

"So that's about it," I said finally. "A fine mess, isn't it?"

To Susie's credit, there were no hysterics, no emotional outbursts. She simply said, "What do you want me to do?"

"Have Irene bring you here right now," I told her. "You can't miss the place—it's right off I-20, about fifty miles from Shreveport. I'll have the jailer release your car to you. Then go back home and wait until I get my attorney to straighten this out." Under my breath I added, "Don't worry, everything will be all right—just wait until I call."

"All right," she said. I heard the catch in her voice and knew she was about to lose her composure. "Will I get to see you when I get there?"

I looked over at the deputy. "My wife's coming to pick up her car tonight. Can I have a few minutes with her?"

"Not on your life," he said. He yawned and looked over his shoulder at the wall clock.

"Sorry, babe," I told her. "The man says no deal. But don't worry, everything's going to be all right. I should have this whole thing cleared up by tomorrow—understand?"

"Do you know what—I mean, do you know how you're . . . ?"

"I think so. I can't get through to my attorney until morn-

ing, though . . . and I have to have him in court. But I'm
sure the deputy will let me make a quick call.'' I threw a
questioning look at Del, saw him frown, then reluctantly nod
agreement.

"Just to your lawyer," he said. "And make it short."

The handcuffs were starting to get uncomfortably warm.

"Look, I gotta go, Susie," I said. "Just get here as soon
as possible, pick up your car and go on back home."

"Ed?" Her voice was small and strained.

"What?"

"I love you. Please be careful."

"I love you too, Susie. And I will. Give Derek a kiss for
me."

I hung up and stood deep in thought as Del came over and
took off the cuffs. He blew on them for a few seconds, then
stuck them in his waistband.

"You'll have to sign a release if you want your wife pickin'
up that car," he said. He motioned me ahead of him, and I
walked back to my cell.

As he locked me in I asked, "Will you be here in the
morning?"

"I'm here *every* mornin'," he replied. "I sometimes think
I might as well move into one of these here cells."

"Then could I call my attorney about eight?'

"Have to be after nine," he said. "I don't get here 'til
nine."

"That'll be fine," I told him. "And I really appreciate it."

"Like I said—keep it short. And only to your lawyer."

Then he turned and walked back into the office, closing
the door firmly behind him.

Once again I started pacing.

Sometime later Del returned carrying a printed release
form. Susie was outside, he said. I signed my name, thanked
him and he went out again. I stretched out on the bunk and
tried to get some sleep, my thoughts filled with tomorrow.

I was up and ready when Del came in a little after nine the
next morning. Another deputy, younger and slimmer, had
brought me what passed for breakfast at six A.M. But I passed
up the gravy and powdered eggs, settling for only the tin cup
of hot, weak coffee.

Del unlocked my cell and jerked his head. "Same procedure, Jones," he said.

We went through the radiator routine again, Del whistling tunelessly under his breath. For just an instant I was tempted to go for his weapon, but resisted the urge. There was no reason to risk either of us being hurt. I only hoped that no one would come in during the next few minutes.

Del finished chaining me and walked back to his desk. I snapped my fingers jut as he was about to sit down.

"Damn!" I said. "I left my address book under the head of my mattress. Could you take this off for a second while I get it?" I knew full well he wasn't going to do any such thing.

He looked at me with obvious disgust. "Just hang loose—I'll get it." he said, and shuffled off through the open steel door and into my cell.

The instant his back turned I removed the altered ballpoint pen filler from my mouth. That expensive Cross pen it had come from was still clipped to my shirt pocket.

In seconds the manacle around my wrist was free. A few seconds more and I had reached the steel door. Del was about ten feet away, one corner of my mattress lifted in the air, peering intently underneath.

I grasped the edge of the door and swung it shut with a crash. Moving quickly I crossed the room and swung over the four-foot-high wooden counter that separated the office area from the frosted glass front door on the other side. From behind me came a high-pitched roar of indignation and rage.

"Whaaaaa . . . Goddamn ya ass!" it wailed. "Goddamn ya asssssss!"

I reached the glass door and cast a quick look over my shoulder. The heavy door was literally trembling as Dell threw his entire weight against it with unsuppressed fury.

"Whaaaaa, Goddamn ya ass!" Boom!

Without further ado I hurried outside and down a short flight of steps. The sidewalk out front was deserted except for one decrepit-looking dog with a torn ear lying chin-down at the edge of the curb. It was cool and overcast, and a brisk wind made me shiver—or perhaps it was from fear that big Del was going to break down that steel door any second.

I turned left and headed up the sidewalk at a fast walk.

The battle-scarred dog cocked one disinterested eye at me, decided I was harmless, then went back to his canine fantasy.

I took a big gamble and ducked into a small drugstore three blocks away. I headed straight for a pay phone at the rear of the store and called Susie collect. She answered on the second ring.

"Head for Texas—now." I told her.

"But . . ."

"The name of the complex is Cambridge Arms . . . it's on Bengle Road in Spring Branch—you got that?"

"Cambridge Arms . . . Bengle Road, Spring Branch . . . but . . ."

"See the secretary and tell her who you are—she'll take care of you."

"But, Ed . . ."

"See you in a couple of days," I told her, and hung up. That took care of Susie and Derek.

Now I had to get myself to Texas.

# CHAPTER 22

It was raining in Spring Branch, Texas. The lowering skies had opened up the night before, and a freezing slush enveloped the city and surrounding areas. A buffeting wind blew the muck against the glass patio doors of our den with an irritating sound like that of dried leaves, causing Susie to shiver involuntarily in spite of the thermostat being set at a comfortable seventy degrees. It was not a good day for the Houston area, and the weatherman had promised more of the same.

Susie directed a final squirt from her can of Endust onto the mahogany surface of the console TV set, polished vigorously, then replaced the eight-by-ten picture of her and Derek, centering it carefully. She walked to the glass doors and stared out at the patio apprehensively, watching the slush bounce from the tarp covering the small pool out there. From beyond the high wooden fence that surrounded the rear of our townhouse came the occasional swish of a passing car cautiously negotiating the flooded street. An extra strong gust of wind shook the fragile glass doors, and Susie shivered again. She turned to me, frowning.

"Do you really have to go out in all this?" she asked. "Why couldn't Jim just take a cab from the airport? I wouldn't be surprised if his flight wasn't canceled anyway. It's awful out there."

"I already called Eastern," I said, looking up from the

sports page. "Everything's on schedule. Planes don't seem to have any problems with weather like this—only cars. And if I made Jim Bailey take a twenty-mile cab trip, regardless of what the weather was like, I'd find myself out of a job before he even finished paying the fare."

I was sitting on the couch near the artificial fireplace, the make-believe log in the grate sending out a pleasant warmth. Susie crossed the room, casually brushed my bare feet from the coffee table and went to dusting it. She dusted everything at least twice a day. Her motto was "If it's stationary, dust it." I was reasonably convinced that if I remained motionless for a full five minutes, I would suddenly find myself drenched with Endust, and there would be Susie, polishing away, leaving me smelling like a freshly squeezed lemon.

"Is the office closed?" she asked.

"Sharon's taking care of it," I answered. "But I sent the leasing girls home. No one's going to be looking for an apartment on a day like this." Sharon was my secretary, and a damned attractive one at that, much to Susie's disgust. She was also married to one of the project security guards, who stood six feet four, weighed two hundred thirty pounds and was a full-time member of the Harris County Sheriff's Department.

I sighed and tossed the paper onto the cushion beside me. The Rockets had lost to the 76ers the night before by a whopping eighteen points, which meant I could say bye-bye to the twenty bucks I had bet with Ted Wright. Ted and his dad owned landscaping companies in Houston, and I had contracted them to take care of our grounds problems—of which there were plenty. We had also become good friends, much to Susie's dismay. Ted was a drinker, gambler and womanizer, and Susie was afraid that his habits might prove contagious. But he was a lot of fun, and we had some good laughs together. He was also the first person I had allowed to get close to me in years.

"Well, better get moving," I said, and headed for the stairs.

"Take a peek at Derek, will you?" Susie asked. "Let me know if he's wet."

The upstairs boasted three bedrooms, the smallest having been designated as the nursery. I tiptoed in, eased over to the blue-and-white crib decorated with Walt Disney's finest and looked down at my sleeping son. He was lying on his stomach, a stuffed giraffe next to his head. I gazed at him fondly, thinking how easy it would be to have him—and Susie as well—taken away from me. I had no illusions as to what Susie would do if I were ever arrested and unable to escape. Which was as it should be, for I couldn't expect *her* to live in a prison. Nor would I want her to. But if I lost her and Derek, there would be nothing left.

And I had come painfully close to doing just that in Louisiana. For three days and two nights I had plowed through that godawful terrain between Ruston and Monroe, freezing my buns off and soaked to the skin. That first night I had spent in a farmer's toolshed, huddled beneath a small stack of burlap bags while an icy rain beat against the tin roof overhead. The next day, under a broken sky, I had continued on, eventually stumbling across an abandoned railroad track. For the next day and a half I had followed the rotting crossties east until at last, famished and exhausted, I had staggered into the city limits of Monroe, looking as wild as a blind squirrel stuck in a drainpipe.

Fortunately, I was carrying nearly two hundred dollars in cash and wasted no time in hailing a taxi and having the driver take me to the local airport. Within two hours I was winging my way towards Houston, praying that Susie had gotten the hell out of Shreveport without anyone following her.

Derek stirred in his sleep, squirmed around and stuck his little bottom in the air. I smiled and felt his Pamper. It was soaked. He had kicked his blanket into a rumpled ball at the foot of his crib. I pulled it over him, lightly stroked the back of his head and slipped out, pausing at the top of the stairs to yell to Susie that the wet-baby situation was affirmative. Then I showered, shaved and got ready to pick up Jim Bailey.

As he had said, Cambridge Arms was a pisser of a complex. In the first month alone I had evicted no less than fifty-six tenants, and they had left one hell of a mess behind. One family of four had been sheltering relatives in the apartment next to theirs—which was supposed to have been vacant. They had simply broken through the bedroom-closet wall, constructed a crude door, then proceeded to take over both units.

Another evicted family had left the carcass of a slaughtered lamb suspended from a makeshift pulley over the bathtub. Sharon, who had been walking the vacant units with me, had fainted dead away at the sight and had since steadfastly refused to enter another vacant apartment.

I finished dressing, slipped into my topcoat and collected Susie's umbrella from the closet. Then I went back downstairs for a final cup of coffee.

Derek was sitting in his highchair in the kitchen, playing patty cake in his oatmeal while Susie looked on in exasperation.

"This kid never eats," she complained. "He just sits there and splatters."

"Squirt him with Endust," I told her. "That'll fix him."

There was a fresh cup of coffee already waiting for me, and I sipped it quickly, while Derek watched with a mischievous smirk on his chubby face.

"Well," I said at last, "time to hit the trail."

"Is he going to be staying with us?" Susie asked.

"Just overnight. He still doesn't believe those dead-bolt locks I had installed didn't cost us anything and wants to check them out himself. He'll be going back tomorrow afternoon."

I looked over at Derek, who was in the process of throttling himself trying to wriggle under the tray of his highchair.

"That's not the way to do it, sport," Susie said, and went to his rescue.

Smiling at this scene of domestic turmoil, I left to meet my boss.

"So tell me about this lock deal, Ed," Jim Bailey said. It was the next morning, and we were in my office, Jim occupying the chair behind my desk. I sat opposite him glancing at the list of figures Sharon had prepared for me. I was ready to answer any questions he might ask, as well as a few he might overlook.

"Well," I began, "have you ever heard of this guy Marvin Zindler? He's with the Channel 7 Eyewitness News Team."

"Is he one of those crusader types that ABC News affiliates are coming up with all over the country?"

"That's right—except this Zindler is probably the most

popular of the lot. He's kind of a cross between Billy Graham and Dale Carnegie, if you can picture that. Has a big following.''

"What about him?'' Jim asked.

''A few weeks ago there were a rash of burglaries at the complex across the street . . . something like nine or ten in one week. But this is a high-crime area for break-ins, right? Everybody's been thinking that it kind of comes with the territory.

"Anyway, one day a couple of weeks ago I'm leaving the office—and damned if I don't run into a camera crew setting up right outside our lobby doors. And there stands Marvin, in deep conversation with a bunch of tenants from our complex as well as from across the street. They were complaining that the apartment owners in the area weren't concerned about their security because the doors weren't equipped with deadbolt locks.''

Jim was toying with my desk calculator. "Go on.''

"So that evening on the six o'clock news, there's Marvin . . . knocking the hell out of every complex in the area—including ours. And we haven't had many problems at all since we hired our two-man security patrol.''

"Is that when you set up your meeting with him?'' Jim asked.

"Right—the next day. Told him I was going to take him to court for misrepresenting Cambridge Arms. I pointed out that statistics showed our complex had a full eighteen-percent-lower ratio of break-ins than any other comparable property in the whole community—which is true.''

"And what did he say to that?''

I paused to light a cigarette, then continued. "He said that if and when I installed dead bolts on all the doors, he would be happy to come back out and do a favorable report—which is all I wanted in the first place.''

"So you decided to buy some locks, right?'' Jim asked. "Seven hundred and ninety-eight to be exact.''

I consulted my sheet of figures. "That's right. But at a good discount . . . forty percent, in fact. It came out that each lock cost us eight dollars and sixty cents. But this was offset by a ten-dollar installation fee charged to each occupied unit, the work being done by my maintenance crew. At the same time I had them install setscrews inside each window. When they were in place, the window could only be raised a total of six inches. If the tenant wanted to raise it higher, all he had to do was back out the screw—which takes about thirty seconds. The end result was that we came out with a practically burglar-proof unit and made a buck forty in the process. The tenants were happy; I was happy, and Marvin Zindler was happy."

"Did he come back out?" Jim asked.

"Three days after the work was completed," I told him. "We got more publicity on that evening's six o'clock news than six months of newspaper ads would have brought."

"So what's the bottom line on all this, Ed?"

"See for yourself," I told him, reaching across and tossing the sheet of neatly typed figures onto the desk. He picked it up and studied it intently, then leaned back and nodded to himself.

"This says you've had better than a two-hundred-percent traffic increase in the last two weeks alone," he stated. "Is that accurate?"

"Very accurate—and it's been ten days, not two weeks. But more important, we've rented three out of every five units shown. Right now I'm down to twenty-one vacancies . . . and I have deposits on four of those. Not bad for a complex that had a hundred and twenty-seven empty three months ago."

I realized that I was probably sounding pretty smug, and Jim's amused look confirmed the thought. But he couldn't argue with success; the figures spoke for themselves.

"And you think this increase was a direct result of your manipulating this Zindler guy and getting TV coverage? You realize, of course, that we've sunk a lot of dollars into renovation work. Don't you think that may have had something to with it?"

"Certainly," I answered. "But you can't alter the fact that we've received one thousand four hundred and eighteen dollars' profit on locks we've already installed—more than enough to cover the price of the eighty-some that haven't been installed yet. I set up a separate account at the bank just for that purpose. The deposit receipts are in the top right-hand drawer—check them out yourself. The locks, areawide publicity and added security haven't cost us one cent. Quite the contrary, we've made a few dollars and rented a few units in the process.''

Jim was silent for several moments, lips pursed, gazing at the carefully prepared document lying on my desk. Finally he gave me a level look.

"You really should have cleared this through me first, Ed," he said. "Regardless of how good an idea it was, you're still not authorized to spend more than five hundred dollars on purchases without approval."

I was ready for that one, too.

"I didn't use project funds, Jim," I said. "The terms with the Corbin lock representative were net sixty days. Every lock I purchased was paid for out of the installation fee. Besides, you were out-of-town then, and I couldn't reach you. It was either jump or forever lose the chance. The timing was critical.''

He drummed his fingers on the desktop for a few seconds, then stood and stretched his lanky frame.

"All right," he said, "I'll buy it. You covered yourself pretty good on this one. But check with me first on anything like this in the future, okay? Otherwise both our asses could end up in a sling. Now, let's walk those twenty-one vacancies and see how that landscape company you hired is doing. Hope you haven't got any other surprises for me."

We spent the rest of the day inspecting the grounds and touring empty units. The weatherman had missed on his forecast for more freezing rain, but the wind was still blowing cold from the north. Jim took some notes, made several suggestions and offered opinions on what might help move the vacancies. I listened dutifully, but my heart wasn't in it. I had passed the hurdle of the lock incident and was still basking in the accomplishment. I knew Mr. Johnson would hear about it and felt that he would be suitably impressed with my initiative. At least I hoped he would. I had at long last found honest employment that I enjoyed and felt qualified in performing. And I was consumed with ambition. Mr. Johnson and I had hit it off from the start, and I still heard the words the imposing old man had said shortly after hiring me:

## Edward Jones

*"I think you can do us a lot of good, young man—and
we're a company that believes in rewarding good people.
And I also believe if there's anything wrong, a Johnson's
going to spot it and fix it!"*

I was determined to be the best damned property manager
Mr. Wallace E. Johnson ever had.

By three o'clock we were once again back in my office,
sipping hot coffee provided by Sharon. Jim had a five-twenty
flight back to Memphis, so I sent one of the maintenance
men to fetch his suitcase from Susie while we summed up
the result of our inspection.

When he was at last ready to leave, Jim surprised me by
saying that he would take a taxi to the airport.

"No point in causing you to get caught up in that freeway
traffic, Ed," he said. "I think the company can afford a one-
way fare. And tell Susan I thank her for the hospitality."

"Will do," I replied. "Give my best to Mr. Johnson."

He gave me a wry smile. "Next time you get one of those
brainstorms, check it out with me first, will you? You've got
a bright future in this business, Ed, and Mr. Johnson's quite
taken with you. But don't dive into the creek until you're sure
no rocks are hidden under the surface—if you know what I
mean. It takes time to climb the ladder, so don't get in too
big a hurry. Just keep that in mind."

Later, as I stood outside the front lobby and watched the
Yellow Cab pull away, I thought about what Jim had said. He
wasn't a bad guy, and he knew his business. But as sound as
his advice was, I just didn't feel that I could afford to take
my time in climbing that ladder. I wanted . . . *needed* . . .
to firmly entrench myself in the inner circle of a major cor-
poration such as Wallace E. Johnson as quickly as possible,
to reinforce my fragile identity with Master Card and American Express and expense-account lunches. I needed to in-
sulate myself against Goldie and those like him who would
tuck me away in a cell for the rest of my life—if they could.
But you aren't aware of that, are you, Jim Bailey? I thought,
as I watched the taxi disappear from sight. You don't realize
that I live in a castle of sand, in constant fear of that one big
wave that might rush in at any time and wipe the whole thing
away. I have to get to higher ground and build a castle of

stone, and in order to make it I'll have to skip a few rungs in that ladder . . . and pray that I don't slip and fall on my face in the process.

A gust of wind sent a smattering of icy moisture against my face, breaking the mood. I pulled the topcoat snugly around my neck and checked the gunmetal sky. It looked as though the weatherman might be on the money after all. Feeling as gray as the day, I turned and headed for home . . . and the warmth and comfort I knew would be waiting.

The months passed quickly. Winter finally fizzled out and was replaced by a late spring. Ted Wright had his Mexican landscapers out in force now, tending the earth that had been so painstakingly cleared and leveled over the past months. Bushes, flowers, small trees and patches of fresh sod were all planted and carefully nurtured. Even a small playground was under construction in the twenty-yard section of bare ground that separated the family units from the singles and young marrieds.

So, all things considered, I was feeling very pleased on this early June morning as I strolled through the complex grounds on the way to my office. I came abreast of the model apartment which served as our leasing office and decided to stop in and see how Ellen and Debbie were doing. They were my leasing girls, and damned good ones. I had promised them a bonus if they could fill the six existing vacancies we had left—a promise that had been approved by Jim Bailey. They obviously had a prospect inside, because a strange Ford station wagon was parked at the curb outside. I noticed in passing interest that it bore Virginia license plates.

I stepped inside and paused with my hand still on the doorknob. Ellen, a heavyset woman in her mid-twenties with a peaches-and-cream complexion, was sitting on the living room sofa going over a rental application.

"Good morning, Mr. Johnson," she said brightly. "Beautiful day, isn't it?"

I was about to return her greeting when I suddenly froze, eyes glued to the small kitchen table in the breakfast nook beyond her. Debbie, a bright young girl only two years out of high school, was sitting facing me, assisting a man in his late forties with an application form. His face was in profile as he sat hunched over the paper in studied concentration. A woman in a green summer dress was seated next to him holding a bored-looking Persian cat.

Debbie looked up, gave me a smile, then went back to helping the prospective tenant with his application. It had been over ten years since I had last seen that face, but even in profile it was one that I recognized immediately. And more importantly, I knew that he would also recognize me!

I turned on my heel and went right back outside, pulling the door closed behind me. I shook my head in disbelief and drew a deep breath, assuring myself that this was no dream. Then, in a state of semi-shock, I shuffled off to my office next door.

I flopped down in the swivel chair behind my desk, leaned my head back against the smooth leather and closed my eyes. This was too much! I thought. Could that really be who I thought it was? . . . who I *knew* it was? In my mind there was no question. But I had to be absolutely certain, so I picked up the phone and dialed the leasing office.

Ellen answered on the first ring. "Thank you for calling Cambridge Arms. May I help you?"

"It's me, Ellen," I said, trying to control my voice. "Are those people still with Debbie?"

"Yes sir," she answered brightly. "I think she's getting a deposit . . . and I just leased six-oh-three a little while ago. Isn't that great?"

"Terrific," I replied. "When they're gone, have Debbie bring me the application right away, will you?"

"Will do," she said, and hung up.

Debbie knocked on my door ten minutes later. I told her to enter, and she bounced through the door exuberantly. She gave me a huge grin and tossed the application form on my desk.

"Only four left!" she said. "I can taste that bonus already." She stood with arms folded and smiled down at me as I scanned the rental form. And there it was, big as life. The name practically leaped at me, printed in bold-faced blue ink.

Mr. and Mrs. Thomas Harmon, of Richmond, Virginia.

My old chain-gang guard from Camp 21.

* * *

# HACKSAW

That night Susie and I sat in the den and discussed the unbelievable event that had taken place that morning. No music came from the stereo, the TV screen was blank, and Derek was tucked away in the upstairs nursery.

The news had hit Susie like a left hook, and she had been quiet and withdrawn all through dinner, speaking in monosyllables and paying an unusual amount of attention to Derek. Finally she gave him his bath, tucked him in and fixed me an uncharacteristic double Scotch on the rocks. What made it uncharacteristic was the fact that I had drastically reduced my alcohol consumption, sometimes going as long as a week between drinks. Maybe she just felt I needed it—which I did.

We were sitting on opposite ends of the couch. Susie looked at me and said, "Maybe it's not the same man. Maybe it's just someone with the same name who just happens to look like him."

"Not a chance, Susie—and you know it. I told you, I checked his application to make certain. His previous employer was the Virginia Department of Corrections, but for the last two years he's been with Brinks Armored Car Service in Richmond. The company transferred him here three days ago. It's him, all right. I'd know him anywhere."

"Well, why don't you just disapprove his application?" she asked, a hint of desperation in her voice. "You're the manager, aren't you?"

"On what grounds?" I asked. "He has excellent credit, a bank account, great references and a perfect rental history. And because of his job, he's also bonded for half a million dollars. How in the hell can I deny an application like that? He would probably insist on a face-to-face meeting with me to find out why—and I wouldn't blame him."

Susie leaned back and sighed, staring out through the glass patio doors. "So what do we do now?" Her voice was low and resigned.

I hesitated before answering, dreading what I had to say. Susie had her eyes on me now, moist and unblinking, knowing what was coming.

"We leave," I said simply. "We have no choice."

She turned her head away from me for an instant, then jerked back to face me again, her face crimson with suppressed emotion.

"I won't go through this anymore, Ed," she said, slowly shaking her head. "Not again. And I won't let Derek go through it, either. He needs a home—and a normal life. And so do I. If we have to leave again, I'm taking Derek and moving back to Shreveport. I can move in with mother—maybe even get my old job back . . . try to pick up my life again. It wasn't very romantic, but at least I knew where I would be tomorrow."

"You don't really mean that, Susie," I said, stunned. "I know this thing has you all upset . . ."

"I *do* mean it, Ed!" she said forcefully. Then, more softly, "I'm sorry, but I really do. I can't take this kind of life anymore—I'm not cut out for it. And it isn't because I don't love you, because you know I do. But I'm not a gypsy, Ed. I want to stay in one place . . . to meet people and have time to make friends. Do you realize how my mother feels since she found out about you?"

"I have a mother too, Susie," I snapped. "It hasn't exactly been easy for her, either. She hasn't even been able to see her grandson . . . or meet her daughter-in-law."

"And whose fault is that!"

I shut up and took a long pull from my glass of Scotch. No wonder Susie had fixed it for me.

She lowered her voice again and spoke slowly, patiently. "All I want is a place for Derek and me to call home. Can't you understand that? Without having to worry about being uprooted every time a ghost from the past springs up."

Her cheeks were wet now, but she didn't bother to brush away the tears. As for me, I sat there in stunned silence, finding it difficult to believe what I was hearing. Like so many husbands do, I had lately started taking her for granted, more or less; it was unthinkable that the time would ever come when she wouldn't be around. But there was no mistaking the finality in her voice.

"Maybe one day you'll be able to find a place where the past won't catch up with you," she said softly. "If you do, you'll know where to find us. Then maybe we can pick up again where we left off. But I'll have to be sure, Ed. Very sure."

She stood and walked slowly to the stairs. I followed her with my eyes until she reached the top and disappeared. A

# HACKSAW

moment later I heard our bedroom door open and close, then the faint sound of water running in the bathtub.

I drained the remains of my Scotch in three long gulps, then studied my reflection in the mirrored surface of the glass. A distorted image looked back, flat and warped. A very accurate picture, I thought. Very accurate indeed.

I drew back and hurled the glass as hard as I could across the room. It hit the far wall and exploded with a burst of flying fragments, leaving an amber-colored wetness on the walnut paneling.

Then I fixed another drink.

Two days later Susie's brother, Danny, arrived. She had called and asked if he would come and help move her things to Shreveport. By then I was resigned to the inevitable. I had pleaded, begged, cajoled—even threatened—her not to follow through on her decision. But it was all to no avail. Her mind was made up, and that was all there was to it.

Danny, feeling awkward about the whole situation, wanted to get the move over with as soon as possible and wasted no time in loading his Chevy pickup with Susie's things. I told her to take everything, TV, stereo, the works. All I wanted were my clothes. Then I sent for one of Ted's gardeners to help Danny load the stuff and went to my office. I couldn't stop Susie from leaving, but I certainly wasn't going to help her.

I told Sharon that I didn't want to be disturbed for any reason, closed the door and flopped down behind my desk. I had three more days before the Harmons were due to move in, so I wasn't worried about running into them. At the moment I didn't much care. I was consumed with frustration, anger and self-pity, and what I really wanted to do was get drunk. Maybe then, for a little while, I could forget that I had just lost another family.

After two hours of moping and soul-searching, I left the office and walked back to the apartment. The pickup was loaded, Ted's gardener had left, and Susie and Danny were sitting out by the pool, solemnly watching Derek totter after a butterfly. They stood as I entered the patio gate. Derek spotted me also and came tripping across the pool apron, giggling. I swung him up in my arms and kissed him, then walked to where Susie and Danny stood waiting.

"So, you're all set, huh?" I said. There was a tightness in my throat that made speech difficult.

Susie nodded, then turned to Danny. "Would you wait for me in the truck, please?" Danny shuffled away uncomfortably. Derek was tugging at my jacket, wanting to play.

Susie gave me a somber look. "Are you sure you don't want the car? Won't you need it to get to . . . wherever it is you're going?"

"I don't know where that is yet," I answered truthfully.

"What about money? You're not keeping very much for yourself."

"I'll get by," I said. "Nine hundred dollars is the best start I've ever had."

She reached out and placed a hand on my arm. "Ed . . . you do understand why I have to do this, don't you? Please say you do."

"Yes, Susie. I understand." And I did. But it didn't make her and Derek's leaving any easier to take.

"Are you going to be all right?" she asked, concerned. "You're not going to do anything foolish, are you?"

"I've been tied up in foolishness all my life, Susie," I said. "Somehow I got in a race with no finish line, and I don't know how to get out of it. But I won't go off the deep end, if that's what you mean."

Derek was getting restless in my arms, squirming around making small noises of protest. Susie reached for him, and he went to her eagerly. The sharp blast of Danny's horn sounded from beyond the patio fence.

"Well," Susie said, hoisting Derek to her shoulder. "Guess I'd better go." She took a quick step forward, stood on tiptoe and planted a brief kiss on my lips. Then she brushed by me and walked hurriedly to the gate. When she reached it, she turned and gave me a final look.

"Call me," she said. "You can reach me at mother's."

Then she was through the gate and gone. I heard Danny start up the truck, then Susie's Malibu came to life. I didn't go to the gate to watch them leave, but stood where I was, staring vacantly at the concrete apron. I heard them as they pulled out of the parking lot, the engine sounds growing fainter as they made their way slowly down the driveway to the Holister Street exit. The sounds grew fainter still, until at last they were gone altogether.

I walked slowly across the patio and entered the apartment through the sliding glass door, stood quietly in the middle of the den and looked around. Like me, the place was silent and empty. I went into the kitchen and took out my fifth of Chivas, unscrewed the cap and took a long straight pull from the bottle. Then I took another, feeling the fiery liquid burn its way to my stomach and bring tears to my eyes. I recapped the bottle, set it on the sink counter and went upstairs to pack.

There was nothing left for me in Texas.

# CHAPTER 23

I LEFT CAMBRIDGE ARMS FOR THE LAST TIME SHORTLY AFTER dawn the following morning, without explanations or good-bys. I jammed my two loaded suitcases into the trunk of the Yellow Cab I had summoned and told the driver to take me to the airport. He asked which terminal and, after a moment of thought made difficult by a king-size hangover, I told him that Delta would be fine.

I looked out at the still-sleeping complex as we rolled out of the driveway and turned onto Hollister. The only people moving were three of Ted's gardeners, already busy watering the freshly planted greenery in the new playground area. It struck me that I had never before seen the property this early, and I marveled at the transformation that had taken place. Gone were the listless gray buildings, scorched grass, barren earth and potholed driveways. The place now had a shiny new look, painted and groomed and pampered, an oasis where once had been a desert. I felt a sense of pride as I watched the grounds slide by . . . pride in the knowledge that for once in my life I had been involved in something constructive and meaningful. This was to have been my beginning, the launching pad for a new life of family and career. But instead I found myself slinking away like the thief I was— once again without family . . . once again alone. The big wave had come and washed away my castle of sand.

A skycap took my bags outside the Delta terminal, carted

them inside and parked them beside the ticket counter. I tipped him and glanced up at the departure board behind the counter. There was a flight leaving for Atlanta in fifteen minutes. Well, why not? I thought. It was a big city, easy enough to get lost in—a prerequisite for any self-respecting fugitive. So I bought a one-way ticket, checked my baggage and made it to the departure gate just as the flight was called for boarding.

Fifteen minutes later I was airborne, the big jet screaming for altitude. The pilot banked left, shallowed his climb and soon leveled off at thirty-one thousand feet. The "Fasten Seat Belt" and "No Smoking" signs went out, and I lit a cigarette, leaned my head back against the headrest and closed my eyes.

"Would you like something to drink, sir?"

I looked at the pretty stewardess with the pushcart of assorted beverages. She stood there smiling down at me, fresh and wholesome in a blue-and-white miniskirted uniform. I thought she looked an awful lot like Susie.

"Bloody Marys, please," I said. "Three of them."

"Rough night?" she asked, reaching for the miniature bottles of Smirnoff's.

"You wouldn't believe it," I said.

I checked into a cheap motel on the lower end of Peachtree Street, paying a week in advance to get the discount. I had no idea what I was going to do, but I had definitely decided that I was no longer going to be Edward Johnson; too many people in Shreveport already knew that alias. So I made up a short agenda of things to do, number one of which was a new identity. Then it was off to the nearest library for a search through the *Atlanta Constitution*'s ancient obituary columns, where I settled on the name Edward James Carlton.

My next priority was transportation, and I solved that problem through a used-car dealership in the Piedmont area. Four hundred sixty dollars bought me an eight-year-old Ford Fairlane of dubious quality, but at least it was wheels and would likely get me from here to there. I was past the stage of trying to impress anyone.

An apartment was next, since it was obvious that I couldn't afford to live in a motel forever, regardless of how cheap the rate. I finally located a low-budget complex in Sandy Springs that didn't require a last month's deposit, paid the sour-looking landlady a month in advance and moved in two days later. It was a one-bedroom unit with mismatched furniture in worse condition than Susie and I had used in Bartlett, but I couldn't afford to be finicky—or much of anything else, either—since I had exactly ninety-four dollars to my name.

But my finances were not my worst state. It was my atti-tude. It had changed drastically: lethargic, uncaring and to-tally without ambition. It's easy to get that way, I guess, once we feel our own personal cataclysm has started and we begin rummaging through the ruins. Eventually we get used to the little tragedies and become emotionally constipated. And that, perhaps, is the greatest tragedy of all.

I met Mary Ann Dawson three days after moving into my new apartment. She was a tall, reasonably attractive woman of twenty-eight who lived in the same building as me and worked as a nurse at Emory University Hospital. We got to know each other while lounging around the pool area, where I was spending most of my days. I hadn't been too interested at first—which is probably what made *her* interested—because I was still brooding about Susie and Derek. But after several days I loosened up and finally asked her out. What the hell, I thought, why should I feel guilty about Susie? She was the one who had done the leaving.

A few weeks later I got another surprise. I had stopped off at a bar called the Pacemaker shortly after midnight to get pleasantly soused. This was a place I had been coming to regularly of late—mainly because the drinks were cheap, and the customers tended to mind their own business, not trying to lay their problems off on you. It was a place of serious drinking and wishful contemplation.

I climbed onto a vacant barstool, nodded to the bartender and waited for him to bring my usual Scotch and water. Bar Scotch, of course. Chivas was now out of my league. I lit a cigarette and studied myself in the bar mirror. A stranger stared back, unshaven and looking shifty as hell. I grinned at the stranger and got a snarl in return. I thought seriously that here was a person I did not like at all.

The bartender brought my drink, and I sipped at it, letting my eyes wander around the dimly lit room. There were fewer than a dozen customers in the bar, and my gaze settled on two men sitting across from each other in a booth along the back wall. They appeared to be in their mid-fifties and were leaning over the table in whispered conversation. There was something familiar about the man on the left. I squinted my eyes, looking at them through the bar mirror. Couldn't be, I thought.

But it was.

I swiveled around and slid off the stool, drink in hand, and walked over to the booth. The two men looked up at me without expression.

I said, "How you doing, Henry? Put on a few pounds, haven't you?"

Henry Miller looked puzzled for a moment, staring at me, then said, "Well, I be damn—Eddie Jones!"

He grabbed my arm and pulled me down beside him, scooting over to make room. The other guy was watching me curiously, giving me the once-over through slitted eyes set in a thin, hawkish face.

Henry threw an arm across my shoulders and squeezed, looking at his buddy. He grinned and said, "John, this here's Eddie Jones—at least that used to be his name. Eddie, meet my partner, John Malone."

We nodded to each other as Henry kept up the chatter. "Me and Eddie did a little time together in Virginia. What's it been now . . . eight, nine years ago?"

"About that," I said.

Henry chuckled. "I gotta tell you, John. Eddie damn near drove those fuckers crazy. Couldn't hold him! He even beat Five Hundred Spring Street . . . and that's a tough bastard to crack."

"I recall having a little help there, Henry," I reminded him.

"Damn little. It was your show all the way. What you drinkin'?"

"Chivas, if you're buying."

"You got it, Cuz."

Henry called for the bartender and ordered drinks all around. He looked extremely prosperous, if somewhat over-weight. He was dressed in a light-brown three-piece suit with a matching polka-dot silk tie. John Malone was equally dapper, though his taste ran to dark blue. Had I not known Henry, I could easily have mistaken them for insurance executives unwinding after a hard day at the office. But I did know Henry.

Our drinks came, and Henry proposed a toast. "To success—which you look like you could stand a little of, Eddie."

"You don't know the half of it," I said, and savored the fine taste of quality Scotch. "So what have you been doing with yourself, Henry?" I asked.

"Robbin' a few banks," he answered matter-of-factly. "Been doin' all right, too. We hit one in Trenton last week for eighty-three grand."

"Sometimes you talk too much, Henry," Malone said, giving him a level look. I got the impression that this man could be very dangerous indeed.

Henry brushed aside the complaint. "Aw, don't worry about Eddie. I've known him since he was knee-high to a four-foot Indian. His stepfather, too. He's all right."

"The man's got a point, though," I said. "He doesn't want his business on the streets."

Malone turned his attention to me. "What line of work are you in?"

"None right now," I told him. "Up 'til a couple weeks ago I was managing an apartment complex in Houston. Now I'm what you might call unemployed."

"Looks like you're broke, too," Henry grunted, taking in my shoddy appearance. "You growin' a beard, or just need a shave?"

I shrugged and downed the rest of my drink. "I haven't decided yet."

Henry reached into his pants pocket and came out with a roll of bills the size of my fist. He peeled off five hundreds and dropped them casually on the table. "Just in case you need razor blades." He grinned, returning the roll to his pocket.

I folded the bills carefully and tucked them into my shirt pocket. "Thanks, Henry. I won't deny I can use it."

"Forget it, you'd do the same for me."

"No question," I said. "If I were ever in the position—which isn't likely."

Malone had been quietly taking all this in, making small

wet circles on the table surface with his glass. Now he looked at me and said, "You interested in a piece of work?"

"I don't think I'd make a very good bank robber," I answered, smiling wryly.

"It's got nothing to do with banks," he went on. "I know this guy in Lauderdale who's looking for some help. If Henry's willing to vouch for you—could be you'd fill the bill."

Henry slapped the table. "Hey, that's right! Joe Morgan." He nudged me with his elbow. "A perfect setup for you, Eddie. Just the thing to get you back on your feet."

"Oh? Doing what?"

"The guy's a jeweler," Malone said. "He also owns an auction gallery. He takes things on consignment—mostly estate jewelry and stuff like that—and auctions them off for a percentage. Right now he's sittin' on more than a million in gems that mostly all belongs to somebody else . . . and it's insured to the hilt."

I nodded in understanding. "And he needs somebody to lift the stuff for him, right? Then he gets it back on the sly and collects all that insurance money to boot."

"You got it," he said. "But that somebody's got to be reliable. That's a lot of ice to let just anybody walk away with. He's got to be reasonably sure of getting it back."

"Why don't you guys just do it yourselves?" I asked.

"Because it ain't worth it to us," Henry said. "Joe's only offerin' twenty grand for the job, and me and John can walk away with at least three times that whenever we want." He paused and ran a finger beneath the starched collar of his shirt. "Besides, we made a little withdrawal out of that area a couple of months ago, and we ain't too anxious to get back right now."

Malone shook his head in exasperation and checked his wristwatch. I noticed with appreciation that it was a gold Rolex. "Look, we gotta get out of here. You want to talk to the man, or what? If you do, just tell me whatever name you want to use, and I'll give him a call to expect you. Better yet, you got a phone?"

"I have a phone," I told him.

"Then give us the number, and we'll have him call you. That is, if you think you can trust us."

I nodded slowly. "Fair enough." He handed me a pen,

and I wrote the number down on the back of a matchbook. "The name's Carlton . . . just like the cigarette."

"Fine," he said, putting pen and matchbook in his jacket pocket. "I'll get hold of Joe, and he'll get hold of you—unless he's already made other arrangements. You ready, Henry?"

We said our good-bys, and I watched as they made their way to the door. Henry stopped, looked back and gave me the thumbs-up sign. I waved in acknowledgment and smiled as he made a show of brushing away some distasteful imaginary object from the sleeve of his fine suitcoat. Then he followed Malone through the door and out into the darkness, probably to climb into some sleek machine with power everything and an interior that smelled of rich new leather. As for me, I ordered another drink and sat back to contemplate the offer John Malone had made.

Joe Morgan called two nights later. I was watching the small black-and-white TV Mary Ann had loaned me, freshly showered and pleasantly looped. Her shift at the hospital ended at midnight, and we had planned on going out for breakfast.

I answered the phone and heard a husky voice that had New York stamped all over it.

"Mr. Carlton?" the voice asked cautiously.

"Yes."

"Mr. Eddie Carlton?"

"There's only one living here," I said.

"Yes . . . well, I believe we have a couple of mutual friends. A Mr. Malone and . . . what is the other gentleman's name?"

"Miller," I told him, smiling at the test. "Henry Miller. And you must be Mr. Morgan, right?"

He gave a nervous laugh. "Yes, that's right. I understand we might be able to do each other some good. Are you interested in the proposition Mr. Malone mentioned?"

I had given some serious thought to that question the last couple of days. Twenty thousand dollars was a lot of money—especially for a job that apparently carried little risk. It might even be enough to entice Susie into coming back to me. We wouldn't need very much; enough for a small place in some out-of-the-way town, surrounded by forests and meandering creeks and where no one had to lock their doors . . . even from me. Perhaps I could even find her little house with the white picket fence.

"I'm willing to talk about it," I told him. "But certainly not over the phone."

"Of course not," he said. "Perhaps you could come to Fort Lauderdale . . . as my guest, of course."

"You pay all expenses?"

"Absolutely."

"When?"

He paused a moment, then said, "Is tomorrow too soon?"

"I'm not doing anything. Where do we meet?"

"There's a motel on Ocean Avenue called the Mark Twenty-one Hundred. Register under the name of William Jennings. I'll call you there at five-thirty tomorrow evening. That should give you plenty of time to get here. Do you have enough to take care of your ticket?"

"I can swing it," I said.

"Fine," he said. "Well . . . guess I'll see you tomorrow then. Remember—William Jennings . . . Mark Twenty-one Hundred Motel . . . five-thirty."

"I'll be there," I said.

I hung up the phone and stood there thinking for a moment. I still hadn't fully made up my mind to go through with this, but I told myself that it couldn't hurt anything to at least talk to the guy. If I didn't like the setup, then I could just take the next flight back to Atlanta and be none the worse for wear. Like I had told the man—I wasn't doing anything. Not anything at all.

I arrived in Fort Lauderdale shortly after eleven o'clock the next morning. I collected my one suitcase containing toilet articles, a change of clothes, and a fifth of Chivas from the baggage-claim area and took a taxi directly to the Mark Twenty-one Hundred Motel. I registered under the name of William Jennings, went straight to my room and hung out the DO NOT DISTURB sign. I unpacked the fifth of Chivas, found the plastic ice bucket in the bathroom and filled it from the ice machine at the end of the corridor. Then I fixed a stiff one, took it into the bathroom and sipped contentedly while relaxing in a hot tub. Later, feeling clean and refreshed, I padded back into the bedroom, turned on the color TV and stretched out on the double bed. Midway through "As The World Turns," I drifted off into a lazy sleep.

I was awakened by the ringing telephone on the nightstand by the bed. I checked my watch, saw that it was five thirty-five, rolled over and lifted the receiver.

"How was your flight?" Joe Morgan asked.

"No problem," I said. "Where are you?"

"Right across the street," he answered. "I'd like to come over, if it's all right."

"Evidently you know the room number," I told him.

"Fine . . . I'll be there in a couple of minutes," he said, and hung up.

I went into the bathroom and splashed cold water on my face, dried off and went back into the bedroom to fix another drink. There were two fragments of ice cubes left floating around in the plastic bucket. I captured them, dropped them into the glass of lukewarm Scotch and watched as they disappeared almost immediately. I took my first sip just as the knock sounded on my door.

Joe Morgan was a heavyset man in his late fifties, dressed in expensive doeskin slacks, a beige silk dress shirt open at the neck and genuine alligator shoes. He wore a heavy necklace of bark gold, a gold Omega wristwatch, a gold bracelet in some intricate rope pattern and a gold pinky ring on his right hand that carried about five karats of cluster diamonds. He was a walking advertisement for his profession.

He stuck out his hand and smiled, teeth flashing brilliant white in his bronzed, deeply lined face. "Okay if I call you Ed?" he asked cheerfully.

"If I can call you Joe," I said, taking the hand and allowing him to enter. I closed the door behind him, motioned to a chair, then took my drink back to the bed and sat down.

"So what can I do for you, Mr. Morgan?" I asked after he had made himself comfortable. "By the way, if you'd like a drink, I have a little Scotch."

"No thanks," he answered, crossing his legs carefully. "If it's all the same with you, I'd like to get right to the point."

"Go ahead."

"I want you to rob me, Ed," he said matter-of-factly. "I have a rather large jewel inventory on hand at my auction gallery—all on consignment, of course, but fully insured. I want you to come into the gallery during business hours, pull a gun on me and take the whole lot. There'll be no interference, no alarm will be sounded until you're well away from the area . . . no one will get hurt."

I studied him carefully and said, "I thought you wanted a theft—not a robbery. That's pretty heavy."

"A theft won't do, Ed," he said. "My alarm system is too good. I need a plain old-fashioned robbery—with witnesses."

"How many witnesses?" I asked cautiously.

"Only three or four. And one of them will be my seventeen-year-old daughter. That should give you an idea of how uncomplicated the job will be. I certainly wouldn't involve my daughter if there was the slightest possibility of anybody getting hurt. The only others will be my two salespeople—a middle-aged man and woman."

I was thoughtful for a moment. "Then what you want," I said finally, "is for me to walk into your place, pull a gun on you, grab a bunch of jewelry and split, that right?"

He said, "Exactly. Only the jewels will be in three trays sitting inside my safe." He smiled. "Naturally, you'll make me give them to you."

"Then what?"

"Then you make us walk up a flight of steps at the rear of the shop—there's a little accounting office up there. Then you leave through the back door that leads into an alley."

I said, "Anybody going to be upstairs?"

"One person, the lady who keeps my books. She'll never know what's happening."

I said, "All right, I'm outside in the alley—what do I do now, hitchhike away with three trays of jewels under my arm?"

He made a face. "Please, don't be crude. You'll drive away in a rented car—I'll give you the money for it. Leave it someplace out of the way, take a cab to the airport and go back to Atlanta. I'll call you in a day or two and tell you where to take the stuff from there. Neat and simple."

I downed the rest of my Scotch and set the glass on the nightstand. "Where do I get the gun?" I asked.

"I got a clean three-five-seven outside in the trunk," he said. "Unloaded, of course."

I gave him a narrow look. "How do you know I won't load it before I come in?"

"I don't," he said. "That's something for you to know and me to wonder about." He sighed and leaned forward, elbows on knees. "Look . . . I'm the one taking the biggest risk here. From the minute you walk through that door, you're holding all the cards. I'm going to be handing you over a million in jewels and trusting that you won't blow holes in everybody before you leave . . . or just keep on going to God knows where with all my shit. All I'm banking on is the word of a man I've known for a lot of years. He says you're all right—which is why we're talking right now. We can both come out on this deal if neither of us tries to fuck the other. And you'll find that I'm a good man to know for future reference. So what about it, can we do business? If not, then say so, and I walk out of here right now and forget I ever met you."

I stood and walked to the dresser and poured another warm Scotch. Then I went back to the bed and sat down, thinking. The man was making a good case for himself, and I couldn't see where he might be trying to set me up for anything. It wouldn't make sense. I thought about Susie and Derek and wondered if twenty thousand dollars would be enough for a new start—assuming that she would be willing to give it another try in the first place. I didn't know the answer to that. But there was one thing I *did* know. I certainly had no chance the way things stood right now.

Joe Morgan was watching me, waiting for my answer. "Tell me something, Ed," he said.

I lit a cigarette and watched the smoke rise lazily to the ceiling. "You got any particular day picked out for this robbery?" I asked.

"Tomorrow," he answered. "In three days I hold an auction, and it'll be too late."

"And when do I get the twenty thou?"

He reached beneath his expensive shirt and withdrew an envelope from his waistband. Smiling, he tossed it onto the bed beside me. "There's ten grand there. You get the other half when the stuff's delivered. You familiar with L.A.?"

I nodded, ignoring the envelope beside me. I had no doubt the count would be right. "If that's where you want me to take it," I said, "that's an expensive trip."

He raised his hands in a gesture of surrender and said, "I'm easy to get along with. Take three or four good pieces for your time. You got a girl?"

"I got a wife," I told him, then added, "I think."

"There you go!" he said. "Stick a two-karat stone on her finger and an eighteen-karat gold timepiece on her little wrist, and you'll know for sure. Just make sure you limit your selection to the smaller stuff, though—right?"

I snubbed out my cigarette, then picked up the envelope. It was fat and bulky, and when I lifted the flap I was greeted by the lovely sight of tightly banded hundred-dollar bills.

"Pretty, ain't they?" Joe Morgan asked.

I stuck the envelope in a drawer of the nightstand and sighed. "They're pretty, all right. But a lot of times what we have to do to get them isn't."

We spent the next hour going over the minute details, which Joe Morgan had obviously worked out long ago. He produced a hand-drawn diagram of the interior of the gallery and pointed out the location of the "jewel room," which was separated from the main display area of Persian rugs, expensive paintings and other objets d'art by an electrically controlled grille gate.

"This is where I'll be," he said, tapping the spot with a neatly manicured finger. "The two salespeople will be in the main room. When you come in, just say that you're interested in looking at some engagement rings. One of them will bring you to me, and I'll let you in the jewel room. I want you to get there at five minutes to twelve."

"Why does it have to be that exact time?" I asked.

"Because my daughter will be there then and one of the salespeople will be having lunch. There's a small kitchen on the other side of the jewel room . . . right here . . . with a curtained doorway between the two. We usually have lunch there every day. Now, right in back of that you'll notice a flight of stairs that leads to the accounting office. And next to that . . . right here . . . that's the rear door. It leads to an alley out back. Have your car parked there, all ready and waiting.''

"How long will I have to get out of the area?" I asked, scooting back against the headboard. Joe had pulled his chair over to the edge of the bed and had the diagram spread out between us.

"I'll see that no alarms are hit for at least a minute after we get upstairs," he replied. "By then you should be half a mile away. You take the car back to the airport rental agency and hop the next flight to Atlanta. I'll call you in two days and tell you where to deliver the stuff in L.A. My man on the other end will give you the other ten thousand, and you can be on your way.''

I nodded thoughtfully and toyed with the .357 Colt revolver Joe had retrieved from his car. It was a wicked-looking thing, powerful enough to send a steel-jacketed slug into an engine block. But, as Joe had said, it wasn't loaded. I hadn't yet decided if that would be the case when I walked into his gallery the next day.

Joe stood up and stretched, exposing a hairy belly beneath the tails of his sport shirt. He glanced at his gold wristwatch and swore. "I gotta be going, Ed. I got a very suspicious wife at home who probably thinks I'm banging some broad over at the Hilton . . . which ain't a bad idea when I think of my wife. Hang on to that drawing. Study it some more and then flush it. Any other questions about tomorrow?''

I shook my head. "All sounds pretty simple. I just hope it turns out that way.''

Joe Morgan said, "Hey! piece of cake," and flashed the smile. He turned and headed for the door.

I said, "Aren't you forgetting something?''

He stopped and looked back, puzzled.

"My expenses," I reminded him. "You *did* say you'd pay them, right? Plus the car rental.''

He said, "Right you are," and reached for his wallet. He took out three one-hundred dollar bills and laid them on the dresser, saying, "That ought to cover it, don't you think?''

"Close enough," I said.

He moved back to the door, opened it, then swung his head around and looked at me, his hand on the knob. He said, "You *will* be there tomorrow—won't you? I mean, I'm no heavy gangster type or anything like that, but I do know a few people. And ten grand won't last you very long."

I felt like asking, he knows so many people, why he didn't get one of them to rob him? Instead I said, "I'll be there."

"Five minutes to twelve."

"I'll be there," I repeated.

He nodded, cocked a finger at me and left, leaving me propped against the headboard fondling the empty revolver and wondering just what I was getting myself into.

Sometime later I put through a call to Mary Ann to let her know I wouldn't be back that night. Her roommate answered and said that she was at my apartment, playing hostess to a group of nurse friends she had invited over for a few hands of bridge. I thanked her and hung up, irritated that Mary Ann would take such liberties without asking. I didn't like the thought of a bunch of strange women roaming through my little castle, poking and prodding and possibly seeing something they shouldn't. So I called my place to see what was going on.

Mary Ann answered on the second ring. Her portable radio was playing at full volume in the background, interspersed with the faint sound of female laughter.

"Sounds like a live bunch you've got there," I said evenly. "What's happening?"

"Whee! . . . Oh, hi there!" She giggled. It was obvious that she was quite drunk. "Where are you?"

"In Florida," I answered patiently, "where I said I'd be. What are you doing with all those people there?"

"We're havin' a . . . hic . . . a hen party. Why aren't you here?"

"How long is that little get-together going to last?" I asked, ignoring the question.

"What?"

"I said . . . oh, never mind. Look, I want you to get your girlfriends out of there as soon as possible . . . you understand? You can hold your card games at your place."

"Oh, don't be such a sourpuss!" she said. "Nobody's goin' to hurt your li'l ole 'partment."

I could see the conversation was going nowhere fast. "Look . . . I'll be back tomorrow afternoon," I told her, holding my growing anger in check. "And I don't want to see any of my things disturbed . . . not one thing. And I don't want to find a mess. We'll talk more about this then.''

I slammed down the receiver and sat there fuming. It occurred to me that I was getting all bent out of shape over nothing, but I couldn't seem to help it. *This whole business is starting to wear on your nerves,* I thought, as I poured myself another Scotch. *The running, the hiding—not knowing who you're going to be tomorrow. You're a loser, Ed . . . a fucking loser! And you know why? Because you don't now what side of the line you want to be on. You think you can combine being a crook and a good guy, depending on the need. But that's bullshit, and you know it—you've got to be one or the other. But you've put off making that decision for so long now that it's warped your thinking. You justify things like what happened in Las Vegas by telling yourself that it doesn't make any difference . . . that you're already wanted anyway, so what the fuck? But that's a cop-out, isn't it? Just like this shit you're planning tomorrow is a cop-out. Where's it going to end—and how? When you stop and think about it logically, there's only one way it can end . . . in a prison or in a grave. And in your case the latter would probably be the better choice.*

On that encouraging note, I decided to see if I could get some sleep.

I entered the Galt Ocean Mile Gallery at exactly 11:55 the next morning, neatly dressed in my tan lightweight suit and with the .357 tucked out-of-sight behind my waistband. Parked in the alley around back was the cream-colored Olds Cutlass I had rented earlier from Avis—after first putting up a two-hundred-dollar deposit for lack of a major credit card.

The interior of the gallery was just as Joe had diagrammed it. Besides the two salespeople he had mentioned, there were three customers present: a middle-aged couple agonizing over a set of sparkling crystal and a fat man wearing a loud sport shirt and smoking a long cigar who was dickering with the salesman over what appeared to be a King Louis sofa. The atmosphere was hushed and subdued, the decor richly appointed—every inch bespeaking wealth and class. Why anyone with a setup like this would need to be robbed was a mystery to me. Business must really be bad, I thought . . . or Joe Morgan was an exceptionally greedy man.

I headed for the saleslady waiting on the middle-aged couple, footsteps echoing faintly as I crossed the gleaming marble floor. She smiled sweetly as I approached.

"Yes sir, may I help you?" she asked.

"I'm looking for something nice in a wedding set," I answered, returning the smile. "Do you carry jewelry?"

"Oh, certainly . . . our jewelry display is in the next room. I'll have Mr. Morgan buzz you in."

She excused herself from the couple, beckoned to me and led the way to the grilled gate at the back of the room. Joe Morgan was arranging a display of gold watches behind a long glass counter. He looked up as the saleslady pressed a small buzzer next to the gate.

"Mr. Morgan? This gentleman would like to see some wedding sets."

He made a little show out of looking me over, nodded, then pressed another buzzer located behind the counter. The gate lock clicked, and the saleslady, still smiling, ushered me inside.

"Thank you, Sally," Joe Morgan said, and she turned and went back to her customers.

He came bustling around the counter and extended his hand. "How are you, sir?" he said. "Joe Morgan . . . now what could I help you with?" At the same time he winked and jerked his head in the direction of a curtained doorway off to my left. I nodded my understanding. I took the hand and spoke loud enough to be heard by anyone back there.

"Ed Colon . . . and I'd like to see something in the two- or three-karat range, if you have it."

"Oh, I think we can satisfy you," he said, moving back behind the display counter. He removed a velvet-lined tray from beneath the glass and set it on top of the counter. It contained eight rows of the most gorgeous diamond rings I had ever seen—perhaps eighty pieces in all—in every imaginable shape and size. They winked at me with a dazzling brilliance that was almost hypnotic in its effect. He selected a three-karat marquise solitaire and held it out to me.

"Now here's something that will warm the heart of any would-be bride," he said.

As I examined the ring appreciatively, Joe reached into the display counter once again and came out with two more trays of exquisite jewelry; pendants, broaches, necklaces—all set with a glistening array of precious stones. He set them beside the tray of rings and gave me a knowing look. These were the items he wanted taken.

Just then the curtain leading to the small kitchen parted, and a pretty, dark-haired girl of about sixteen peeked through. She smiled shyly at me and addressed Joe Morgan.

"Dad, your sandwich is ready whenever you are."

"Be there in a minute, honey," he said. "I'm taking care of this gentleman right now."

"Would you like a cup of coffee or something?" she asked me.

"No, thanks," I said. "I'm in kind of a hurry."

She smiled again and closed the curtain, disappearing back into the kitchen. Joe waited a few seconds, then came around the counter and glanced through the grille gate into the main room. Satisfied, he hurried back, stacked the three trays of jewelry one on top of the other and nodded back to me.

I gathered the trays under one arm, pulled the .357 from my waistband and leveled it at his chest. His face paled slightly as he raised his hands shoulder high and cocked his head to one side, trying to see if the chambers of the revolver were empty.

"Just turn around and move," I said in a normal voice, not seeing any particular reason to satisfy his curiosity. He did as instructed and headed for the curtained doorway, with me following close behind feeling like an incongruous Jesse James.

His daughter was sitting at a small table, sipping a diet soda and chatting idly with Sally, the saleslady, who was standing at the sideboard pouring a cup of coffee. They both looked our way as we came through the curtain and froze when they saw what was happening.

Joe said, "Please—everyone just stay calm, it's all right," his voice trembling, really doing a good job. "Christie, Sally . . . go on upstairs." He looked over his shoulder at me. "Just don't hurt anybody, okay? Or I swear you'll never get out of the city." Threatening a guy pointing a .357 at him. Beautiful.

"Just turn around and move," I said, waving the gun and sounding dangerous.

The girl stood up and moved stiffly to a flight of steps at the rear of the kitchen, still carrying her can of soda. The saleslady, both hands pressed to her mouth, followed, throwing quick tentative glances over her shoulder. I nudged Joe Morgan in the back with the gun barrel, and he fell in behind.

I stood at the bottom of the stairs and watched until everyone was out of sight, then turned to the service door behind me, released the bolt lock and stepped out into the alley.

I had the rental car pulled up close against the building. I tossed the jewel trays and magnum onto the passenger seat, jumped behind the wheel and roared off . . . and ran into trouble right away.

I reached the end of the alley just as a white delivery van was turning in, and we both slammed on the brakes to avoid a head-on collision. The driver glared at me and leaned on the horn, not about to give ground. He was blocking two thirds of the alley, leaving me no room to go around. And I sure wasn't going back.

The fool driver finally let up on the horn and leaned his head out the window. "You some kind of fuckin' nut or what, pal?" he said. "Back that sonofabitch up!"

I picked up the magnum, not having time for this shit, opened the door and stepped half out the car. I rested my arm across the top of the door and thumbed back the magnum, pointing at a spot just above the bridge of his nose.

I said, "You got five seconds to get that thing out of the way."

The head jerked back, and he peeled rubber backing out of there, nearly plowing into another car that was going by. I slammed the door and left some rubber of my own as I went around him, accelerated to the end of the block and made a right turn onto Ocean Boulevard. The incident had cost me more than a full minute, and by now, in spite of Joe Morgan's assurance, I had to assume the alarm had been sounded. Even worse, I was sure the driver of the van had gotten my license number. Fortunately, I had rented the car with the Edward Johnson license instead of my current one.

I hadn't traveled two blocks before I saw a police car making the turn onto Ocean Boulevard from up ahead. That was quick. I slowed and scrunched lower behind the wheel as he went roaring by with his red lights and siren going. No sooner had he zipped by than another came into sight, coming from the same direction. Soon the entire area would be crawling with police.

I was only a dozen or so blocks from the Mark Twenty-one Hundred Motel, and it was there that I decided to return. It was just a matter of time before a complete description of the Cutlass—along with its license number—was circulated to every police officer in the city. I had to get it off the streets.

I reached the motel without incident, turned in and drove to the far end of the parking lot. I reached into the back set for my suitcase, brought it forward and crammed the jewel trays and magnum inside.

The air was filled with distant sirens as I stepped from the car and walked hurriedly with suitcase in hand back to my room, which was located on the ground floor at the rear of the building. I still had the room key in my pocket and wasted no time in getting the door open and ducking inside, breathing a sigh of relief as I pushed it closed behind me . . . a temporary haven from the madness outside.

I took a few moments to collect myself, then tossed the suitcase onto the freshly made bed and removed the one change of clothing I had brought, a pair of dark blue polyester slacks and a yellow pullover shirt. I changed quickly, stuffed my suit into the crowded bag, then went over to the window for a quick look outside. No cause for alarm yet.

I walked over to the nightstand, took out the phone directory and looked up the number for Yellow Cab. Then I called and asked to have a taxi sent as soon as possible, giving a room number several doors down from the one I was actually in.

I was watching from the window five minutes later when the cab pulled into the driveway and cruised slowly towards the end of the building. I grabbed my suitcase, bounded through the door and met the driver before he was halfway down the line.

"Pier 66 Motel," I told him, climbing quickly into the back seat. He started the meter, took forever getting the cab turned around and moving in the right direction, then turned left onto Ocean Boulevard, heading for downtown Fort Lauderdale.

I slumped low in the corner and kept a wary eye on the passing scenery as the taxi wended its way through the thickening midday traffic, ignoring the bearded young driver's attempt at conversation. He finally gave up, found Elton John on the small portable radio hanging from the dash and began thumping the steering wheel in time to "Someone Save My Life Tonight," lost in a world that didn't include surly passengers.

Ten minutes later he dropped me off in front of the Pier 66, looking surprised at the five-dollar tip I gave him. "Hey . . . thanks, man!" he said, and drove away happy. When he was out of sight I walked to a nearby taxi stand, climbed into a Checker Cab and told the driver to take me to Miami International Airport, feeling somewhat better about the situation.

Within the hour I was boarding another Delta flight back to Atlanta, my cargo of jewels and gun stored in the belly of the Boeing 727. But as I fastened myself into the seat at the rear of the plane, a hollow spot beneath my breastbone told me that I had made an unpardonable mistake.

The plane touched down in Atlanta in the midst of a gigantic thunderstorm. I claimed my suitcase from the baggage area, ducked into a waiting cab outside and gave the driver my address.

I relaxed in the back seat during the long trip to Sandy Springs, reflecting on the events of the day and lulled by the steady *slap slap* of the windshield wipers. More thunderstorms came wanging and banging across the surrounding countryside, leaving behind steaming blacktop and metallic sunshine. One of the storms brought a roar of hail the size of garden peas and such a blackness that drivers had to turn on their lights. It beat against the metal roof of the cab with unrestrained fury, bounced high off the asphalt, battered at soggy tissues caught in roadside grasses and cracked a few dozen feet of neon tubing—so that later, when the signs came on, they would spell out agreeable nonsense.

I was caught up in an atmosphere of impending doom, and my thoughts were depressingly gloomy, which belied the fact that I had half a million dollars or so in gems tucked away in my suitcase. The fact was that I wanted to get rid of them as soon as possible—minus the few select pieces I would keep, that is. Just get them to wherever in L.A., collect my other ten grand and pretend the whole thing never happened. Then I could make my pitch to Susie and see how she reacted. But I just couldn't shake that feeling that somewhere along the line I had made a terrible, terrible mistake.

There was a note propped on the scarred coffee table in the living room when I got back to my apartment. It was from Mary Ann, complaining about how mean I was to her on the phone the night before. I couldn't help smiling as I read her tiny scrawl:

> *As you can see, your precious apartment is squeaky clean . . . which is better than the way I found it!!! Am going to Morvan with Julie to spend the weekend with her folks—will be back late Sun.—maybe! Hope you're in a better mood then. M.A.*

Crumpling the paper in my hand, I walked into the kitchen, tossed it into the empty grocery bag under the sink and made myself a drink. Then I went into the living room, sat down on the faded couch and opened the suitcase.

I examined the loot closely, mesmerized by the glitter of it all. I was no expert, but even a novice could see that this was top-quality merchandise. Joe Morgan had made a very good deal. With a heavy sigh I began selecting the pieces I would keep, limiting my choices to four rings—all within the three- to five-thousand-dollar range—and one eighteen-karat-gold bracelet in an intricate rope pattern with a price tag of seventeen hundred. Behold, Susie, I come bearing gifts. Now can I have you and my son back? Or will you think even worse of me for trying to buy you?

I removed everything from the suitcase, except the gun, put the three trays of jewelry back inside, then took the bag into the bedroom and shoved it under the bed. It would be safe there, I decided, unless Mary Ann got in the mood to go exploring. Thankfully, I wouldn't have to worry about that for the next couple of days, and after that I would be long gone, and she could throw all the parties she wanted.

I stripped off my clothes and padded into the bathroom for a much-needed shower, that sensation of alarm I had experienced earlier still tugging at my consciousness. But once again I shrugged it off. After all, Joe Morgan was covering for me . . . wasn't he?

A little later I decided to go out for pizza and beer, since I hadn't eaten all day, and was just walking back in the door when the phone rang. I set my purchases on the kitchen table and went to answer it, thinking it was Mary Ann.

"Ed?" The voice was unmistakably Joe Morgan's.

"What's up?" I asked, instantly wary. "You said two days."

"Nothing to worry about," he said. "But I think it would be a good idea if you left for L.A. as soon as possible. The FBI's been called in, and they're snooping around heavy."

"What are they doing in this?" I asked, surprised. "That's a local matter . . . the feds don't get involved with local matters."

"They do if it looks like interstate transportation is involved," he answered.

"And why would they think that?"

He hesitated before answering, then said, "Because they found the car. They traced it back to Avis and know it was rented to an Edward Johnson, of Memphis, Tennessee. Goddamn it! Did you have to pull that stunt in the alley? Throwing down on a delivery driver, for Christ's sake!"

"Where are you calling from?" I asked sharply.

"A phone booth . . . *I've* got a little sense!"

"Look," I said, holding my anger in check. "Just tell me where you want the stuff delivered and get off my back about what happened in the alley . . . it couldn't be helped."

"You know where the International Hotel is in L.A.?"

"Yeah, it's right across from the airport."

"Room eight-twelve," he said. "There'll be a guy waiting. You flying or driving?"

"Driving. I'm not taking any chances on my luggage ending up in Boston. Give me three days. And make sure he has the rest of the money."

"He'll have it." He waited until the noise from a passing truck faded in the background, then said, "I've covered you as best I can from here. I told them the guy who hit me was a few inches shorter than you, with brown eyes and a scar on the right neck. I don't know how far they can trace you, but that should help. When you leaving for L.A.?''

"Tonight. I should be there Monday.''

"Then we don't need to have any more conversations," he said. "We never heard of each other.''

"Why Joe," I chided. "I thought you were such a good man to know. Isn't that what you told me?''

"Not anymore—not since that shit in the alley. I got you pegged as some kind of maniac. Just get my stuff to L.A., collect your money and we're even—fair enough?''

"Whatever you say," I told him. "Anything else?''

He paused again. "Yeah, just one. Were there any bullets in that fuckin' cannon? Tell me the truth.''

I grinned into the mouthpiece. "All the way around, Joe," I lied. "What else would a maniac do?''

Still grinning, I hung up, the sound of his disgusted "Go to hell!'' fading in my ear.

My temporary humor vanished an hour later, however, when the FBI showed up.

There were two of them, just getting out of a tan Plymouth as I was coming back from the laundry room with an armload of socks and underwear. I paused in the act of unlocking my door and watched apprehensively as they walked toward me, casual and confident in their narrow suits. They stopped a few feet away and looked at me curiously, the short stocky one reaching into his jacket for I.D.

"Mr. Carlton?'' he asked, showing the dreaded badge.

"Yes?'' I answered, feeling a sudden coldness run through me.

"FBI. My name's Jim Hart, and this is agent David Modine. We'd like to have a few words with you, if you don't mind. Could we come in?''

"Sure," I said. What else could I say? You don't tell the FBI to get lost when they ask for *a few words* with you. They have alternate methods of accomplishing the same end . . . without being nearly as polite.

I let them inside, dropped my bundle of clothes in a heap by the door and motioned them to the sofa. They made themselves comfortable, waited until I was settled in a chair opposite them, then got straight to the point.

"Do you know a man by the name of William Jennings?" Hart asked.

So they had found the motel room, too! Now I realized what my biggest mistake had been. The phone calls to Julie and Mary Ann. Damn that delivery driver anyway! Because of him I had had to change everything, ending up right back where I had started—and leaving my home phone number for the FBI. Brilliant, Ed! But maybe I could bluff it through yet. It was obvious they weren't sure who they were talking to; otherwise I would be in handcuffs and on my way downtown. So they were still fishing. Maybe I could supply them with a little more bait.

"I know him slightly," I said, hedging. "What's all this about?"

Modine, a taller and younger version of his companion, took an envelope out of his inside jacket pocket and withdrew a folded sheet of white paper with perforated edges. He smoothed out the creases and handed it across to me. It was a computer drawing of a man's face.

"Is this him?" he asked.

I looked at the electronically prepared sketch carefully, trying to organize my thoughts. It was supposed to be me. But it certainly didn't look like me.

"It looks a little like him," I said, frowning in mock concentration. "But I can't be sure with this thing. Does he have brown eyes and a small scar on the right side of his neck?"

The two agents looked at each other, then back at me. "Yes, he does," Hart said. "You do know him, then?"

"Not all that well," I told him, my thoughts racing. "We've gone out together a few times . . . he used to date my girlfriend's roommate."

Hart produced a worn notebook and thumbed through the pages. "Would that be Mary Ann Dawson or Julie Cataris?" he asked.

"Julie Cataris," I answered, putting a puzzled expression on my face. "How did you know? And what is this all about anyway?"

He ignored my question and asked another of his own. "When was the last time you heard from Mr. Jennings?"

"He called last night," I answered, feeling uncomfortable as Modine calmly dissected me with his eyes. He was paying special attention to my neck. "He wanted to know if I'd seen Julie. He was a little upset because some guy answered the phone when he called her apartment . . . claimed it was her brother and that he was just using her place for the night."

Hart nodded slightly, as if that explained the other phone call. "And was it her brother?"

I shrugged. "I don't know. I think she has one, but I've never met him."

"Where is Miss Cataris?" Modine wanted to know.

"She and Mary Ann took off yesterday afternoon to spend a few days with her parents. Said they would be back sometime late Sunday. Mary Ann and I had a big fight yesterday morning, and I stormed out in a huff. When I got back a few hours later she was gone."

"Then how do you know where they went?" Hart asked.

"She left me a note. I've been on her case lately about not leaving dishes and things like that lying all over the place, and yesterday it came to a head. I got pissed, told her to clean the place up and went out for a few drinks. When I got back I found the note . . . like I said."

"Could we see it?" Modine asked.

"Sure."

I went into the kitchen, dug the wadded paper from the trash bag under the sink, brought it back and handed it to Modine. He looked at it briefly, nodded and passed the note to Hart.

"Would you guys mind telling me what this is all about?" I asked, returning to my chair. I decided it was about time to take the offensive—the way any ordinary innocent citizen would do.

Without asking permission, Hart took a stubby cigar from his breast pocket, lit it and blew a cloud of foul-smelling smoke at the ceiling. "Your friend Bill has been a pretty busy fella, Mr. Carlton. He hit a place in Fort Lauderdale yesterday for better than a half a mil in jewels—with a gun. We're talking big-time armed robbery here. By the way . . . you happen to know anybody named Edward Johnson?"

"No," I told him. "And Bill Jennings isn't a friend . . . I just happen to know him."

"Do you know where he lives?" Modine asked.

I shook my head. "All I know is that he dated Julie, and a couple of times Mary Ann and I went out with them. The only other thing I know is that he drives a maroon Dodge . . . a '74, I think it is."

Hart scribbled some more in his notebook, looked questioningly at Modine, who shrugged without comment, then turned his attention again to me. "I'd like to keep this note, if you don't mind."

"Help yourself."

They asked a few more questions, saw that I wasn't going to be of much more help, then prepared to leave. I walked with them to the door, and Hart handed me a card.

"If you hear from this guy Jennings again . . . or think of anything else that might have slipped your mind, give us a call. Meanwhile, I want you to keep this visit to yourself."

I assured him that I would cooperate in every way, escorted them outside and watched from the walk as they climbed into the Plymouth and drove away. I gave a little wave as they reached the end of the driveway and turned right onto Roswell Road, feeling like a condemned man who had just been given a last-minute reprieve.

As soon as they were out of sight I bolted back into the apartment, went to the bedroom and collected my other suitcase from the closet. I packed hurriedly, taking only what was necessary, leaving behind everything that wouldn't fit into the single piece of luggage. Then I retrieved the jewel-laden suitcase from under the bed, took both bags into the living room and carefully scrutinized the parking area from the window. When I was reasonably certain there were no FBI agents lurking about, I left the apartment for the last time.

I tossed everything into the back seat of the old Fairlane, got behind the wheel and spun gravel as I backed from the parking slot. Soon I was heading east on Roswell, following the path taken by the agents not ten minutes earlier. It was then I thought about the revolver in my suitcase. I had to get rid of it.

A few miles further I spotted the decaying chimney of an abandoned house rising above a stand of pine trees to my right. A weed-infested driveway gave access to the place, which was situated some fifty yards back from the road. I swung into the driveway and sent the Ford bouncing along the pitted surface until I broke into a wide clearing.

The house was old and dilapidated, the front yard now used as a place for citizens to deposit their refuse. I noticed that the trash was piled highest around a tilted sign that read POS-ITIVELY NO DUMPING! I stopped the car, fumbled around in the suitcase until I had the .357, then got out and began searching for a good-size rock. I found one, used it as a hammer to break the firing pin, then wrapped the revolver in an oilcloth and jammed it beneath a pile of trash. If anyone found it, they certainly wouldn't be killing anyone with it. For all I knew it was entirely possible that the weapon could be traced to me, and all I needed was to be wanted in con-nection with a homicide.

I got back in the car, turned around with difficulty and bounced my way back to Roswell Road. Soon I was on I-20, headed west.

I had to talk to Susie.

# CHAPTER 24

I PULLED INTO A SLEEPY HAMBURGER JOINT ON THE OUT-skirts of Shreveport and called Susie's mother. It was a little after five o'clock in the evening on a sticky day of misty sun and no wind. I had driven all the previous day and most of the night, pausing only long enough to pull into a roadside rest area shortly before dawn. A few hours later I was back on I-20, coaxing the ancient Ford along at a steady clip. This time I made certain that I stayed well within the posted speed limit. The old Fairlane wouldn't do much more than sixty anyway without gagging on the fuel.

I reached Irene in the middle of dinner. She was reserved in her conversation, telling me that she had to keep it short because of J.W. in the dining room. She hesitated when I asked for Susie, then finally told me that she was no longer living there. She was also reluctant to give me her new address but relented when I explained that it was urgent that I see her. It turned out to be an apartment complex on Youree Drive in South Shreveport, apartment 213. But please don't upset her, Irene asked, she's been through enough as it is.

I thanked her, promised there would be no ugly scenes, and hung up. I was aware of the risk I was taking in showing my face in Shreveport again, but I didn't care. In my mind was a fixed objective: I wanted my wife and son back—at any cost.

I had no difficulty locating the apartment complex. I cruised slowly through the rows of parked cars until I spotted Susie's Malibu. There was an empty slot next to it, and I pulled in and cut the engine. The tired Ford sputtered a few times, gave a grateful sigh and died.

Number 213 was a ground-floor unit located in the middle of the third building. A small red tricycle was lying on its side next to the walkway leading to the door. I recognized it as one I had bought for Derek only a few months before. I picked it up and set it gently on its wheels, feeling an emotional tug in my throat. Then I rang the doorbell and waited to see what kind of reception I would get.

Susie opened the door almost immediately. She stood framed in the entrance wearing white shorts and a red halter. There was a solemn expression on her face, and she didn't look surprised to see me at all.

"Hello, Ed," she said. There was no emotion in her voice.

"Hello, Susie. I guess Irene called you, huh?"

She nodded, nibbling at her lower lip the way she always did when undecided about something.

"Well, are you going to let me in, or not?" I asked.

She stepped aside, and I brushed past her into the living room. She closed the door, put on the night chain, then turned to face me, arms folded across her small breasts. We stood that way for several moments, staring at each other across six feet of beige carpet, neither knowing quite what to say.

I was trying to think of something witty that would break the ice when suddenly she let out a great sob and launched herself at me. I caught her on the second hop and held her as she squeezed my neck and uttered little choking sounds. Her tears were wet against my neck, but I didn't mind at all. Her greeting said more than words ever could and gave my hopes for the future a much-needed boost. Maybe there was still a chance after all.

Finally, she pulled away and led me to the familiar chocolate brown divan. We sat down, and Susie went about composing herself, producing a Kleenex from somewhere and blowing daintily into it.

"I worked so hard on my eyes, too," she said with a nervous little laugh. "Now they're a mess!"

"They look fine," I said, gazing at her fondly. "Everything about you looks fine."

She turned to face me. "I never should have left, Ed. I know that now. All I've been is miserable . . . and Derek runs around all the time going da-da, da-da—and then I get even more miserable."

"Then leave with me," I urged. "Tomorrow. Anyplace you want to go. I have enough money to give us a good start . . . and no more running."

She looked at me suspiciously. "Where did you get it, Ed? The money, I mean."

"Where's the Little Man?" I asked, countering her question. "Taking a nap?"

"Ed! Where did you get the money?"

I looked down at the carpet and sighed. "Fix some coffee, will you? I'll make a quick trip out to the car and then tell you all about it."


We sat at the kitchen table, me sipping the chicory-laced coffee she made so well and Susie staring in wide-eyed disbelief at the contents of the open suitcase in front of her. She had listened in stunned silence as I unfolded the Fort Lauderdale incident, occasionally dipping a tentative hand inside the bag to explore the glitter.

Derek was awake and tripping around the kitchen with joy, grinning hugely. He was determined to remain the center of attention and was busy showing me his toys. He would disappear into his room, return with a prized plaything and lay it at my feet. "Thee!" he would lisp, then promptly toddle off for another. Eventually he became bored with the whole thing and trudged off to the living room to see what he could get into there.

"Are these things really real?" Susie asked, at last finding her voice.

I reached into my jacket pocket and took out the rings and gold bracelet I had selected for her. "As real as these. And I guarantee they're *very* real. They're also yours."

She took them hesitantly, almost fearfully, her eyes drawn to the price tags I had so crassly failed to remove.

"Oh God, Ed! I don't know . . . ."

"What's to know?" I said encouragingly. "I mean, they

*were* given to me. Besides, I always heard that diamonds are a girl's best friend.''

I took her arm and gently pulled her to me. She sat in my lap and rested her cheek against my forehead, sighing.

''I really . . . I just don't know, Ed. Things like these are fantasies—they're nice to dream about but kind of scary when you actually have them. I wouldn't look right wearing thousands of dollars' worth of jewelry . . . or feel right.''

''Then keep one nice piece, and we'll sell the rest,'' I told her. I took a beautiful karat-and-a-half solitaire from her hand and held it up. ''How about this one? I've been picturing it on your finger ever since I first saw it.''

She took it away from me, placed it and the other pieces on the table. ''Just let me think about it, okay? About everything. Right now I don't want my mind cluttered with anything but you.''

There was a loud crash, and I leaped involuntarily from my chair, dumping Susie in an unceremonious heap on the kitchen floor. She let out a squeal and bounced to her feet, eyes wide and frightened.

Derek was standing on tiptoes, clutching the edge of the table and gazing solemnly at the overturned suitcase at his feet. A fortune in gems lay scattered on the linoleum floor like so much spilled popcorn. He had finally found out what mommy had been so interested in. He immediately sank to the floor and made a beeline for a large pendant with a canary diamond in the center.

''Vin bunk!'' he shouted with glee.

''I'll bin bunk you,'' Susie squalled, reaching for him. ''You know better!''

I laughed with relief and sat back down. ''Go easy on the Little Man, Susie. At least he's got good taste.''

It was shortly after dawn the following morning, as I lay in heavy slumber beside Susie in our familiar bed, when I was awakened by yet another loud noise. For an instant I thought Derek had gotten into the suitcase again—until I groggily realized I had placed it on top of the bedroom dresser, where Derek couldn't possibly reach.

The haze lifted, and I bounded from the bed and was halfway across the floor when the room suddenly blazed with light.

"Right there, asshole!" somebody shouted, just as half a dozen armed men charged into the bedroom. "One more step and you've bought it!"

I froze in mid-stride and turned to face the invaders—grim-faced men in suits and ties, their weapons poised and ready. Susie screamed and leaped from bed also, heading for the hallway that led to Derek's room. He was crying loudly, and the sound spurred her into mindless action as she charged through the milling men, nightgown billowing. Someone stepped in front of her, blocking her way.

"She's just going to our son," I said, still rooted to the spot. "Leave her alone, she's no danger to you."

"Let her go," the man closest to me ordered. "But watch her."

One of the men followed her from the room while the others converged on me. Hands grabbed me roughly by the arms, twisting them painfully up behind my shoulder blades. Handcuffs were clamped around my wrists and locked into position.

The obvious spokesman of the group—a youthful, nattily dressed man of average height and build—holstered his weapon and took out a small card from the breast pocket of his jacket. In a flat voice devoid of emotion, he began reading me my rights. The others started poking about the bedroom, looking under the bed, rummaging through the closet and dresser drawers. One of them lifted the lid of the suitcase and whistled.

"I want to see some identification," I said stiffly. I was standing nude in the middle of the floor, feeling like a lab specimen on display.

"Gladly," the spokesman said, producing a leather folder from his inside jacket pocket. He held it before my eyes. "Special Agent Thomas—FBI. And I don't need any identification to know who you are—Mr. Jones. A lot of people are anxious to talk to you. Especially about the contents of that suitcase."

I was finally allowed to dress—under the watchful eyes of three agents holding .38s at the ready. The FBI doesn't believe in taking unnecessary chances. Thomas carefully examined each piece of clothing personally before passing it to me. Then I was cuffed again and taken outside, one agent carrying the incriminating suitcase.

They led me to one of three unmarked cars that were triple-parked in the driveway. Other men materialized from the gray shadows surrounding the building and joined us . . . silent sentinels of doom hazily outlined in the early morning dawn.

From behind me I heard Susie call my name. I paused beside the open rear door of the first car and looked back. She stood framed in the doorway of her apartment, the lights from within outlining her slim figure through the transparent nightgown. She was holding Derek to her shoulder, comforting him, his arms wrapped tightly around her neck. Then hands were pushing me into the car, and the door closed and locked behind me.

I pressed my face to the window and stared out at my wife and son, vaguely aware of the sounds of slamming car doors and coughing engines that invaded the early-morning stillness. Then we were pulling away, and an obstructing building blocked Susie and Derek from view. But their afterimage remained: a vision of utter despair and anguish, of broken dreams and empty promises—and the terrible knowledge that our fairy tale would have no happy ending after all.

I was taken straight to the city jail in downtown Shreveport. We entered the five-story concrete building through an underground garage, where we were met by three uniformed deputies. They led us to a waiting elevator operated by a black trustee in gray coveralls. He stared at me, chewing on a paper match in silent insolence as the car ascended.

We got out on the third floor, where one of the deputies produced a large ring of keys and let us through two barred gates. He slammed them shut behind us and led the way along a narrow corridor to a booking office, where two other deputies were waiting. I was getting the impression that the entire jail had been waiting.

Agent Thomas turned me to the booking counter and re-

moved the handcuffs. I rubbed my wrists gratefully, trying to
restore lost circulation.

"This is Mr. Edward R. Jones . . . a.k.a. Hacksaw,"
Thomas said wryly, speaking to the waiting jailers. "He has
a bad habit of disappearing, so give him the best room in the
house, will you?"

"We'll take good care of him." The speaker was tall and
well built, with Sergeant's stripes on the shoulder of his uniform. A name tag above his breast pocket said his name was
Leon. He grinned at me without mirth and added, "We ain't
lost one yet."

The second deputy rolled a sheet of paper into an ancient
typewriter. "Charge?"

"Interstate transportation will do for now," Thomas answered. "I'm sure a bunch of others will be coming later,
though."

Leon addressed one of our escorts. "Take care of him,
Stoney."

Stoney was small and wiry and spoke with a deep Louisiana drawl. "Awright, ever'thing outta yer pockets an' on
the counter. Then turn 'round an' spread 'em. The belt goes
too."

I followed instructions and felt Stoney go through the familiar routine of patting me down. He had me kick off my
loafers and inspected them thoroughly, looking for false
heels, loose insoles. Thomas watched while he fed the
booking officer additional information. The other agents
were milling around with the jailers, swapping lies and telling war stories.

Stoney finished and told me to relax. He sorted through
the items I had placed on the counter and whistled as he
flipped through the roll of hundred-dollar bills. Thankfully, I
had left most of the ten thousand Joe Morgan had given me
with Susie.

Leon recorded everything on a property sheet, had me sign
it, then gave me the pink copy. Everything nice and legal and
proper. Then he told Stoney to take me to a small room
across the corridor to be fingerprinted and photographed.

Thomas stopped me as I was being led away. "You've had
a good run, Jones. But it's over now. Save yourself a lot of
grief and don't start any shit while you're here. These boys

aren't going to play games with you. And don't try spending any of that money just yet, 'cause we're putting a hold on it."

I gave him a level look but said nothing. Speech would have been difficult with a wadded hundred-dollar bill in my mouth. I had palmed it while Stoney was examining my shoes. It's amazing what that amount of money can buy inside jail. I gave him a bright, beaming smile to show just how worried I was about the whole thing, then turned and went with Stoney into the little room across the corridor. But I was worried, all right. Very worried indeed.

They didn't put me in a tank with other prisoners. I was taken instead to a secluded area one floor above and placed in what was called "Max Cell One," one of three such cells located on the west side of the building. The rest of the floor consisted of two tanks that served as trustee quarters and a small desk next to the desk leading to the Max Cell area. Two jailers worked the floor: one controlling the in-and-out movements of the twenty or so trustees, and one supervising the Max Cells.

They dressed me in a bright orange jumpsuit and gave me a bedroll of blanket, sheets and towel. The only other item I was permitted to have was a styrofoam cup. Toothbrush, toothpaste and toilet paper would be furnished on request, I was told.

I tossed my bedroll on the steel bunk and sat down. There was no mattress, and the metal was cold through the thin jumpsuit. I leaned my back against the steel wall and looked around. I wasn't encouraged by what I saw.

The back of the cell was enclosed by bars, beyond which was a narrow passageway with fluorescent light fixtures in the ceiling. There was also a closed-circuit TV camera angled downward to cover the interior of the cell, which contained a metal toilet/sink combination, a tiny shower stall and the steel bunk. The door was also solid steel, with an oblong tray slot in the middle. Escape looked hopeless.

I stood and walked to the back of the cell, glancing upward at the TV camera in the passageway ceiling. I could imagine some bored deputy in the control room downstairs sitting in front of a monitor, watching my every move. He would be smug and confident, secure in the knowledge that this bug in a mason jar wasn't going anywhere. But there had to be a way—I was convinced of it. All I had to do was find it.

I let myself slump to the floor, turned my back to the bars and looked over my shoulder at the camera again. As I had thought, I was in a blind spot that the angle of the camera couldn't cover. It was small consolation, but at least it was a start. I made use of the opportunity to remove the hundred-dollar bill from my mouth and transfer it to my sock. Then I stood up, smiled without humor at the unwinking eye of the camera and stretched out on the bunk to think.

"Cell one!"

The voice caught me off guard, since I had assumed that I was alone. It came from one of the other two cells.

"Hey . . . cell one!" the voice called again.

I rolled from the bunk and went to the bars. "I'm here," I said. "What's up?"

"Got a cigarette?"

"Can't help you, pal. They took everything."

I heard him clear his throat and spit. "You must be the guy they was talkin' about a couple hours ago. They had some trustees cleanin' the place up. You s'pose to be some kinda escape artist or somethin'?"

"Or something," I said, hooking my arms through the bars.

"How many joints you beat?"

I thought for a moment and smiled to myself. "Not enough, apparently. Where the hell you at anyway?"

"The end cell," he said. "The one in the middle's empty. You sure you ain't got no smokes?"

"I'm sure—but I'll see if I can get some."

We spent the next hour or so in aimless conversation, both grateful for the diversion. He was called Cochise, and he said he was in for murder. He was doing a life sentence in Angola for hacking a man to death with a meat cleaver six years earlier and was back in Shreveport for a new-trial hearing.

"Fuckin' funny farm, that's what that joint is!" he complained. "A bunch of fuckin' loonies runnin' 'round stickin' shivs in each other. Man's gotta carry a piece every minute just to stay even."

I thought this was a rather incongruous statement to be coming from someone who had chopped another man to death with a meat clever. But prisons are full of incongruity; all you have to do is enter one, and the absurdity of it all is apparent. The accent is to place one on temporary hold while the rest of the world goes by—teaching a minor offender how to make license plates, for instance, and calling it vocational training. Then, years later, the guy returns to society and begins looking for a place to apply his new skills—only to discover that the only place license plates are made is in prison. If that isn't absurdity, I'd like to know what is.

I heard the sound of jingling keys, and a moment later the door at the end of the passageway opened. Leon stepped inside, a sardonic smile on his face. He stood aside to let another man enter, and I felt a cautious dread as I recognized the figure.

George D'Atoris—Shreveport's chief of police.

He paused outside my cell, hands clasped behind his broad back, and gazed impassively at me through the bars. He stood that way for a moment, nodding his head in silent appraisal. The little cellblock had suddenly become as quiet as a cemetery.

D'Atoris finally broke the silence. "Well, Jones—I've been wondering when we'd run into each other again. Had a hunch it wouldn't be long . . . soon's I found out Susie was back. Figured you'd be sniffin' around. Well, you made a bad mistake. Everybody in town was on the lookout for your ass."

I turned away and went back to my bunk, determined to ignore him.

"Cat got your tongue?" he asked. "Seems to me you used to do quite a bit of talkin'. I ain't forgot that mornin' over at the Alamo Motel. I knew then that somethin' wasn't right about you. Just couldn't put my finger on it. And you even had the balls enough to use your real name!"

He stepped closer to the bars and made a sweeping motion with one hand. "So, what you think of our little old hotel? Kinna nice, ain't it. Even got its own private shower, and I tell you that's somethin', yessiree." He lowered his head and scratched at his nose. "Oh—one thing. You don't get no visits, so don't be expectin' Susie to pop up. You ain't gonna be here that long anyway.''

I kept my eyes glued to the opposite wall, trying to keep my cool but feeling the heat rising up the back of my neck. I didn't say anything.

D'Atoris stepped back, gave his pants a hitch and looked at me, amused. He said, ''I hear you got some kind of escape rep—got outta practically everything they put you in, they say. Well, it don't work that way here. I don't know what kind of places you been in, but this one's top of the line. You can't cut these bars with no hacksaw blade. And Leon here just pure loves it when somebody starts actin' like a hardcase. You'd best remember that.''

He stared at me a few moments, then turned on his heel and walked out. Leon straightened up from the wall he'd been leaning against, gave me a wink and followed. The noise of the door clanging shut echoed inside the small passageway.

Cochise laughed, spit again and said, ''I don't think that dude likes you, man. But he's right 'bout this fuckin' joint. Shit, Angola's easier to beat.''

''Means we can forget about those cigarettes,'' I said, and lay down on the bunk. I laced my hands behind my neck and stared at the ceiling, thinking D'Atoris might be right. I certainly couldn't cut tool-proof steel, even if I *could* get my hands on a hacksaw. But no jail or prison is escape-proof. There's always a way out; all you have to do is want it bad enough.

I wanted it very badly.

It was two days later when the idea first took shape. I had been prowling about the cell, half-listening to Cochise dribble on about his ill-fated life and all the shit he'd had to take. But I was thinking about the jail routine I'd been watching the last couple of days. There was a flaw in it that had definite possibilities.

Each of the past two mornings had been the same. I would wake up at 5:30 to the sound of the tray slot in my door being opened. A trustee would set a paper plate of the day's special in the opening, then move on to Cochise's cell and do the same. Another trustee would follow with a plastic spoon and a styrofoam cup of watered coffee. Then they would leave, and the Max-Cell deputy, a heavy-set guy about forty named Stroizer, would close and lock the outside door. Thirty minutes later Stroizer would return, accompanied by the same two trustees. He would unlock my door and stand outside while they swept and damp-mopped my floor, during which time I was expected to sit at the far end of my bunk, in full view of the TV camera. When the trustees were finished, they would collect my breakfast utensils and move on to Cochise's cell, where the procedure would be repeated. The Shreveport City Jail was as sanitary as it was secure.

I had questioned Cochise about the routine, and he assured me that it was the same each day.

"But if you're thinkin' 'bout jumpin' Stroizer, forget it," he warned. "Those trustees would be on you like stink on shit. And that fuckin' camera's watchin' you every second. All that fool in Control has to do is push one button . . . *just one fuckin' button!* . . . and it freezes every lock in the joint—not to mention the elevator."

But he wouldn't know what was happening if I could do something about that camera, I thought. I was willing to chance jumping Stroizer . . . trustees and all . . . if I could only checkmate the Control Room deputy for a couple of minutes.

I stopped my pacing, walked over to the bars and squatted down in the blind spot. In my pocket was a thick rubber band I had found stuck in the shower drain that morning. I pulled it out, examined it thoughtfully, then glanced up at the fluorescent light fixture in the passageway ceiling. With a little luck, it just might work.

I stood and turned to the bars. "Hey, Cochise!"

"What?"

"You still got those two plastic drinking glasses?" I asked.

"I got 'em . . . what about 'em?"

"How about sliding one down to me, will you? But keep to the bottom of the bars so the camera doesn't pick you up."

"Awright," he grumbled. "Wait'll I get off the shitter."

A few minutes later I heard the toilet flush, then shuffling sounds as he moved about.

"Here it comes," he said. "I don't know what you want

it for, but you didn't get it from me. If anybody asks, tell 'em one of the hacks gave it to you.''

The glass bounced once, rolled around and came to rest against the back wall opposite my cell. Cochise had wrapped it in toilet paper to cushion the sound. Keeping low against the bars, I slipped out of my jumpsuit and used it to fish in the glass. I now had one rubber band and a piece of clear, hard plastic to work with. Two inconsequential items that might very well spell the difference between success or failure.

I was very busy the rest of that day. Whoever was watching the monitor must have decided I had a thing about water. On four separate occasions I had stepped into the shower, towel draped around my waist, spending fifteen to twenty minutes inside the small enclosure each trip. But I wasn't showering. I was fashioning what I hoped would be my escape tools. I had broken the six-inch drinking glass and honed a section of the tough plastic against the cement shower floor until it resembled a crude knife. Then I had wrapped one end with a strip of bed sheet to serve as a handle.

The rubber band had also been broken, a small square of sheet now connecting the parted ends. It wasn't the best slingshot in the world, but hopefully it would serve the purpose. For ammunition I had pinched off eight small pieces from a bar of lye soap, rolled them between my fingers until they resembled amber-colored marbles, then left them to dry. If all went well, I would have an unexpected surprise waiting for Stroizer in the morning.

The following morning dawned heavy with thunderstorms. Outside the two screened windows opposite my cell the sky was still black, punctuated by occasional flashes of lightning. Booming thunderclaps rolled across the invisible sky and echoed within the small cellblock. It was a fitting backdrop for what was to soon take place.

I ate my breakfast hurriedly, now and then cutting my eyes upward to the camera. I was fully dressed, the makeshift slingshot and soap balls in my pocket. My dangerous-looking knife—which would have had difficulty passing through warm butter—was lying beneath the folded blanket at the bottom of my bunk.

I scraped up the last bite of powdered eggs, set the paper plate and plastic spoon inside the tray slot and stretched out on the bunk, closing my eyes against the glaring passageway light that never went out.

A trustee came by a few minutes later, removed the items from the tray slot and slammed the cover shut. From Cochise's cell came the sounds of heavy snoring. He always went back to sleep after breakfast, only to be awakened shortly afterward by the cleaning crew. So I listened to his snores and sweated the passing minutes, preparing myself for what was to come and hoping my mental clock was right. From this moment on, timing would be the most crucial factor.

Five minutes before I judged Stroizer and his trustees would return for the morning cleanup chores, I rose from the bunk, stretched, then sauntered over to the bars. I made a show of yawning, turned my back to the bars and sank slowly to the concrete floor.

Out of sight of the camera, I removed the rubber-band slingshot and chunks of lye soap from my pocket. I wrapped the rubber band around my thumb and forefinger, loaded a soap ball and took careful aim between the bars at the light fixture in the passageway ceiling. I held my breath and let fly.

The soap ball struck the outside of the metal casing with a dull *thunk* and bounced harmlessly away. I loaded another, adjusted my aim and fired again.

This time the missile was on target. It struck the middle of the three fluorescent tubes squarely, and a shower of falling debris rained noisily to the floor below. The remaining tubes flickered and dimmed, their harsh brightness now reduced to an ineffective glow. Whatever image the camera picked up now would be nothing more than an indistinct blur.

"What the fuck's goin' on?" Cochise yelled.

"That's what I like about you, Cochise," I replied evenly. "You really know how to mind your own business. I got tired of that damned spotlight shining in my eyes and put it out. That all right with you?"

"Well, how the fuck you do that? I want to take care of mine too."

"Hold up!" I hissed. "I hear keys!"

I heard the telltale jingle as a key was fitted into the lock of the corridor door, accompanied by faint snatches of conversation. The voices grew louder as the heavy door opened. Someone laughed.

Everything normal.

I moved quickly to the foot of my bunk, threw back the blanket and grabbed the "knife." A twilight haze had fallen over the interior of the cell, and the only sound was the muted hum coming from the wounded light fixture.

Stroizer was now unlocking the door to my cell. I flattened myself against the wall and waited, gripping my inadequate weapon in a slightly sweaty hand. I felt no emotion whatsoever, only a calm acceptance of what I had to do. Then the lock turned, and the heavy door swung outward.

I spun away from the wall and slammed my shoulder against the opening door, throwing every ounce of my two-hundred-pound frame into the steel barrier. It flew outward, ricocheted off a startled Stroizer, then clanged against the outside wall.

The impact spun the deputy around and sent him staggering. I bounded through the doorway, clamped my left arm around his thick neck and rested the point of the sharpened plastic against his throat.

"One wrong move, Stroizer," I said, "and things are going to get real messy."

Before he had time to think about it, I swung him around and sent him lurching through the open door of my cell. The keys were dangling from the lock. I slammed the door shut, shot the bolt and turned to face the two trustees.

They were in a state of semi-shock, pressing against the opposite wall of the corridor, staring wide-eyed at the crazy man confronting them with a knife in his hand. Their cleaning props were in a jumbled heap at their feet.

"First one makes a move in my direction gets opened up like a can of beans," I said. "Now get to the end of the corridor and stay there."

They nearly collided with each other in their haste to obey. They had little choice, since the corridor door was locked, and I had the keys.

The second key on the ring opened this barrier. I stepped

through quickly, relocked the door behind me and took stock of the situation. I knew that somewhere on the floor there was another jailer—the one responsible for overseeing the trustees—but he was nowhere in sight. Probably on the back side of the trustee tanks, I thought, which was a break for me.

I turned to the desk next to the door, grabbed the telephone cord and ripped it from the wall. Then I moved quickly to the two gates leading to the elevator. Another key opened these. I stepped through, pushed the call button and waited impatiently for the car to arrive.

The doors finally opened, revealing the same trustee operator as before perched on a stool in front of the control panel. His mouth opened in amazement as he noticed me standing poised with my wicked-looking knife. He cringed backward, hands reaching out instinctively.

"I'll take it from here," I told him, reaching through his outstretched hands and grabbing a fistful of coveralls. I heaved and sent him lunging through the elevator doors. He slipped, caught himself, then took off running through the open gates. I stepped inside, pushed the ground-floor button and watched the doors slide shut with agonizing slowness. The car lurched once, then started down.

It was my intention to run the elevator directly to the lobby floor and bolt through the front door, counting on surprise and my make-believe weapon to neutralize anyone who might be posted there.

But it wasn't to be that simple.

Unexpectedly, the doors opened on the third floor—the nerve center of the jail—where I was suddenly face-to-face with two deputies ready to get on. Apparently they were heading for the fourth floor to check on my defunct camera. They drew up short at the sight of me.

"Hey! . . . what the fuck!" the first one said, and immediately lunged for me.

I lashed out with my foot and caught him squarely in the chest, sending him stumbling backward into the second deputy. They both went down, arms and legs flailing. By the time they untangled and regained their feet, the elevator doors had closed, and I was again descending.

The G button on the control panel glowed yellow, and the

car doors began opening onto a spacious, carpeted lobby—just as a deafening clanging sound coming from somewhere inside the building shattered the early morning calm. At the same time I heard a strange clinking inside the elevator control panel.

They were freezing it!

I made a desperate leap from the car—a fraction of a second before the doors slammed together. I sprinted across the lobby, burst through the double glass doors and came out on Texas Street.

The morning was gray and hazy. The rain had stopped, leaving the streets and sidewalks shiny with wetness. I was filled with wonder at having not run into anyone in the lobby. Then I remembered that it was Sunday, and most of the ground-floor offices were closed, their occupants slumbering peacefully in warm, comfortable beds. I couldn't have picked a better day.

My thoughts were interrupted by screeching tires and angry sirens as a string of police cars peeled out from the underground garage on the far side of the building. I ran across Texas Street and ducked into an alley behind the State Office Building, which emptied into a wide field covered with tall grass and assorted debris. Some fifty yards ahead a steep embankment angled sharply upwards, at the top of which was a tall hurricane fence. On the other side was Interstate 20, and I could plainly hear the sounds of struggling semis and swiftly moving cars, their tires humming on the wet blacktop as they sped through the city. I certainly wouldn't find refuge there.

Now the air was heavy with the sounds of pursuit. First they would seal off the area, make it so tight a cockroach couldn't slip through. Then they would flood the area with men, try to flush me out. Helicopters would be brought in—maybe even dogs. I had no illusions about what lengths D'Atoris would go to in order to get me back. The only thing for me to do was find a hole and wait for the search to wane.

I turned right and sprinted through the high grass, heading for a cluster of junked automobiles a hundred yards away. Halfway there I changed my mind; they would be too conspicuous to offer effective concealment. Then where?

Off to my left, lying isolated in the middle of the field, was a small pile of rotting boards, perhaps three feet high. As a hiding place it didn't look very promising, but its very unlikeliness might work to my advantage.

I made a dash for it, fell to my stomach and worked my way under the soggy wood, wriggling and squirming like a berserk worm. It took some doing, but at last I was reasonably covered. I curled into a fetal position and pressed my face into the spongelike earth.

And there I waited.

It didn't take long. From everywhere they came, calling to each other and receiving instructions over their hand-held radios. Thudding footsteps shook the ground as they lumbered across the open field like stampeding cattle, drawing closer every second. There most be scores of them, I thought, and pressed closer to the ground.

Then they were all around me—so close I could hear the sharp intake of their labored breathing, the faint *squish* of shoes against drenched earth.

"Take a good look at them junk cars," I heard a voice call. "He can't be far."

Then they were past me, footsteps receding, heading for the jumbled mass of wrecked automobiles in the distance. Gradually I emptied my lungs in a prolonged sigh, giving silent thanks to whoever would hear. But I wasn't out of the woods yet. Not until dark would I be able to risk movement. So I burrowed a little deeper into the damp earth and resigned myself to the uncomfortable hours ahead.

I had been right about the helicopters. Within fifteen minutes there were two of them, the steady *thump thump thump* of their rotary blades beating the air as they circled slowly overhead. They would move off in different directions, sweeping close to the ground, then bank and come back again, crisscrossing the area in ever-increasing circles. But gradually the sounds grew fainter as they moved away, widening their search pattern, and then eventually died altogether.

Patiently, I continued to wait.

Sometime later, along about three in the afternoon, the cramps started to hit. I had maintained my fetal position for hours and the muscles in my back, shoulders and thighs were knotted with pain. I had heard no hostile sound since the helicopters had withdrawn, and my body was screaming for relief. I also had to urinate in the worst way—which was exactly how I was going to do it.

Slowly, I stretched my aching legs and hunched my shoulders. With my right hand I fumbled for the zipper at the front of my jumpsuit. The motion dislodged a few of the smaller pieces of wood and sent them sliding from the top of the pile. I located the zipper and pulled it up, moving my hips forward in order to free myself.

"You got ten seconds to come outta there, or I turn that stack of wood into kindlin', mister!"

I froze, feeling my heart jump. *Not now!* I thought . . . *not when I'm so close! Tell me that was just my imagination . . .*

"You got five seconds left!"

So much for imagination. It was all over . . . everything for nothing. And that unknown voice had sounded very serious indeed.

With the taste of defeat bitter in my mouth, I slowly rose, brushing aside the rotting wood like some giant jack-in-the-box. I raised my hands to shoulder level and stared icily at my captor.

He was a young patrolman, no more than twenty-three or twenty-four. He stood about ten feet away, crouched in the classic combat position taught by police academies everywhere, a .38 revolver centered on my chest.

"All right, cocksucker!" he said. "What did you do with the fuckin' keys?"

I smiled and said nothing, determined to gain one small victory from what had proved to be a disastrous day.

D'Atoris was enraged. He stood in the passageway behind the bar of Max Cell One and proceeded to explain in detail the heritage of my ancestors. Earlier, as I was being escorted through the underground garage by a horde of uniformed police, two federal marshals had to restrain him physically from attacking me. His courage had been heightened further by the fact that my hands had been securely fastened behind my back. Even now, the only thing preventing him from having Leon and his crew bounce me off the walls was the stern warning he had received from the same two marshals, who were directly responsible for me since I was a federal prisoner. But that warning didn't restrict his verbal abuse.

"I'll see you never hit the streets again—so help me God!" he was saying. "And if you do . . . I swear I'll come lookin' for you personally! Attack my jailers! Scare the shit outta my trustees? That officer shoulda blowed your fuckin' brains out, that's what he shoulda done!"

I was sitting on the bunk, breathing slowly because of the burning pain in my ribs. When my captor had put in a call for assistance, no less than two dozen police officers had converged on the scene. And they were extremely upset. They had pounced on me like a swarm of angry hornets, stinging me with fists and feet, demanding the whereabouts of Stroizer's keys. I had tossed them somewhere during my flight through the rain-drenched field, but I was damned if I would tell them that. But I had paid a high price in pain for my silence.

I looked at D'Atoris. "Why don't you save that concerned act for somebody who'll buy it," I said. "You don't give a damn one way or the other about your trustees—or jailers either, for that matter. All you care about is your damn king-size ego. That, and your precious escape-proof jail. Well, you can't make that claim anymore, can you, D'Atoris? You let your mouth overload your ass, and now it's eating your guts out. And if the truth were known, I'd be willing to bet that you belong behind these bars as much as anyone in here . . . maybe more."

I could see the fury building in him as I spoke. His jaws clenched, and his face grew battleship gray. He reached out and gripped the bars with both hands, struggling for words.

"You miserable sonofabitch," he whispered, "I'll see you in hell—you hear me? I'll see you in hell if it's the last thing I ever do!"

I turned my back to him, stretched out on the bunk and closed my eyes. "Go away, D'Atoris," I said. "You bore me."

D'Atoris went away, It was either that or kill me.

Three days later I was removed from the city jail by two deputy U.S. marshals. They strip searched me, placed a chain around my waist and secured my wrists to the chain with two sets of handcuffs. Then they took me downstairs and placed me inside a government van. A short while later we were on the road, heading for Florida. But I wasn't totally unprepared. Taped against the back of my right forearm were two hacksaw blades—compliments of a greedy trustee and an overlooked hundred-dollar bill.

# CHAPTER 25

THEY TOOK ME TO THE FEDERAL CORRECTIONS INSTITU-
tion in Tallahassee, Florida. We drove up a winding blacktop road set back from the highway and parked in front of
the Administration Building, a two-story structure of concrete and brick that looked like a bunker with windows. An
old-fashioned belfry jutted high above the roof, while directly across from the entrance, spiraling upward like some
ancient lighthouse, was a gun tower. Other towers, sta-
tioned about a hundred yards apart, surrounded the prison,
overlooking two fourteen-foot-high hurricane fences. Between the fences, stacked one atop the other, were thick
coils of razor wire, which could cut you to pieces if you got
caught up in it.

It was my first look at a federal prison.

I was unchained in Receiving & Discharge and given a
tattered set of green army fatigues and a thin pair of canvas
slippers. The two hacksaw blades taped to the back of my
forearm felt conspicuous as hell when I stripped and put on
my prison clothes, but nobody even came close to finding
them. Like they say, nothing is so well-concealed as that
which is most obvious.

Because of my escape history they decided to put me in
the isolation block. I would have to stay there until the marshals from the Southern District of Florida showed up to take
me the rest of the way to Fort Lauderdale—which I was told

would take about a week. Meanwhile, I was to be held totally incommunicado. It was highly illegal, but I was in no position to protest. The Constitution only applies when those charged with enforcing it so choose.

The isolation section was a separate wing which branched off the main corridor of the prison. Officially it was known as "I-Block." I was placed in the first cell, one of thirty such cells lining one side of the building.

It was a typical prison cellblock, the kind always depicted in TV and Hollywood movies. But no actor or camera can come close to projecting the decayed atmosphere of reality that lies within. The true essence of prison must be *felt*—not visualized. Only by experiencing the phenomenon firsthand can one gain a true appreciation for the word despair.

My new home was a five-by-nine-foot steel box with a barred front. Other than the standard metal toilet/sink combination attached to the back wall and one filthy two-inch mattress on the littered concrete floor, the cell was bare. The walls bore silent testimony to the passing of countless other occupants who had come and gone: "Cool Sam From Burminham' " (sic) . . . "Slick Willie" . . . "Gator Man," and others. Someone had drawn a huge nude on the wall above the toilet, her gaping vagina encompassing the flush button. The name "Windy" had been scratched into a crude heart next to her head, which was thrown back in wild abandon. The drawing was surprisingly good, full of detail and well proportioned. But the face wasn't right. It was dead and listless, totally devoid of emotion—as if resigned to the obscene posture of her body and the carnality it suggested. The drawing was a mirror that reflected the soul of the unknown artist; anatomically correct, but without feeling.

Up and down the length of the cellblock, caged men were calling to each other. Everyone seemed to be talking at once, shouting not so much to be understood as to just be heard. One prisoner two cells away was chanting like an Indian praying for rain. Someone screamed for him to shut the fuck up, which of course only served to make him chant the louder. Farther down the line, a match bomb—created by pulling the heads from several books of matches, compressing them into a ball, then flinging them with force against the concrete floor of the tier—went off with an explosion more deafening than a shotgun blast.

Just an average, normal day.

I unpeeled the strip of masking tape from the back of my forearm, removed the hacksaw blades and tucked them beneath a corner of the mattress. Then I turned my attention to the cell bars.

The steel was not top-grade and wouldn't be difficult to cut, I thought. By removing two bars from the bottom I would have enough room to squeeze through out onto the tier. From there I would have to saw through a steel cross-frame in one of the windows opposite the cells. Nearly all of the panes had been shattered by flying objects to allow more air into the cellblock, so I wouldn't have that problem to contend with. What concerned me more was what I would do once outside the cellblock itself.

In the afternoon, a guard showed up and began letting the men out one at a time to use the shower at the back of the tier. Each was allowed ten minutes, after which time the guard would return, lock the prisoner back in his cell and let another one out.

My turn came in the early evening, but I didn't use the time to shower. Instead, I walked slowly along the length of the cellblock gazing through the smashed windows. I could feel inquisitive eyes giving me the once-over as I passed along the row of cells, but I kept my attention focused outside. Prison etiquette prohibits even the most casual glance into a man's "house." There is an invisible curtain drawn at all times, and he resents anyone peeping inside.

Outside was a small fenced-in exercise yard, approximately twenty yards in back of the Administration Building, through which I had entered earlier. From my vantage point, I could just make out the top of the gun tower on the other side. I let my eyes wander along the twin hurricane fences branching out from each end of the building, the dying sun glinting from the coiled razor wire stacked between them. Somewhere in that maze would also be an alarm wire that would alert the tower guards to an intruder's presence. I was positive there would be alarms on the roof of the Administration Building as well. Getting out of the prison without being seen wasn't going to be easy.

# HACKSAW

I carefully checked the back side of the Administration Building, paying attention to the upper and lower windows. They were covered with bars, while those facing the front were not. But at the far end, on the ground-floor level, was one that didn't have bars. It was covered instead with an air-conditioning unit that was bolted to the casing.

I thought I might have found my way out.

Later that evening I coated the teeth of the hacksaw blades with soap and started on the bars. The guard's station was on the second tier, just outside the barred gate, and I had to be careful in case he made a surprise round. I wasn't too worried about the other prisoners hearing anything; they were making so much noise that nothing short of an explosion was likely to get their attention. Still, I took it slow and easy, so that after several hours of stop-and-go sawing, I was only halfway through the first bar. And I still had to make a second cut before it would be ready to come out.

It wasn't until after one in the morning that the men began to settle down for the night. I was finished with the first cut and halfway through the second by now, so I decided to call it a night and flopped down on the mattress, tired. I was drenched with sweat, and the fingers of my right hand were cramped and blistered. But I was pleased with my progress. If all went well, the fruits of my labors would be borne the following night.

I finished with the bars by late afternoon the next day. I filled in the tell tale cuts with loose dirt scraped from the floor, blew away the residue and sat back to examine my handiwork. Only a thin section now held the two bars in place—which would give way with the slightest pressure. I was convinced that it would require close inspection to reveal that they had been tampered with.

Satisfied that all was in readiness, I tucked the blades away and, using a roll of toilet paper for a pillow, stretched out on the mattress to think.

I tried to shut out the cacophonous noise within the cellblock and concentrated on Susie and Derek. What were they doing at this moment? Had Susie tried to see me? Did she even know where I was? And did she realize—as did I—that our bubble had finally burst? Tonight's outcome wouldn't alter that . . . *nothing* could alter that. I had been foolish to come to her in the first place, bearing false hopes, counterfeit dreams and a suitcase filled with fantasy. It would never have worked . . . and deep down inside I had probably known as much. Only I hadn't wanted to admit it. And what could I offer her and Derek anyway? Absolutely nothing. Sooner or later the past would catch up again and out would come the suitcases—if there was enough time. Then another city, another name, another lie—all the while erecting about them an impenetrable wall of abject hopelessness . . . a wall that would hold them captive in a prison far worse than any I had ever been in. Well, it was time that I commuted their sentence.

When there are things you don't want to think about, the mind slips down the nearest back alley and deals with the problem in its own way. Sometimes it just wanders along, whistling and kicking cans as a diversion. Or it may regress back to some absurd moment of the past and play around with that for a while. I suppose that when the mind stays in the alley long enough, there are those who will say you've gone mad.

I stayed in the alley for quite a while that night.

Three A.M. I knew that was the time because the bell in the belfry above the Administration Building had just told me.

I lay quietly on the thin mattress inside the now-darkened cell and stared at the ceiling, wishing desperately for a cigarette and listening to the night sounds of the sleeping cellblock.

It was quiet. So quiet I could almost hear the silence bouncing from the steel walls of my cell. An occasional cough or grunt would come from one of the other cells down the line, reverberating along the empty tier with a clarity in sharp contrast to the uproar that had prevailed earlier. But I was waiting for different sounds—the soft, shuffling footsteps and gentle clinking of keys that would signal the approach of the cellblock guard as he made his hourly rounds.

And then I heard him.

Footsteps slowly descended the iron stairway from the tier

above. Then the grating of a key in the gate, the squeak of protesting hinges as the guard entered the cellblock.

I closed my eyes and feigned sleep as he passed my cell, the glow from his flashlight flickering briefly across my eyelids. He walked the length of the cellblock, turned around and came back. The light danced across my eyes again. Then he was gone, relocking the gate behind him. Echoing footsteps as he ascended the stairway, the faint scrape of a chair on the upper tier.

Silence.

I moved to the front of the cell, knelt and grasped the two cut bars and pushed firmly. They came out with a small *snap!* Quickly, I retrieved my hacksaw blades and crawled through the opening.

Cautiously, I made my way to the last window at the back of the tier and went to work, taking one of the bars with me to use as a lever. At best, I had less than an hour to work my way completely out of the prison.

The cross-frames were tougher than I had expected; they were so flat that I was having trouble getting the hacksaw to bite. I also had to be careful of the noise, so I gritted my teeth and tried to time the strokes to coincide with the chorus of snores coming from the cell behind me.

I judged that twenty minutes had passed when the frame at last parted. I picked up the bar, placed one end between the severed frame and concrete sill and slowly applied pressure.

The section broke away with a metallic sound that echoed up and down the tier. I caught it before it fell to the floor, and froze, alert to any sound of danger. When it appeared that no one had heard, I carefully set the frame against the wall, climbed onto the sill and dropped to the ground outside.

I paused for a moment, huddled close to the wall, then sprinted across the small exercise yard and scrambled over the surrounding fence. The Administration Building loomed darkly in front of me, outlined by the evenly spaced vapor lights coming from the perimeter fences on either side.

Keeping low, I darted over the shadowed ground until I reached the window with the air conditioner. I examined it carefully, paying close attention to the support bolts holding the unit to the frame. There were only two—one on either side.

I immediately attacked them with one of the hacksaw blades. The air was heavy with humidity, and I soon became drenched with sweat, but eventually I cut through the bolts and freed the small unit from the frame.

I braced both hands against the back of the air conditioner and pushed with all my strength. Inch by inch it slid inward. I stopped for a moment, looked around, then braced myself again and gave a final heave. The unit teetered on the inside sill, hung there for a second, then fell with a dull thud onto the carpeted floor.

I wasted no time waiting to see if the small noise had been heard, but hoisted myself through the opening and tumbled into the room, banging my knee against the fallen air conditioner in the process. I got to my feet and peered cautiously out the window, breathing heavily and rubbing my sore knee. There was no sound and no sign of movement.

Relieved, I made my way to the other side of the spacious room. A faint glow filtered in through the far window, outlining a large desk with an engraved nameplate neatly aligned on the front edge. The letters were clearly visible in the dim lighting, and had the moment not been so serious I would have laughed.

I had broken into the office of Warden Z.S. Grzegorek.

I knelt beside the far window and peered through a crack in the drawn curtain. I looked up at the thick glass windows encircling the top of the gun tower and tried to spot the guard inside, but the interior was pitch dark. For all I knew, he could be looking directly at my window that very moment. Or he could be asleep.

I wouldn't know until I went through that window.

And then the bell in the belfry began to strike four, and I had no more time to think about it.

I released the latches at the top of the window, threw it open and literally dived through the opening onto the grassy lawn five feet below. I landed on my shoulder, rolled to my hands and knees and jumped to my feet.

Then I ran.

I ran like all the demons of hell were at my heels, jabbing at my buttocks with flaming pitchforks. In a matter of seconds I had reached the outer darkness on the back side of the gun tower in an all-out gallop for the sheltering woods across the highway.

A shot rang out from behind me. Then another. Then an entire fusilade. The night became alive with lead insects in search of a fleeing body. Even in the covering darkness, some came uncomfortably close.

I reached the highway, bounded across without so much as a glance in either direction and went crashing into the underbrush on the other side. Gratefully, I felt the forest close around me.

The prison would be in an uproar now. Soon the woods would be crawling with hunters, and with them would be my greatest fear—bloodhounds. Somehow I had to throw them off, and the only way to do that now was to reach a populated suburb, where my scent would mingle with that of other humans.

I continued my plunge through the dense undergrowth, struggling through vines and thornbushes, brushing aside clutching tree branches. I winced as a sharp pain went through my right ankle, but I paid it no mind. Cuts and scratches are a small price to pay for freedom—regardless of how fleeting.

A short while later I came upon a small clearing and paused to catch my breath. I was feeling lightheaded and nauseous, and a burning sensation was building in the area of my right ankle. Something was wrong.

I sat down with my back against a large cypress tree and raised my pant leg. A touch of panic hit me as I gingerly fingered the two tiny red punctures just above the outside anklebone. The area was puffy and streaked with pinkish red lines that ran halfway to my knee.

Snakebite! And definitely poisonous.

The canvas slippers had been torn to shreds, so I ripped them off and tossed them aside. I leaned my head against the smooth bark of the cypress and tried to slow my racing heartbeat, which was speeding the venom through my body. The dizziness and nausea persisted, and I craved water. *If I can just rest for a few minutes . . . If I could just have a nice cold drink of—something! Anything! Gonna waltz right out of these fucking woods . . . yessiree! Soon's I rest a few minutes.*

*Ain't no goddamned coral snake—is it? If it ain't a coral snake I'm all right . . . but I don't want it to be no coral snake. But what the fuck's the difference? Nothing left anyway. Susie . . . Derek . . . Dee Dee . . . Mom—all out of reach. Why not just go to sleep and forget about all this shit? . . . that's one way of beating them. It's hot! You hot, Tugboat? What the hell am I thinking about? Fuck it . . . just close your eyes and rest . . .*

Something wet and rough was rubbing my face. I wanted to brush whatever it was away, but the effort seemed too great, so I peeked through my eyelids to see what it was.

It was a bloodhound. Licking my face and wagging his tail as if disappointed that the game was over. *Hi there, boy. Be a good doggie and go 'way, will you?*

I closed my eyes again and drifted back into the world of gray mist. Voices were speaking from far, far away. Hands lifted my body . . . turning me . . . drawing my arms behind my back. Metal bands circled my wrists, feeling cold against my feverish skin. I couldn't have cared less.

Then consciousness faded altogether.

I awoke in the prison infirmary, an IV bottle feeding fluid into my left arm. I blinked away the remaining mist, raised my head and looked down at my feet protruding from beneath the sheet. My right ankle was swathed in bandages and elevated by a small green cushion. The left was secured to the bed with a thick chain and padlock.

Feeling a sickness in the pit of my stomach that had nothing to do with snake venom, I let my head fall back onto the pillow and surveyed the room—which was only slightly larger than a standard cell—with disinterest. There was the inevitable toilet/sink combo on the wall to my right, while above my head was a barred window through which poured bright sunshine. It reflected harshly from the surface of a metal nightstand to the left of the bed. The locked door across from me was made of heavy wood instead of steel, with a small viewing window at eye level.

Welcome home, Ed.

I spent the next three days in a state of lethargy, a vacant creature who stared at blank walls and said nothing. I drank little and ate less, and stirred from bed only long enough to carry out normal bodily functions, which the heavy chain around my leg barely permitted. A few times each day a white-coated medical assistant came in and took my vitals. He voiced approval at my condition and, on the second day, removed the IV and ankle dressing. I bore it all with stoic indifference, refusing to respond to any questions or attempts at conversation. Day and night melded as one, and I spent the time in a world of daydreams and remembrances. They flicked across my mind in endless succession, filled with sound, color and rushing event. A point in time where the lost was recovered, the forgotten recalled, and where tomorrow was as meaningless as yesterday's shadow.

On the morning of the fourth day I had a visitor. He walked in looking very suave in highly glossed tan boots, fawn-colored slacks and white cardigan sweater, full of swagger and self-assurance. A tiny set of gold handcuffs dangled from the left side of the sweater.

He signaled the guard to close the door behind him, then walked over to the bed and stood looking down at me. "I'm Warden Grzegorek. How you feeling?"

I turned my head away and said nothing.

"If you don't want to talk, it's fine with me," he said. "Actually, I just wanted to get a look at you—see who this Houdini was everybody's talking about. What they call you? . . . Hacksaw? Guess I can see why."

"Now that you've had your look, Warden, why don't you just leave me alone?" I said, still looking away.

"Well, so you *can* talk," he said. "Doctor Wingfield was thinking maybe some of that snake juice had paralyzed your vocal cords."

He moved to the foot of the bed, picked up a length of the chain and casually fingered the lengths. "You're a lucky man, Jones. That bite came within a smidgen of hitting a vein. If it had, you wouldn't be here right now. If you're interested, Doc thinks it was a copperhead . . . or maybe a cotton-mouth."

He dropped the chain and walked slowly around the bed. I turned my head the other way.

He gave a short laugh and said, "You're really something, you know that? One by one, you're putting the nails in your own coffin. That little escapade in Shreveport is going to cost you five years. And this latest stunt? That's another five. When are you going to learn that you can't win? We have to discourage this kind of thing."

I swung my head towards him angrily. "And you think that's the way to do it? That's all you people know, isn't it? *Time!* Years . . . decades . . . centuries! That's the great cure-all, isn't it? You dump a man in one of these cesspools, let him rot for years and put him through every indignity you can think of, until eventually he feels about as useful as a piece of whale shit. If he's a good boy and doesn't get in your hair, and if he agrees with your idea of what's right and wrong, then you turn him out and tell people he's rehabilitated. But if he doesn't go along with the program, then you pile on more shit . . . give him more time and tell everybody he's incorrigible. Meanwhile, he sits and festers—the hate and bitterness growing all the time. He's too concerned with his own survival in this shark tank you've put him in to even consider what he's going to do once he gets out . . . *if* he gets out. But he will—if he's lucky enough to survive and keep his sanity. And then you have a different kind of monster on your hands, don't you? He's a misfit. Nobody wants him living next door, dating their daughters or working in their companies—because the fact of the matter is that society has no use for prison survivors. Next thing you know he's gone back to the basic principle of 'survival of the fittest' that you people teach so well, and everybody wonders why. And *that*, Warden, is the real crime . . . one that few people will ever understand—certainly not you."

He folded his arms and looked at me in silence for a moment before replying. "You really believe all that, don't you?"

"You're goddamned right I believe it!" I answered hotly. "I've lived it . . . I've seen it! That chain you have around my leg? That's an unnecessary indignity—and you know it. What am I, an animal? Where am I going? You've got a guard right out there in that hallway who looks in here every ten or fifteen minutes. That's just one way you people get your jollies—chaining a man up like a wolf. But you know what a wolf does when he gets caught in a steel leg trap? He gnaws the leg off and limps away . . . and becomes meaner than ever. Is that what you want?"

"The chain is necessary, Jones. You have this nasty little habit of not staying put."

"That's because a cage is an unnatural environment, Warden. You can't put man or animal in one and expect him to act natural. And it's only instinct to want out."

He gave an impatient nod and looked at his watch. "Well, this has all been very stimulating, but it isn't getting us anywhere."

"I never thought it would."

"Anyway, there's another reason I came up. There are a couple of FBI agents downstairs who would like to see you. Want to talk to them?"

"What about?"

"Something about some missing jewelry, that's all I know."

I thought about it for a minute, wondering what it was all about. What missing jewelry? What kind of game were they playing now? My curiosity got the best of me.

"Why not?" I told him. "Might as well break up the monotony some way."

"Good enough," he said. "They're in my office now. I'll have them brought up."

He went to the door and pecked on the viewing window. A guard quickly appeared and opened up for him. He turned and looked back at me.

"I don't know when you'll be leaving," he said. "But you're staying right where you are until you do—which is better than the isolation block. Just don't go gnawing your leg off."

"Anything you say, Warden."

Then he was gone, and I was left to wait for the FBI. But I was grateful for his visit, because it *had* been stimulating. Perhaps he was right . . . maybe I couldn't win. But his conquering attitude had at least brought me out of the back alley.

And what made him think it was going to be that easy anyway?

The FBI came in about ten minutes later. Two Ivy League types in soft-colored suits carrying leather-bound file folders under their arms. They greeted me with hail-fellow-well-met smiles, clucked in sympathy over my misfortune with the evil snake and said they certainly hoped I was feeling better now. I told them that I was feeling fine, but would they please get on with the business at hand and tell me what this was all about. Whenever the FBI opens with smiles and condolences, it's a lead-pipe cinch they either want something, or they're about to shoot you. Since I knew they weren't armed, I figured it had to be the former.

They stood at parade rest at the foot of the bed and flipped through their notes. The younger agent, who was about my age, took out two neatly typed documents and handed them to me.

"Mr. Jones, this is a copy of the list furnished to us by the owner of the Galt Ocean Mile Galleries. That's the establishment you're alleged to have, uh, robbed. As you can see, it details the individual items the owner says were taken at that time."

I looked the list over carefully, noting with interest the wholesale and retail prices beside each item. There were a hundred thirty-eight pieces in all, and by a rough mathematical guesstimate, I judged the total retail value to be well over one million dollars. One particular piece that caught my eye was a ten-karat diamond solitaire with a retail price tag of sixty thousand dollars.

"Is this for real?" I asked, handing the papers back.

The agent tucked them back in his folder. "That's the information we received from the owner, yes sir."

"Are you saying that isn't an accurate inventory?" The second man asked, who was older than his companion by at least ten years.

"That's exactly what I'm saying. Somebody's padded the hell out of it."

The two agents looked at each other knowingly, then turned their attention back to me. Again, it was the older man who spoke.

"Mr. Jones, let's just say for the sake of argument that that list is correct . . ."

"I just told you—it's *not* correct," I interrupted.

"Just for the sake of argument," he continued, "that's all. I'm not asking you to admit anything. But if it *is* correct— then that means there are still roughly seventy pieces of jewelry missing, right?"

"According to the list—about that," I agreed.

"Because I believe you had a total of sixty-eight pieces in your possession at the time of your arrest. Now, *Assuming* that those seventy pieces are still missing . . . and *assuming* the person who took them could tell us where they were—or take us to where they were—then that person could do himself a lot of good. We're talking nearly half a million in jewels here, Mr. Jones. Giving that up could buy a whole lot of goodwill in court."

I glared at him. "Look, I don't know how else to put this . . ."

I broke off in mid-sentence and looked away, trying to cover the sudden excitement that hit me. *Take* them there? The picture of a dilapidated house in the middle of a litter-filled yard came to mind—a .357 magnum wrapped in an orange oilcloth tucked in among the debris. An empty .357 magnum with a broken firing pin.

But they wouldn't know that.

"Well, what do you think, Ed?" the younger agent said. "You mind if we call you Ed?"

I shook my head, my thoughts two hundred forty miles away.

"So, does that sound like a good deal to you, Ed?"

I looked at each in turn, sighed and said, "Yeah . . . it sounds like a good deal. What the hell, it isn't doing me any good anyway. But it was dark when I stashed the stuff . . . I don't think I could give you good enough directions."

"I'm sure you know how to get to it," the older one said.

"Oh, I know how to get to it," I told him. "I just don't know if I feel up to making the trip or not. I still feel pretty queasy."

The young agent smiled reassuringly. "I'm sure you'll be fine in a couple of days, Ed. We'll get things squared away with the doc first."

He sat on the edge of the bed and took out pen and notebook. "Now, let's see if we can pin the spot down. What city is it in?"

"Atlanta," I said, "about a mile from my apartment, off of Roswell Road. There's some little turnoff on the right that leads to an open clearing, but that's about all I can tell you. Like I said, it was dark, and I was in kind of a hurry, and there are dozens of little turnoffs on the right.''

"But you would recognize which one if you saw it?"

"I'd recognize it. But let's get something understood before we go off on this treasure hunt. I want three things from you."

"Such as?" the older agent asked.

"Number one—I want a guarantee from you right here and now that any judge I go in front of will know I was a good boy and gave the stuff back voluntarily. Agreed?"

They nodded in unison.

"Number two—I don't want you people carting me off in public wearing prison rags."

"We'll see that you get a suit from R&D," the young agent said. "What else?"

"Number three—I want some cigarettes. I'm having nicotine fits."

"What kind?"

"Marlboros. And if you could see your way clear to maybe sneak in a fifth of Chivas . . .''

"Let's not go overboard," the older man interrupted. "All right, Mr. Jones—you've got a deal. We'll get this on the wire to Atlanta and set things up on that end. Don't jack us around on this, now. Just work with us, and we'll work with you."

He motioned to his partner, who stood and put away the notebook and pen.

"You'll be hearing from us in two or three days. Meanwhile, just relax and get your strength back. Oh . . . and don't think about trying any hanky-panky, okay? We don't want anybody hurt."

"Neither do I," I told him. "Neither do I."

Within thirty minutes after they had gone, the guard came in and handed me a carton of Marlboros. I lit my first cigarette in days, inhaled deeply and closed my eyes in thought. Would I really be able to pull this off? These boys didn't play games. I had no illusions about what would happen if the slightest thing went wrong. They would kill me on the spot. But the alternative was even worse, the very real probability that I would spend the rest of my life in prison. Too many jurisdictions wanted my scalp, and there just wasn't that much of me left to go around. So I *had* to try. Would I be able to get to my inoperable gun without getting shot? And if so, would they really let me get away with it? It didn't seem likely.

But I *was* able to get to it.

And they *did* let me get away with it.

# CHAPTER 26

*Six Flags, Georgia*
*September 18, 1975, 1:35* A.M.

**I** BOLTED UPRIGHT IN BED AND LOOKED AROUND AT THE
unfamiliar motel room, momentarily confused. It took several seconds before I caught up with myself and remembered
where I was . . . and what had happened. The only sound
was that of the steady hum coming from the air conditioner
under the window, the artificial breeze causing the drawn
curtains to ripple and sway in a gentle motion. There was a
chill in the room, but my forehead was damp with cooling
perspiration, and the pillow was soaked. Chasing memories
is an easy thing, but reliving nightmares can be draining.

I got up and turned off the air conditioner, then went to
the dresser and poured the remainder of the Scotch. My mouth
was parched, and the fiery liquid tasted terrible without ice.
I recalled seeing a machine in the little alcove just down the
hall, so I scooped up the plastic bucket from the little tray on
the end of the dresser and headed barefoot for the door.

The corridor was deserted as I walked the short distance
to the alcove. I filled the bucket with tiny cubes, bought a
bag of Fritos from an adjacent vending machine and hurried
back to my room. As I reached it, the door across the hall
opened, and a young couple stepped out. They glanced at me

suspiciously, and I smiled to show that I was harmless. They nodded stiffly and went on their way.

Back inside, I iced down my drink, took it over to the bed and lay down on the rumpled covers. I lit a cigarette and thought about my next move.

First thing was to get as far away from Atlanta as possible. Houston would be the place to go; once there I could count on Ted Wright, my landscaping contractor at Cambridge Arms, for whatever initial help I would need. The FBI didn't know about my connection with him. I still had nearly thirty dollars of Hart's money in my pocket—enough to keep me eating until I got there, if I could find transportation.

My best bet would be to get to the nearest truck stop, strike up a conversation with some of the drivers and hitch a ride west. After that I would just have to do the same as always, play it by ear. Drop in on the local library, dig up ancient obituaries, reincarnate yet another ghost. This shit was getting old—and I was tired. Seventeen years. Jesus! Maybe I'd go to New Zealand or somewhere, herd kangaroos or whatever they had over there. Get the hell away from here, they know me too good. What was it Napoleon said? Oh yeah . . . never fight with the same enemy too often or you will teach him your way of doing battle. Was that before or after Waterloo?

I thought about Mom. What had the years done to her? Why hadn't I been able to contact her? Had time, circumstance and lost contact dulled her memory of the son she *once* had? Or had she become the biggest victim of all in this charade of madness I had started so many years ago? In my heart, I knew the latter to be true. And it hurt.

I turned my thoughts to Susie and Derek. Should I try to contact them? I didn't think so. I was through dangling carrots and promises. Well, maybe one quick phone call. Just long enough to sever the cord and make yet another inadequate apology—which was fast becoming a desperate, incurable habit.

I shook off the melancholy, gulped the rest of my Scotch and concentrated on sleep. Tomorrow would be a long day, and I needed rest. I considered getting up and turning off the table lamp in the corner, but decided it wasn't worth the effort. So I closed my eyes and soon drifted into an exhausted slumber so deep that even my troubled thoughts couldn't follow.

Something cold was pressing into my neck. Reflexively, I attempted to wriggle away from it, but the cold weight persisted, so I struggled upward through the dark void of sleep to see what was bothering me.

"One move . . . one blink . . . and it's all over, dude," a voice said.

I came awake in a hurry, eyes flying open. But I didn't blink. I didn't want to risk making the very large figure standing over the bed angry. He wore a black flak vest over his suit and held a short-barreled riot gun pressed just below my left jaw. It didn't look like it would take much for him to pull the trigger.

I cut my eyes to the door, which was standing wide open. Somebody had snipped through the nightchain with a pair of bolt cutters or something—Jesus, I hadn't even heard them—and the room was crowded with serious-looking men holding guns.

Jim Hart was there, standing at the foot of the bed with a satisfied look. I almost didn't recognize him without the cigar in his mouth. He holstered his revolver, walked around the bed and told me to roll over and put my hands behind my back.

When the handcuffs were in place he grabbed me roughly by the shoulders and twisted me onto my back again. Other guys were systematically searching the room, rummaging through drawers, checking under the bed and nightstands. The big guy in the flak vest was standing six feet away, riot gun held at the ready.

Hart sat on the edge of the bed and waved a pudgy finger in my face.

"I got one question to ask you, mister," he said deliberately. *"Who put that fucking gun there?"*

I lay there quietly for a moment, staring at the quivering finger a few inches from my nose, then looked at him.

"Tell you what," I said. "I'll tell you who put the gun there if you tell me how you knew I was here."

"Gladly!" he said. "Did you happen to watch yourself on

the twelve-thirty News Wrap-Up this morning? And I just know you did.''

I nodded.

''And do you happen to recall running into a couple of people out in the hallway a little later?''

I turned my head and sighed. ''So that was it.''

''Got the picture now? They watched News Wrap-Up, too. Now, tell me about the gun.''

The others had finished their search and were standing in a semicircle around the bed. There were eight of them altogether, the only other one I recognized being Modine, who stood glaring at me over Hart's shoulder.

''Funny thing about that gun,'' I said to no one in particular. ''I just happened to look down, and there it was. Of course, I could see right away that it wasn't loaded . . . not to mention the fact that the firing pin was broken. I guess that's why somebody threw it away. But I said to myself, 'What the hell, only somebody who knows guns will notice, so I can probably get away' . . .''

''Get him outta here!'' Hart snapped, rising from the bed and striding angrily to the door.

Eager hands yanked me to my feet and hustled me from the room. I was marched down the hallway and out the side exit, where half a dozen plain cars were blocking the driveway. A small crowd of onlookers had gathered outside, craning their necks to see who was being led from the building.

I was unceremoniously shoved into the back of the second car, sandwiched between Hart and the agent wearing the flak vest. I closed my eyes and rested my head against the seat back as we pulled away, feeling vaguely detached from it all. The reality of the situation had not yet fully penetrated my fogged brain; maybe this was just another nightmare that I would awaken from at any moment—sweaty and shaken, but still safe. But as the car turned onto the on-ramp of I-20 and gradually picked up speed, I opened my eyes and looked first at the granite block of humanity sitting to my right, then at the grim features of Jim Hart on my left—who felt my gaze and returned the look. A slow grin crossed his face; more of a grimace, really, for Jim Hart did not have a face made for grinning. Then he turned away, and I closed my eyes again, and that's when the fog started lifting.

I was taken to the Fulton County Jail in Atlanta. The normal booking procedure was dispensed with, and I was led through a maze of winding corridors and barred gates to a solitary-confinement cell in the back of the jail, accompanied by Hart and four deputies. Another jailer was waiting for us, holding the cell door open. Hart ushered me inside and had me stand facing the wall while he removed the handcuffs. Then he stepped out, and the jailer slammed and locked the door, giving it a forceful shake to show it was secured.

Three of my escorts left. The other two stood a respectful distance away and watched as Hart unwrapped a stubby cigar and peered at me through the bars.

"I can't make up my mind about you, Jones," he said. "You're either the gutsiest sonofabitch I've ever seen, or the dumbest."

I sat down on the bunk and leaned back against the steel wall. It was cold and slightly damp. "Well, you know what they say, Hart," I told him, displaying a bravado I didn't feel. "A scared man can't gamble, and a jealous man can't work. Anyway, what's the difference now?"

"There never was any jewelry out there . . . was there?" he asked. "I had it pegged right from the start."

"It seemed like a good idea at the time."

He stuck the cigar in his mouth, rolled it around until it was good and wet and stuck his hands in his back pockets. "It did, huh? You'll find out how good of an idea it was before it's all over."

He looked at the two deputies. "I want somebody sitting in front of his cell twenty-four hours a day 'til he leaves here."

"Way ahead of you, Mr. Hart," the one with the cell keys said. He pointed to a straight-back chair against the wall directly across from my cell. "We already got the word."

Hart nodded and turned back to me. "And that's how it's gonna be from now on . . . at least 'til you get to the joint. Eyes watching every move you make twenty-four hours a day. What do you think of that, Hacksaw?"

I stared at the opposite wall and said nothing.

He nodded to the other deputy and turned to leave, but I stopped him.

"Hart?"

He walked back to the bars. "Yeah?"

"What happens now?" I asked softly. "Where do we go from here?"

He removed the wet cigar and studied the tip. "To Fort Lauderdale, first . . . to stand trial for armed robbery. Then I imagine they'll shoot you over to Tallahassee on an escape charge—then to Shreveport for that one back there. Then back here to answer to that shit you pulled the other day—and that's going to be a biggie. You're looking at a lot of time, my man."

"And where will I end up?"

"What prison?" He laughed. "The big one right here in Atlanta . . . the Big A. You like busting out of places so bad, let's see how you do there. It's as tough to crack as Leavenworth."

"Then I won't be going to Virginia?" I asked.

"Virginia? That's the least of your worries. They're going to have to stand in line—for quite a while."

I looked at him with a hint of a smile on my face, imagining how unhappy Captain Aaron Goldie up in Richmond would be. "Thanks, Hart."

"Oh, you're quite welcome," he said sarcastically, and walked away shaking his head.

The next few weeks went pretty well the way Hart had predicted. Three days after my capture, at 4:30 in the morning, I was taken from the Fulton County Jail in the company of four deputy U.S. marshals, put on a chartered twin-engine Cessna at Hartsfield Airport and flown to Fort Lauderdale. They locked me in a tiny cell in the Broward County Jail, where I was kept under visual guard around the clock.

Then they began meting out the years.

First I was marched into federal court, where U.S. District Judge Norman Rottger handed me eight years for interstate transportation of stolen goods.

Next came the State of Florida, which brought me to trial for stealing the goods. It lasted five days and was a virtual circus. Each day I was brought into the courtroom in chains and leg irons, surrounded by half a dozen stony-faced bailiffs who sat in a semicircle behind me during the entire proceedings. Joe Morgan was the star witness. He took the stand and described to a horrified jury how I had held a cocked pistol to his head and threatened him with death, and then walked away with over a million dollars of his jewelry—half of which, he said, had never been recovered. When the prosecuting attorney asked if he could point out the culprit, he aimed a trembling finger in my direction, looked me dead in the eye and said, "That's him! That's the man!" and never flinched once. When all the testimony had been given, the jury deliberated exactly thirty minutes before reaching a verdict: guilty as charged. The presiding judge immediately sentenced me to fifty-five years in state prison, banged his gavel and said, "Take him away."

Then it was on to Tallahassee, once again by chartered plane and in the custody of four deputy marshals. I was whisked into federal court, pleaded guilty to one charge of escape and had five more years tacked on. I was back on board the Cessna before the engines had cooled, and we were soon airborne for Louisiana.

I was in and out of Shreveport so fast that I didn't have time to even think about calling Susie—had I been allowed to, which I wouldn't have been. Another federal court, another guilty plea for escaping from George D'Atoris' jail, another five years.

Then it was back to Atlanta for The Biggie, as Jim Hart had promised. The charges were escape, assaulting federal officers and theft and destruction of government property. Guilty on all counts—sentenced to an additional ten years.

Finally, during the evening hours of November 22, 1975, I was escorted by an entourage of federal marshals up the wide concrete steps that fronted the imposing fortress of Atlanta Federal Prison to begin serving a sentence that totaled eighty-three years.

# CHAPTER 27

CHRISTMAS DAY IS UNUSUALLY QUIET IN PRISON; MORE OF a quietness of spirit than of sound, but even that isn't the same. Most prisoners lock themselves inside their own special thoughts and memories while at the same time going about the mechanical motions of life inside the walls. But the laughter is too forced, the conversation too strained, and you don't really want to watch TV because it only serves to remind you that families and loved ones are gathering out there, caught up in the mutual pleasure of giving and sharing, and all you can think about is that you aren't part of it. So you slip off to your cell at the earliest opportunity, fall out on the bunk and switch on the radio. But every station is playing "I'll Be Home For Christmas" or "Silent Night," so you switch it off because there's a tightness in your chest, and your throat feels funny and you tell yourself that you never really liked Christmas carols anyway—all the while remembering the times so long ago when you used to sing them yourself. So you grab pen and paper and start a letter to some special person in your life, but after several lines of gibberish you find that you want to get emotional, to try to describe the dead spot that's inside you this day, hoping that the awful emptiness will ease under the illusion of sharing with the unseen reader. And that's when the gut-wrenching pain wells up in earnest, hangs for a moment, then slams into you full force—weighting you with its misery until you bend like a beggar with a too-heavy sack. Because in struggling to find the right words, you realize too late that you have brought to the surface the very things you have fought so hard to keep buried. So you rip the unfinished letter to shreds, flush the pieces down the toilet and throw yourself back on your bunk. You feel like crying simply because there's no other way to relieve what's inside. But that wouldn't be macho, would it? Spoil the image. So you lie there for a while and cry inside, where nobody can see . . . which is the worst kind of cry because it doesn't let anything out.

Such is Christmas day in prison.

I was walking back to my cell after a noon meal of roasted Tom with all the trimmings when I heard my name called over the P.A. system: "Inmate Jones, 97961, report to the visiting room."

I paused at the entrance to "D" Block and wondered who would be visiting me here on Christmas day. I thought of Mary Ann. Thanks to the local news media, I had no doubt that she knew where I was. And in the four weeks since I had arrived, I hadn't been in contact with anyone on the outside. I didn't think I was ready for that. Not just yet.

I walked along the wide corridor that separated the four main cellblocks of the prison and stopped in front of a locked wooden door where a guard was waiting.

I stood with arms outstretched while he patted me down, then he unlocked the door, and I went inside.

The visiting room was laid out cafeteria style—without the service line. Inmates and visitors sat together around small Formica-topped tables, talking and holding hands, sipping sodas and munching snacks purchased from the vending machines at the back of the room. All very pleasant and civilized. Here, there were no panels of bulletproof glass to deprive one of the sense of touch, no telephones to distort a loved one's voice. But when the good-bys are said and the fantasy of togetherness ends, the parting hurts just as bad.

The guard sitting just inside the door listed my name and number in a logbook and motioned to a table near the center of the room. I followed his gaze, expecting to see Mary Ann. My eyes fell instead on a smaller figure staring silently at a can of 7-Up in front of her.

Susie.

She stood as she saw me coming, weaving my way through the packed tables. Her hands were clasped tightly to her breasts, and her eyes were wide and solemn.

I stopped a foot away from her, and we looked at each other for a moment without speaking. Except for a slight redness at the corners of her eyes, she looked as lovely as I remembered.

"Hello, Susie," I said softly.

She didn't say anything, just reached out her arms for me to hold her, and I did. We stood that way for a while, her face buried in the hollow of my shoulder, then slowly disengaged and sat down at the table.

Susie was wearing a cream-colored suit and matching high heels that didn't seem to make her any taller. She took a tissue from her jacket pocket, dabbed at her eyes and gave me a hesitant little smile.

"It seems like every time I see you lately I have to cry," she said. "I'm going to have to stop wearing eyeliner."

"Or stop seeing me," I suggested. "What are you doing here, Susie? Why aren't you home with the Little Man and your family? You do know what day this is, don't you?"

"I know. Mother took Derek to spend Christmas with Danny and Earleen, and I . . . well, I thought I'd like to spend it with you."

Her voice faded at the end, and she looked down at the crumpled tissue in her hands.

"How did you know where I was?" I asked gently. "I haven't exactly broadcast my whereabouts."

"It was in the papers. Seems like everything you've done lately is in the papers. Only they . . . they keep calling you that stupid name—that Hacksaw name. And they always blow things out of proportion."

She paused for a moment, then looked up at me. "Why didn't you write me, Ed? Why didn't you let me know where you were—what was happening? I tried to see you the day after they took you away, but that damn George D'Atoris wouldn't let me! And then . . . when they brought you back . . . I called the marshal's office, only they told me you were already gone. And I didn't know anything at all about you escaping anymore until J.W. cut it out of the newspaper. I was going crazy, not knowing what was happening."

I reached over and covered her hand with mine. "I couldn't let you know, Susie . . . not then . . . not until they put me in here. And then I guess I just didn't know what to say. They gave me eighty-three years, Susie—eighty . . . three . . . years!"

She looked down at her lap and nodded. "I know. I couldn't believe it . . . I still can't believe it. You didn't kill anybody—or even hurt anybody."

"There are none so vindictive as those with wounded pride, babe," I said. "And you're wrong . . . I *did* hurt somebody—a *lot* of somebodies. I've hurt you . . . Derek . . . my daughter . . . my mother . . . "

"Have you told your mother yet?" she asked, raising her eyes.

"I don't know how to get in touch with her. I tried a couple of times a while back, but she and Dick had moved, and they weren't listed in the directory."

"Isn't there anybody you could ask? Don't you have an aunt and uncle back there?"

I nodded. "But the phone company doesn't have a listing for my uncle either, and my aunt got married again, and I don't know her last name. Anyway, I've already caused enough shit for Mom as it is, and if it's all the same with you, I'd really rather not talk about it." I smiled to take the sting out of my words. "It's a sore spot."

"Do you want a drink or something?" Susie asked, reaching into her jacket pocket and pulling out a handful of change. "They made me leave my purse in a little locker out front."

I shook my head no, then asked, "How's Derek?"

"He's fine. I've got some really cute pictures in my wallet I wanted to show you. Mother bought him one of those little carousels—you know, that plays music? It plays Old Mac-Donald. Anyway, it has all these farm animals on it, and Derek just *loves* the goat! He'll sit there and watch it turn, and every time the goat goes by he'll go 'baaa, baaa' . . . you know, real cute. I took one of him doing that. And the stinker's getting too big for his crib. I caught him climbing over the side one morning . . . I keep the Polaroid on his dresser most of the time for this reason . . . and he was half in and half out, just kind of dangling there with his little hiney sticking in the air. I got just a precious picture of him looking around at me and saying, 'oh, oh!' like he knew he was caught in the act. Then he flopped back inside and laid there grinning at me. He's such a mess, I tell you. One day I found him . . .''

"Susie," I said, squeezing her hand. Her eyes were getting moist again, and she dabbed at the corners with the tissue, looking somewhere across the room.

"It's really over this time, isn't it, Ed?" she said quietly, more statement than question. "There's no point in pretending anymore . . . is there? So tell me, what do we do now?"

"Look, Susie," I said. "I'm not going to be juvenile enough to sit here and plead with you to play the faithful-little-wife routine until they decide to let me out in fifteen or twenty years . . . and I wouldn't expect you to be juvenile enough to go for it if I did. I know how the scene goes. Before long the frustration sets in—then the bitterness—and the letters get fewer and farther between. The next thing you know you meet somebody, and the juices start flowing . . . you remember how it used to be sharing a bed with a warm male body. So you think, 'Why should I punish myself—deny my own womanhood—because that jerk went and got himself tossed in Atlanta?' and you'd be right. And that's when all the good intentions go flying out the window, and you wake up one morning, stretching and yawning, and notice with a shock that there's a strange man lying next to you. Then you feel a little guilty, and then curse me for making you *feel* guilty—maybe even start hating me a little . . . or a lot.''

"That isn't a very nice way of putting it, Ed," she said. But she wasn't looking at me when she said it. She was looking at a spot somewhere over my left shoulder. Somewhere far away.

"There isn't any nice way to put it, Susie. The facts speak for themselves. I'm facing a hell of a lot of years inside—might not ever get out, unless I escape. And I know now that I can't ask you to run with me anymore. So where's the hope? Contrary to what some idiot once wrote, absence does not make the heart grow fonder—absence makes the heart *forget*. So I'd rather face this thing head-on right here and now, so there won't be any guilt complexes later. Doesn't that make sense to you? Because maybe . . . just maybe, we can still be friends.''

Susie slowly pulled her hand away and looked down at the table. She started toying with her half-finished 7-Up, making little wet circles on the Formica. When she spoke, her voice was little more than a whisper.

"I think . . . I know what you're saying, Ed. And I think that's one of the reasons I came here today." She gave me a quick look. "Not that I didn't want to see you, too. But I had to find out for myself just how real this nightmare is, so that I can—you know—have some idea of what to expect. But everything is so . . . so mixed up that I just don't know *what* I'm going to do."

"You do what you have to, Susie," I said, trying to sound brave but not quite succeeding. I thought my voice sounded a little huskier than I would have liked. But I had to give her an out. "I just want you to know where I'm coming from, and that it's all right . . ."

"All *right*, Ed—I *know!*" she said, leaning toward me. She offered a weak smile of her own, sniffed once and went for the tissue again, looking at me through lowered eyelids.

"Are you going to be okay?" she asked, giving her hair a quick toss. "I asked you that once before, and you went out and robbed a jewelry store—or helped rob it."

I lit a cigarette and looked out over the crowded room, at the false gaiety and painted expressions—like picnickers trying to ignore the ants.

"If you're asking if I'm going to try to get out of here," I said, "you know the answer to that as well as I do. And what's more, *they* know it. But not now, not until they lighten up a bit. They're pretty paranoid—shaking me down all the time, watching every move I make. But that'll change . . . eventually. After a while they'll let down, and I'll be just one of the boys."

Susie frowned, concerned. "Do you think you can? I mean, isn't this supposed to be one of their most secure places?"

I shrugged. "I don't know. All prisons are secure—to a point. All you can do is look for a weakness and hope for a little luck when you think you've found it."

"I don't want you getting yourself killed, Ed," she said, serious.

"I don't either. But I'm a little bit dead already."

We talked for another hour or so, keeping it light, avoiding as much as possible the touchy subjects that might cause emotional hemorrhage. Then the guard stood up and announced that visiting hours were over, and it was time to leave.

We stood close together, and I rested my hands on her shoulders, looking down at her. I felt a slight tremor go through her body as she lifted her eyes to mine.

"I suppose," I said, "that the customary thing to say at this point is 'Don't worry—everything's going to be all right.' But that won't work, will it? Because we both know it isn't. So I'm going to say that I love you and that I'm sorry, and that I hope you find some happiness in your life—because you deserve it. I think, in a way, we've been good for each other. And we did produce a good-looking kid, didn't we?"

She buried her face in my chest and nodded.

"You bet we did," I said, holding her. "So you go on home, grab the Little Man and give him a big hug and kiss for me—and think about how lucky we were to have him. Raise him right, and watch him grow, and send me a picture from time to time. And when he's old enough to understand, tell him about me. Will you do that?"

She nodded again. I placed a hand beneath her chin and lifted her face. It was tear-streaked, as I knew it would be. I leaned down and kissed her softly on the lips. She threw her arms around me and held me fiercely, returning the kiss with unexpected fury. Then she broke away and, without a word, turned and walked quickly through the crowd of lingering visitors. I watched as she reached the guard's desk, saw him open the door and turn her over to the corridor guard, who would escort her back up front. I didn't expect her to look back, and she didn't. The door closed again, and she was gone. I had the feeling that it was for good.

Merry Christmas.

In mid-January I set out in earnest to learn all I possibly could about the Atlanta Federal Prison. This task was made easier by the elevated status my reputation had gained for me among the other prisoners. Everyone seemed to know me, and I quickly learned that wagers were being made as to how long it would take before I tried to escape. Word had it that

Gary Lamberth, the joint bookie, was laying eight-to-five that I wouldn't make it—and wasn't getting many takers.

I never had to ask for information concerning the prison's complex security systems; this was given freely by old-time cons who would seek me out, wanting to compare notes and see what all the fuss was about. I was accepted with a respect that bordered more on curiosity by the most influential of the prison's two thousand inmates and was invited to a cell on the fifth tier of ''D'' Block, which was referred to as Cadillac Row because of the East-Coast mafia figures who resided there. As might be expected, anyone with a dozen successful escapes to his credit is much in demand in a maximum security prison. For those who stand little chance of ever being released, he represents a last-ditch hope for freedom. But in Atlanta, that hope was fragile at best. In the prison's history, which dated back to pre-Depression days, only two men had succeeded in beating the walls. Which wasn't surprising when one realized that Atlanta was a duplicate of Leavenworth.

Despite my unsolicited notoriety I kept pretty much to myself, preferring not to become involved with the high-visibility types that made up the majority of the prison population. Organized-crime figures were the norm, made up of an international clientele that read like a ''Who's Who'' of the underworld elite. Pornography and narcotic kingpins, international terrorists and hit men, smugglers, gun runners and—naturally—the ever-present Mob. Atlanta was strictly big time, no lightweights allowed, and its collective membership controlled literally hundreds of millions of dollars outside the walls.

Which caused me to ask myself two questions: What in the hell was *I* doing here? . . . And what made me think I could escape from the gray stone fortress of Atlanta when those of this ilk could not? These guys knew every trick in the book. Hell, they *wrote* the book!

But I still felt I could do it, even though I had thus far found no chinks in the armor. Quite the contrary; the more I looked, the more impossible it seemed. Still, I knew there had to be a way. There is *always* a way. And sooner or later I would find it.

Of all the inmates in Atlanta, I became friends with only two. Jimmy Buck was one. He was serving twenty-five years for bank robbery and was the leader of the Country/Western band, which I had joined in an effort to fill up the dead spots. During the teeth-clenching times when thought became too painful and the prison stench too overpowering, I would make my way to the small band room on the second floor of the recreation building. There I could escape for a while into a world of twangy guitars and clapping hands, where I would flail away at the ancient set of drums as though it were the source of all my woes. It was good therapy, and inevitably I would leave after a couple of hours feeling sweaty and drained, but considerably smoother around the edges . . . especially if some of the dozen-or-so regulars who sat around listening happened to break out a few joints—which was usually the case.

Jimmy Buck was one of the most colorful characters in Atlanta, and at age fifty looked at least fifteen years younger. He was short and slender, with thinning blond hair combed straight back and a quick way of moving that made you think he was always in a hurry. Jimmy loved to crank up his red electric Fender, pack his lower lip with Happy Days snuff and try to sing like George Jones—and the regulars loved it. He smiled a lot, called everybody "young 'en" and could heap insults and curses on the toughest cons in the joint and draw nothing but chagrined smiles in return.

My other comrade was Brian Copeland, who was the exact opposite of Jimmy: tall and gangling, quiet and unassuming, with a perpetual look of boredom on his narrow face. He was nearer my age, but nine consecutive years in Atlanta had caused premature baldness and brought a stoop to his shoulders. Brian was doing forty years for trying to land a crippled DC-3 loaded with three tons of high-grade Colombian in an Alabama cow pasture. An amazed farmer had pulled him from the twisted wreckage and saved his life, but nothing could save him from the DEA and a steely-eyed federal judge. Now he played bass in Jimmy's band and refused to touch the stuff when the regulars posted a lookout at the door and pulled out their little baggies.

It was late March, and I was walking the huge recreation yard with Jimmy and Brian. The thing was huge—big enough to hold all of Virginia's 500 Spring Street. It was also pretty deserted at 9:30 on Saturday morning, not many wanting to brave the biting wind that swooped in over the forty-foot wall. We were on the jogging track that circled the grassy infield, hands jammed into the pockets of our pea jackets.

Jimmy was talking, making an effort to walk slow so Brian and I could keep up. "You know what your problem is, young 'en?" he said to me. "You're startin' to believe your newspaper clips, this escape-artist shit's startin' to go to your head. You can't just waltz into a joint like this and expect to just waltz right back out. I'm tellin' you right now this jailhouse is *t-o-u-g-h!* Ask Brian you don't believe me. Tell 'em, young 'en."

"This jailhouse is tough," Brian said, his chin buried against his chest.

"Fuckin' right it is," Jimmy continued. "And it's held some good ones. I did my first stretch right here . . . been damn near thirty years ago . . . and I remember they brought that asshole Capone in after they got him on that tax rap. Brought him right in through the East Gates in a boxcar and unloaded him outside of Industries. There was a bunch of us standin' round watchin' when he stepped out on the dock, lookin' all keen in a pinstripe suit, snap-brim hat cocked sideways and chompin' on a fat cigar. They marched him 'cross the yard to R&D—marched him right past us—and you know what the bastard said when he walked by? He looked at us grinnin' all crazy-like and said, *I got a million dollars waitin' for the man who puts me on the other side of that wall.* He stayed there eight months before they shipped him off to Alcatraz, and you know somethin'? He never got one taker the whole time he was here. That tell you anything?"

We stepped aside to let a couple of joggers in heavy sweatsuits pass, then resumed our pace. I pulled the collar of my pea jacket tighter around my neck and smiled.

"That tells me he was a damn fool for running his mouth like that," I said. "No wonder they sent him to Alcatraz."

Jimmy let loose a brown stream of snuff spittle that made me and Brian duck our heads. "Yeah, well I was makin' a point, in case you missed it—which you obviously did. That prick had all the money in the world, and he ended up dyin' in the joint."

"Slow down a little, Jimmy," Brian said, giving a little skip to get back alongside.

"You long-legged sonofabitch!" Jimmy complained. "Legs all the way to your brain, and you can't keep up." But he cut it back a notch.

"Why do you have to be so negative, Jimmy?" I asked. "You sound just like somebody else I once knew back in Virginia. 'You'll never make it,' he said, 'It'll never work.' In fact, I've heard it so much I'm sick of it. Besides, all I'm doing right now is getting information—trying to learn the place. You can beat any security with enough time and information."

"I ain't negative. But I ain't a dreamer, either. And I ain't sayin' you *can't* get out of here. All I'm sayin' is don't be so intense about it . . . lighten up a little, and don't let it take up all your thinkin'. You're makin' your time harder."

"Relax and enjoy, huh?" I said. "Just keep pushing 'D'-Block garbage out to the compactor twice a day and wait for the walls to fall down, right? That's going to really make my time easier."

"What, you bored? Hell, I'll get you in the Plumbin' Shop with me—or how about you work with Brian on the Loadin' Dock? Little more exercise'll do you good, take your mind off the streets."

"No thanks, I'll stay in the block. Gives me more time to look around."

"Jimmy, will you slow the fuck down?" Brian said.

"Well, goddamn!" Jimmy said, spitting out another stream of juice. "Why don't me and Ed just stop a while and let you get a good lead?"

Brian cut his eyes at him but didn't say anything. The two joggers came by again, and we made way for them. One slapped Jimmy on the back as they passed and got a "Hey there, young 'en!" in return.

We were passing beneath the southeast gun tower, which rose fifteen feet above the rim of the wall. I looked up and saw the guard's head behind the bulletproof glass. He gazed down at us for several seconds, then turned his attention back to the infield, where some prisoners were playing tackle football. Fifty yards ahead of us was another tower, and fifty yards beyond that, another; a total of eleven altogether, surrounding the prison like airport control towers. Twin strands of wire, six inches apart, ran along the top of the wall, which was rounded to prevent grappling hooks from getting a bite. The gusting wind caused them to give off a faint whistling sound that only intensified my depression. They would signal an alarm in the towers if a warm body came within one foot of them.

"How long have those alarms been there?" I asked.

"Ever since Morris Johnson went over six years ago," Jimmy answered. "And there's two big-ass fences on the other side—also put up six years ago."

"Forget the wall," Brian said. "It's too tight now. Nobody's going over it anymore without getting their ass shot off."

I thought for a moment, then said, "I still say the boxcars have possibilities. What about it, Brian? You help load them."

"Oh, I could probably get you in one. The problem would be getting out. Them things have to be loaded by three o'clock, then they lock 'em and put these numbered wax seals on 'em, and they sit there 'til eight the next morning— through six head counts. Then they pull 'em between the East Gates, check the locks and seals, make sure they ain't been fucked with . . . and believe me, they can tell if they've been fucked with. Now if you can figure how to beat the locks, the seals and the head counts, you might have something. Any ideas?"

"What about a dummy? Worked once before."

Jimmy snorted. "Try that and *you'll* be the dummy! You ought to know by now they want to see *skin* when they count, ain't no lumpy blanket gonna fool nobody—and four o'clock's a double count, so you got *two* of 'em to beat. Oh, one other thing about this dummy shit you ain't thought about yet. Every hack in the joint knows you by sight, you can believe that. When they count, they're gonna want to see your smilin' face on the other side of those bars. So what next, Gen'ral?"

Brian, exasperated, said, "Jimmy—goddammit, will you slow . . . aw, the *hell* with it!" . . . and took off jogging, long legs gliding effortlessly over the gravel track.

Jimmy stopped and looked after him, amazed. "Ain't that a bitch? Can't walk but the sonofabitch can sure run, can't he?" He looked at me and grinned. "Ass looks like two Volkswagens tryin' to pass each other. We'll just wait here for him and go on in."

* * *

I hadn't thought much about the counting procedures as they might apply to me; I just assumed they were the same throughout the prison. So over the next week I set out to test Jimmy's theory, making it a point to have my face turned during the four o'clock count. I sat on the toilet with my nose buried in a magazine; I pretended to be sleeping with my head partially covered; once I was in the act of urinating, my back turned to the bars. Each time the lead guard would halt outside my cell, call my name, and wait until I showed my face before continuing the count. The second guard would do the same thing. So much for assumptions.

But at least the shakedowns were becoming less frequent, my movements scrutinized with less suspicion. For all intents and purposes I was a model prisoner, carrying out my duties as cellblock orderly without complaint, keeping my nose clean and addressing the staff in a polite and respectful manner—when I had to address them at all. In prison, you don't want to be seen engaging in too many conversations with The Man. Someone just might get the idea you're talking out of school, in which case you would soon be found on the back of a tier with a bloody grin carved in your throat.

I also helped my cause somewhat by requesting a cell change. Cadillac Row made me uncomfortable, and I felt out-of-place among the mafioso types on the fifth tier, where the cigar smoke hung like permanent smog and narrow-eyed guys with slick hair and unpronounceable names sat around all day playing pinochle. Most of the dope that came into the prison moved through them, either directly or through an agent, which brought a lot of heat to the tier from the cellblock guards. And heat was the one thing I could most do without. So Brian invited me to move to the third tier, where there was an empty cage two cells from him. The Housing Lieutenant looked at me squinty-eyed when I asked, trying to figure if I had some ulterior motive he hadn't thought of. But he gave the okay, and I moved in the same afternoon.

In Atlanta, you don't live on any tier unless the occupants want you to. Oh, you can move into a vacant cell without asking anybody's permission. But if for some reason your neighbors decide they don't want you on the block, you'll get the message real quick. The first hint will be if you come in one day and find that your cell has been burned out. Ignore that warning, and the next order of business will be an iron pipe wrapped around your skull. A rather innovative way of preserving the neighborhood.

Brian came in around three-thirty one afternoon, looking smudged and beat from loading boxcars all day, and sauntered into my cell. I was sitting at the little square table with the swing-away stool, hunched over a letter I had gotten from Susie—which was only the third in six months.

"Watcha got?" he asked, leaning against the bars and nodding to a newspaper clipping lying on the table. "More propaganda?"

"Not about me," I said. I picked up the clipping and handed them to him. "Sit down and read this. It's going to blow your mind."

Brian sat down on the bunk and crossed his long legs, blinking at the headlines. He looked up at me, then back at the paper.

"That's right," I said. "My old buddy George D'Atoris. Remember I told you and Jimmy about him a while back? Well, seems he went out and hired somebody to kill a Shreveport city councilman because the guy started some kind of investigation on him."

"Heavy," Brian said, squinting his eyes at the fine print. "Had him blown away with a sawed-off shotgun. That would do it."

"The good part's still to come. When they came after him, the sonofabitch barricaded himself in his house and threatened to shoot anybody who came in. Forty cops stood around outside for six hours 'til they finally talked him out. Had it been me they would have blown the house up."

Brian grunted. "Says here they got him when he hired somebody else to knock off the trigger man. Guy went straight to the state attorney's office and blew the whistle on the whole thing. Is this fool for real?"

"Oh, he's for real, all right. Ask me. I *knew* that bastard wasn't right—I could feel it. And you know what? He'll probably get away with it."

"Wouldn't surprise me," Brian agreed, handing me the clipping. "You said at lunch you wanted to talk to me about something."

I lit a cigarette and put away Susie's letter—which was filled with how's-the-weather? small talk and little else. She had signed it *love,* but I could tell by the way the *L* overlapped the *S* in her signature that it had been an afterthought. I didn't think there would be many more letters.

"What do you know about a guy named Vincent Papas?" I asked Brian.

"The Frenchman? What do you want to know about him?"

"Well, he caught me when I got back from the compactor this morning. Invited me to his cell, made me a cup of coffee, then went about telling me how bad he wanted out—in no uncertain terms."

Brian looked surprised. "Over the wall?"

"Over, under, through—he wasn't finicky about how. Said he could see to it I never had to work again if I could do something about it. What's his story anyway?"

Brian leaned back on one elbow and looked out at the tier, busy now with prisoners passing back and forth and shouting to each other, the way it was every weekday after three-thirty and all day on weekends and holidays. Peace and quiet are two luxuries no amount of money can buy in prison.

"You remember that movie made Gene Hackman so popular . . . *The French Connection?*" Brian asked.

I nodded.

"Well, Papas was the so-called mastermind in that shit. Oh, in the movie the guy that was supposed to be him got away—left Popeye Doyle really pissed because Mr. Big *e-lud-*ed him, as they say. But that was just so they could make another movie where Gene could terrorize all the pedestrians in New York roaring through the streets in his souped-up Plymouth. Truth is, they got the guy along with everybody else, and that guy is Papas, and he's got eighty years to prove it. So what else you want to know about him, aside from the fact that he's bad news."

"Eighty years, huh? No wonder he wants out. But why come to me? All the money he's supposed to have, looks like he could work something out easy enough."

"If this was a state joint—maybe," Brian said. "But he's not going to buy his way out of this system. Nobody is, unless they do it before the judge bangs that gavel. And as for why he came to you—well, let's just say you're a victim of your own reputation. Somebody gets the idea, knowing all the times you've split, maybe he can ride on your wave.''

"Well, I'm not making too many waves right now. Didn't know I was giving that impression.''

"You're not. But everybody knows it's just a matter of time before you try. You might not know it, but you've got some guys watching you closer than the hacks, only they're cool about it. But if you make a serious move, you better not stop to take a shit, 'cause they're going to be there to wipe your ass if you do.''

"Think they'd move in on my play?'' I asked.

"In a heartbeat—if they knew about it. What did you tell him?''

"Papas? What do you think I told him? Said I was being a good boy and trying to make parole. He just nodded, told me to keep it in mind, and I left.'' I thought for a moment, then added, ''Why did you say he's bad news?''

He shrugged and looked away, scratching absently at a knee. "Word has it he might be thinking of making a deal with the FBI. All that nice white powder they had stored in the property room of New York's Finest? Well, it disappeared—all hundred and forty million worth. Some say he knows who did it and might be willing to share the information. The kind of people supposed to be involved, they're probably pretty nervous right about now. So, all things considered, guess it makes sense, talking to you like that.''

"Well,'' I said, just as three sharp whistle blasts signaled count time, "we all have our problems, don't we?''

Brian got up and grazed his knuckles against the ceiling, stretching. "We surely do, buddy. Every last one of us.''

He was going out the door when I said, "Hey, Brian?''

He looked back.

"How about you?'' I said. "Would you go if you had the chance? If you thought you could make it?''

He thought about it, his expression serious, then said, "Nope. Not my nature. Some people just have a knack for that sort of thing, others don't. I'm one that don't . . . I'd fuck it up. I can set a DC-3 down on a thousand-foot dirty path in a snowstorm . . .'' He grinned, thinking of Alabama.

"If my rudder don't break. But that wall scares hell outta me. Know what I mean?"

I was nodding as he walked out, thinking I knew exactly what he meant. It scared hell outta me, too.

Then two days later I got The Letter, and all thoughts about the wall were put on hold.

# CHAPTER 28

I SAT ON THE EDGE OF MY BUNK AND STARED AT THE PLAIN white envelope in my hands, holding it reverently, as though it were some delicate treasure of incalculable worth. Which, in a way, it was. The handwriting was slanted and uneven, not at all like the neat scrawl I remembered. But I recognized the hand nonetheless, even without benefit of the return address in the upper-left-hand corner.

I turned it over and examined the back, then flipped it over to the front again, noted the neat slit along the edge where it had been opened and inspected by the mailroom guard. Dragging it out, both dreading and anticipating the contents. Finally, with trembling fingers, I took out the folded sheets of unlined writing paper and started reading.

*My Dearest Son,*

*Thank God I have found you at last. I have been so worried about you for so long, wanting to hear from you and to see you again. I have prayed and believing God for an answer and He did. I will always be praying for you My Son. That you will take Jesus into your heart and life and work with Him daily, just as I do, for without Him I could not have made it these years.*

*Your grandmother, that is my mother, died of a stroke several years ago. And your grandfather, that is my father, died a short time later also of a stroke and heart failure. And then I lost Dick too a few years ago, he had a sever heart attack. You may not believe it but Dick was Saved in the Lord about 2 years before he died. He turned his life over to the Lord and loved to read the Good Books of Prophecy and he had gotten so when friends came to see us, he would start talking to them on the Bible and the belief he had in the things that were in it. I was real proud of him.*

*Your daughter Dee Dee graduated from high school in June. I went to her graduation with her. She was so afraid I wasn't going to be able to go. She is a very beautiful girl now, she spent 4 days with me last summer. I was real proud of that. She looks just like you 20 years ago. She and her boyfriend were here Saturday before Thanksgiving and had supper with me. She called me Christmas and talked a while. She said she would be back to see me sometime after the first of the year. I think she is planing to get married in the spring. She knows all about you and talks about you a lot, she always asks me questions about what you were like. She says she would love to see you very much.*

*I've been a little sick for a while but I'm better now. All I want to do now is see you again. Will that be alright? If I come to where you are will they let me? Please let me know and I will come as soon as possible and bring Dee Dee with me.*

*Well My Son, I will close for now. Please answer soon and call me if you can. If you can't then please please write and let me know you're alright. Son, I love you with all my heart and I always will and I will never give up on you. So until I hear from you, may God Bless you and keep you in His care.*

*All my love forever*
*your mother*

*PS Please write to me soon Son.*

I sat there for a long time afterward, oblivious to the cell-block sounds around me. Her words danced and blurred before my eyes as I shuffled the pages back and forth, reading the lines over and over again. I think Brian stopped by my cell, the way he usually did after coming in after work, but I couldn't swear to it. If he did, he probably stuck his head in, saw the look on my face and just kept on going. I remember hearing the count whistle and the doors clanging shut up and down the tiers as the men were locked in, but I never saw the guards when they came by making little check marks on their clipboards. I was too busy blinking at five sheets of paper a little lady three states away had poured her heart out on; pictured her sitting there someplace, alone, listening to the clock on the mantelpiece while she struggled to find the words. There was a sick feeling inside my guts that made me lean over and hug myself, and I wanted to vomit because maybe it would make me feel better. Like that was all it would take to make the gut pain go away. God! What had I done to her?

Brian found me like that, after they announced count clear over the PA system, and the cellblock guard had unracked the doors. I didn't notice him at first, standing outside the cell peering in at me.

"You all right?" he asked.

I straightened up and tucked Mom's letter back in the envelope, laid it on the metal table. "Yeah," I told him, "I'm all right."

"Anything you want to talk about?"

I shook my head.

"Well," he said, looking awkward, "guess I'll go ahead and eat. Don't suppose you're going, huh?"

I got up and went to the sink, turned on the cold water. "I'm not hungry," I said. I bent over, sloshed a few handfuls over my face and toweled myself dry. When I looked up Brian was still there, puzzled.

"You coming over to play tonight, then?" he asked. "Packie's supposed to have some good shit—might make you feel better."

"Not tonight," I told him. "Tell Jimmy I got to write a letter. A long one."

"All right," he said, and started down the tier. Then he backed up and looked in at me again. "Ain't none of my business but . . . didn't nobody die, did they?"

I rummaged through the metal locker on the wall, found a Bic pen and writing pad and dropped them on the table.

"Yeah," I said, sitting down. "I think so. And I think I was the executioner."

Brian looked at me like he wanted to say something else then thought better of it and walked away. I sat there a long time, just staring at the blank recycled writing paper the government issued its prisons, trying to organize my thoughts. Finally I picked up the pen, paused a moment, then took a deep breath and started writing.

*Dear Mom . . .*

I came striding into "B" Block and took the iron steps two at a time up to the fourth tier. Brian was right behind me, telling me to slow down, I wasn't going to a fucking fire. Jimmy was standing outside his cell a third of the way down the tier, leaning on the upper rail and looking out through the barred windows that faced the parking lot at the front of the prison. He saw me coming and grinned.

"Well, ain't you the cat's meow?" he said, taking in my freshly pressed khakis and black spit-shined shoes. "Damn, young 'en! You goin' on a visit or a date?"

"Seen anything yet?" I asked, stopping next to him. I stood on tiptoe and leaned forward over the railing, trying to hide my nervousness. From this height I could see over the rim of the wall beyond the cellblock windows, out to the gravel parking lot off to the left and the circular turnaround at the front of the building, where the long driveway leading from McDonough Boulevard forked around the main guntower island across from the entrance. Traffic was thin on Boulevard, but every now and then a car would slow down, turn in between the giant concrete columns that said UNITED STATES PRISON and make its way to the gradually filling parking area. It was ten thirty-five on a Sunday morning, six weeks after I had answered Mom's letter, and Sunday was a heavy visiting day for the inmates of Atlanta.

"I ain't seen no green-and-white '74 Ford yet," Jimmy said. "Least I don't think so. Sure it ain't blue and white? Two or three of them out there. Check it out."

I squinted and gazed out at the assorted cars, vans and trucks parked grille to grille fifty yards away. I didn't recognize anything that fit Mom's description.

Brian, just now ambling up, fell in beside me and propped

a foot on the lower rail. "If you'd moved that fast in Talla-hassee," he complained, "that snake wouldn't have had a chance. You're getting as bad as somebody else I know."

"She said between ten and eleven," I said, keeping my eyes peeled. "I want to see them before they get in."

"You daughter's comin' too, huh?" Jimmy asked. "How long since you seen her?"

"Not long," I said. "Only about eighteen years. You got a cup of coffee?"

Jimmy stepped inside his cell and turned the hot water on in the sink, saying, "Yeah, I got coffee. Hell, I got tea, I got hot chocolate, I got Pepsis . . . I'm a regular fuckin' Seven-Eleven. You want, I'll get you some wine—anything to make you stop leanin' nine yards over that rail—you're makin' me nervous."

He came out with a plastic cup of instant Nescafé and handed it to me. "Here—calm yourself. Want a dip of snuff?"

"This'll do," I told him. "Thanks. Think maybe they're having a hard time finding the place?"

"Ray Charles could find this place," Jimmy said. He turned around and hooked his elbows over the rail. "I had a visit a couple of years ago. Ex-old lady come to see me. Man, was she a mess! All drunked up, hair like a dust mop—lookin' all crazy. First time I'd seen her since that judge said twenty-five years . . . never even got a letter from her. So I go in there, sit down, and the first thing she does is kick me dead in the knee under the table. So I say, 'What the fuck you do that for?—you ain't even said boo in damn near three years!' And she says, 'That's for doin' this shit to me, actin' like Jesse James and walkin' in First National with a gun bigger than Clint Eastwood's.' Said we was doin' just fine with me drivin' a UPS truck and her makin' fishhooks and sinkers at the Cullen plant, and there wasn't no need for me to do such shit. Now she says she's gettin' a divorce, sellin' the house and truck and movin' to Minnesota, so there. Then she gets up and staggers out and leaves me sittin' there like a damn fool. Whole thing took about four minutes, and I never got to say a word except to ask why it was she kicked me in the knee." He shook his head. "Took her three years to work up the nerve."

"The point, Jimmy," Brian said.

Jimmy pulled out his can of Happy Days snuff and packed his lower lip. "I dunno there is one. I just happened to think about it, that's all." He put the can away and turned around and stared moodily out the window. Brian and I looked at each other with raised eyebrows, wondering whether to grin or play it straight. With Jimmy you couldn't tell.

"Green and white, right?" Jimmy asked.

"What?" I jerked my head back and followed his gaze— and there it was, just turning into the driveway, yellow blinker light flashing. It moved slowly, tentatively, toward the parking lot, like the driver wasn't quite sure where to go. I watched, fascinated, as the car turned into the front row and found a vacant spot next to a gray van.

"Black-and-white license plate," Brian mumbled, craning his neck. "That Virginia?"

I nodded, too tense to speak. A young girl got out on the driver's side, walked around and opened the passenger door. She was tall, with shoulder-length brown hair, dressed in a tan pantsuit. Even from this distance I could tell she was quite pretty. She leaned down and helped out a middle-aged woman in a long lavender dress with a white shawl about her shoulders. They looked around, getting their bearings, then the girl took the woman by the elbow, and they walked slowly across the gravel parking lot. The three of us watched without speaking until they disappeared around the corner of the building.

"That them?" Jimmy asked.

I stood there looking at where they had passed from sight, feeling things I couldn't describe. "I don't know," I said. "Ain't that a hell of a thing? I mean—I know it has to be . . . but if I passed them on the street right now, I just wouldn't know."

"Yeah," Jimmy said, and took the cup of forgotten coffee from my hand. "It gets like that sometimes. Guess you need to be kicked in the knee too, don't you?"

They were sitting at the back of the packed visiting room, next to the sandwich machine, and didn't see me when I first came in. I stood beside the guard's desk and stared at them across the room, feeling like I was looking through the back end of binoculars. Mom was folding her shawl in her lap, making it into a neat little triangle. Dee Dee was searching her jacket pockets for something, every once in a while brushing her hair back from her forehead with slender fingers.

I never took my eyes off them as I threaded my way across the room. Dee Dee saw me first. She leaned over and said something to Mom, who looked up just as I reached the table. I eased into the vacant chair sitting there, pulled it close and without a word put my arms around her.

We sat that way for several minutes, hugging and rocking, not really needing to say anything. Mom kept patting my back and touching my hair like she was trying to reassure herself that I was real. But there were no tears, no big emotional outburst. Just a quiet touching. Out of the corner of my eye I could see Dee Dee looking on solemnly.

When the hugging was over I sat back holding her hands and studied her carefully for the first time. She had changed, looking older than her fifty-eight years. And tired. Her face was lined with deep wrinkles, and her loosely curled hair was mostly gray. But where it really showed was in her eyes. They looked back at me from behind wire-rimmed glasses with an expression that said she had seen and felt it all. Like a wounded deer looking up at the hunter who's about to blow its heart out.

She smiled and wrinkled her nose at me and said, "Hi, son. How's my baby?"

"I'm fine, Mom," I told her. "Did you recognize me?"

"Of course I recognized you. You haven't changed at all."

"You have," I told her seriously. "You've been worrying yourself to death, haven't you? About me."

She patted my hand and said, "It'll be all right, now. Besides, I wouldn't be . . ."

"You wouldn't be a mother if you didn't worry—I know. Sounds like a pretty rough job, being a mother."

Dee Dee went "Ahhummm! Remember me?" and I turned and saw her looking at me with raised eyebrows.

"Only from baby pictures," I said, grabbing her in a bear hug. "And that's been a while back." I took her by the shoulders and held her at arm's length, taking in the sight of her. "God, you're beautiful—you know that? Guess I did something right, huh?" And I hugged her again. It was hard for me to believe that this almost-grown woman was my own daughter.

Dee Dee pulled away, and I was surprised to see a slight blush on her cheeks. She smiled shyly, brushed her hair back from her forehead, then pulled a handful of change from her jacket pocket and dumped it on the table.

"They said we could only bring change in—for drinks and stuff. I want some coffee, and I know Grandma does. You want some?"

"Cream and sugar," I told her. "It's got to be better than we get here."

I watched her as she got up and walked stiffly over to the coffee machine and started feeding it quarters. Several inmates sitting nearby cut their eyes to her, trying not to be obvious about it, taking in her trim waist and snug-fitting pants. It made my angry, knowing what was in their minds . . . a really strange sensation. The instinctive father-image being protective of his girl-child.

"She's really grown, hasn't she?" Mom said, then put a fist over her mouth and coughed several times, patting her chest when the spasm ended.

"Yeah," I said, watching her. I pulled her chair a little closer and put an arm around her shoulders. "Where did you get that cough?"

"Oh, just my emphysema acting up. Had a little bronchial trouble lately. Doctor made me quit smoking."

Dee Dee came back with three paper cups of coffee and set them carefully on the table. "That's hot, Grandma, so watch it. Here, Edward."

I gave her a look as she sat down. "Edward! What's with this Edward stuff?" I gave Mom a grin. "How you like that? Talk about no respect! That the fad out there now? Should I start calling you Heddie?"

Dee Dee peered at me over the rim of her cup, embarrassed. "Just give me a little time. I just found out about you three years ago. Right now it just seems so . . . you know . . . strange."

"To call me 'Dad'? That's strange?"

Mom put a hand on my knee. "What she means is that it's hard to call two men 'father.' " Like she was explaining to a child. "Just give her a chance to get used to you."

It bothered me a little, but I tried to make light of it, pretending to think about it for a while. Then I grinned at Dee Dee and said, "Okay, you got about three hours. How's that?"

"We'll see," she said. "Grandma tells me I've got a half-brother. What's his name? Derek?"

So I sat back and told them all about Susie and Derek, filling in details about times and places and events that I didn't have room for in my letters to Mom. Each time I mentioned a new city, Mom would close her eyes and nod her head, as though saying to herself, *so that's where you were then*. They listened attentively, throwing in an occasional question when I became overly vague, wanting to know it all. I spoke only of the better times, leaving out the jails and the prisons and the things I shouldn't have done, until finally there was nothing left to tell. I started winding it down on our third cup of coffee, wanting a cigarette in the worst way but resisting the urge because of Mom's obvious breathing problem. Every so often she would be hit with another fit of coughing, until Dee Dee had to give her a little white pill from a vial she had in her jacket pocket—which seemed to help. But it caused me concern.

I asked Dee Dee about it, when Mom wanted to know where the ladies' room was, and I watched her make her way slowly through the jumble of tables, casting dubious glances at some of Atlanta's rougher elements.

"I don't know, Edward," she said, watching me light a quick cigarette while Mom was gone. "She's been that way the last few years, maybe not as bad as lately, though. She can't walk a block without getting all out of breath and having to rest. I know she's taking a lot of medicine—for emphysema."

"Is she seeing a doctor?" I asked.

"Yes . . . two of them, I think. She's had a bad time ever since Dick died. I was glad to see her move to New Kent, where she can be close to her brother and sister. You remember Nettie and Hunka, don't you? Well, they don't live too far away, and they come by once in a while." She gave me an accusing look. "Do you know how long she looked for you?"

I crushed out my cigarette in the tin ashtray and fanned the air with my hand. "I know, Dee."

"Well, it was a long time . . . a lot of years. She was going *crazy* thinking she'd never see you again. She finally got in touch with some detective-guy Dick used to know and asked him if he could find out anything. That was about a year ago, I guess. Then he called one day and told her you'd been sent here—something about tracing you through a detainer Virginia had on you. She was a nervous wreck for a while after that, but real excited at the same time because—you know—she'd found you and at least knew that you were alive."

I had been sitting there listening to her, fooling with the tin ashtray. "You're pretty rough, you know it?"

She reached over and covered my hand. "I'm sorry, I didn't mean to . . ."

"No. That's all right. Most things we need to hear we really don't like to listen to. You think I haven't thought about her? About you? You think maybe I've *liked* this shit? You don't know the half of it, Dee . . . not a *tenth* of it. I could tell you things that happened to an eight-year-old kid that would make your eyebrows curl—things that still seem clear as yesterday. A few other things I could mention while I'm at it, but I won't go into all that. I'm not copping out, not trying to say I couldn't have done things a little different. But a lot of shit happened before I really knew how to deal with it, and by the time I did it was too late. Even so, I can accept what I do to myself. But when I think of what I've done to Mom, it hurts, when I think what I've done to you, it hurts, and there's a pretty damn good woman and a little baby in Shreveport that I think about quite often, and that hurts too. But tell me, what can I do about it? What? I'm open to any and all suggestions, Dee."

She didn't get a chance to answer because Mom was coming back. I held her chair as she sat down and beamed at us. "You two getting acquainted?" she asked.

"We're getting there," Dee Dee said.

We spent another hour talking and trying to put the years into some kind of perspective, my arm draped around Mom's shoulder. Dee Dee confirmed the fact that she was getting married in June—two months away. I told her she was too young to be getting married, to which she replied that I was a fine one to talk, seeing as how her mother and I had run off to South Carolina when we were even younger than her. She was going to be living in Greenville, North Carolina, and thought she might be singing with a group playing weekends at a local night spot. She had it all mapped, she said: get married, have two or three babies, buy a double-wide trailer and live happily ever after. I told her to go for it, if that was her dream, but to make sure she knew what she wanted. Those who can't do, teach.

Visiting hours were nearly over, and some prearranged signal must have passed between Dee Dee and Mom, because Dee Dee looked at her watch, excused herself and headed for the ladies' room, a dozen sets of male eyes following her. Mom leaned close to me and took one of my hands, her expression serious.

"Edward," she said, "I know they gave you a lot of time."

"A lot of time, Mom," I agreed, looking across the room. "But it wasn't like you think. How much do you know anyway?"

"I know you're supposed to have robbed somebody," she said. "And I'm not going to ask if you did or didn't."

"I didn't, Mom," I told her. "Not for real. But I did do something wrong, and I went into it with my eyes open . . . at least I thought they were open."

"Well, that doesn't matter now," she said. "What's done is done, and I don't know all the whys and wherefores of what might be done legally to get your sentence reduced. But I want to tell you . . . look at me, son . . . I want to tell you something Richard Repp told me a few days ago. You remember him?"

"Yes."

"Well, he knows all about your troubles, and he called me and said that he heard Virginia was going to drop all charges against you."

I gave a short laugh. "A lot of good that's going to do now. Chances are they'd never get a shot at me anyway."

"Maybe not," she said. "But it's something—it's a start. And there's always a chance that things will work out, regardless of how bad it might seem. I don't know how you feel, but I have an awful lot of faith in the Good Lord, and I know what He can do. And I want to ask you to do me one favor—the only one I'll ever ask.''

"Name it, Mom," I said seriously.

"I want you to promise me right here and now that you won't try to escape, that you'll give my faith a chance. I asked you that once before—when you were back there in Spring Street. You didn't say then that you would or you wouldn't, but I knew in my mind what you were going to do. But this time, Edward, I'm asking you to promise me. I'm begging you. I've never asked you for much, have I?''

I shook my head, watching her eyes blinking at me behind the wire-rimmed glasses, seeing what it meant to her. Feeling it.

"Then promise me, Edward," she said, giving my hand a quick squeeze. "Tell me what I've been waiting to hear for fifteen years . . . that you'll stop running and not put me through this anymore. Because son, I honestly don't think I can take it again.''

She waited for an answer, searching my face with anxious eyes. It was her look that really did it—I would have promised her anything to escape that wounded-deer look.

"All right, mom," I said. "I promise. We'll try it your way.''

"You mean that, Edward?''

"I mean it. We'll see what happens.''

A big smile lit up her face, and a few years seemed to disappear from it. "That's my baby. Can I get a hug on it?''

"You can get all you want," I said, and hugged her. Over her shoulder I could see Dee Dee just coming out of the ladies' room. She saw us and stopped, then changed course slightly and sauntered over to the vending machines, pretending to study the cellophane-wrapped sandwiches.

"We got a spy," I said into Mom's ear.

Without turning her head, Mom said, "I know. Ain't she sweet?''

When visiting hours were over I walked them to the guard's desk, where others were gathering, saying good-by. Mom said she would be back in two or three weeks and would keep on coming because we had a lot of catching up to do. Dee Dee promised to come when she could, depending on her wifely duties. But in any event we could write often, couldn't we? You'd better believe it, I told her.

I gave them another hug as the visiting room door opened and the visitors were asked to file out. Mom let go with an effort, stepped back and gave me a look.

"Don't forget your promise," she said, and I told her I wouldn't. Then they left, giving a final over-the-shoulder wave, and the door closed.

I took a seat at one of the tables and lit a cigarette, waiting for the shakedown crew to arrive and strip search us before letting us out. I let myself slip into the deep depression I knew would come and ignored the milling prisoners, some already in the process of removing their clothes. I thought about how nice it would be if I could let my mind go into that back alley again and tune out everything, where I wouldn't keep seeing Mom's eyes or hear Dee Dee call me "Edward." But reality had leaped out at me in 3-D, and nothing was going to lift the curtain of guilt that threatened to smother me. I didn't think it was likely to get any better.

When the strip search was over I walked back to "B" Block, went up the steps to the fourth tier and stopped outside Jimmy's cell. I paused by the rail and looked out at the parking lot. Mom's car was gone. So were most of the other vehicles, now that visiting hours were over.

Jimmy stepped out of his cell and said, "They left about ten minutes ago, young 'en." He was freshly shaved and smelled of Mennen aftershave, which was the only kind they would let us have since there wasn't any alcohol in it. "Have a good visit?"

I leaned my forearms against the rail and stared down at the flats below, seeing guys roaming back and forth, a few tables surrounded by poker players. Two skinny black guys were sitting off to themselves, their backs against the wall, sharing a joint while they looked up and down the range for the guard. Every once in a while one would reach over and feel the other's crotch, not caring who was watching.

"It was good and bad," I said, still feeling depressed. "Least I didn't get kicked in the knee. But I think I took a pretty good shot in the heart."

"Same difference," Jimmy said. "I was just puttin' it another way."

I gave him a quick look, saw him standing there fanning his cheeks with his hand, drying the aftershave. Jimmy wasn't one to show much emotion, this being about as close as he was likely ever going to come.

"By the way," he said. "Some pretty heavy shit went down a couple hours ago. Three guys hit Papas on the back of five tier in 'C' Block. One of 'em had a fuckin' hatchet. He was a mess."

I wasn't really surprised. I didn't think Papas was either. I asked Jimmy, "What you think—contract?"

"No question. Somebody figured they better not take a chance. Personally, I don't think he would of said anything." He sighed and turned around. "Well, they don't have to worry about it now. Better get on to your house, young 'en, be count time soon."

"Yeah," I said, and walked away thinking about the poor bastard getting hacked to pieces with a hatchet. But by the time I reached "D" Block I had put it out of my mind. Like Brian said, we all had our problems.

## CHAPTER 29

Saturday nights were the biggies for the fans of Jimmy Buck's Country Swingers. They would come bounding up the stairs to the little band room around six-thirty in the evening and scramble for the dozen-or-so folding chairs that were available. The overflow, which on these nights numbered at least another dozen, would line the walls with knees drawn up to their chests, jostling and bullshitting and unloading all manner of contraband—usually weed, with a sprinkling of multicolored pills and spray bottles filled with pruno thrown in for good measure. The spray bottles were fun—guys sitting around seeing who could hit whose open mouth with a stream of forty-proof home brew from six feet away. The pills were another matter, since everything had been crushed up and packed into empty antibiotic and cold capsules issued from the hospital. You didn't know if you were getting uppers, downers or Ajax. Guys would just down a couple and sit back to see what happened.

Packie Sunstrum was the biggest marijuana dealer in Atlanta. Packie always had weed, though no one was quite sure how he got it. It was suspected he had a guard on the string, giving him a cut of the action. But it wasn't anybody's business but Packie's, and he kept a few Dixie mafia boys around for the purpose of discouraging nosiness. He sold the stuff for ten bucks a tablespoon, but on Saturday nights he passed out pin joints to the Country Swingers Fan Club and got everybody pleasantly stoned. Then he would kick back and listen to Jimmy try to sing like George Jones, nodding his big head with the beady eyes and snapping his stubby fingers out of time. The goon squad could have shown up at any time and busted everybody in the room, despite the lookout posted at the door. But as long as nothing serious went down and everybody kept mellow, they looked the other way. Jimmy had three rules that anyone coming upstairs was expected to follow: no weapons, no fighting and no hassling the band. It was a good place to come and unwind, to let your hair down for a couple of hours, and anybody who wanted to come was welcome. But violate the rules and somebody would bounce you down the stairs like a pogo stick.

It was during one of our Saturday night sessions that Jimmy decided to make a speech, after we had tuned up and turned our black piano player loose on our theme song, "Sweet Georgia Brown." As usual the place was packed, with so much marijuana smoke hanging in the air that Brian cracked open the back window, complaining he was getting a contact high.

Jimmy stepped up to the microphone and said, "All right you mother-fuckers, listen up a minute!" and pulled a folded piece of paper from his shirt pocket. He opened it up and waved it at the laid-back audience.

"What I got here," he said, "is a thing from the *National Enquirer* that came out yesterday, and I *love* that paper! Now, I ain't gonna bore shit out of you by goin' through the whole thing, but you gotta hear this headline, and by God I'm gonna read it to you, and then I'm gonna read you the last paragraph." He looked back at me and said, "Give me a drumroll, young 'en."

I knew what was coming but didn't see any way out of it, so I gave him a few tats on the snare and a pleading look that did absolutely no good whatsoever.

"Thank you," Jimmy said, and turned back to his audience and started reading. " 'The Amazing Exploits of America's Most Incredible Prison Escape Artist' . . . somebody called Hacksaw Jones. Ya'll know anybody like that?"

Everybody went, Who? Who? like a bunch of owls, and I felt like sliding down behind the bass drum.

Jimmy grinned, loving the attention, and said, "I don't

know Who Who either, but this thing says he's beat every joint he's been in . . .''

Cheers and whistles, guys squirting spray bottles.

''. . . but Hogan says he can't get out of Atlanta!'' Jimmy finished, raising his voice, which brought a chorus of boos and hoots.

''I ain't shittin','' Jimmy said, getting wound up. ''Listen to this last paragraph—and I quote . . . 'I'm aware of Jones' escape record,' said warden Marvin Hogan, 'but this is a maximum security federal prison. Havin' him inside these walls solves that problem . . .' unquote.''

More boos and hoots. Somebody in back hollered out, ''Let Hogan get on these nuts!'' Which brought another roar.

Jimmy held up a hand, and the noise level dropped a few decibles. ''Now I ain't tryin' to start no shit, but is Hogan right?'' and everybody went Noooo! ''Think my young 'en back there's gonna end up makin' a liar out of him?'' They cheered again, most of them so stoned they didn't even know what he was talking about.

Jimmy stepped back and made a production out of handing me the paper, saying, ''There you go, young 'en,'' still grinning and thoroughly enjoying himself. ''That oughta be all the incentive you need. Start yourself a scrapbook.''

I stuck the article in my shirt pocket and glared at him as he turned back to the microphone, knowing I was in for a lot of ribbing and steamed at Jimmy for bringing the whole thing up. I already had a copy of the story in the first place, Jackie Stencil having brought one by my cell that afternoon. Jackie— whose prison name was Norma Jean—was always coming by my cell, swishing back and forth along the tier, batting his magic-marker-accentuated lashes and asking if I was *positive* there was nothing he could do for me. Jackie wanted to do something for *every*body, but never had much luck because he was probably the third ugliest person in Atlanta.

Jimmy had everybody loose now—as if they needed it— and told them to get out their handkerchiefs because here's one they might remember. Then he kicked off ''I'll Be Over You When the Grass Grows Over Me,'' and by the time he started on the second verse I had decided it was time I filled him in on the situation.

So I talked to him about it, the next morning after the cell doors opened. I went down to "D" Block and up to the fourth tier and caught Jimmy sitting on the edge of his bunk in his underwear, sipping coffee and listening to Bill Emory interview Donna Fargo on his portable Panasonic. He looked at me bleary-eyed and said, "Come on in, young 'en, make yourself a cup. Ain't your momma comin' today?"

"No," I said, and walked over to the sink and let the water run hot while I measured out a double spoon of Nescafé. Then I sat down at the little metal table and lit a cigarette.

"I wanted to talk to you about last night," I told him.

"Aw, you ain't pissed about that, are you? I was just funnin'. Besides, you been mopin' around goin' on two years now—like this fuckin' time's killin' you. Somethin' on your mind, shit, talk about it."

"The thing is, Jimmy," I said, trying not to sound corny, "you remember the first time Mom and Dee Dee came up?"

"Yeah?"

"Well, I kind of promised Mom I wouldn't try to escape. She's been through a lot on account of me, and I don't want her worrying anymore. She's scared to death I'm going to get killed."

Jimmy scratched his chest and said, "Hell, that it? I figured you was all in the dumps 'cause you couldn't figure a way out. You was all gung ho when you first got here—one scheme after another. I just figured you needed a little boost. How come you didn't say nothin'? Wasn't no need keepin' somethin' like that a mystery, tellin' your momma you wouldn't escape."

"I didn't want you or Brian thinking I was using it as an excuse . . . you know, acting like that's all was keeping me in here."

Jimmy, looking disgusted, said, "Well, hell, if you *had* of told me I wouldn't of put you on the spot like I did last night. Want me to clean it up?"

"Naw—don't worry about it," I told him. "I don't need my actions explained to anybody. I just wanted you to know where I was coming from."

"So now I know. Say your momma ain't comin' today? Been a couple months now, ain't it? Anything wrong?"

I tossed the cigarette butt in the toilet and right away lit another. Lately I had been smoking them right down to the filter.

"She's been sick, Jimmy," I said. "Dee Dee says it's her emphysema getting worse, but since she got married and moved to North Carolina I don't think she really knows. Mom's been in the hospital twice now in the last five months. Last time she came up she acted like she could hardly breathe . . . and she's coughing a lot."

"Think maybe that trip's getting too much for her?" Jimmy asked. "It's a good drive from Virginia."

I got up and walked out on the tier, stood looking out the window for a minute like I was expecting to see Mom's Ford pull up any time. But I knew from her last letter that it wouldn't be today. The last time had been seven weeks ago, when my aunt had made the trip with her. It was the first time I had seen Nettie in nearly twenty years, but she was the same bright-eyed, bouncy lady I remembered from my teen years, though heavier and grayer now. And Mom hadn't looked good at all, though she kept trying to play it down. Three weeks later she was back in Richmond Memorial and had just gotten out last week. For tests, she said. Like somebody had to spend nineteen days in a hospital for tests.

I went back in Jimmy's cell and sat down again, seeing he had his pants on and was fooling around with his red guitar, playing single-note lead while Donna Fargo sang about being the happiest girl in the whole USA.

"I'm scared, Jimmy," I said. "Really scared." He stopped playing and looked at me, seeing I was ready to talk. "I think Mom's sicker than she lets on—at least to me. And the last three or four times she'd been up she's acted like she was right on the verge of telling me something, but never does. It's like she changes her mind in mid-thought, then steers the conversation to some point in the past. Lately she's been bringing up Beaumont a lot, asking me funny questions about what kind of place it was and all that."

"What's Beaumont?" Jimmy asked.

"Reform school back in Virginia," I said. "Funny. I spent four years of my life at that place, but Mom and I never were able to talk about it. She couldn't, and I wouldn't. Now she's got a thousand questions, and I can't figure it out. Personally,

I think it's just her way of ducking the issue about the nature of her sickness.''

"You worried about her, Ed," Jimmy said, "why don't you go see the Chaplain and ask him for a call. He'll give you one for somethin' like that. They got a fuckin' FTS line they can call all over the country on, don't cost 'em nothin'.''

"Her last letter just said she wasn't feeling too good, Jimmy," I told him. "I wouldn't say he'd classify that as an emergency.''

"Maybe not, but I'll lay odds he gives it to you anyway—especially you tell him about her just gettin' out of the hospital and all. Hell, Ed, you know well as I do that guys go up there all the time runnin' games on him to get calls—and he knows it. But he goes along with it, long's nobody gets carried away. In your case it ain't even a game, and he'll know that too. You're worried about your momma and want to make sure she's all right.''

I thought about it for a minute, really wanting that call. In the back of my mind was a nagging uneasiness that wouldn't go away.

I looked at Jimmy and said, "You think he would, huh?''

"I know damn well he will," he said, and started picking the guitar again. "Now get your ass on outta here and go see him.''

I nodded, got up and walked out, and was three cells away when Jimmy stuck his head out and said, "And come back and let me know somethin' when you're finished.''

The chapel was upstairs above the cellblocks—right across from the auditorium, where movies were shown once a week on Friday nights. I sat down on a short bench outside the chapel entrance next to the closed door that said *R.F. Thomes, Chaplain* and waited until early-morning services were over. It felt strange, sitting there listening to a bunch of cons inside singing hymns and praising God, knowing maybe five of them were serious. The rest would be roaming the cellblocks and haunting the rec yard later, looking for dope or pruno—maybe hook up with somebody and spend fifteen or twenty minutes under a bunk somewhere. Next Sunday they would be back again, testifying and quoting scripture and making sure Reverend Thomes had their names. The Parole Commission would be suitably impressed.

When it was all over and the last of the congregation had filed past, Chaplain Thomes came out, saw me sitting there, walked over and asked if he could help me. He was young, tall and thin, with a prominent Adam's apple that made a lump in his white collar. He had nice eyes and a firm handshake, but he gave me a dubious look when I told him why I was there—until I pointed out that I had been in Atlanta nineteen months now and never once asked him for a call. He thawed at that, took me in his office and sat me in front of his tiny desk that still took up half of the windowless room. Saving souls didn't have high priority in Atlanta.

I gave him Mom's number and watched him dial, after first dialing nine and triple-eight to gain access into the FTS line. Then he handed me the receiver, pulled out a ledger book and began checking off the names of the faithful who had attended service.

I let it ring an even twelve times before handing the phone back, feeling more uneasy than ever. She could have gone to the store—maybe dropped in to see Nettie or Hunka, but I didn't think so. I knew Mom. If she was too sick to visit me, then she wasn't going to be visiting anybody.

Chaplain Thomes hung up the phone and said, "Nobody home?"

"No, guess not." I thought a moment. "Okay if I try another number? My aunt should know something."

I didn't know Nettie's number but Chaplain Thomes got it from Information, dialed it and handed me the receiver again. This time I got an answer on the third ring, a young girl's voice that turned out to be my sixteen-year-old cousin, Heddie May. Nettie had named her after Mom, though I had never met her.

"Oh, hi," she said shyly, after I told her who I was. "Are you out, or something?"

I laughed and said, "No, honey, afraid not. Is your mom there?"

"Not right now," she said, "she went up to the hospital to see your mother. She'll probably be back . . ."

"Wait a minute—what hospital?" I asked, starting to get that numb feeling again.

"They took her to Henrico Doctor's this time. I think they were going to do a bron . . . a broncus . . ."

"A bronchoscopy?"

"Uh huh—to see if they could find any more tumors, I guess."

And there it was. Out of the mouth of a sixteen-year-old who obviously thought I knew all about it. Lung cancer. Maybe I had known all along, or at least suspected, but just wouldn't admit it. The signs had certainly all been there—the coughing, the wheezing, the shortness of breath. How long had *she* known? Living with that awful thing inside her that was slowly killing her, wanting to tell me about it but not wanting to put that burden on me. It was fine for me to worry her to death for twenty years, but she wasn't going to do it to me.

A voice I didn't recognize said, "Heddie May, do you have that number?"

"Uh huh, it's right here. Phone number and room number."

"Give it to me," I said, grabbing a pencil and paper from the desk, and as soon as she did I hung up. Chaplain Thomes had stopped making marks in his ledger and was looking at me curiously.

"I need to make another call," I said, not making it a question.

"Certainly," he said, and reached across and picked up the paper I had already forgotten about. This time he waited for someone to answer, then said, "Just a moment, please," and held out the receiver. I took it like it was something to be feared.

"Room 301, please," I said.

The lady at the switchboard asked, "Are you a relative?" and I said yes. She put the call through, and Nettie answered on the first ring, saying hello in a low voice.

I cleared my throat. "Nettie? It's me—Edward. What's happening with Mom?"

It caught her off-guard and she didn't quite know what to say. Finally she just sighed and asked how I had found out.

"I just finished talking to Heddie May. Guess she didn't realize it was such a big secret—especially from me. Why didn't you tell me, Nettie?"

"Because your momma didn't want you knowing," she said. "Not right now, anyway—until they finished all the treatments and stuff and could tell her . . ."

"Tell her what? Tell her how long she's got to live?"

"That's the way she wanted it, Edward. There was a chance it might go into remission, and she didn't want to take a chance on you doing something . . . rash until she found out for sure. Don't blame her, she had good reason for doing what she thought was right."

She said it gently, but I caught the message. "I'm not blaming anybody, Nettie," I said, resigned. "Where's Mom? Can I talk to her?"

"She's sleeping right now—from some medicine they gave her a while ago. She don't rest worth a durn anymore. Doctor says it's anxiety, mostly."

"How . . . bad is it, Nettie? How many tumors?"

"Just the one, so far—it's in her right lung. But it's in a bad spot, and they think it's spread. Her emphysema don't help matters any."

"What are they doing for her?" My hand was starting to ache where I was gripping the receiver so tight, and I had to concentrate to loosen up a bit.

"Keeping her on medication—mostly steroids," Nettie said. "And they got her on oxygen. Yesterday Doctor Belsic tried laser surgery, but like I said, it's in a bad place. She had a pretty rough time."

There was silence for a while, faint static buzzing over the line, then Nettie said, "She's in a bad way, Edward—no two ways about it. And she's had thirty-some radiation treatments that didn't help worth a durn to boot." Her voice trailed off. "I just don't know."

"Look . . . when can I talk to her, Nettie? Damn it, I've got to talk to her!" starting to lose it, feeling something inside me trying to get out.

"You'll get to talk to her, Edward," she said, "just take it easy. But she can't talk to anybody right now—it's all she can do to whisper."

"Then when?"

She thought about it, then said, "How about day after tomorrow? Maybe around noon. Give her a chance to bounce back a little."

"All right," I said, not having a choice. "Tuesday noon." Then I remembered Chaplain Thomes and gave him a quick look. He was watching me with a solemn expression, having heard enough to understand the situation, and nodded in agreement.

Nettie was saying, 'I'll tell her you called when she wakes up and that you'll talk to her Tuesday, then—okay? I'll be here in case she needs help with the phone or something."

"Thanks, Nettie. And tell her . . . tell her I said I love her, will you?"

"I'll tell her. You just keep your chin up and don't go doing anything stupid."

"Yeah," I said. "That would be a switch, wouldn't it? Bye."

I let the receiver droop from my hand, and Chaplain Thomes reached over and took it, placed it gently back in the cradle.

"Cancer?" he asked.

I leaned forward and stared at the floor, nodding, noticing how hot it was in the little room and how hard it was to swallow. After a short silence Chaplain Thomes said in a soft voice, "Would you like to pray?"

And I said, "God, yes!" and started crying like a baby.

I was waiting outside the entrance to "D" Block at eight-thirty the next morning when Warden Hogan came by on his way to the Lieutenant's office. I stepped out in front of him and said, "Warden, can I talk to you a minute?"

"Certainly," he said, and we moved to one side of the corridor. He was tall and trim, with neat salt-and-pepper hair and a fondness for narrow tweed suits regardless of the season. He folded his arms and gave me a speculative look.

"My mother's in the hospital," I told him, getting right to the point. "Lung cancer . . . from what I understand, it's pretty bad."

"I know," he said. "I'm sorry to hear it." He probably had a full report from Chaplain Thomes on his desk right then.

"Well, I wanted to ask you about this policy the Bureau of Prisons has about bedside visits. I heard they sometimes allow it—if it's a member of the immediate family who might be . . . terminally ill.''

He nodded his head and said, "That's true. If the illness is serious enough and confirmed through the hospital. The inmate has to pay all expenses though, including transportation and security. Are you asking to be considered for one?''

"Yes sir, I am. I think I can get the money.'' Thinking about Ted Wright back in Houston.

He gazed down the corridor for a moment, then looked back at me. "You know, there are other considerations we have to take into account. We don't allow just *anybody* to take trips into the community—escorted or not. And in your case, I'm afraid we'd have to say no. I'm sure you can understand why.''

"Look, Warden, I don't care how many people you send with me or how many chains you put on me—whatever you want to do. A couple of months ago you let a guy doing life for kidnap and murder visit his sister. Who's a bigger threat to the community, him or me?''

Hogan tensed up over this. "In the first place, Mr. Jones, these decisions are made through Washington—which I can assure you will turn thumbs-down on your request. And in the second place, it's not your position to question who does or does not go out of this institution. I'm sorry about your mother, but a bedside visit just isn't feasible. Now if you'll excuse me, I have a meeting to go to.''

He stepped around me and walked stiffly down the corridor, leaving me staring after him with a look I really wouldn't have wanted him to see.

I was still seething when I arrived outside the chaplain's office at eleven-thirty the next morning and knocked on the door. Getting no answer, I took a seat on the wooden bench and tried to compose my thoughts. How should I handle it? Be upbeat and encouraging about it? Tell Mom they can do amazing things nowadays and to just hang in there, that everything was going to be all right? Or ask her to tell me straight out just how bad it was—to stop worrying about me and think about herself for a change—and then take it from there. Either way it wasn't going to be easy, and by the time

Chaplain Thomes showed up twenty minutes later, I still didn't know.

This time he stepped out of the office and left me alone, after getting through to the hospital switchboard and handing me the phone. I watched him through the crack of the nearly closed door as he sat on the little bench and crossed his legs, fingering a tiny silver cross that hung from his neck—still able to hear what I said but not being obvious about it.

The phone rang twice in room 301, and then Dee Dee answered.

"Hi, honey," I said. "What are you doing there?"

"That you, Edward?" she asked, speaking soft. "I came down to see Grandma for a couple of days. I'm staying over at mother's. How are you doing?"

"About what you'd expect—scared. I thought Nettie was going to be there."

"She and Hunka went downstairs to get some coffee," she said. "We've been here all morning. Nettie said you'd probably be calling, so I waited here."

Not able to prolong it anymore I said, "How's Mom, Dee? I mean really."

"Well . . ." She hesitated, and I knew from the change in sound that she had placed her hand over the mouthpiece. Then she was back, saying, "Edward? Just a minute, Grandma wants to talk to you. But be patient. They put her on a respirator last night, and it's hard for her to talk. They . . . they had to do a tracheotomy."

Quickly I said, "Dee. Why don't you go on and have some coffee with Nettie and Hunka, if Mom can handle the phone—okay?"

"I was going to. Here she is."

The next sound I heard was breathing, labored and rasping, like wet pebbles falling on cardboard. I shut my eyes and clenched my teeth, seeing a phrase I had often read in books but never heard firsthand: death rattle. Once you hear it, there's no mistaking it.

In a voice barely a whisper she said, "Hi, son," and I had to press the receiver tight against my ear to make out the words.

"Mom, honey, why didn't you tell me? Didn't you think I'd find out sooner or later? When you're sick, I want to know it.'' There was a silence for a moment, except for faint static and that horrible breathing, and I thought she hadn't heard me. ''Mom?''

''I'm here,'' she said. ''I have to poke my finger over this dadgum hole they cut in my neck. Come to the hospital to get my throat cut, ain't that something?''

''What do the doctors say, Mom? And don't pull any punches—please.''

''I guess it's bad enough, son,'' she said, serious now. ''I was going to tell you about it as soon as I could find out what could be done.''

''What can be done?'' I asked.

''Well, you know doctors . . . always saying this and that. But I don't guess there's a whole lot they can do. Just a matter of time.''

I couldn't believe it, sitting there listening to Mom telling me—in her own way—that she was going to die. Actually going to *die!* I was having trouble making it register, looking aimlessly around the little office that seemed to be getting even smaller, finally focusing on an eight-by-ten face of Jesus on the wall behind the desk. It seemed to be staring at me.

''Edward?'' Mom said.

I cleared my throat, turning my attention back to the phone. ''Mom . . . don't be talking that way, honey. They've got procedures nowadays—''

''You asked me not to pull any punches, son. There's just nothing they can do. I got worse faster than I thought.'' She paused a moment, and I could hear her trying to get her breath. Then she said, ''I don't suppose they'll let you come see me, will they?''

I didn't say anything, trying to figure out a way to keep from bursting that last bubble of hope.

''I didn't think so,'' she said. ''In that case I want to ask you something here and now.''

''Mom, why don't you just let me talk a while, and you get your breath back, okay? You're tiring yourself out.''

''I'm doing okay,'' she said. ''But I want to ask you . . . do you think the years you spent at Beaumont so young . . . caused you to have all this trouble? You know, things that have happened since?''

I couldn't understand; she was back on that again. "Mom, why is that so important to you? That was a long time ago."

"Did it?" she insisted.

I thought back over the years, considering it, seeing it really meant something to her. I decided, after conjuring up discarded images, that I truthfully didn't have an answer; it was something I had never given much thought to. But she was waiting, it was important to her and I had to say something.

Feeling my way along I said, "I don't think so, Mom. If I was still twelve or thirteen and doing all this stuff, maybe. But I've been grown up a long time now, I know the difference between right and wrong, and I have to accept responsibility for my own actions. That's what it boils down to, isn't it—free choice?"

I almost thought I heard her sigh, but it could have been a gasp. "You sure?"

"I'm sure. Mom, what is all this?"

She paused. "That judge talked to me . . . before."

"What?"

"Before he sent you there . . . he talked to me. He said you really needed more male supervision . . . keep you from running around the streets getting in trouble. He scared me . . . said if somebody didn't straighten you out quick . . . you'd end up in prison, or worse."

I said gently, "Mom, you can hardly breathe, don't go doing all that."

"I'm doing okay," she said. "I thought he might be right . . . you not having a father and me working all day. One time—you remember?—you almost drowned. Six years old and they found you laying on the . . . bottom of the pool at the YMCA."

"I remember," I said, going back in my mind. "I woke up in the hospital, and you were sitting there, holding my hand and scared to death. They told you I might not make it."

"Dadgum right I was scared. And then you took up with those Church Hill boys . . . all of them older than you. Twice you ended up in Juvenile Hall . . . playing hooky and stealing that battery from that service station. Then, when they picked you up on Broad Street with those rings . . . the judge took me in his room and talked to me. He said he had to send you to Beaumont for a while . . . or a foster home. Left it up to me. I didn't want either one, but I had to choose. He said Beaumont was a boy's *school*, that you'd get good learning there.''

I was starting to get the picture. ''Mom, don't say anymore.'' Then I lied. ''I know all about it.''

''You do?'' she asked, confused. ''How?''

''That social worker told me when she was taking me there. Said it was standard procedure in cases like that—the parent had to choose. Beaumont or foster home.'' I was getting into it now, needing to convince her, wanting to take this thing off of her that she'd been carrying—how long?

''And I'll tell you something, Mom, it's a good thing you didn't choose a foster home. All I would have done is run away, maybe think you didn't want me. I'll admit I wasn't too crazy about Beaumont either, but at least I figured I did something to get there. It was a little rough, but not all that bad. And you were there every weekend, just about.''

She paused a moment. ''I really didn't want you in a foster home. Afraid I wouldn't get you back.'' She hesitated again, breathing heavier now, talking becoming more of an effort. ''Did I make the right choice, Edward?''

''Absolutely, Mom,'' I told her. ''Is this what's been eating at you all this time? Thinking you had something to do with it?''

''I'd thought about it.''

''Well, you don't have to think about it anymore, right?''

This time there was no mistaking the relief in her voice when she said, ''Right . . . I guess not.''

Chaplain Thomes, whom I had absolutely forgotten about, was standing in the door now, leaning in. He caught my attention and motioned to his watch. I looked at him, covering the phone with my hand.

''Going to have to wind this up, I'm afraid,'' he said gently. ''I have three call-outs waiting to see me. If you like I can let you call back Thursday morning. About the same time?''

I nodded reluctantly, took my hand away and said, ''Mom, I have to go now. Chaplain Thomes says I can call you again Thursday. That okay?''

After a short silence she said, ''I guess that's okay. You

behave yourself, hear? And don't worry . . . the Good Lord will look out after me. He looks out for all of us."

I lifted my eyes again to the wall behind the desk, where the framed face was still staring at me—how? Accusingly? . . . compassionately? . . . or with deep pity? I decided it could be any of the three—depending on what was really in the heart of the soul looking back. I thought—in my case—accusingly.

"I love you," I told her. "You know that, don't you? I never meant for all this to happen. I just wish to God I could go back and do it all over again—try it one more time."

"I know, son, and I love you too . . . more than anything in the world. But just remember, everything happens for a reason. No matter what we might think of it."

"I'll remember," I said. "Now please get some rest, and I'll talk to you Thursday."

"I'll rest," she said. "Better than I have in a long time. Bye for now."

"Good-by, Mom." I said, and waited with the phone to my ear until I heard the distant click that told me she was off the line. Then I slowly hung up the phone, thanked Chaplain Thomes and went to find someplace where I could be alone.

It was a little after eight the next morning—after a sleepless night of cigarettes and instant tap-water coffee—and I had just parked the big metal trash dumpster with wheels at the back of the cellblock. The wakeful hours were catching up, and I was still puffing from hauling the metal bin to and from the giant trash compactor on the far side of the prison. By two o'clock the bin would be full again, piled high with accumulated garbage and litter collected during the course of the day. Then I would have to do it over again; nineteen months of disposing of prison waste from a cellblock smelling of urine and disinfectant.

I started up the back steps on the way to my cell when I heard the PA system: "Jones, 97961, report to the chaplain's office."

I wondered about it, as I checked out with the cellblock guard, walked down the corridor and up the six flights of stairs to the chapel area, not liking the feeling I was getting.

I paused outside the closed door, fisted hand raised shoulder high, then rapped lightly.

"Come in."

I entered and closed the door softly behind me, nodding at Chaplain Thomes seated behind the desk. He was reading from a white leather-bound Bible open in front of him, making notations in a 2-by-3 spiral notebook. He looked up at me, marked his place in the Bible with a strip of red silk attached to the binding and set it aside.

"Sit down, please," he said.

I sat down in the chair next to the desk and watched him pull a small slip of paper in front of him.

"The Warden asked me to let you call"—he looked down at the paper—"a Mrs. Nettie Hall." He looked up at me. "That's your aunt, isn't it?"

"Yes," I said, watching him pick up the phone. "What's it about? She at the hospital?"

He shook his head, dialing. "I don't know . . . I think this is her home number."

He waited for the ring to start on the other end and handed me the phone, then swiveled his chair around until he was in profile, hands steepled beneath his chin.

"Nettie? . . . Edward. What's going on?"

"Where are you now?" she asked. "In an office or something?"

"Yeah," I said, getting tense. "The chaplain's—why?"

"Edward—your momma went into a coma yesterday afternoon. You could tell she was pretty bad, couldn't you? She was suffering horribly—you wouldn't believe how much. She even had holes in her lung, causing—"

"What do you mean *had,* Nettie?" I heard myself say.

She hesitated. "Your momma died at seven-thirty last night, Edward. There was nothing anybody could do."

I sat there, hunched forward with the phone pressed against my ear, listening to Nettie's voice saying sharply, "Edward! *Edward!*"

"I'm here, Nettie."

"Then listen to me." Softer now. "I know how you feel, it's hard on all of us. But believe me, it's a blessing, the way she was. You just don't know. But, Edward, she died in peace.

And she was ready. I think your call had a lot to do with it. And she's not suffering anymore. Are you all right?"

"Yeah," I said. "I'm all right." The feeling hadn't hit yet. Not really. Like a bullet wound, the real pain would come later, after the shock wore off.

Nettie was saying, "You talk to the chaplain before you leave. And don't worry, Hunka and I will take care of things out here." She paused. "I don't suppose they'll let you come to the service, will they?"

"No," I said. "They wouldn't let me see her when she was alive, I know they won't now."

"Uh huh . . . well—everything will be taken care of, rest easy on that."

"I know it will. Listen, I better go now."

"You're going to be all right?"

"Yeah, Nettie . . . I'll be fine. Just fine. Take care."

I handed the phone to Chaplain Thomes, who swiveled back around and hung it up. He sat looking at me, hand still on the phone.

"She pass away?"

I nodded and said, "Yeah," then stood and turned to the door. I had it open before he spoke again.

"Would you like to talk about it?"

"No," I said, and started out the door . . . then stopped and looked back, at the Jesus face hanging on the wall. The eyes were still watching me. But this time I saw pity, like the eyes knew something I didn't. Take care of her, I thought. As much as she believed in You—trusting and loving to the end—You had better take care of her. Then I left, hearing Chaplain Thomes say, "I'm sorry," to the closing door.

# CHAPTER 30

"THE FUCK'S A *DEATH* MASK, ANYWAY?" JIMMY ASKED, LEANing against the sink with his arms folded, tonguing his lip of snuff. "You know what you're doin' with all that shit?"

I was squatting on my cell floor surrounded by three plastic baggies of dry plaster of paris; a one-gallon can that once contained Del Monte peaches but was now filled with powdered lab stone stolen from the dentist's office; a green plastic pitcher half-filled with hot water; an open jar of Vaseline—which Jimmy was *very* concerned about; two short lengths of quarter-inch rubber tubing; a wooden mixing spoon; and a shaker of salt.

"Yeah," I told him, now emptying the baggies of plaster into the pitcher of water. "I know what I'm doing. Mind moving a little bit? You're in my light."

Jimmy pushed away from the sink, edged around me and walked to the bars, where my blanket now hung, blocking the cell from outside view. "Jesus, *Vase*line!" He eased back a corner of the blanket and peeked out, making sure Brian was on the job, then edged back around me and sat down on the toilet. "Can't you hide that shit when you ain't usin' it? . . . shove it under the bed or somethin'?"

"Relax, Jimmy." Stirring the plaster now. "Nobody's going to see it."

Jimmy spit in the toilet. "Goddamn, bad enough I gotta be in here with that blanket up, guys walkin' by." His voice trailed off, and he sat watching me. "You still ain't told me what a death mask is."

"It's like a mold of your face," I told him, "and they call it a death mask because the person's usually dead when they do it. You've seen these bronze busts of somebody sitting on tables or pedestals? Well, like that. Only this one's going to be made out of lab stone . . . like teeth models that dentists make. Got the picture?"

"I don't know—sounds fucked up to me."

"Let's hope not," I said, lifting a spoonful of thick plaster and letting it dribble back into the pitcher. About right. "Okay, now for your Vaseline."

I sat on the edge of the bunk and began smearing my face and neck with Vaseline, being liberal with it, close around the hairline, all the way to the back of my ears. Jimmy watched, fascinated, as I adjusted two towels over the pillow, took off my shirt, inserted the rubber tubes in my nostrils, then stretched out on the bunk with the back of my head nestled into the towels. "Okay," I said. "start pouring."

Jimmy, looking dubious, picked up the pitcher and knelt beside the bunk. With his arm extended, pitcher poised six inches above my face, he said, "You sure about this?"

"Just pour," I told him. "And don't get any down the tubes, I won't be able to breathe. Do it slow and let it build up—don't worry about spillage."

"Shit looks like pancake mix," Jimmy said. "You ready?"

He started pouring. I closed my eyes and mouth and felt the warm paste trickle over my face, hoping I had enough Vaseline on my lips and eyelids so that when the mold hardened it would come off without taking them with it.

After a few minutes Jimmy said, "Well, that's it. You're covered. You all right?"

I made an up-and-down motion with my hand.

"I'm gonna slide all this shit under the bunk then and go out with Brian. How long before it dries?"

I raised my hand and flicked my fingers three times. The plaster was already beginning to tighten. I carefully reached up and made a small adjustment to my breathing tubes.

I felt Jimmy slap me on the leg. "Fifteen minutes. I'll be right outside. Don't go nowhere, now."

I heard the faint rustle of the blanket as Jimmy left the cell, then low conversation as he and Brian began talking outside, watching for approaching guards, as they propped against the rail.

I lay still under the mound of darkness, feeling a touch of claustrophobia as the cast continued to tighten, breathing slowly and trying not to swallow. I pictured the rubber tubes getting blocked, the rocklike mask frozen to my face in spite of the Vaseline—slowly smothering while I struggled to rip the thing off but unable to. I reassured myself by touching the tubes again, making sure they were firm, then tried not to think about it anymore.

Instead, I drifted back over the last four-and-a-half months, ever since Mom's funeral that, naturally, I wasn't allowed to attend. It had been difficult to deal with, and at first I thought I might not make it. Prison grief isn't the same as street grief. There isn't anyone to share it with, not really; no way to really let out the emotions in that fishbowl environment. So you keep the feelings inside and handle it the best you can, walking the track with clenched hands and a fixed expression while the tower guards stare down at you. They know, and they're waiting for you to lose it and maybe make some kind of mad dash for the wall. As if you could actually climb four stories straight up just like that.

Jimmy and Brian had let me know they were there when-ever I felt the need of company, but for the most part they left me alone—for a while, anyway. In prison you're expected to cope with skinned knees and personal tragedies on your own.

We all have our problems.

Then had come anger, after the pain faded enough to allow room for it. I lay back and let it grow, pregnant with it, wanting to hurt back. I could only do it by escaping.

Then the weeks of thinking, watching, eliminating—searching for the weakness everyone and everything has. Probing and prodding at the defenses . . . until finally decid-ing on a method of attack. Then more weeks of collecting, gradually assembling the necessary tools . . . bringing Jimmy and Brian into the picture, both skeptical yet intrigued by the possibilities.

"Knock, knock—you in there?" Jimmy said, tapping on the outside of the cast now hard as cement. I thought, 'Scare the shit out of me why don't you, Jimmy,' then reached up and felt for myself. It was firm.

"Feels pretty good," Jimmy said. "Want to take it off now? Be a bitch if we couldn't, huh?"

Yeah. Be great.

Together we wrestled with the chunk of heavy plaster, wriggling it back and forth, breaking loose from the suction created by my damp, greasy face. It came away with a few stray eyebrow hairs embedded inside, but no other damage.

I removed my nostril tubes and wiped my face with one of the towels, feeling tiny bits of dried plaster around the hairline. Then I sat on the bunk again, the cast resting on my knees, and smeared the inside with Vaseline, covering every nook and crevice.

Jimmy, looking on from his seat at the table said, "What you doin' now?"

I said, "Greasing the inside so the lab stone won't stick. I mix it up, pour it in the mold and let it set 'til it's hard. Couple of hours ought to do it. When it comes out we should have a death mask."

Jimmy, still working his snuff, said, "Yeah," but not sure about it.

There was a hard crust of dried plaster lining the inside of the green pitcher. I half-filled it again with hot water, mixed in a third of the powdered lab stone, added some salt and poured the concoction into the mold.

"What's the salt for?"

"Heat. Helps it harden faster."

He nodded, sitting there with his legs crossed, hands laced around one knee. "You finished with that Vaseline?"

"Jimmy, I'm finished with all of it," I told him, setting the mold—now weighing about ten pounds—on the floor and sliding it carefully beneath the bunk. Jimmy reached down, picked up the jar of Vaseline that was making him so nervous, screwed the lid on and placed it on the shelf above the sink— behind the Johnson's Baby Powder. He stood watching while I pulled the tucked portion of my sheet from under the mattress and let it dangle along the side of the bunk, hiding what was underneath.

"Can I take that blanket down now?"

I said, "God, yes," and started tossing everything into a

number-ten grocery sack. In the morning it would all go into the big compactor, arriving there with the rest of "D" Block's considerable trash.

Jimmy had the blanket down and was folding it into a square. Brian, leaning on the railing outside, looked up.

"That it?" he said.

Jimmy dropped the blanket on the foot of the bunk and walked out on the tier, looking up and down self-consciously. He said, "I'll catch ya'll later," and was gone. Brian looked after him with a half-grin as I came out with the grocery bag under my arm . . . then swung his head in my direction as I brushed by him going the other way.

Brian said, "Hey, where you going?"

"Taking out my trash," I said over my shoulder.

"Yeah? Well, when am I gonna get a look at this master-piece?"


We all got a look about thirty minutes before lock time that night. This time Jimmy acted as lookout while Brian hung the blanket and sat down at the table. He watched without comment, a lazy expression on his narrow face, as I sat on the floor and eased the chunk of solid lab stone from the plaster shell. Holding it in my lap I stared down at the rock-face that was me, feeling awed. Eyes closed, a somewhat pensive set around the mouth . . . Christ, I *did* look like I was dead.

Brian leaned forward, elbows on his thighs, getting a closer look. "You seen those carvings in Mount Rushmore?" he said. "Reminds me of one of those. Not bad."

Brian switched places with Jimmy, who stood gazing over my shoulder as I examined myself from various angles, fi-nally letting me rest faceup in my lap again. It crossed my mind that this was the first time I had ever seen myself with my eyes closed.

"Yep," Jimmy said, "that's you, young 'en. Little hair and paint, shit. But you ain't got no ears."

"Don't need 'em," I told him, now wrapping my image in a white bath towel. "What they're going to see is me lying there sleeping with a set of headphones on. I've been doing it for weeks."

Jimmy sat on the edge of the bunk and thought about it.

"Yeah, I can see it. I've done that myself. Where you gonna stash it?"

"Up there," I told him, nodding towards the eight-by-twelve-inch steel-mesh air vent above the mirror. The two setscrews holding the metal frame to the wall had been doctored so they could be removed with a pair of fingernail clippers. "Along with a few other little items I already have in there."

"What kind of items?"

"Oh, some hair, pair of tweezers, roll of masking tape, glue."

"How 'bout paint? Got any of that?"

"Not yet," I said. "I got to talk to you and Brian about that."

After the mask had been tucked away in the vent and the blanket removed, we talked about it. Brian sat at the table, leaning against the wall with his long legs stretched out crossed at the ankles. Jimmy was sitting on the toilet where he could spit between his knees, while I lounged on the bunk, cigarettes and ashtray next to me.

"The problem is," I told them, "I don't know shit about painting. Especially something like this. We're talking artwork here, somebody knows what they're doing. You know it?"

Brian said, "Got to look real, no question. Jesus—three feet away, that's how close they're gonna be."

Jimmy said, "What about the body? Don't forget that. You can't just fluff up some shit under a blanket and expect it to pass. It's harder'n you think, making a good outline."

I said, "You don't need much outline when you're flat on your back with one knee raised. Gives you a tent effect."

"That how you been doin' it?" Jimmy asked.

"Most the time. So far, no problems. They're so used to seeing me like that every day, I think they'd be surprised if I was doing anything else. Four o'clock's the hardest, because of the double count and the light from the windows. Nine o'clock's a little easier, only one man and the tier lights to worry about. Midnight on is pure gravy—the tier lights are off, and the guy just uses his flashlight. And when that thing is finished, I guarantee it'll beat a flashlight every time."

I paused and lit a Marlboro, ready to hit them with the

clincher. I dropped the match into the ashtray and slid my hand beneath the pillow. "And here's my ace in the hole"— and withdrew it as the sound of nasal snores, deep and muted, filled the cell.

Jimmy and Brian exchanged looks, then Brian reached over and lifted the pillow to see the small cassette recorder I had stolen from Education.

"You like it?" I asked.

Brian let go of the pillow and slumped back against the wall. "Sounds like you got sinus."

I said, "But it works," and reached under the pillow and hit the STOP button. "I've already tried it on the four and nine o'clock. Several times. They never batted an eye. It'll go for thirty minutes, plenty time to finish counting. After midnight it won't matter."

Jimmy spread his knees and spit a brown stream into the toilet. "How come you sleep with your head next to the bars? Why don't you get on this end where you ain't so close?"

"I don't want them to have to look too hard . . . and they can hear the snoring sooner—before they ever get to the cell. What I'm hoping for is an illusion; they come down the tier making their little check marks, hear snoring five feet before they get here, see me dozing with earphones on—and I mean *me*—and keep going, don't even slow down. They see *skin*, they *see* me, they *hear* me. And I know damn good and well it'll work."

"If you can solve the paint problem," Brian said.

"Right. If I can solve the paint problem. Which is why we're holding this conversation. Any suggestions?"

Brian and Jimmy gave each other another look. Jimmy grinned, and Brian hunched his shoulders and recrossed his ankles, studying his white sneakers like he was trying them on for style.

Brian said, "Welllll, could be somebody. Used to be a makeup artist on the street. Solid, too—never say a word."

I said, "Great. Who is it?"

Brian, deadpan, said, "Jackie Stencil."

Jimmy spit and laughed at my expression as I stubbed out the cigarette and said, *"Norma Jean?* You serious?"

Jimmy said, "Let me tell you somethin' about Norma Jean, young 'en," and I saw Brian roll his eyes, ready for another war story. ''That bitch probably robbed more banks than any four guys here put together. Used to dress in drag, long blond wig, miniskirt, spike heels—the whole nine yards. Only picked male tellers, standin' there at the counter battin' her false eyelashes while the guy melted . . . 'til she come out of her shoulder bag with a big-ass three-five-seven and threw it on him, smilin', and say in that sweet little-girl voice she uses sometimes, 'Give me the money, motherfucker, or I blow your throat out.' Really freak the poor bastard out, you know? FBI thought they was lookin' for a foxy broad, and that took some doin', considerin' how ugly Norma Jean is. They even called her the Go-Go Bandit. Then she comes out of Peachtree Crocker one day after makin' a decent withdrawal and runs right into two off-duty FBI men just happen to be comin' in. Right away they recognize her from all the camera pictures 'cause by now she's a fuckin' star. Right outside the revolvin' doors they stop her, 'Excuse me, Miss—just a minute,' and start reachin' for badges. Norma Jean, hand still inside the shoulder purse, comes out with that three-five-seven and starts blastin'. Only she can't shoot worth shit, and the first two miss while they're divin' out the way and wounds a MARTA bus pickin' up passengers at the curb. The third one catches one of the FBI men in the knee and likes to take his fuckin' leg off. The fourth one takes out a whole plate-glass window from Peachtree Crocker. The fifth one—after Norma Jean swings around tryin' to get a bead on the other guy who's divin' behind the bus-stop bench—goes right through a fire hydrant and sends water everywhere.''

Jimmy stopped to spit and get his breath, taking his time. Brian gazed at the ceiling, looking bored, probably having heard the whole thing a dozen times.

''Then what?'' I said.

Jimmy shrugged. ''That's all she had—five. She drops the three-five-seven and runs over to where the guy's rollin' around holdin' his knee, wantin' to get his piece, and catches two in the back from the guy under the bench. Damn near killed her. But she hung on and got forty-five years. Newspapers called it 'High Noon On Peachtree Street.' '' Jimmy paused and spit again. ''Anyway, that's Norma Jean. Got more balls than a pool table and stand-up as they come . . .

and that's who you need to bring that thing to life. You want, I'll talk to her."

I said, "Yeah—do that," as a guard in a blue shirt and gray slacks strolled by outside the cell. He stopped, looking in, then glanced at his watch.

"Five minutes to lock time," he said, looking at Jimmy.

Jimmy said, "I'm gone, boss," and the guard walked away.

As they were leaving I tapped Jimmy on the arm. "Look here. If Norma Jean does this, she's not going to expect me to . . . ah, you know . . ."

He frowned, giving it his serious look. "Naw," he said. "I don't think so." And left.

That was on Wednesday.

Sunday, during the evening meal of pressed turkey, greens, mashed potatoes and gravy, Brian and I sat hunched over metal trays waiting for "B" Block to come in. The mess hall was huge, seating nearly eight hundred men who moved cafeteria-style through twin serving lines at the back of the room. Guys in T-shirts and white paper hats circulated among the four-man tables with damp towels, cleaning up the mess left behind as the tables were vacated. The noise was constant: raised voices, bursts of laughter, metal against metal as guys on their way out emptied what was left on their trays into the garbage cans next to the dishroom. Three sweaty cons on the other side of the counter took the empty trays, cups and spoons as they were handed over and ran them through the big Hobart machine; if the Hobart hadn't been sabotaged—as it often was. Sometimes the dishroom guys would just say "fuck it" about ten minutes before mealtime and break a gear or jam a cog, then give the civilian steward "who me?" looks when he came back raising hell. Then the meal would have to be served on paper plates, and the dishroom crew could go watch "Wide World of Sports" on TV.

Brian, looking up, said, "Here he comes . . . Who's that with him?"

I followed his gaze and saw Jimmy coming in followed closely by a wiry-looking black guy wearing a gray sweatshirt and a black watch cap. They moved in single file with several other guys up the right-hand serving lane, picked up trays, cups and spoons and sidestepped their way through the line, sliding their trays along in front of them.

"Beats me," I said. "Looks like they know each other though. Probably came in on the bus this afternoon."

Jimmy and the black guy, their trays full, came down the middle aisle and worked their way over to our table. Jimmy straddled the swing-away stool to my left while the black guy, looking a little self-conscious, eased in next to him.

"How ya'll doin'?" Jimmy said. "Want you to meet a friend of mine just came in from FCI Miami. Name's Choco. Choco? . . . that there's Brian, and that's Ed. You can call him Hacksaw, if you want."

"What's happenin'?" Choco said, and shook hands with me and Brian. He smiled, showing a silver front tooth, then swung his head slowly in a half circle, taking in most of the mess hall. He turned back again and said, "Big mother-fucker, ain't it?" and started on his food.

Jimmy said, "Choco and me go back a ways . . . did some time together in Raiford. When was that, Choco—sixty-seven?"

"Sixty-eight," Choco said around a mouthful of mashed potatoes.

Brian said, "This your first federal bit?"

Choco nodded, swallowing. "Been down 'bout a year. Busted with a little cocaine at Miami Airpo't comin' in from the B'hamas."

"Wasn't a lot," Jimmy said, "about eleven million worth."

Choco showed his tooth again. "They say I was dealin'. Shit, I tell 'em it was for personal use. They get me for dealin' anyway. Thirty years." He shrugged. "It be like that sometime."

"Choco got some news you might be interested in, young 'en," Jimmy said.

"Oh yeah?" I said, looking across at the black guy. He was somewhere in his early forties, built like a wide receiver, with what appeared to be a medium afro peeking out beneath the rolled watch cap. Bright, alert eyes showing traces of humor. "What kind of news?"

He said, "You the one got hooked up in that jewel robbery in Lauderdale couple of years back? Dude named Morgan owned the place?"

"Uh huh," I said.

"You know he got busted 'bout six months ago?"

"No. What for?"

"Dude had another store over in Hollywood, right? So one day these two dudes come in, tap him on the head with a gun and walk out with five million in ice. Witnesses and all see it go down, see the dude get his head cracked. But the *po*lice gets a tip it's bogus—some reliable source—and they start checkin.' FBI gets in it, they start checkin' too. Come to find out this dude's been robbed six times in five years, three times in eighteen months. This dude, shit, he been robbed more'n First National. When it all comes out, the dude finally cops, say it's all a setup. By now they got so much shit on 'im he ain't got no choice but to cop a plea." He squinted his eyes at me. "Know what he got?"

"I bet it wasn't sixty-three years," I told him.

*"Five* years," he said. "Pro*ba*tion!"

I held his gaze a moment, then glanced over at Jimmy and Brian, everybody waiting for my reaction. I said, "Figures," and went back to my food.

"Well, shit," Jimmy said. "That all you got to say . . . figures?"

"What else am I supposed to say?"

"You might could get a new trial out of this," Brian said. "Shows what the guy really is. Get a good lawyer, file a habeas corpus . . ."

"Brian," I said, tired. "Don't you think the D.A. knows all about this shit? Don't you think the *court* knows? You see anybody trying to get hold of me? saying 'Gee, Mr. Jones, you might have got a little raw deal here. So we're gonna reopen the case and see if maybe you were hit too hard on just this asshole's word and maybe readjust the sentence— how's ten years sound? Defrauding an insurance company.' The guy got *five years,* Brian. Pro*ba*tion. What's that tell you? For stealing five million. It tells me he's got somebody on the string. Ray Charles could see that. I had my day in court, and nobody believed me, case closed. I'm not going to beat my head against a wall anymore. Not that one, anyway."

Choco was scraping his tray, getting it all. "He probably

right," he said. "I know for a fact I coulda walked if it been state got me. Happen all the time, you got enough grease."

Jimmy dropped his spoon in his half-empty tray, finished. "Well, all I know is if it was me I'd be screamin' my ass off."

"You do that anyway," Brian told him.

Jimmy said, "Yeah, but you still love me, don't you, young 'en? Come on, Choco—goddamn, they gonna feed breakfast. You didn't get arrested, you got *rescued*." Looking at me he said, "Choco's a drummer—which I need bad since it don't look like you're comin' upstairs anymore. Keep tryin' all them rookies, shit, they get back there and start beatin', sound like they're sendin' home for money."

Brian and I sat there sipping lukewarm coffee after Jimmy led Choco away. The mess hall was thinning out now, guys breaking down the serving line, running push brooms and mops over sections of the tiled dining area.

Brian, studying me, said, "So nothing's changed?"

"Why should anything change? Norma Jean's coming over after five o'clock to put the finishing touches on the mask—which by the way is looking pretty good. And tomorrow you and me got a date in Industries, right?"

Brian nodded. "Make sure it's eleven-thirty. Only one foreman around at lunch, and he mostly stays in the office. We should have twenty, twenty-five minutes, anyway."

"That's enough," I said.

Brian looked off across the room, coffee cup poised, then back at me. "You know, if they find you between the East Gates while they're shaking down those cars, they're liable to turn that man in Four Tower loose on you and blow your ass away. You're already outside the wall then and that's a killing zone. They don't fuck around, Ed. Anything at all go wrong it could be 'Katy, bar the door.' "

"Yeah," I said. "Well, nobody has a written guarantee on anything, do they?" I looked at my watch and drained my cup. "Ten to five. Better go catch Norma Jean. You coming?"

Brian said, "Yeah. Nothing else to do, Jimmy out playing tour guide." He smiled. "You gonna need somebody holding point anyway while you're behind the blanket with Norma Jean.''

"Fuck you," I said.

Norma Jean, sitting at the table in my cell, said, "Honey, I can make you look good as I *want* you to be."

He was hunched over the mask with a shaving brush in one long fingernailed, delicate-looking hand, brushing the painted face with some powdered concoction he had mixed in one of Jimmy's snuff cans. The blanket was up, and Brian was outside on the tier, the sonofabitch really enjoying himself, every once in a while saying, "Ya'll all right in there? Breathing awful loud." Really in a smart-ass mood.

I said, "I don't want you to make me look *good,* I just want you to make me look *natural* . . . What is that shit, anyway?"

"Honey, this is my special blend of Cover Girl mascara. Red and brown drawing chalk—crushed very fine." He was brushing under the eyes now. "Dash of talcum powder. Some cigarette ashes . . ." now brushing lightly over the painted lips . . . "and a little shaved shoe polish for consistency. Neutral, of course. I think I'll patent it when I get out. Put Revlon right out of business. Oh, this is *fun!*"

I sat on the edge of my bunk, bent forward, looking over Norma Jean's right shoulder. Even from this angle you could see he was no prize, with flared ears jutting from an almost perfectly round head that even his stringy, mouse-colored hair, parted in the middle and nearly shoulder-length, couldn't hide. From the front he looked like Peter Lorre on a bad day—at least in the face. The body was another matter, slender and delicate, with a tiny waist, gently curving hips and a tight, saucy ass that he loved to swing. Sitting there, bent over the table in deep concentration, it stuck out over the metal stool in tight khakis in a way that would fool you if you didn't know better. Nature had made a bad mistake with Jackie Stencil. Like it wasn't quite sure which way to go, then said the hell with it and threw in a little of everything. Now he had to go through life paying for it. Maybe he was making a statement, standing out there shooting up Peachtree Street in the middle of the day and not even trying to run.

# HACKSAW

Norma Jean put down the brush and used a finger to highlight the cheek bones, blending and smoothing.

"There!" he said, leaning back, head cocked at an angle. "How's that? I think you look gorgeous. Except for the hairdo, of course, and that's simply *horrid!*"

"What did you expect," I said defensively. "It come off the barber shop floor. I'm not trying to look mod, just natural. But it looks good, Norma Jean, damn good."

"It's the pigmentation that's important," he said, adding a few quick touches with the brush. "Otherwise you'll look dead, and we can't have that now, can we?"

"Oh, absolutely not. How about the eyebrows and lashes? They look all right to you?" I said, then thought, Jesus, listen to me.

"Fine," he said. "You did good there. But that *hair!*"

I stood, reached across his shoulder and picked up the head. I laid it carefully on my pillow, drew the sheet up around the neck and stepped back, looking down at me. And it *was* me. Even without earphones hiding the missing ears and in the harsh light coming from the light bulb above the mirror, it looked unbelievably real. When it was all set up, any guard spotting it for a dummy would deserve to be warden.

"Norma Jean?" I said, still staring at my clone, "you're a genius."

"Ain't it the truth, baby?" he said, swiveling around on the seat. "You look so real I could just kiss you." And he did. He leaned over, tight little ass six inches off the stool, and planted one right on the painted and powdered lips. He sat back again, smacking his lips on exaggerated pleasure, looked up at me and grinned.

I grinned back. "How was I?"

"Not bad, honey, not bad. Gives me a wonderful idea. Why don't we make a cast of something else for me to remember you by? I'll help."

# CHAPTER 31

**B**RIAN WAS WAITING FOR ME AT THE SIDE DOOR LEADING into Industries at eleven-thirty. It was a three-story, red brick building with a hanger-like basement area used for assembly and storage of Atlanta's main product, canvas mailbags and mail carts, which they sold to the U.S. Postal Service. Four hundred cons worked piecemeal on the assembly lines eight hours a day, five days a week, year in and year out, and still they couldn't keep up with the orders. And there were nine other prisons in the federal system doing exactly the same thing. Total everything up, and the Postal Service was buying something like one million, two hundred thousand mail bags and four hundred sixty thousand mail carts every year. I wondered what the hell they were doing with all of them. No wonder stamps kept going up.

Brian opened the door as I got there, and I followed him inside and down a short flight of steps leading to the basement. When we reached the bottom, I stood behind him while Brian eased the door open and peeked inside.

"Okay," he said, "it's clear." He looked at me over his shoulder. "Remember, we don't have long. Stansberry's in the office down on the other end eating his lunch. If he comes out and starts moving around, you're gonna have to get the hell out of here. If he sees you he's gonna be suspicious as shit."

# HACKSAW

"Well, let's go," I said. "We already wasted two minutes."

Brian pushed through the door and moved quickly to his right, with me close behind. From the corner of my eye I could see the wood-and-glass-partitioned office at the far end of the long basement, maybe a hundred feet away. A gray-clad figure was sitting inside, reared back with his feet propped on a metal desk, concentrating on a sandwich. He was in profile, facing the left side of the building.

We crossed twenty feet of open space, then ducked in between two rows of assembly tables and paused. Now we were out of sight of the office, blocked from view by a towering pile of cut canvas that stretched a third of the way across the concrete floor. I looked around at the rows of waist-high wooden tables, seeing the assorted nuts and bolts, cut canvas and U-rod frames that went into building the mail carts. There were no tools visible; they were counted and locked in the foreman's office until the men returned from lunch—I checked my watch—in about twenty-two minutes. I turned and looked at the wall behind me, where rows upon rows of completed mail carts were stacked one inside the other, eight high, waiting to be loaded and transferred to the warehouse outside the walls.

Brian gave me a nudge. "Over here," he said, and we moved to the back row of tables closest to the completed carts. Here the final phase of assembly took place, attaching the thick wooden bottoms and caster wheels to the bottoms of the carts, several of which were waiting now, lying upside down along the length of tables, their canvas sides stretched tight around the U-rod frames.

Without speaking, Brian and I lifted one of the bottomless carts from the tables, carried it over to the nearest row of completed mail carts and set it down. Then we went back and got another.

I waited while Brian eased out to where he could see around the pile of cut canvas, checking the foreman's office at the other end. He hurried back.

"It's still cool," he said. "Let's get it done."

Working fast, we tilted one of the stacks of mail carts onto its side and pulled out the first five. We stuck the two bottomless carts together, placed them inside the remaining three,

375

then topped the stack off with three of the completed carts we had taken out. We tilted the stack upright again and made sure it was neatly aligned with the others in the row. Then we rolled the two good carts over to where a group of other recently completed ones stood, and that was that.

Brian said, "Come on, let's get the hell out of here."

We got out of there.

I was waiting for Jimmy and Brian to finish up in the music room, where they were going over some numbers with Choco. Stretched out on my bunk, leaning on an elbow, lost in thought while the portable Sanyo on the shelf next to my head played parlor music. Trying to think of anything I might have forgotten, playing the scenes—the way they were *supposed* to go—over and over in my mind. I would picture something going wrong, like the headphones sliding off the dummy and leaving me lying there with no ears. I made a mental note to tighten the tension on them after Jimmy and Brian showed up . . . if they ever got here. Seven-forty now, and Jimmy said no later than seven-thirty. Mail call! Now *that* was something I had overlooked. If I had a letter in the office and didn't pick it up, the cellblock guard would bring it right after count. I could see him standing at the bars, "Hey, Jones, you want this letter or not? Hey!" . . . I'd have to make sure Brian checked before count, pick it up if one was there.

Not that I was getting much mail lately. A two-page letter from Dee Dee two months ago, telling me she was pregnant and asking how I thought I'd like being a grandpa. A cute little card from Susie shortly before Mom died that was signed *As ever,* with a recent picture of Derek sitting on a green lawn in a red-and-yellow-rubber swimming pool, grinning at the camera. That was it.

"What kinna shit you got on that jukebox, young 'en?"

I looked up as Jimmy and Brian walked in, Jimmy's motions slow and deliberate as he walked over and sank down onto the toilet. I swung my legs over the bunk and sat watching him suspiciously as Brian took a seat at the table.

"You're stoned," I told him.

Jimmy looked at me, glassy-eyed. "Fuckin' A. What's wrong with that?"

"Nothing," I said, getting up and shaking out the blanket

that was lying folded at the foot of the bunk. "Long as you're in shape to watch for the man while I fix this thing up for Brian."

"Shape? Hell, I can see. Go ahead and do your thing. Let me get some coffee. Got anything to eat?"

I told him I didn't.

Jimmy fixed a cup of coffee and then oozed out to the tier while I hung the blanket and turned to Brian.

"Okay," I said, "show time."

I knelt down and pulled the towel-wrapped head from under the bunk and arranged it carefully on the pillow. I reached under again and slid out a gray sweatshirt, the sleeves and torso stuffed with toilet paper. After pulling down the top sheet, I placed it on the bunk beneath the head. Once more under the bunk, this time coming out with a pair of toilet paper-stuffed khakis, the right leg bent and tied so that the knee was elevated at a forty-five degree angle. I placed this beneath the stuffed sweatshirt, made a few adjustments, then pulled the sheet up and over the body, letting the folds settle naturally over the outline. I stepped back, examining the effect, moved in again and made another adjustment around the shoulders and below the neck, then stepped back again. Perfect.

I turned to Brian. "Look good to you? The body, I mean."

He nodded. "That'll do it."

I reached across the bunk and picked up the set of GE headphones from the shelf by the radio, bent the headpiece to narrow the fit and eased them gently over the head. I plugged the jack into the Sanyo outlet, and the parlor music abruptly ceased.

I stood with hands on hips, gazing down at my double, hearing Brian say, "Man, that thing's alive."

"Yeah," I said. "Whole setup took less than five minutes. Think you'll have any problems? I want it covered with that blanket though, not just the sheet. It's cold in here . . . less likely to slip off, too."

"I won't have any trouble," he said. "What about the recorder?"

"Under the pillow—already set. Just reach under and push the PLAY button." I looked at him. "Oh, make sure you check the board to see if I have any mail. If I do, pick it up.''

"Want me to forward it to you?" He grinned.

Just then Jimmy's voice, low and urgent, came from outside the cell. "Shit . . . the *man!* Clean it up, he's almost on you!"

I reached over and ripped the blanket from the bars and tossed it under the bunk . . . now seeing Jimmy on the tier, face set, leaning stiffly with his back against the rail. I made a move for the dummy, heard Jimmy say out of the side of his mouth, "You'll never make it," paused . . . then dived headfirst under the bunk.

I rolled over and came to rest on my stomach, pressed against the wall, looking out through the bottom bars. A pair of legs came into view, less than three feet away. Gray pants and black spit-shined shoes. The voice that went with them said to Jimmy, "How you doing?"—the legs pausing a moment. I held my breath for a count of five, and then the legs and shiny shoes were moving again, going away. Jesus!

Half a minute went by without anyone speaking, the three of us frozen in position. Finally Jimmy said, "All right—he's gone."

I crawled from under the bunk, pulling the blanket with me, and tossed it in a corner . . . and in record time had everything tucked out of sight beneath the bunk.

"Christ, Jimmy!" I said, sinking down on the mattress. I looked out at him standing there with a guilty grin on his face, dangling the now-empty coffee cup from one finger. He walked into the cell, placed the cup on the shelf above the sink and sat down on the toilet. Brian and I were both watching him now, stone-faced.

Jimmy said, "Sorry 'bout that. Guess I got to trippin' a little."

Brian said, "A hundred feet of tier and you let him walk right up on us. Dumb shit, you almost got us busted."

"Well ex*cuuu*se me!" Jimmy said. "I said I was sorry—what you want me to do, kiss your ass?"

"Never mind," I said, calmer now. "What did he do, Brian? When he stopped."

Brian looked off, then back at me, still disgusted. "He asked Dumb-ass there how he was doing, and Dumb-ass just grins at him, can't think of anything to say, which has got to be a first. Then he looks at me sitting here picking my fingernails, and we nod. Then he looks at you—what's supposed to be you . . ." He paused a moment. "And then he walks away. He just fucking walks away."

"He get a good look?" I asked.

"You kidding? Stared dead at you. Then just walks away. Shit, I still can't believe it."

Jimmy had a thought and perked up some. "See? I actually did you a favor. Now you know it works—even with this light on."

Even Brian had to smile at that.

I lit a cigarette from the pack on the table, picked up the ashtray and scooted back on the bunk with my legs folded under me.

"All right," I said, "let's go through it again real quick. There's two lots of mail carts being loaded tomorrow afternoon—right, Brian?"

"Right after lunch," he said. "They're going in the second car. Got twenty-five thousand mailbags going in the first one—and we're loading those in the morning."

"So I meet you same time, same place . . . eleven-thirty, side door, Industries."

Brian said, "Yep. We get you in the carts, you go up in the freight elevator and into the boxcar—I told you, no problem, once you're inside the carts."

"Don't let anybody else grab that stack, they'll notice the difference in weight."

"I'll be with you every step," he assured me.

"And don't tip him over," Jimmy put in, slouching on the toilet with his arms folded.

"Well, if I do, Jimmy," Brian said sarcastically. "I'll get one of the hacks there to help me pick him up—okay?"

"All right," I said, before they started again. "Now I'm in the boxcar. Give me the rest of it."

Brian leaned his head back against the wall and gazed at the ceiling. Sounding like he was rehearsing an alibi, he went through the rest.

"The boxcar's locked and sealed. I come in around three-thirty and check see if you got any mail. Dumb-ass meets me at my house, and we get here by three-forty. Then I set up the thing while—'' cutting his eyes at Jimmy—''*he* watches. And if the man walks up on me I'm throwing him off the fucking tier.''

Jimmy, looking off, nodded absently, lost somewhere. He would be fine tomorrow, and acting as Brian's lookout was the only major role he had.

Brian continued. ''After the doors open—assuming the count clears—I pick my shot and slide the thing under the bunk. At eight-forty Jimmy watches while I set it up again for the night. Six-fifteen the next morning I tear everything up, bust the head, take everything down and stuff it in the trash—which by now's gonna be pretty damn full. At ten to eight I push it out to the compactor and bring the bin back. Gonna make me a little late for work, but nobody'll give a shit. End of scene.''

I stubbed out my cigarette and immediately lit another, thinking. Brian had his part down, which was basically simple, once he wheeled me into the boxcar. Outside the walls, when the car was pulled up to the warehouse loading dock, the mail carts would be unloaded by forklift. When the civilian operator left for lunch, I could pop up like a jack-in-the-box and walk away. Yeah, that was simple too. But I wasn't fooling myself. Simplicity is an illusion that can only be made possible by perfect timing.

Brian was looking at Jimmy, who was starting to nod out on the toilet, his chin on his chest.

Brian, tired, said, ''Guess I'd better get *this* dummy home. I don't think he can find 'B' Block by himself.''

''What's he been smoking?'' I asked.

Jimmy, jerking his head up, said, ''Fuckin' Thai weed, and it ain't bad.''

''I can tell,'' I said.

Jimmy fumbled around in his shirt pocket and came out with a bent joint. He held it up between thumb and forefinger, looking like a white S. ''For you,'' he said. ''Help you sleep.'' He reached over and tucked it under a corner of the mattress.

''C'mon, smiley,'' Brian said, getting up, ''let's go home.''

Jimmy stood and looked around, patting his pockets. ''The fuck's my snuff can?''

Brian said, ''At home,'' and steered him towards the door.

"See you at breakfast," I said.

When they were gone I undressed and got into bed, the light still on, and draped the headphones over my head—on the off chance that the guard got to thinking about it and decided to come by for another look.

Later, after nine o'clock count, I sat in the corner next to the bars and smoked the Thai joint, using my shaving mirror to keep watch on the tier. I started getting melancholy about halfway through it, drifting a little, lulled by the semidarkness and the parlor music still coming from the Sanyo. The overhead tier lights slanting through the bars made zebra-striped patterns on the concrete floor. I stared at them, trancelike, as I sucked in the sweetish-tasting smoke, held it, then slowly exhaled. Jimmy was right—it wasn't bad. Put you right up there where the 747s are, take you anywhere you want to go.

And a few places you don't want to go. I didn't want to go back to Beaumont again, but I did. Then skimmed over tree-tops and rushing landscape until I reached Camps 15 and 21. I hovered there a while, seeing familiar faces, then zipped on over to Five Hundred Spring Street, where I cursed Goldie and flailed away at Red Miller with a softball bat. A runaway videotape, stuck on fast forward. Lingering for a while on Susie and Derek, equal time to Dee Dee . . . coming to a dead stop on Mom.

Jesus!

I got up and flushed the roach that was burning my fingers down the toilet, climbed into the bunk and plugged in the headphones . . . jumped up again and blew a puff of Johnson's Baby Powder into the air to kill the weed smell . . . then back into the bunk again.

The tape was still on stop. A soft, wrinkled face with wounded deer eyes, surrounded by the sounds of string instruments and muted horns. It took a while before I realized what the song was. An instrumental version of "Silver Bells." I had completely forgotten that Christmas was six days away.

There was little talk around the breakfast table, the three of us concentrating on our powdered eggs, sausage patties and farina, washing it down with sips of black coffee while we darted knowing looks at each other over the rims of our cups.

Jimmy was first to finish, pushing his tray away and draining his cup. He gave me a long look, sitting there with his hands in his lap.

"You need anything?" he asked.

"No. Just a little bit of luck."

"You'll make it," he said. "Least you'll make it outta the walls. Last night made a believer outta me."

"Tell Norma Jean I said thanks again, will you? She did a good job."

Jimmy said, "I think she wants to keep it—the head, I mean. Fell in love with it."

I said, "Yeah, but I don't want Hogan knowing how I got out . . . if I get out. I want him to go crazy thinking about it."

Jimmy looked at me a moment, thoughtful, then said, "Well, I'm gone," dumping his cup and spoon on the metal tray. He stuck out his hand and grinned. "You take care now—you hear?"

I took the hand, squeezing hard. "You know it. Thanks for your help, Jimmy."

He said, "Behave yourself," gathered up his tray and walked away, moving through the tables, grinning and slapping guys on the back. Jimmy Buck. The Good Humor man.

Brian left a few minutes later, saying he would see me at eleven-thirty. I watched him all the way to the dish room, his lanky frame relaxed and unhurried. He wouldn't tip me over, I decided. Not Brian. He would be as good as All-State.

I finished my coffee and went to take out the trash for the last time.

There was a cold drizzle falling when I met Brian at the side door to Industries. I was dressed in new khakis over a grey sweatsuit, two pairs of athletic socks under Adidas tennis shoes and my heavy pea coat. A blue watch cap was pulled low over my ears. Tucked beneath my waistband was an empty plastic milk bag and a Sue Bee Honey jar of water.

Brian looked me over, then turned without a word and led the way inside and down the steps to the basement. He eased the door at the bottom open, and we both peered through the opening, down to where Stansberry was sitting in the foreman's office, looking like he hadn't moved since yesterday.

We slipped inside, hurried across the open floor until we were hidden by the jutting pile of cut canvas, then moved with purpose over to the waiting columns of mail carts against the side wall.

Working fast, we tilted the doctored stack onto its side and pulled out the top two carts. I got down on my hands and knees and squinted into the dark opening. I would have about three feet of head room.

Brian, urgent, said, "C'mon, we don't have all day."

I said, "Sure you can push it back up with me inside?"

"You'll never know 'til you get in."

I crawled inside, turned onto my side and made myself as small as possible. Brian eased the two carts back into the stack, and I was surrounded by darkness. I felt myself being lifted, the cars tilting upward, a jerk and a lurch as Brian got a new grip, trying to keep the wheels from rolling out beneath him, then a final rush of movement as the stack landed upright on its casters. Brian rolled me around a little, lining me up with the other stacks, then all motion ceased. I was lying on my back, knees drawn up, head tilted against the opposite end. Uncomfortable as hell, but not nearly as uncomfortable as Atlanta Federal Prison.

Brian, his voice somewhere close behind me, said, "You all right in there?"

"Everything's fine," I said to the darkness.

"Okay, looks good from here." The voice was further away now, like he had stepped back a few paces. Now it was close again as he said, "Don't worry. I got you all the way. I'm gonna get out of here now and come back with the others. Don't move any more than you have to . . . and no noise. See you in a little bit."

"Brian?" I said.

"What?"

"Thanks. I couldn't have done this without you."

"Oh, I dunno," he said. "You'd probably think of a way . . . I'm gone."

And I was left alone in the cramped darkness.

* * *

The basement was coming alive now: big exhaust fans in the side of the building winding up; the sound of mini-tractors *putt-putting* around, hauling wagonloads of canvas bolts, casters, U-rods, and other odds and ends to the assembly tables; guys yelling back and forth, some within a few yards of my hiding place.

I reached down between my legs and picked up the penlight I had stolen from the hospital, clicked the little button on the end and checked my watch in the tiny beam of light: twelve-oh-five. I clicked it off and set it down again, next to the plastic milk bag and honey bottle of water. I hugged my knees and waited.

"Here we go, loop de loop . . ." Brian's voice, singing, right behind me now. "Here we go, loop de la ah ah ah—think I'd make it on TV, Beatle?"

And Beatle, close by, said, "Maybe, you sit real still and don't fall off."

Moving now, the rumble of casters on concrete as Brian rolled me across the floor, then more rumbling as other guys grabbed more stacks and fell in behind . . . over to the freight elevator next to the stairway and inside. Then we were going up, the whine of the elevator motor loud in my ears. A lurch as the car stopped, then moving again, out of the elevator and onto the loading dock . . . past the two guards who would be standing to either side of the open boxcar doors, keeping tally on clipboards. The pitch of the casters changing now, echoing inside the steel confines of the boxcar, a gentle *thump* as Brian parked me against the rear wall, then whispering as he left, "You're on your own."

I was in.

I clicked the penlight and checked my watch: four-sixteen. They would be through counting in the blocks. I adjusted my position, able to risk movement now that the boxcar was locked and sealed, and pictured alert guards walking by my cell, stopping at the bars to do a double take—"Hello there . . . what's this?"—then start tearing the place apart. First spot they'd hit would be the boxcars. Getting by the four o'clock count was the most critical phase; the two guards would be out to impress each other with how diligent they were. About now they would be calling in their totals to the

Lieutenant's office, where they would be put on the Sentry computer that went straight to Washington. If everything tallied, Sentry would display two words on the monitor screen: count checks. If not, one word would appear: recount. Either way the control room officer would announce the verdict over the PA system—I checked my watch again: four-twenty—any time now . . . any time . . .

The PA system came to life, the control room officer's voice reaching me clearly. "Count clear, count clear—four twenty-one P.M."

I felt so relieved that I opened the milk bag and urinated, not realizing I had to go so bad.

A violent jar sent me lunging forward, causing my head to bang painfully against the undercarriage of the cart directly above. Voices outside, faint, somewhere at the front of the boxcars. Then another lurch, more gentle this time, a deep rumbling sound from up ahead . . . now moving slowly forward. Quickly I checked my watch—eight-ten—and let out a long breath, realizing what was happening. They had brought in the locomotive and coupled the boxcars to it, and now we were heading for the East Gates.

Somehow during the night, in spite of my cramped position and the deepening cold, I had fallen asleep, though I couldn't remember when. I was approaching the final barrier now, the last hurdle before leaving the walls.

After several minutes the car stopped. I was inside the East Gates. Voices and a jingling of keys came from outside the boxcar door . . . a heavy rasping sound as the sliding door was pulled back. I held my knees and took shallow breaths as what sounded like two men entered the car and started climbing over the rows of mail carts, grunting and swearing, wanting to get it done because they weren't really expecting to find anything in the first place. One stepped into the top cart of the stack to my left, and I could actually hear him breathing as I rolled my eyes upward through the darkness. Then he scrambled back over the stacks to the door and jumped out.

Somebody yelled to the tower directly above, "Open one!" and a few moments later I was moving again, slowly at first, then gathering speed as the boxcars cleared the outer gate and wound their way around the curving tracks that led to the huge warehouse fifty yards away. I thought, "I'm out! Really out!" not able to believe everything had actually worked exactly the way it was planned. I felt like laughing, shouting, beating my chest—anything to release the tension that was screaming to get out.

I removed the plastic cap from the honey bottle and gulped the remaining water—dropped it next to the knotted urine bag and inhaled deeply for the first time in more than twenty hours. The rest would be easy; one civilian forklift operator unloading the cars, not expecting anything, the warehouse loading dock shielded from view of any guard towers. Walk right out the door and head across the field in back of the prison—*Jesus!* not even having to *run*. Wouldn't even be missed until four o'clock, and then they would spend hours searching the entire prison thinking I was hiding out. By tomorrow morning they would have to advise Washington that apparently I had escaped. I pictured the conversation. Washington would say, *"Apparently?* What's this *apparently* shit? Did he or didn't he?"* . . . and Hogan saying, "Well, if he's here, we can't find him—and if he got out, we don't know how." Then Washington saying, *"What?* You sayin' you don't know if he's in or out? Ain't that a *bitch!"*

Yeah. I guess I did feel pretty good at that.

# CHAPTER 32

THREE HUNDRED YARDS IN BACK OF THE ATLANTA FEDERAL
Prison is a gently rising hill, at the top of which is a large
clearing the size of a football field. The grass grows wild and
unkept here, the back side of the clearing sloping downward
to join with a thick stand of young Georgia pines. There is
nothing to distinguish this clearing as being any different from
thousands of others similar in nature, though one might wonder in passing about the evenly spaced mounds which line
the earth like small grassy waves. The clearing is Atlanta's
version of Potter's Field, the final resting place for dozens of
Atlanta's inmate population who had died or were murdered
inside the walls. Here lie the unmourned and the unclaimed,
those who were unable to escape the shadow of prison even
in death—which is perhaps the final indignity.

I stood among these unmarked rows and looked back at
the prison, hands jammed into the deep pockets of my pea
coat, collar turned up against the wind and the drizzle that
was still falling. The walls looked small in the distance, and
it was a weird feeling to be standing here in the midst of the
unknown dead, looking *in* instead of *out*. The elation was
gone, replaced by a sense of wonder . . . and the futility of
it all. So I was out. Big deal. Now what? Where do I go from
here? Back to more of the same? And for how long this time?
Doing life on the installment plan.

Jesus—get morbid, why don't you, I thought. I danced

around a little, stomping warmth into my feet, considering options. I had a ten-dollar bill in my pocket, enough to get me out of Georgia. Call Ted in Houston, he'd help me get on my feet. Find some out-of-the-way place and pull the zipper—forget about it. The hell with that. What was the point in getting out of one prison only to lock yourself away in another? So take it as it comes, then; get laid, have a few laughs, a few drinks, see what happens next. How's that sound to you?

Great. Something to do, anyway.

I opened a button on my coat and reached into my shirt pocket for my first cigarette since yesterday morning . . . and pulled a folded piece of paper out with the pack. Almost forgot about it. I lit the cigarette and opened the *National Enquirer* article, the paragraph Jimmy had read to the Country Swinger Fan Club circled in red. I smiled as I read it, enjoying the words and the cigarette, seeing Hogan's face as he opened his mail about two days from now. I'd send a card with it; something with a big Santa Claus on the front. Mail it on the way out of town.

I put the paper away, stomped out the butt and looked off in the distance—past the gray prison squatting in the drizzle to McDonough Boulevard. Traffic was thick this morning, heavy with the lunch-hour rush. People whispering by in the rain, secure in their little metal worlds, craning their necks at the tall cellblock windows as they drove past the entrance to Atlanta. *Now Robert, you little shit, I swear if you don't stop that whining I'm going to march you in there and hand you to the warden, tell him to keep you! That's where they put bad little boys.*

I turned and walked down the hill towards the stand of young Georgia pines, thankful I wouldn't be spending this Christmas in prison.

I WAS RECAPTURED ON MAY 2, 1979, IN OCEAN BEACH, CALifornia, just outside San Diego. The FBI, after receiving a tip that I was in the area, traced me to a leased apartment on Santa Cruz Avenue, and another year and a half of semifreedom came to an end. I remember stepping out of the 1977 Monte Carlo that was three payments short of being mine, and seeing four guys with short-cropped hair in Ivy League suits moving toward me with weapons drawn. They were flanked by two Ocean Beach squad cars, and I decided right then and there that there was no percentage in offering resistance. The guys with the badges don't tell you to lean against the car and spread 'em anymore; that went out with "Hawaii Five-O". These days it's face down and spread-eagle in the middle of the street, and the hell with mud-puddles and traffic. They almost seemed disappointed to find out I wasn't armed.

They took me to Metropolitan Correctional Center, a twenty-two story high-rise jail for federal prisoners in downtown San Diego. They had a cell already waiting for me on the fifth floor, normally reserved for violent mental patients and those running on PCP. It had stainless steel inserts lining the concrete walls and double-thick steel mesh screens covering a narrow window of quarter-inch-thick Lexan. For good measure they parked a guard at a small table just outside the cell so he could watch me through the little oblong window in the door.

They didn't know it, but there was no need for all the theatrics; not anymore. I was tired of it all, burnt out, exhausted from a nineteen-year marathon that had finally caught up with me, at least mentally. Behind me were another eighteen months of dodging shadows, zipping in and out of cities, odd jobs, borrowed identities and temporary relationships until the images had begun to blur—like a carousel gone berserk. Maybe it was time to get off.

So I paced and thought, occasionally lifting my gaze to the serious-looking guard outside the door who was already reared back with his feet up on the table . . .

Fourteen escapes . . . fourteen! And here I was right back where I started. It gradually dawned on me that if a person couldn't achieve a specific goal in that many attempts, then he'd better try something different. By the following morning I'd made up my mind.

I wasn't going to run anymore.

My escape from Atlanta cost me another five years, imposed by a stern-faced federal judge in San Diego who said that actions such as mine had to be discouraged. I now had a grand total of thirty-four years federal time, and fifty-five with the state of Florida for "robbing" Joe Morgan. Amazing, I thought, how quickly things can start adding up. It was going to take some effort to get off the carousel.

A succession of prisons followed; Lompoc, California; Marion, Illinois; Chicago, Illinois; Otisville, New York. For the first three years I was kept in total lock-down status, relegated to tomb-like cells for twenty-three hours a day, with one hour for exercise and a shower. I spent the time writing letters and reading everything I could get my hands on. I reestablished contact with Susan and my daughter Dee Dee. Susan was still living in Shreveport, trying to cope with a sprouting Derek. Dee Dee was married and living in Goldsboro, North Carolina—and about to make me a grandfather.

Jesus—where does the time go!

In 1982, Bureau of Prisons officials in Washington, D.C., finally placed me in open population in a prison at Butner, North Carolina. One man was responsible for this move; an Assistant Director of the BOP named J.D. Williams, who for some strange reason believed me when I gave him my word that I would not attempt to escape, something I had never said before. I simply wanted to be near at least some members of my family. I spent another two years there, passing some pleasant hours in the visiting room with Dee Dee and my brand new granddaughter, Stephanie . . . trying to catch up. Because of the distance, Susan and Derek were unable to visit. But we did spend a lot of time on the phone, where I was able to become buddies with Derek, who was nearly twelve now. He was also old enough to ask some pretty heavy questions that demanded some deep, soul-searching thought. Kids have a knack for cutting through the verbal bullshit in a way that makes all excuses sound hollow even to yourself.

As for Susan and I, it was quietly understood that our previous relationship would never be revived. A big chunk of our lives would always be missing, and no effort on our part could ever fill in the blanks. But we could still be friends, and are to this day, and perhaps that's even more important.

But all this family reunioning was making me long for the outside world in a way I never had before . . . because now I truly knew what I was missing. I wanted to take Derek fishing and to ball games, rough-house with him on a green lawn and talk to him about those marvelous mysteries called girls. I wanted to take Stephanie to circuses and county fairs, buy her frilly dresses and cuddly dolls, and tell her bed-time stories while holding her until she finally fell asleep.

Talk to me about punishment.

I decided to hire an attorney and see if anything could be done about that fifty-five-year Florida sentence for "robbing" Joe Morgan, and maybe, while he was at it, do something about the accompanying eight-year federal sentence for carrying "stolen" property across state lines. But I wanted a good one, not some Smiling Jack who would lead me on with hearty assurances while holding out his hand for more money.

After some extensive checking I was told that the man I needed was David Rudolf, of Beskind & Rudolf Law Offices in Chapel Hill, North Carolina. He would be expensive, but there was no one better in the entire South. I figured, well, you get what you pay for, and called him. An agreement was reached, Dave took the case, and immediately went to work.

The first thing that had to be determined was how the District Attorney's office in Broward County, Florida, felt about possibly reopening the robbery case in light of Morgan's subsequent conviction. Investigative reports showed that he had reported six large-scale robberies within a five-year period (including the one involving myself), three of them occurring in eighteen months. Transcripts of his testimony during my trial also showed that the man had committed perjury by testifying that I had taken six trays of jewelry. A Fort Lauderdale police officer, however, testified that Morgan had told him only three trays had been taken. But the D.A.'s office wasn't interested in reopening anything, evidence or no evidence. They had a good conviction on the books and by-God it was going to stay there.

David Rudolf, a transplanted New Yorker who bears a mild resemblance to Al Pacino, got feisty after that and rolled up his white shirt sleeves. "All right," he said, "fuck 'em. We'll go after the parole board. We'll hit them with so much information they'll go cross-eyed trying to read it all."

And he did. And a year later, in October 1984, the Florida Department of Probation and Paroles paroled me to my federal sentence. I would not have to worry about Florida anymore.

Things were moving at last . . . and so was I. The Bureau of Prisons first ordered me transferred back to MCC San Diego, then to a new prison in Phoenix, Arizona. By this time J.D. Williams was no longer in Washington, having made a lateral move to take over the BOP's Southwest Regional office in Dallas, Texas—probably because he got tired of all the back-stabbing that goes on at the Central Office in Washington, D.C., which is mostly comprised of a bunch of pseudo-intellectuals who know more about politics than they do about running a national prison system. J.D. Williams has more correctional savvy packed in his pipe than they have in their collective heads.

While all this was going on David Rudolf was launching a two-prong assault on my federal sentences. He offered the same information to the U.S. Parole Commission that had been presented to the Florida Commission. At my hearing on August 14, 1984, a two-man panel recommended that I be paroled on July 4, 1985, my eligibility date. But the recommendation was rejected by the National Commission in Washington D.C., which eventually set a presumptive date of February 16, 1991. The main reasons offered in their Notice of Action stated that this was because ". . . you committed an armed robbery in which you transported stolen property in excess of $500,000 across state lines." Apparently they had not read one word of the reports which had been submitted to them, preferring instead to rely on the sole word of the "victim." Small wonder that Congress is putting them out of business (effective November 1st, 1987, the U.S. parole commission will be abolished to all offenders sentenced after that date). During the ten years of their existence they've given themselves more power than the United States Supreme Court.

Dave then brought in Tom Maher, a recent addition to the law firm, to help file suit against the U.S. Parole Commission in federal court. Not only was he young and bright, but an expert in the rules and regulations by which the Commission is governed. That suit is currently pending before the Ninth Circuit Court of Appeals in San Francisco, California.

Meanwhile Dave was petitioning United States District Judge Norman C. Roettger in Fort Lauderdale, who had sentenced me to the eight-year sentence for Interstate Transportation of Stolen Property in 1975. He was asking the conviction be vacated in light of substantial new information relating to the "victim," Joe Morgan.

I am currently awaiting the results of a hearing of this petition conducted by Judge Roettger in open court two weeks ago. If my request is granted, then the U.S. Parole Commission will be obligated to reconsider my case—this time without being able to consider that eight-year sentence. Which could mean that I might very well be released by mid-1988 . . . truly free for the first time in twenty-seven years.

What a thought.

Now let me make one observation and then I'll be finished,

and it comes as a result of more than two decades of rubbing elbows with the kept and keepers alike.

The official stated position of the United States Bureau of Prisons is that rehabilitation does not work. They have gone to a great deal of time and effort to sell this theory to Congress and the American public as well. In a word, this is pure bullshit. It doesn't even comport with common sense, and one minute of serious thought would show the lunacy of that statement. If rehabilitation indeed does not work, then it follows that every offender who enters prison is relegated to a lifetime of crime. Yet ten years ago, when prisoner rehabilitation was a top priority, the recidivist rate for federal offenders was one in four. Today, at the peak of the anti-rehabilitation movement, it's two in four—or twice as many. In that same time period the federal prison system has nearly doubled from 24,000 in 1977, to 45,000 today. The projected annual increase in the federal system alone is estimated at 8% over the next five years, and who knows after that . . . and these are U.S. Government figures, figures that many experts feel are far too conservative.

It doesn't take a genius to figure out we had better rehabilitate somebody, and be damn quick about it.

What federal prison officials are really saying is that they don't want rehabilitative programs in the first place, that they don't have the qualified personnel to administer them in the second, and that they wouldn't recognize the results if you waved them before their eyes on a color-coded graph in the third. They would rather spend their appropriations money by building twice as many prisons and hiring twice as many correctional officers, doubling that figure approximately once every decade, until eventually the number of federal prisons in this country will outnumber MacDonald's Restaurants. Their logo could be a golden arch of razor wire and a flashing sign that reads: OVER ONE MILLION SERVING!

The age-old fallacy of quantity over quality.

Another fact: each dramatic increase in the prison population is directly reflected by an increase in the membership of organized street gangs in the community, and in case you haven't noticed, they're becoming more and more violent each and every year (in Los Angeles alone the number of homicides committed by these gangs is over 300 a year and growing). And their recruiting and day to day activities are controlled almost exclusively from behind prison walls. And prison officials, in their all-knowing wisdom, try to solve the problem by spreading it around. Five days a week, two Boeing 727s owned by the U.S. Bureau of Prisons criss-cross the country, depositing gang members in prisons from California to New York, from North Carolina to Washington state. There, like cancer cells, they take roots and multiply, reorganizing and recruiting, sending their released brothers into unsuspecting local communities who are totally unprepared to deal with them.

While prison gangs become more and more sophisticated, prison officials become less so. Once again quantity over quality. Staff turn-over within the BOP is a whopping 85%. Consequently their recruiting efforts for correctional officers is as intense as that of the prison gangs themselves, and they're not very choosy about who they hire. Got a high school education and no felony convictions? Welcome aboard. That's all it takes. But it doesn't take long before the brightest of even these become disillusioned with the low pay scale, inadequate training and constant stress, and decide that they can do a lot better. I'm not saying there aren't any good corrections personnel in the United States Bureau of Prisons, because there are, I'm just saying they're as scarce as the California Condor.

Obviously these ideas are not going to make me very popular with many prisoners or officials. I'll make that one of my major goals in life, becoming popular with prison gangs and BOP officials. And you don't have to accept the opinion of a guy who's broken the law and deserved to come to prison; I accept the responsibility of my own actions, as well as the consequences. But it's an opinion shared by many outside professionals as well, and someone had better listen to them. One of the nation's foremost authorities in the field of criminology, Dr. Karl Menninger, psychiatrist and founder of the Menninger Foundation in Topeka, Kansas, probably said it the best during a recent interview with Ann Landers concerning the making of a criminal.

Said Dr. Menninger:

"Some of the most hardened and dangerous criminals in society come from prisons. The penitentiaries in our country are a disgrace. Instead of being institutions of rehabilitation, they are places that teach people how to steal, maim and murder. Until something is done to change the system, it will get far worse before it gets better.''

Well put, Dr. Menninger. Because until society demands a drastic change, then the functions of our nation's prisons will remain nothing more than an exercise in futility . . . just as my escapes were.

EDWARD R. JONES,

      Petitioner,

v.

UNITED STATES OF AMERICA,

          Respondent. /

UNITED STATES DISTRICT COURT
SOUTHERN DISTRICT OF FLORIDA

CASE NO. 83-6325-CIV-NCR

FINAL ORDER

THIS CAUSE is before the Court on Motion of PETITIONER, EDWARD R. JONES, to vacate PETITIONER's conviction and sentence.[1]

Upon consideration of the record and after evidentiary hearing in this cause, it is

ORDERED AND ADJUDGED that PETITIONER's Motion to vacate his conviction and sentence is GRANTED.

PETITIONER pled guilty in this Court on November 12, 1975, to interstate transportation of stolen property . PETITIONER received an eight (8) year sentence.

---

1. PETITIONER is a legendary escape artist with the nickname of "Hacksaw." PETITIONER's early career featured repeated escapes, culminated by a clever escape from Atlanta penitentiary while serving the instant sentence; apparently this skill hasn't been exercised in recent years. PETITIONER has been exercising, instead, the skill of a writer and PETITIONER's second book will soon be published.

PETITIONER has been convicted for escapes subsequent to this instant offense and is serving a lengthy sentence.

PETITIONER brings the instant suit under 28 U.S.C. 2255 (2255), to have his conviction and sentence set aside. Since PETITIONER pled guilty F.R.Crim.P. 11 (Rule 11), which governs the taking of guilty pleas, applies.

Violations of Rule 11 warrant 2255 relief in one of four circumstances: (1) when the violation is jurisdictional or constitutional, (2) when the violation constitutes a fundamental defect resulting in a complete miscarriage of justice, (3) when the violation is not consistent with fair procedure, or (4) when the violation presents exceptional circumstances. U.S. v. Timmreck, 441 U.S. 780 (1979); and see Keel v. U.S., 585 F.2d 110, 114 (5th Cir. 1978) (en banc) (prior to Timmreck but consonant therewith); Lilly v. U.S. , 792 F.2d 1541 (11th Cir. 1986).

The standard of review in a 2255 proceeding is the "cause and actual prejudice" standard. U.S. v. Frady, 456 U.S. 152, 167 (1982). Under the "cause and actual prejudice" standard a petitioner in a 2255 proceeding must show good cause for collaterally as opposed to directly attacking his conviction, Frady, supra, at 167-68, and must show a fundamental error in his conviction which prejudiced the petitioner and resulted in a miscarriage of justice. Id.; U.S. v. Addonizio, 442 U.S. 178, 185 (1979) (quoting Hill v. U.S., 368 U.S. 424, 428 (1962)).

In the case at bar PETITIONER alleges, first, that he is entitled to relief under 2255 because there was no factual basis

for PETITIONER's guilty plea. PETITIONER alleges that this Court
was substantially misled as to the existence of a necessary
element of the charge to which PETITIONER pled guilty.

PETITIONER pled guilty to 18 U.S.C. 2314 (2314). 2314
says in pertinent part: "Whoever transports in interstate
commerce any goods, wares, [or] merchandise. . .of the value of
$5,000.00 or more, knowing the same to have been stolen, shall be
guilty of an offense. . ." (emphasis added). One essential
element of this offense is that the property transported be
stolen. <u>Dowling v. U.S.</u>, 105 S.Ct. 3127, 3132-33 (1985).
"Stolen" is a broad term meant to reach all the ways by which a
rightful owner of property is wrongfully deprived of the rights
and benefits of ownership. <u>U.S. v. McClain</u>, 545 F.2d 988, 992
(5th Cir. 1977).

PETITIONER asserts that the property he transported was
not in fact "stolen," because the property was transported with
the owner's consent. PETITIONER says that he pled guilty to
section 2314, and did not seek relief until several years after
his conviction, because PETITIONER did not know until now that
the consent of the owner of property vitiates a federal
theft-based charge.

In reviewing PETITIONER's Motion the Court feels
constrained to note the circumstances surrounding the taking of
PETITIONER'S plea. The circumstances were unique, and the
pressures generated by the circumstances can only be described as

"hydraulic." The circumstances of PETITIONER's plea have much to do with the instant Motion.

At the time of his plea PETITIONER was something of a legend due to his numerous successful escapes from custody. PETITIONER had in fact only recently been recaptured at the time of his plea. Just prior to his recapture and plea PETITIONER left three FBI agents and federal marshals handcuffed together while PETITIONER drove off in the Government car.

On the day of PETITIONER's plea PETITIONER was brought into the federal building in leg irons, waist chains, and handcuffs, under heavy guard. Security in the courthouse was unusually tight. A Fort Lauderdale Police officer stood guard with a shotgun. The goal, of course, was to insure that PETITIONER did not complete yet another escape.

Under these circumstances and just prior to taking PETITIONER's plea the following conversation between the Court and PETITIONER took place:

THE COURT: (referring to the Government's proffer) Mr. Jones, is that what happened?
PETITIONER: Everything except the statement that I myself personally committed the robbery.

(Tr. p. 10)

Because of the circumstances surrounding PETITIONER and his plea the Court did not grasp the significance of PETITIONER'S statement. Without further inquiry, the Court accepted PETITIONER's plea.

400

Unknown to the Court when the Court took PETITIONER's plea, PETITIONER had previously elaborated on his in-court statement that PETITIONER did not commit the robbery. PETITIONER had stated at the time of his arrest on July 12, 1975, that the "robbery" was really "an inside job which was accomplished with the assistance of the owner" of the property, Joseph Sirgany (Sirgany). PETITIONER's statement that the robbery was actually an inside job was related by Milton Simmons, Chief Probation Officer for the Western District of Louisiana, in a letter to the United States Parole Commission. PETITIONER's statement was not made known to this Court.

PETITIONER testified at the evidentiary hearing in the instant cause that Sirgany, the owner of the jewelry store which PETITIONER pled guilty to robbing, called PETITIONER regarding an insurance scam. Sirgany allegedly offered to pay PETITIONER, in jewelry, to pretend to rob the store so that Sirgany could collect the insurance proceeds.

The likely veracity of PETITIONER's testimony that the "robbery" was orchestrated by Sirgany is borne out by the following events and circumstances which became known or occured subsequent to PETITIONER's plea:

(1) PETITIONER has consistently alleged from the day of PETITIONER's arrest to the present time that the "robbery" was an "inside job."

(2) PETITIONER felt strongly that he was not guilty of robbery as charged by the state, but apparently thought he was

guilty of the Federal crime because PETITIONER did transport the
jewelry across state lines.

Therefore, although PETITIONER feared that a jury would
believe Sirgany, a local buisnessman, rather than himself,
PETITIONER ignored his attorney's advice and pled not guilty to
robbery charges brought by the state of Florida. Jones asserted
that the "robbery" was part of a scheme concocted by Sirgany to
collect the insurance proceeds. PETITIONER was convicted but
later paroled by the state of Florida, see point (6), _infra_.

(3) Sirgany was convicted in July, 1981, of faking an
armed robbery of Sirgany's own jewelry store as part of an
insurance scam (Sirgany was sentenced to 5 years probation).

(4) The mode of the July, 1981, insurance scam for which
Sirgany was convicted was identical to that described by
PETITIONER regarding the July, 1975 "robbery" for which
PETITIONER was convicted.

(5) Investigation by the Florida Parole and Probation
Commission (Commission) revealed the "great possibility" that
Sirgany set up the 1975 "robbery" for which PETITIONER was
convicted. The Commission based this "great possibility" on the
facts that (a) Sirgany had reported 6 robberies of the same
nature, including 3 within 18 months of each other, (b) Sirgany
had been convicted of faking a robbery in order to collect the
insurance, and (c) Sirgany reported 6 trays of stolen jewelry to
his insurance company after the 1975 "robbery" for which
PETITIONER was convicted, when in fact only 3 trays were taken.

(8)   The Commission recommended on the basis of its investigation that PETITIONER be paroled from the state conviction (PETITIONER was so paroled).

(9)   Judge Paul Marko III, Circuit Court, 15th Judicial Circuit, Palm Beach County, Florida, who was the presiding judge at PETITIONER's trial on the state robbery charges, stated after Sirgany's conviction that "[PETITIONER's] story has always been consistent," and forwarded a letter from PETITIONER to the Broward County state attorney's and public defender's offices so that either or both of those offices could, if they chose, investigate whether the 1975 "robbery" was in fact a robbery.

This Court can say without reservation that if this Court had been aware at the time of PETITIONER's plea that PETITIONER had stated upon arrest and continued to maintain that the "robbery" was an inside job, the Court would not have accepted PETITIONER's plea.[2]  Absent the unique pressures and

---

2.  This Court remembers that Jones' Pre-Sentence Report showed several convictions and sentences for escapes but not a single conviction for any other crime.  This track record of Defendant seemed not only bizarre— as it truly was— but also completely unique among defendants.  Additionally, this track record seems incompatible with the events surrounding the "jewel robbery."

circumstances surrounding the taking of PETITIONER's plea the Court would have caught the significance of PETITIONER's statement that he personally didn't commit the robbery. Certainly, events known or occuring after PETITIONER's plea show the "great possibility" that PETITIONER'S testimony is true, that the property in PETITIONER's possession was not "stolen."

Given the evidence in this cause it appears to the Court that the "stolen" character of the property is in grave doubt. Accordingly, the Court finds no factual basis for PETITIONER's plea to the charge of transporting stolen property, "knowing the same to have been stolen." Quite the contrary, PETITIONER knew that, allegedly, Sirgany had paid PETITIONER with jewelry to "rob" Sirgany's store.

Lack of a factual basis for a plea constitutes a fundamental defect which is a miscarriage of justice, a violation inconsistent with fair procedure, and an exceptional circumstance. See Timmreck, supra. Accordingly, PETITIONER's Motion for relief under 2255 for lack of a factual basis for PETITIONER's plea is GRANTED.

PETITIONER alleges, secondly, that he is entitled to relief under 2255 because PETITIONER did not understand the nature of the charge to which PETITIONER pled guilty. PETITIONER says that he pled guilty because he did not know and was not informed that property transported across state lines is not within the statute- and cannot be "stolen"- when taken with the owner's consent. PETITIONER admits a scheme to fake a robbery but PETITIONER alleges that he did not understand the legal significance of such a scheme, i.e., that PETITIONER could not be guilty of transporting "stolen" property if PETITIONER had the owner's consent.

Rule 11, which governs the taking of guilty pleas, is designed to insure, _inter alia_, that a defendant understands the nature of the charges to which he pleads. _U.S. v. Bell_, 776 F.2d 965, 968 (11th Cir. 1985), _cert. denied_, 106 S.Ct. 3272 (1986). A guilty plea entered voluntarily and understandingly precludes any further inquiry into the question of guilt. _Moore v. U.S._, 425 F.2d 1290 (5th Cir.), _cert. denied_, 400 U.S. 846 (1970).

If a plea is voluntary and knowing, then mere technical noncompliance with or a "formal" violation of the requirements of Rule 11 will not serve as a basis for relief in a 2255 proceeding. _Adams v. Lankford_, 788 F.2d 1493, 1496 (11th Cir. 1986); and see _Timmreck_, _supra_. However, relief can be granted if a defendant did not understand the offense to which he pled and the defendant was prejudiced thereby. _See, e.g._, _U.S. v. Scott_, 625 F.2d 623 (5th Cir. 1980).

The importance of an understanding plea was addressed in _U.S. v. Dayton_, 604 F.2d 931 (5th Cir. 1979), where the court noted that, while guilty pleas serve many desirable legal and societal goals, one of the "most dangerous" pitfalls of guilty pleas is that a man might plead in ignorance. The _Dayton_ court stated that a defendant must "know[] what it is he is admitting,

so that he does not mistakenly consent to be punished for a crime
he did not commit." _Id._ at 935. Rule 11 was designed in part to
protect against ignorant pleas. _Id._ at 936.

It is clear, from PETITIONER's testimony and other
evidence, _see_ this Order, _supra_, at pp. 2 - 6, that PETITIONER
did not understand the nature of the charge to which he pled.
PETITIONER did not understand that property obtained by consent
of the owner can not be "stolen" property. This lack of
understanding is underscored by PETITIONER's statement at the
plea that all the evidence against him was true "except the
statement that I myself personally committed the robbery."
PETITIONER pled guilty and consented to punishment in ignorance
or from confusion equivalent to ignorance.

2255 relief may be warranted when a petitioner pleads and
proves that the petitioner would not have pled guilty if he had
understood the nature and elements of the offense. _U.S. v._
_Patterson_, 739 F.2d 191 (5th Cir. 1984). _And see_ _McCarthy v._
_U.S._, 394 U.S. 459, 470 (1968) (defendant entitled to plead anew
where, facing charge of "knowing and wilful" attempt to defraud,
trial court accepted guilty plea without inquiring whether
defendant understood nature of offense, and where defendant
insisted that his acts were "neglectful," "inadvertent," and
without any attempt to defraud).

PETITIONER has pled and proved to the Court's satisfaction
that PETITIONER would not have pled guilty if PETITIONER had
known that property taken with consent can not be "stolen

property" within the meaning of the statute, even though said property is subsequently transported across state lines. PETITIONER's lack of understanding and the prejudice PETITIONER suffered as a result thereof constitute a fundamental defect which resulted in a miscarriage of justice and which does not comport with any concept of justice and fair play. Accordingly, PETITIONER's Motion for relief under 2255 for lack of an understanding guilty plea is GRANTED.

WHEREFORE, and for the reasons stated in this Order, PETITIONER's Motion to vacate PETITIONER's conviction and sentence is hereby GRANTED.

DONE AND ORDERED this __25__ day of _____Nov_____, 1987.

UNITED STATES DISTRICT JUDGE
NORMAN C. RUETTGER, JR.

cc: counsel of record